ALL SHOOK UP

ALL SHOOK UP

The Shifting Soviet Response to Catastrophes, 1917–1991

NIGEL A. RAAB

McGill-Queen's University Press
Montreal & Kingston • London • Chicago

ISBN 978-0-7735-5002-5 (cloth)
ISBN 978-0-7735-5003-2 (ePDF)
ISBN 978-0-7735-5004-9 (ePUB)

Legal deposit first quarter 2017
Bibliothèque nationale du Québec

Printed in Canada on acid-free paper that is 100% ancient forest free (100% post-consumer recycled), processed chlorine free.

This book has been published with the help of a grant from the Canadian Federation for the Humanities and Social Sciences, through the Awards to Scholarly Publications Program, using funds provided by the Social Sciences and Humanities Research Council of Canada.

McGill-Queen's University Press acknowledges the support of the Canada Council for the Arts for our publishing program. We also acknowledge the financial support of the Government of Canada through the Canada Book Fund for our publishing activities.

Library and Archives Canada Cataloguing in Publication

Raab, Nigel A., 1968–, author
All shook up : the shifting Soviet response to catastrophes, 1917–1991 / Nigel Raab.

Includes bibliographical references and index.
Issued in print and electronic formats.
ISBN 978-0-7735-5002-5 (cloth). – ISBN 978-0-7735-5003-2 (pdf). – ISBN 978-0-7735-5004-9 (epub)

1. Disasters – Soviet Union – History – 20th century. 2. Disasters – Social aspects – Soviet Union – History – 20th century. 3. Disasters – Political aspects – Soviet Union – History – 20th century. 4. Soviet Union – History – 20th century. I. Title.

4DK266.R32 2017 303.48'5 C2016-906624-X
C2016-906625-8

This book was typeset by True to Type in 10.5/13 Sabon

To my wife, Carolyn Peter

Contents

Figures

Abbreviations

AES	Atomic Energy Station
ASSR	Autonomous Soviet Socialist Republic
NEP	New Economic Policy
NGO	non-governmental organization
RSFSR	Russian Soviet Federative Socialist Republic
TASS	Telegraph Agency of the Soviet Union
UAS	Ukrainian Academy of Sciences
USSR	Union of Soviet Socialist Republics
VOOPIK	*Vserossiiskoe obshchestvo okhrany pamiatnikov istorii i kul'tury* [All-Russian Society for the Preservation of Historical and Cultural Monuments]

Acknowledgments

Take Interstate 5 north of Los Angeles to the junction with Route 166, then drive west, past Maricopa, and then a little further up the hill until you can take a right on Soda Lake Road. Drive about twenty minutes past abandoned farms and former cattle fields, and then turn right onto a dusty road. Continue a few minutes more and you will find a beautiful quiet picnic spot at which to write a thank you note – right atop the San Andreas Fault.

Gone are the days of the isolated thinker waiting for that eureka moment – a book only surfaces with the help and assistance of friends, colleagues, and the right environment. Thus, *merci beaucoup* to Lynda O'Donnell, who controlled the wayward French; *danke* to Alice Raab, who ordered the German; and *spasibo* to Maria Lentsman for the Slavic touch. Where would this book be without the efforts of our interlibrary loan librarian, Orlando Penetrante, who made me feel as if our library had as many books as the Library of Congress? A special thanks to the state archivists in Moscow and Kiev who have been helping me for more than a decade. With utmost efficiency, they kept the documents coming without a glitch. And a big thank you to colleagues in the Department of History at Loyola Marymount University, who pushed for more clarity whenever cloudiness flowed from my pen. Klaus Gestwa in Tübingen and Marc Elie in Paris were instrumental with commentaries in earlier stages of the project, and Katja Doose in Berlin had ground-level insights into Tashkent. Of course, the wonderful anonymous reviewers made important suggestions: they didn't like everything and they still won't, but they vastly improved the pages that follow.

The experts at MQUP have been tremendous. A special thank you to Jonathan Crago and all the conversations we have had about what makes a book more than just a study of some academic topic. Joanne Richardson did a superb editing job, and David Drummond designed a wonderful cover. Ryan Van Huijstee kept the whole thing moving forward throughout the production period.

Since writing a book is not a disembodied experience, I had to be somewhere to put everything together. Liudmila Zhavoronkova had a warm place to stay in the heart of Moscow, and this enabled me to walk to the archives. The Gatineau River just north of Ottawa is also part of the story. Thanks to Joseph and Simone Maingot who provided me with a room with a view so I could wake up to a sunrise over an icy river before tip-tapping on my keyboard.

The unseen constant behind all of this – much like the air we breathe – is family. Ever since I first embarked on my historical journey, I received crucial support from my parents, and they are still there for me. My sister and her family have kicked in extra energy when my own has been lagging. And then there is the lady to whom this book is dedicated – may she always be by my side.

Carrizo Plain, California
October 2016

ALL SHOOK UP

Introduction

Nature has its own ways. Despite tremendous human efforts to tame it, humans have not been able to dominate it. Throughout the industrial world confident men and women believed that the earth was theirs to conquer by channelling the energy of rivers, whether with cement on the bottom of the Los Angeles River or by implementing a revolutionary vision of technological advancement with a massive dam on a Ukrainian river. Yet these vast projects only touched upon a tiny part of the earth's surface. Even if humans of the industrial age have polluted huge expanses, the projects themselves focus on limited areas. These visions of grandeur ignored the fact that nature still could do as it chose on all the oceans and almost all the land.

Only in the past two or three decades have scholars and activists concerned themselves with the limits of human control. After Hurricane Katrina in 2005, the Haiti earthquake in 2010, and the Fukushima tsunami and nuclear meltdown in 2011, claims about control are ill-advised; rather, these disasters expose a non-responsive state and a racist legacy, a colonial pattern that goes back centuries, and an overconfident technological society forced to rethink basic energy assumptions. In looking at these recent disasters, it is difficult to tell whether our planet has become moodier – shaking, spewing, burning, blowing – but whatever the case, confidence has been undermined.

This applies to the Soviet Union as much as it does to other countries. In hindsight, the Soviet confidence in its ability to overcome nature was equally out of place. Not only did its engineering projects cause environmental harm, but even the best laid plans could not prevent natural disasters from spreading across vast spaces. Despite claims to the contrary, the Soviet Union was a very dangerous place.

In the Far East, vast land masses were subject to flooding and regular subterranean tremours. In the Eurasian heartland, the rivers rose in the spring and the forests burned in the summer. At the Central Asian periphery, the earth shook and mountain streams were transformed into rushing mud flows as they raced to inhabited areas in the plains. In many instances, no impact was registered on human communities. The great Tunguska meteor, which demolished about two thousand square kilometres of Siberian forest a few years before the Bolshevik Revolution, had little bearing outside the expeditions of curious scientists. Unfortunately, however, this was not always the case: throughout the entire history of the Soviet Union, cities and villages suffered the terrible consequences of both natural and human-made disasters. From the smallest case of people getting lost in snowstorms, a classic trope so ably portrayed in Vladimir Sorokin's recent novel *Snowstorm* (*Metel'*), to earthquakes that killed thousands in republican capitals, the Soviet Union was no stranger to unexpected calamities.

In the limited personal accounts of earthquake experiences, it is clear that industrial and modern confidence could not eliminate thoughts of disaster from the minds of inhabitants. Valentin Ulomov, the former head of the Tashkent seismological station, knew the long history of seismological activity in Uzbekistan but he also knew earthquakes from personal experience as a young boy. He experienced his first disruptive tremour in 1946 and watched how "all the inhabitants fled their swaying homes" because these homes were made out of loam.[1] In this case, the epicentre was way up in the Chatkal mountain range, where fewer people lived. In remembering the 1966 disaster in Tashkent, eyewitnesses expressed a lingering unease that no slogans could undo. Rustam Sagdullaev was a sixteen-year-old who experienced "no fear" himself but who was aware of a "sense of fear" in those around him. However, this fear soon dissipated and residents became so accustomed to tremblers that they did not even react to anything under a 5 on the Richter scale. Interestingly, Sagdullaev was involved with a film at the Uzbek film studio at the time of the major earthquake. Although he claimed little fear as a young man, he and his colleagues made every effort to avoid the studios of Uzbekfilm because they were terrified that the building would collapse. Such concerns cannot be considered unusual for someone who lived in a seismologically sensitive zone.[2]

Even if one never suffered directly from a disaster, the possibility of doing so was never far from the surface. In one form or another, disasters appeared in popular culture, reminding readers and viewers of historical catastrophes and potential dangers. Towards the end of Il'f and Petrov's *Twelve Chairs* (*Dvenadtsat' stul'ev*), published in the 1920s, the main characters are caught in Yalta during an earthquake. Leonid Gaidai's early 1970s film version shows the theatre collapsing from the earthquake. Natural disasters were not as popular a subject as were revolutionary themes or heroic tales of the Second World War, but they linger just below the surface. Indeed, for most Soviet citizens, disasters were never far from their minds.

Despite the regularity of disasters large and small, little research has been done on the disaster profile of the Soviet Union.[3] In one breath, Paul Stronski mentions disasters in Ashgabat, Tashkent, and Chernobyl but only cursorily so as to make the traditional claim that the Soviets were unable to master natural phenomena despite their monumental aspirations; he pays little attention to how the response changed over time.[4] Disasters open doors to subtle interpretive possibilities: they should not simply be seized upon to further a narrative of Soviet failure. For at least two decades, German- and French-language historiography has studied disasters in all sorts of contexts, but even here the Soviet side has been neglected.[5] Chernobyl is the exception, this disaster having been studied in isolation and mostly from the perspective of science. Thus the following history offers new empirical terrain that enables us to challenge common stereotypes about the Soviet Union. With the recent onslaught of natural disasters from the Mississippi delta to the shores of Japan, a history of Soviet disasters adds a critical dimension to environmental change in the third millennium. As environmentalists and politicians across the globe gain a new respect for the ability of the natural environment to impose its will on human decision making, the historian can add to this conversation by offering a glimpse into the tragedies that influenced the policies and fate of a twentieth-century superpower.

Whenever calamity occurred, the Soviet state had to respond and provide citizens with the means to overcome it. In some cases, such as with a single car crash, the state could take care of the issue with a quick report; in other cases, more substantial resources were required. Floods regularly required the evacuation of citizens and the allocation of temporary housing. Earthquakes, which could destroy downtown cores in seconds, forced city planners, architects, construction crews, and medical personnel to take care of young and old. In Ashgabat in 1948 and in Tashkent in 1966, massive earthquakes required the reconstruction of both cities; large numbers of Soviet citizens were shipped in to help with the reconstruction process. The urgency was even more extreme in April 1986, when the reactor in Chernobyl exploded. The Soviet Union had to mobilize its entire resource base to bring the situation under control.

Arguments and attitudes changed depending upon the specific disaster and the needs of the specific groups responding to it. This not only highlights the diversity of experience within the authoritarian parameters of the Soviet Union but also indicates that not all disasters were created equal. Whereas certain disasters became major media affairs, others were ignored entirely. In 1957, a radioactive explosion, far less destructive than the Tashkent earthquake, was cloaked in secrecy and only became the subject of discussion after the Chernobyl explosion in 1986.[6] In 1975, a massive storm swept through Odessa bringing the city to a standstill. Although destructive winds in the 1970s were politically much less sensitive than was a radioactive explosion in the 1950s, local newspapers only provided information five days after the storm. In contrast, the 1966 Tashkent earthquake was reported immediately and remained a major news item for months. Interestingly, the earthquake was not the only natural disaster to hit Uzbekistan in 1966; a few months later, river flooding caused further destruction and even more fatalities than did the earthquake. Although the river flooding was reported and sympathies were expressed for the evacuees, it never developed a lasting media presence. Much like the falling tree in the heart of the forest, this and many other disasters went unheard. By looking at disasters in this way, this study goes beyond simple talk about censorship to show how each situation required a unique media response. This perspective offers a stark contrast to that of Ellen Mickiewicz, who suggests a Soviet reluctance to broadcast information about disasters.[7] The Soviet response really depended on local circumstances and national needs. Bearing this in mind, we should use caution when equating the Gorbachev period with the most diverse disaster coverage.[8]

Since disasters require the spontaneous mobilization of vast resources, they provide critical insights into the nature of the Soviet state. First and foremost, disasters upset the best made plans of centralized states and therefore created an atmosphere of improvisation both within the Communist Party and without. The Soviet Union has long ceased to be considered a static state, and historians have indicated, both culturally and socially, how citizens had opportunities to forge an individual lifestyle within the larger Soviet experiment.[9] When an earthquake destroyed a city, it gave unexpected opportunities to architects, youth, volunteers, artists, media outlets, and others to experience life beyond preordained frameworks. These disasters, themselves spontaneous, evoked spontaneity within the population, spurring the regular citizen into action. In different forms, from active participation in recovery operations to the donation of money, citizens had an opportunity to act outside the regular parameters of Soviet life. This did not affect everyone, and it had its limits, but a disaster almost always evoked societal flux. Furthermore, the response to major disasters depended upon the policies of the time. Just as a Stalinist response to an earthquake differed immensely from a Brezhnevite response, so these catastrophes provide another dimension to our understanding of Soviet politics during specific eras. A study of disasters disabuses the reader of the notion that Soviet society was a static organism with little room for improvisation.

While disasters occurred regularly throughout the Soviet Union, I select major disasters from separate time periods in order to focus on important social, cultural, and political transitions during different periods of Soviet rule. To this end, chapter 1 conceptualizes disasters so as to position them within a comparative framework. This demonstrates how disasters relate to critical interpretive issues such as the fragility of the authoritarian state, perceptions of time, the role of linguistic usage, and the nature of volunteer work within a coercive environment. Thereafter, it continues with the Crimean earthquake of 1927, when inexperienced Soviet authorities worried that the entire coast, the sanatorium of the Soviet Union, might slip into the sea. In the waning years of the New Economic Policy (NEP), when the economy was still decentralized, local authorities in the Russian Soviet Federative Socialist Republic (RSFSR) took much of the responsibility for rebuilding the tourist-rich coast. While the Crimean earthquake occurred before the Stalinist takeover, the Ashgabat earthquake of 1948 destroyed the city during one of the harshest periods of Soviet rule. In Ashgabat, a city with a population of 120,000, the earthquake killed tens of thousands of people and instantly demolished the city.[10] The human toll was much larger than that in any other twentieth-century earthquake in the Soviet Union. The outset of the Cold War required the Soviet Union to present itself as a strong power to the external world. It therefore had to take certain measures, but Stalin and his advisors never exploited the earthquake as a propaganda event. After the Second World War, the Soviets had other rebuilding concerns, and its resources were focused in other directions. This low-key response contrasts with the mobilization of enormous resources to rebuild Tashkent in 1966.

The Khrushchev years were fortunate since, with one exception, no major natural or human-made disasters occurred. Economic decisions concerning the area of the Virgin Lands were about to blight the landscape, and industry was taking its toll on the natural environment, but no event required the spontaneous mobilization of Soviet resources. The exception, of course, was the radioactive disaster in the Cheliabinsk region in the Urals in 1957, the same year in which the Soviets sent Sputnik into orbit. The Soviet response to the disaster was slow and, because of the sensitivity of nuclear science, never became a news item. The authorities eventually evacuated thousands of people, and many more were affected by radiation sickness. Although Soviet officials posted roadside signs warning about radiation levels, the disaster was quickly hushed up.[11]

Of course, a regime cannot choose when it wants to respond since earthquakes and explosions happen at unexpected moments. In April 1966, the earth's crust shook right below downtown Tashkent. Thus, months after the Central Asian capital had been the focus of global diplomatic attention for a meeting between the heads of India and Pakistan, the earthquake destroyed the centre of town. The response from Aleksei Kosygin and Leonid Brezhnev, the effective leaders of the Communist Party, was immediate. Far different from Ashgabat, where Joseph Stalin and his advisors kept a measured distance from reconstruction efforts, the leadership in the post-Khrushchev era realized it could turn a disaster into a media event that would trumpet the values of the Communist Party. Media outlets followed the rebuilding process much as an American television network might follow the exploits of a traveller embarking on a year-long adventure. Readers had regular updates in regional and central newspapers. The Soviet Union was renowned for large engineering projects and the reconstruction of entire cities. Tashkent offers one of the largest instances of an entire city being rebuilt from the ground up.

In 1966, the Tashkent earthquake took place in a media environment that was radically different from that of 1948. In the early Brezhnev years, Lazar' Karelin wrote a novel about the experiences of a film crew during the Ashgabat earthquake. Despite the subject matter, only minimal visual reporting of the Ashgabat earthquake was made available to the public.[12] In the 1960s, however, television and film had emerged as popular aspects of Soviet life. With the increased production of more popular and less ideological films, film studios were adjusting to a changed media landscape.[13] During the Tashkent Conference in January 1966, Soviet authorities beamed views of Tashkent to television viewers around the Union of Soviet Socialist Republics (USSR).[14] After the earthquake, the Communist Party took further advantage of these technologies.[15] Malik Kaiumov's film *Tashkent, Earthquake* (*Ташкент, Землетрясение*) appeared in theatres in 1968 and gave a complete visual introduction to the earthquake.[16]

To respect the social importance of the visual media, the discussion of the Tashkent earthquake is followed by a chapter dedicated to the representation of disasters in film. The highpoint of disaster film production came during the Brezhnev years, so these films are integrally related to the aftermath of Tashkent. From Kaiumov's film (mentioned above) to the production of insurance films and to the embrace of the American disaster film genre, directors had a variety of stories to tell. Implicitly, the increased presence of disaster films on television and in movie theatres during the Brezhnev era helped Soviet citizens anticipate worse disasters down the road. Explicitly, the films demonstrate a variety of attempts at shifting public perceptions of disaster, whether in fiction or "real" life. As visual evidence promises to become increasingly important in historical analysis, this chapter is clearly warranted.

The Brezhnev years have often been considered a period of stagnation, especially in the latter half of his rule when commentators began to speak of a gerontocracy. Yet recently historians have started to put more effort into trying to understand the more vibrant and creative aspects of these years,[17] which, in turn, leads to a better understanding of the contemporary nostalgia for the Brezhnev period. The analysis of Tashkent contributes to this discussion because it indicates the energy and determination that the state invested in the project and the opportunities the various rebuilding projects offered to citizens around the USSR. Even if the earthquake lasted a matter of seconds, the rebuilding project and the energy it sustained went on for years.

The notion that the government provided adequate response mechanisms in Tashkent links disasters with more general questions about the nature of the Soviet Union. If the response in Ashgabat was rather haphazard and disorderly despite the presence of the Stalinist state, why were Brezhnev and Kosygin able to mobilize such energy and organization in the case of Tashkent? How had the Soviet state matured to the point at which it could remain unfazed by such a calamity? If Chernobyl contributed to the collapse of a superpower, why did Tashkent have almost the opposite effect? Although the Tashkent earthquake precedes the economic problems of the 1970s, it nevertheless highlights the ability of the Soviet Union to respond successfully, albeit selectively, to disasters. This does not mean that the reconstruction of the city was flawless – problems cropped up every step of the way – but the city was rapidly rebuilt.

If Brezhnev transformed destruction into glory, Gorbachev was less fortunate. At the onset of perestroika, about a year into Gorbachev's rule, the nuclear reactor in the fourth block at Chernobyl exploded, causing a catastrophic incident of global interest. Earthquakes were isolated in specific regions, whereas the spread of radiation and the persistence of high radiation levels made the Chernobyl incident unique. Chernobyl had a global significance that went well beyond the singular response of the Soviet Union and, this being the case, has been studied extensively. Scholarly works were already appearing within months of the explosion, and many of the criticisms from 1986 have not lost their saliency: the failure of Soviet authorities to publicize the accident when they knew that the radiation was spreading; the May Day parade in Kyiv that was held despite the high radiation levels; the lack of available medical treatment for victims; and the downplaying of the human danger.[18] In independent Ukraine, research has been compartmentalized to reflect the needs of the young state. Ukrainian scholars have focused on the response of the Ukrainian Academy of Sciences and the lives of first responders who suffered after their work was done.[19] Chernobyl remains politically sensitive to this day. Nikolai Ryzhkov, the former head of the Council of Ministers and the highest-ranking official to have visited the area in 1986, defends the Soviet response and suggests that only a great power could have been in a position to take care of such a calamity.[20]

Chernobyl has, however, been presented as an isolated incident. Although the nuclear element has special meaning in the context of twentieth-century science, Chernobyl gains another dimension when seen within a comparative perspective. It underscores how many elements in the early perestroika years of Gorbachev were drawn from years of Soviet experience, thus emphasizing continuity over change. A comparative look at rebuilding practices, remuneration of "volunteers," media usage, and the role of scientists indicates the overlap between Gorbachev and his predecessors. And, if comparing Chernobyl to

Tashkent shifts our understanding of the Gorbachev era, then comparing Tashkent to Chernobyl shifts our understanding of the early Brezhnev years. Thus, doing so performs a doubly useful function.

This comparative perspective is further enhanced by looking at the Armenian earthquake that occurred in December 1988, about thirty months after Chernobyl. While Chernobyl occurred during the earliest period of perestroika, the Armenian earthquake destroyed cities just as the tectonic foundations of the Soviet Union were shifting. Fewer than three years apart, the Armenian disaster took place in a radically different political climate than did Chernobyl. Ethnic tensions had already surfaced between Armenians and Azerbaijanis in February 1988; nationalist movements in the Baltic states were gaining momentum by November 1988, when Estonia declared itself a sovereign republic; and, under the rule of Gorbachev, Eastern Europe was quickly drifting away.[21] For officials in Moscow, however, the two catastrophes were deeply linked since, in late 1988, Soviet authorities were still dealing with the aftermath of Chernobyl.

Despite the distance that separated Ukraine from Armenia, as far as local authorities were concerned, the incidents were related. Ukrainian building crews went to help resurrect Armenian villages at the same time that Armenian citizens went to help with the building of housing for Chernobyl evacuees. While this aid fit the general parameters of a traditional response, both Ukrainian and Armenian officials saw the disasters as opportunities to renegotiate their political relationship with Moscow. As radioactive levels in Ukraine continued to hamper normal life in vast regions, Ukrainians increasingly sought to solve their own problems. The Soviet system was weakened by the incredible resources required to deal with this double tragedy, and this allowed Armenian authorities to push for help from the expatriate Armenian community.

These Soviet catastrophes occurred decades apart, but they were all inextricably linked through the history of the Soviet Union. Chernobyl occurred twenty years to the day after the earthquake in Tashkent, and responders who had been active in Tashkent were also present in Chernobyl.[22] In the aftermath of Chernobyl, the memory of the Crimean earthquake of 1927 was resuscitated on the Crimean peninsula when it became the site of active protests against the further construction of nuclear power plants. Despite public disapproval, the Communist Party pushed ahead with its plans to build a nuclear power plant on seismologically sensitive territory in the Crimea. Protesters and scientists mobilized their opposition around the historic possibilities of great shifts under the earth's surface. With all the overlapping of events, disasters were neither discrete in time nor isolated in space as they became reference points in contentious discussions.

On a land mass of more than 22 million square kilometres, with a spectacularly diverse natural environment, thousands upon thousands of natural catastrophes have occurred over the eighty-four-year history of the Soviet Union. Faced with this multitude, the historian has to make choices in order to provide a qualitatively rich assessment of the influence of these disasters on Soviet society. The source base influences the selection of disasters presented here; they are the best documented in Soviet history. Smaller disasters may have been recorded, but the documents either only provide insights into the scientific nature of the phenomenon or only reveal trace elements of local dynamics. The documentation pushes one towards more densely populated areas and, even in cases in which the disaster affected a vast territory, the most significant sources come from that territory's urban areas. This is not surprising; however, as is evident in this study, it (albeit unwittingly) shifts the debate onto urban ground.

The careful selection of disasters in Crimean cities, in Ashgabat, in Tashkent, in Chernobyl, and in Armenian cities serves to establish a base for extending the analysis while still taking smaller areas, such as the villages of Armenia, into consideration. The recovery in the larger cities offers a perspective on almost every imaginable social group. The selection of these cities and their experiences of disaster opens avenues for understanding youth, educated professionals, workers, and party members in a way that would not have been possible with the limited sources available for smaller areas. Journals of architectural associations, regional newspapers, the minutes of Komsomol youth meetings, individual complaints to party leaders, discussions within construction companies, the work of film studios based in urban areas, and a variety of other sources ensure a multifaceted view of these phenomena.

Just as the Soviets could not predict where the next disaster would strike, so the work of the historian is guided by where that disaster did strike. Although this may introduce a degree of randomness into the selection, it has the advantage of taking the analysis beyond the traditional capitals of Moscow and St Petersburg. It is fortunate that the five chapters on disasters focus, respectively, on five different Soviet republics and thus reveal specific aspects of local political culture.

The aim in analyzing the above disasters is not to provide a compendium of misfortunes that struck Soviet citizens but, rather, to focus on those unexpected disasters that provide insights into important socio-political aspects of the history of the Soviet Union. This being the case, a number of disasters are beyond the purview of this study. The recurring bouts of famine, such as the one that occurred in the early 1920s and the Holodomor of the early 1930s, during which millions of Ukrainians died, have been left aside not only because these phenomena deserve treatment in their own monographs but also because the nature of the events were different.[23] The famines were the direct outcome of Soviet policy and can hardly be considered spontaneous or accidental. Soviet cities also suffered catastrophic damage in the context of the Second World War, but this is a subject that has already been studied.[24]

Importantly, however, the discussion pays close attention to disasters of lesser magnitude. Smaller tremours and storms required the mobilization of forces, albeit on a lesser scale, and complete the disaster profile of the Soviet Union. In a state trying to modernize, industrial explosions, train accidents, and plane crashes occurred more regularly than those in power might have wished. An auxiliary focus on these lesser evils provides temporal continuity to major catastrophes, which tend to hog the spotlight.

Disasters have even been credited with the dismantling of a fragile state. For example, the nuclear accident in Chernobyl has been considered the catalyst that led to the ultimate collapse of the Soviet Union. This is debatable; however, it is true that, during times of disaster, strengths and weaknesses are exposed in a way that they are not during normal times. Not only did disasters upset the Soviet narrative, but they also provide the researcher with a closer, if unsettling, glimpse into the functioning of the Soviet state and the people who lived within it. In investigating these disasters, one begins to see the "accidental" nature of Soviet life. Because the Soviet state could not prepare for every eventuality, moments of disaster reveal the Soviet Union stripped of its polished veneer. But the rawness of the state's responses should not lead to a hasty condemnation of Soviet practice; rather, it should function as an opportunity to analyze the evolution of disaster responses and to examine how Soviet citizens explored their own, sometimes quite diverse, options in these harrowing circumstances.

In the aftermath of the Soviet collapse, Martin Malia wrote about the Soviet tragedy, referring to the human deprivations of the Soviet period and the tragic disregard Soviet officials had for the well-being of their citizens.[25] The history that follows, hardly a day trip for optimists, is no less tragic. At each turn in the story, people perished under rubble, had to evacuate their homes, lost family members, were forced to resettle thousands of kilometres from home, suffered irremediable sickness, and had their lives altered forever. Yet beyond these tragic stories lies a web of issues that indicates the complexity and dynamics of a state that has all too often been depicted in monochrome.

1

Conceptualizing Disasters

Disasters have drawn the attention of writers for centuries, and over the centuries attitudes towards these calamities have changed. With their ability to upset societal rhythms, disasters have been explained in any number of ways. Enlightenment thinkers were shocked by the destruction wrought by the Lisbon earthquake in 1755. Voltaire wrote his famous *Poem on the Lisbon Disaster*, which provides a humbling assessment of humankind's ability to face such calamity.[1] No providential being was going to help, and humans were hardly in a position to help themselves: evil would persist in the world. In the next century, new sciences (such as seismology) and professions (such as engineering) emerged, and a confident industrial society believed it could prevent great catastrophes. The modern state of the nineteenth century, with its well-informed bureaucracies, took it upon itself to ensure the safety of its citizens even if it could not always fulfill its promises. These trends continued into the twentieth century with the design of earthquake-proof buildings and the management of flood plains. The cementing of the Los Angeles River in the late 1930s is an example of a large engineering project designed to prevent flooding.

Disasters can thus be perceived from numerous angles. What follows considers these angles within a comparative perspective and then integrates with the themes that emerge in the context of Soviet studies. Given the strong emphasis on state power, the next paragraphs explore how sociologists have conceptualized the role of the state and provide a sense of how Soviet actions, rather than being unique to the communist state, are not unlike the practices of liberal states. The Soviet state had its peculiarities but it was not unusual. Nor were disasters atypical events. In thinking abstractly about disasters it is critical to consider how they fit within the social and cultural fabric of individual Soviet communities. Time and language have been studied extensively, and it is interesting to see how disasters intersect with them. For example, disasters enable us to look at the presentation of time and to investigate linguistic usage that goes beyond common platitudes about an *hors texte* or the manipulation of language. They allow us to take a nuanced look at how the idea and slogan "friendship of peoples" shifted in meaning from disaster to disaster. Throughout the Soviet Union, disasters required that citizens engage in extensive volunteer activity. Of course, the word "volunteer" is controversial because detractors question whether volunteering is even possible in a coercive state. Still, disasters provide us with a nuanced look at the choices individuals made when volunteering. Even if these choices don't correspond to an idealized version of free will, they nonetheless indicate the range of opportunities with which citizens were presented when they had to make important decisions. Finally, disasters expose differences between the urban and rural contexts of Soviet life. All these issues reappear in specific contexts throughout the rest of the work.

If the modern state could not prevent a disaster, it had to respond to it. In the 1940s, Pitirim Sorokin argued that disasters elicited totalitarian behaviour from governments. In this view, "in response to the impact of war, pestilence, floods, earthquakes, devastating explosions or fires, and similar catastrophes, more rigid governmental control at once takes place in the form of martial, siege, and other emergency laws."[2] He then describes the Canadian government's authoritarian response to the Halifax explosion in 1917, which destroyed most of the city. A similar thesis is advanced by Andreas Ranft and Stephan Selzer in a collection of essays that focuses on how cities recover from disaster. They equate times of disaster with the rise of bureaucratic activity.[3] Contrary to suggestions concerning the totalitarian aspects of bureaucratic disaster response, disasters provide some of the least authoritarian moments in Soviet history and offer a glimpse into the haphazardness of the authoritarian state. This reverses Sorokin's thesis; rather than a loosely organized parliamentary state shifting to authoritarian means, we see an authoritarian state being forced to shift to looser means.

It has been common practice to view disasters as discrete events in the history of a given society. In *When the Planet Rages*, Charles Officer focuses on disruptive volcanic eruptions and destructive earthquakes, such as the one that ruined Lisbon in 1755.[4] His analysis does not, however, look at the interaction between local cultural practices and the destructive force of a natural disaster. From the opposite direction, Kenneth Hewitt argues that most natural disasters are characteristic rather than accidental features of the societies in which they occur.[5] Friedrich Nietzsche took flooding in his stride when he undertook a dangerous trip from the Swiss Alps to Turin to complete *Twilight of the Idols*.[6] If we look at the Swiss literary heritage, we see that many authors wrote about the possibility of avalanches in the Alps.[7] Across the European parts of Russia, floods were as much a part of some seasons as snow was of winter. In *Crime and Punishment*, Svidrigaylov hears the St Petersburg cannons announcing flooding and mocks the regular procedure of people, "dripping wet and cursing," who "drag their rubbish to the upper floors."[8] Thus, when we discuss Alexander I's reaction to the flooding of St Petersburg in 1824, we must realize that this natural phenomenon could not have come as a surprise: floods were common throughout the Russian Empire. In rural areas, peasants took floods for granted, and the Imperial bureaucracy regularly took note of floods and fires. As Cass Sunstein notes, "*people are far more willing to tolerate familiar risks than unfamiliar ones, even if they are statistically equivalent*."[9] In the mines of eastern Ukraine, a methane explosion was just part of the job. Disasters are not unexpected events with a short lifespan but, rather, integral geocultural elements with which residents live and learn to cope. Earthquakes in Central Asia were only spontaneous in so far as residents did not know when they might occur; everybody understood that they *would* occur. This perspective encourages us to establish links between isolated disasters and to explore behaviour both before and after any given calamity.

At about the time Hewitt was writing, Ulrich Beck published his famous work on risk society.[10] Beck wanted to shift discussion away from an outmoded standard analysis. He saw risk as the fundamental source of societal conflict, contending that how societies related to risk, and the associated social ruptures that came about when managing it, revealed the most significant modern tensions. In his native Germany, Beck had seen acid rain destroy the forests of Bavaria. This scourge transcended geopolitical borders, thus proving that risk had a global dimension.[11] Although Beck has more patience with scientific detail than does Hewitt, he analyzes human-made disasters with a sociological eye, seeing how they affect specific social groups. In his discussion of Villa Parisi, a polluted chemical town in Brazil, he notes:

"the devil of hunger is fought with the Beelzebub of multiplying risks."[12] Impoverished countries gamble with the lives of their own citizens in the belief that Western companies, such as Union Carbide, will ultimately modernize dilapidated communities. Much like Hewitt, Beck understands that you have to look beyond the scientific achievements of the West to capture the full meaning of disasters.

Since that time, a wide range of scholars have studied the local dimension of disasters and have integrated upheavals into the life experience of the victims. A decade ago, Anthony Oliver-Smith wrote about the anthropology of disaster and brought up the concept of vulnerability, building upon both Hewitt and Beck. He argues that numerous catastrophes traditionally associated with "natural causes were more than likely generated, at least in part, by human practices, both collectively and cumulatively."[13] It was not just a matter of weakness before nature but also of systemic weaknesses within society: stratified societies evinced stratified experiences when disasters struck. This, of course, is a central theme in Marc Elie's work on the Azeri communities after the Armenian earthquake in December 1988 (in this case, the stratification is along ethnic lines).[14] In a different vein, Oliver-Smith studies vulnerability in the face of such pending disasters as the inevitable submersion of homes once a major hydroelectric plant dams the flow of water. The calculation of compensation costs follows averages and norms and ignores "the breakdown of community or the loss of cultural or spiritual resources."[15]

Eric Klinenberg's study of the Chicago heat wave mirrors this approach. In this sociological study, Klinenberg pays special attention to the elderly to demonstrate that the heat wave could only be categorized as a disaster because existing municipal policy made it incredibly difficult for less mobile citizens to seek help. Policies that housed senior citizens close to drug addicts made them afraid to leave their homes and thus less likely to seek external help when needed.[16] Moreover, the social habits of elderly men, who were reluctant to exhibit signs of weakness, put them in a higher risk category than women. Klinenberg's sociological approach has led many scholars to look at the direct experience of smaller communities. While the Soviet cases that I address deal predominantly with cities, scholars such as Jean-Christophe Gaillard and Virginie Le Masson look at remote mountain villages to understand how responses to disasters are conditioned by social factors.[17] Obviously, their narratives do not focus on scientists or leading corporate or political figures. Although the database for Soviet history does not always permit such a penetrating look into the lives of individual victims and close-knit communities, similar themes emerge in all instances.

All these approaches to disaster are critical and are generally designed to illuminate disparities in the human condition and to undermine the hubris that has been such a part of Western society for the last century. Of course, these approaches also undermine the hubris that emerged from the Soviet leadership. Yet not all disaster theories are necessarily negative. Scholars have also highlighted the positive benefits of a timely disaster. In his work on the Hamburg fire of 1842, Dirk Schubert argues that the fire ultimately encouraged the modernization of the city and led to widespread reform that went well beyond the simple reconstruction of buildings. The fire had "uncovered fundamental flaws" in municipal governance and, although radical reform was not on the agenda, city fathers invited the Englishman William Lindley to broaden roads and build a city with proper sanitation, fire protection, and transport.[18] Schubert is effectively writing about "Bettering the City."[19] While one has to be careful about overly optimistic assessments, his work reminds us not to ignore the occasional silver lining. The outcomes of Soviet disasters were never rosy but, in many cases, groups and individuals did seek and find betterment of one sort or another.

If disasters can only be conditionally referred to as discrete events in a long cultural trajectory, then how should we understand the meaning of an event? How long does an event last? Who or what starts an event and what determines its end point? In his work on nationalist movements in the Soviet Union, Mark Beissinger carefully elaborates the significance of an event as a catalyst in the eruption of nationalism. He borrows inspiration from Hannah Arendt and Michel Foucault to categorize the type of action that belongs to the event. Far from a passive occurrence, events are tumultuous and sometimes even revolutionary. Beissinger writes that events are "contentious and potentially subversive acts that challenge normalized practices." Further, "events are purposeful forms of action whose perpetrators aim to transform rather than to reproduce, to overturn or alter that which, in the absence of the event, others would take for granted."[20] This definition separates everyday pursuits from disruptive actions and energizes those who choose to engage in the latter.

As a means of promoting the endeavors of nationalist groups during the final days of the Soviet Union, this definition has its merits. It also, however, has its limitations because critical events must have their source in individual actions. In other words, what happened at Chernobyl cannot be defined as an event unless someone purposefully sought to initiate a nuclear disaster. Except for the Soviet judiciary, which sought scapegoats for the catastrophe, few would ascribe intent to Chernobyl. Thus an anthropocentric definition of *event* ascribes purposeful actions to human beings and sidelines external factors such as the natural environment from the political equation. Despite the references to Foucault, this attitude towards events bears traces of Enlightenment thinking in so far as the actions of rational (in the sense of purposeful) human beings transcend the influences of their natural surroundings.

In a reverse perspective, problems arise when a disaster is presented as a scientifically qualifiable moment or as an event in natural history. A scientific timing of events implies discrete actions, such as the moment an earthquake strikes. But, much like the philosophically contested idea of the present being a single moment in time, an event as a single moment in time omits the long-term social and cultural aspects of the phenomenon. The Chernobyl reactor can be said to have burst at a measurable moment in time, and astronomers can determine the alignment of the stars when the reactor exploded. In Tashkent, photographs of clocks tell us when the earthquake happened. But disasters are not necessarily cotemporaneous with this scientific measurement of time. As Hewitt notices, the tendency to refer to natural catastrophes as events separates them from human experience, much as Beissinger's definition separates human beings from the natural environment. Therefore, if we continue to write of events, the natural environment must be considered in tandem with human action, and events must be considered, perhaps not in the longue durée, but certainly in a longer durée.

Classical etymology has been overshadowed by the linguistic turn and offshoots such as *Begriffsgeschichte*, yet it can still play a useful role in qualifying terms. "Event," for example, has Latin roots in words such as *venire* (to come) and *ventus* (wind) and is also related to the Spanish *ventana*, that is, the English window, which is related to the German *Wind* and possibly the German *Wende* (turn). (And if we push the linguistic play a little bit further, the German verb *wenden* is related to catastrophe – χαταστροφ in early ancient Greek.)[21] In English, "vent," when employed as a verb, can mean exposed to air. All these roots and variations impart motion and movement. Technically, a window does not block air or refer to a hole in the wall; rather, it refers to the motion of elements, such as the wind, which passes through that hole. If we think of events in such fluid terms then they become ubiquitous and stretch over longer periods of time. An event is not an isolated moment in time, a single measurable uprising or protest, but a long drawn out thread of interconnected occurrences.

In his exploration of the Chicago heat wave in 1995, Eric Klinenberg promotes a version of the aforementioned approach. In the aftermath of the heat wave, a commission appointed by the mayor of Chicago concluded that "the heat wave was a unique *meteorological event*."[22] Klinenberg argues that the heat wave was not a single event reducible to scientific analysis; rather, he treats "the city as a complex social system of integrated institutions that touch *and* interpenetrate in a variety of ways."[23] When Klinenberg couples this approach with the principle that "institutions have a tendency to reveal themselves when they are stressed and in crisis," he is able to wrest the disaster from institutional control, amplify the muted voices of the marginalized, and highlight the multiple sociological layers of so-called natural disasters.[24] The death toll was a function not merely of the rising mercury but also of endemic social ecologies. The data available for a study of Soviet disasters is very limited when compared with the data at Klinenberg's disposal, yet his methodological approach takes earthquakes beyond the pronouncements of Soviet seismologists. The Soviet state did not reveal itself through scientists but through the workers it sent to rebuild destroyed areas, the Komsomol youth who were supposed to rejuvenate ancient cities, and the state media that reacted to the destruction.

In American fiction, this idea of portraying the normal as the unique is illustrated in *The Wonderful Wizard of Oz*, which takes a tornado – a regular meteorological phenomenon of the Midwest – and transforms it into a moral paradigm. Although the twister is presented as having fantastic qualities as it whisks the characters into the Wizard's realm, the tornado per se is no more unusual than a wardrobe in a bedroom or a devastating snowstorm in a short story by Pushkin. Of course, *The Wonderful Wizard of Oz* quickly removes the reader from the social setting of the actual tornado, but this should not detract from the commonplace attributes of the tornado itself.[25] Similarly, the history of the Soviet Union is filled with disasters and accidents that emerged from the flow of ordinary life. In the early 1930s, Mikhail Zoshchenko tells the story of a drunken man during the Crimean earthquake to create a parable that merges a natural disaster with the common cultural phenomenon of drunkenness.[26]

Of course, simply because tornados in the American Midwest and earthquakes in the Crimean peninsula are common phenomena, it would be foolhardy to suggest there is little difference between smaller and larger incidents. Fortunately, the slippery slope of the relativist has no application here. Just because tornadoes were expected does not mean that, if they were large enough, they didn't frighten, shock, and surprise the local population. Too often, however, larger, more significant disasters are presented in isolation. The 1994 Northridge earthquake had a much more devastating effect than did various tremours in Los Angeles, yet it cannot be fully understood without being aware that the citizens of Los Angeles constantly deal with earthquakes, whether through earthquake drills or noticing the cracked walls left by smaller tremours.[27] Although we must grant full respect to larger disasters, we need to be sure that the smaller ones linger in the recesses of our minds.

Beyond nuancing our attitude towards events, disasters enable insights into the perception of time. Historians have become sensitive to the flexibility of time and have ceased to portray time as a fixed entity outside of human experience. Norbert Elias long ago argued that historical figures did not experience time as "an even, uniform, and continuous flow."[28] In his classic study of church bells in nineteenth-century rural France, Alain Corbin links the religious marking of time with sound.[29] The physical act of ringing the bell at a specific time was incidental relative to the set of social symbols and practices the sound evoked. When Einstein's concept of relativity is paired with recent notions of the social construction of reality, time becomes relative to specific events. In the history of science, historians have challenged the notion that scientists were conducting objective experiments because they worked within the parameters of socially constructed devices such as clocks.[30] Although this last conclusion runs roughshod over basic realist elements in Einstein's theory, it does sensitize readers to the importance of time not as an absolute value reflected on clock faces but, rather, as a piece of the social fabric whose meaning is subject to change depending upon circumstances. In a Soviet context, Stephen Hanson explores the relationship between time and revolution in the communist leadership.[31]

In discussing earthquakes, commentators liked to point to street clocks that have been frozen at a particular moment of time. Of course, the mechanical breakdown of a wall clock cannot stop the passage of time, so the reference is clearly metaphorical. Nor do the frozen hands of a wall clock imply that all the wristwatches in the region stopped as well. The contrast between the stoppage of time on public clocks and the continued movement of the second hand on private wristwatches suggests how perceptions of time could be linked to the public and private spheres. Whereas the centralized state preferred to believe that time was measured by public devices and promoted this idea at times of disaster, wristwatches were not necessarily linked to such notions of time. Thus, the idea of time offers interesting perspectives as we attempt to understand the strategies of the authoritarian state and the people who lived within it.

At Chernobyl, time shifted to accommodate the scientific parameters of the catastrophe. The spread of radiation right after the explosion did not create any immediate physical damage so the clocks kept ticking in Pripyat, the city built to house Chernobyl workers. In the affected villages surrounding the nuclear power plant, the measurement of time – whether done according to sunrise or a Soviet watch – was unaffected. Yet the aftermath of the disaster was measured in scientific terms based upon the half-life of radioactive elements. The abstract idea of a half-life introduced a scientific measurement of time that was foreign to many villagers.

In looking at the role of time, it is tempting to write about a discourse of time. No doubt citizens spoke about time and had expressions to categorize it, but one should not exaggerate the link between language and time. The visual experience of looking at a clock, wristwatch, or other time measurement device is vastly different from how time is expressed in Russian grammar. As cognitive linguists have demonstrated, language plays its own games with time, and if the historian wishes to make claims about the discourse of time, she must pay close attention to verb tenses and other aspects of verbs before drawing any significant conclusions — it is not enough to simply mention an overblown postmodern notion about how language limits experience.[32] In other words, without extensive additional linguistic research, there is no evidence to suggest that an earthquake or nuclear explosion changed grammatical representations of time.

The perfect or imperfect expression of a verb remains unaffected whether or not the state makes efforts to harness time for its own needs. Of course, the reference to a discourse on time links the analysis to the claims made about language in Soviet historiography.[33] It has become popular to claim that the Soviet state, particularly in the 1930s, controlled language and thus broke down the barrier between the public and private spheres. State expressions such as "enemy of the people" (*vrag naroda*) transcend private and public spaces and effectively limit the ability of citizens to think other than they do.

At both empirical and theoretical levels, the proposition that the Soviet state controlled language and thus blurred the division between public and private rests upon a very narrow view of language, one that is hard to associate with disasters. Language consists not just of the words we use but also of the expressions we invent and design based on the grammatical possibilities inherent within any given language. Plagiarists, for example, can be caught because we understand that people rarely write identical sentences even though they may be expressing the same idea. Similarly, one can hardly claim that the state controlled language simply because it had mastered a few slogans. Any citizen capable of saying "enemy of the people" had the ability to say the opposite: "not enemy of the people." In English and in Russian, it is always possible to grammatically negate a sentence (Everyone who claimed to love Stalin had the linguistic ability to say that they did not love Stalin). If it never occurred to a speaker to utter the negated sentence, this was not a function of language. Much recent linguistic research highlights the public importance of language but not at the cost of the private sphere. In his *Philosophical Investigations*, Ludwig Wittgenstein famously argues that there is no such thing as a private language. He does not, however, imply that individuals cannot have secrets or develop independent thought.[34] In other words, the language of disaster was important, but, as we shall soon see, not in a way that completely blurs the distinction between public and private.

Beyond these limitations, certain linguistic conventions offer contours for understanding disasters. The Russian language distinguished and distinguishes between a spontaneous natural occurrence and an unfortunate accident that has its origins in human failure. Russians could describe a disaster however they wished, but generally the choice was between two terms – one spoke either of a *stikhiinoe bedstvie* or of an *avariia*.[35] A *stikhiinoe bedstvie* was a natural, uncontrolled, and often spontaneous calamity and the term was used to describe phenomena such as earthquakes and flooding. Interestingly, the root of the *stikhiinoe* is related to *stikh*, which appears in *stikhotvorenie*, or poem.[36] On its own, *stikh* can mean verse or moodiness, a moodiness that suggests the fluctuating rhythms of a poem. Linked to disasters, *stikhiinoe bedstvie* refers not only to the moodiness of nature but also to a rhythm, suggesting that these were recurring phenomena.[37]

In contrast, an *avariia*, or accident, connotes a human-made problem.[38] Chernobyl was referred to as an *avariia*, and therefore it was linguistically linked to mining disasters, bus crashes, and other such misfortunes.[39] Officials did argue about the appropriateness of these terms. Chernobyl, for example, started as an *avariia*; however, as cracks developed in the political structure of the Soviet Union, activists pushed to have it referred to as a catastrophe (*katastrofa*).[40]

The word "catastrophe" also had specific connotations in the Soviet Union. According to Dal', it came to Russian via French in the early nineteenth century, so it had a shorter etymological history in Russian than it did in French or German. But even without a long history, its usage was careful and specific. In the Soviet Union, only certain events could be referred to as catastrophes. The word "catastrophe" could be freely used with respect to war but not with respect to natural disasters. Publication laws had strict restrictions with respect to using the term "catastrophes" because, unlike disasters, catastrophes were closely linked with human casualties, industrial fires, and calamities that might be the consequence of direct human error. Broader, more challenging, references to catastrophes only rose during Gorbachev's glasnost. Now one could write not only about economic catastrophe but also about environmental catastrophe – and, of course, the Chernobyl catastrophe.[41] One might even be tempted to say that "catastrophe" became a popular word.

The linguistic distinction between *stikhiinoe bedstvie* and *avariia* was not unintentional; indeed, it can be seen in the response of the Communist Party. A spontaneous calamity did not require the party to find a guilty person; rather, it became a test of the will to overcome the forces of nature with the progressive means available to an advanced communist state. Normally, in an *avariia*, there was nothing to overcome. An *avariia* required committees to determine its cause.[42] Whether a bus flew off a bridge and into a river or a reactor exploded at Chernobyl, the party found convenient scapegoats. Although the parameters of the response, whether to the *stikhiinoe bedstvie* in Armenia or to the *avariia* in Chernobyl, were very similar, the political repercussions were distinct and thus require exploration.

These distinctions were not unique to the Soviet Union: American political debates have been framed within similar terms. Deborah Stone indicates that, "as one side in a political battle seeks to push a problem into the realm of human purpose, the other side seeks to push it away from intent back toward the realm of nature."[43] This thesis indirectly explains the popularity of the weather channel. As one of its scientists notes: "One thing people always loved about the Weather Channel was that it was nobody's fault."[44] The recent attention to global climate change has increased the awareness of humanity's role in environmental catastrophes, but placing the blame on nature had, and has, its political benefits. In the Soviet Union, there was only one official side in the political battle, but the Soviets nevertheless understood how to push the problem outside the realm of human purpose.

Disasters and the words chosen to categorize them indicate the shifting policies and priorities of individual Soviet administrations. Disasters are not, however, a purely political phenomenon as each disaster reveals particular socio-cultural elements of any given society. In a Soviet state that took pride in its ethnic diversity, disasters were an opportunity for members from all the ethnic republics to come together and contribute to the building, or rebuilding, of a Soviet city. The notions "brotherhood of peoples" and, after the mid-1930s, *Druzhba narodov*, or "friendship of peoples," were key elements of the Soviet project.[45] Dating back to Lenin's statements about national self-determination right after the revolution of 1917, Soviet authorities were fully cognizant of the ethnic diversity of the Soviet Union. Officially, the Soviet Union supported national diversity, although not to the point of self-determination. Yet the policy towards nationalities was a mixed bag, promoting certain cultural features while denying others.[46]

At a number of levels, the response to disasters was also deeply intertwined with the policy on nationalities. Soviet authorities had little control over the timing and location of disasters (even a conscious policy to place nuclear power plants in Ukraine did not mandate a disaster in that part of the USSR), so the rescue and recovery mission took place throughout the vast expanse of communist territory. More important, the dynamic of the response changed over time. If the Crimean earthquake in 1927 was largely the responsibility of authorities of the RSFSR, by the time of the Ashgabat earthquake in 1948, the Soviet state took responsibility and began to make direct appeals to the friendship of peoples. Friendship in this context had a less fundamental calling than it had in Tashkent in 1966, when Brezhnev and Kosygin repeated the slogan at every opportunity.

The state and other participants recognized the political potential – both positive and negative – of disasters and reacted accordingly. In the case of Tashkent, Soviet authorities promoted their efforts at creating a globally significant multi-ethnic Central Asian capital. It was not, however, always this way. Traditionally, earthquakes were not a Russian problem because they occurred on the periphery of the Russian Empire. Imperial authorities were more concerned with traditional Russian problems, such as fires and flooding, than they were with earthquakes. The response depended upon the immediate interests of the state, and, for this reason, an evident hierarchy of disasters existed and persisted.

If the Russian Empire was a multi-ethnic state, it was also a multi-disaster state. Countries such as Switzerland have been able to incorporate avalanche dangers into their national identity because their mountainous regions are dominated by a single geological feature.[47] The Russian Empire, however, was too vast for this, even though it pretended otherwise. At the end of the nineteenth century, an earthquake wreaked havoc in Tashkent, and Imperial authorities had to deal with the problem. But having to deal with an earthquake was the exception rather than the rule: more often than not it was fires, not earthquakes, that destroyed Russian cities.[48] In 1842, a massive fire destroyed entire sections of Kazan, an important city on the Volga River.[49]

Since cities had to be reconstructed, architects became involved with the relief effort to transform a devastated landscape into a vision of the Soviet future. The extent of architectural influence depended upon the nature of the disaster and the importance that Soviet officials gave to the recovery of the particular area in question – architects had little to do with rural flooding but were instrumental in redesigning urban areas. When Tashkent crumbled to the ground, architects were immediately ushered in to reconstruct the city on paper, then in mock-ups, and finally in the central areas of the demolished city. Given the general Soviet desire to refashion the urban environment of the Homo Sovieticus, plans for the reconstruction of Tashkent were already in the air, so for some the earthquake was seen as convenient. Whatever individual architects felt about the tremour, it called for extensive design models in which Western influences were clear to see. The neon lights that were glowing in Moscow had a distinctly Western tinge, and the desirability of Western designs was felt in Tashkent as well.[50] Through these extensive design models, historians have an opportunity to re-evaluate the spatial and visual values inherent in an important Soviet city. In particular, they allow the researcher to juxtapose Western influences with indigenous Central Asian styles

– a juxtaposition that would seem to challenge the notion of what constitutes a Soviet city.[51]

The atmosphere surrounding the reconstruction of cities turns disasters into greater issues. The response that emphasized the friendship of peoples did not differ from the response to many large engineering projects. Although the Dnepropetrovsk dam in the 1920s was constructed using predominantly Russian and Ukrainian labour, the construction of the BAM railway in the 1970s leaned on the idea of the friendship of peoples.[52] Disaster response reflected larger socialist proclivities and was often business as usual. Moreover, the friendship of peoples was not a static concept. In the late 1940s, the Soviet government had specific tasks for specific peoples, and the concept was reserved for the peoples of Central Asia; by 1966, however, it encompassed all the republics in the Soviet Union. In Chernobyl in 1986, however, the concept shrank and only a handful of republics participated. Unlike in the Tashkent earthquake, in Chernobyl the Central Asian republics played only a secondary role. And, of course, as perestroika wore on, the concept of the friendship of peoples collapsed altogether. There are ample reasons to take a cynical view of Soviet nationalities policies, but disasters permit us to take a closer look at the changing profile of this slogan/concept.

The concept of the friendship of peoples forced individuals far and wide to help with emergencies; a Latvian travelled thousands of kilometres to help in Tashkent in 1966. This population movement did not just fill the requirements of a Soviet-era slogan: it also contributed to the long-term migrations that emerge as a result of disasters. The earthquakes and Chernobyl caused population movements, suggesting that the Soviet population was not stuck in one place. Yet migration patterns came in many forms. In some instances, the volunteers who arrived in Tashkent from Ukraine and other republics never returned. They settled into a new life in the Uzbek capital, once again shifting the demographics of this Central Asian city.[53] In the reverse direction, evacuees from Tashkent arrived in Ukraine to find a new life in Ukrainian towns and villages. Each incident of migration was linked to new social problems, even though the original disaster was now thousands of kilometres away.

Disasters are times when communities, both local and national, are called upon to volunteer their services to aid the affected. Typically, "assistance to the victims comes first of all from the other survivors, with the means used by the authorities contributing to the emergency only to a very little extent."[54] Ample examples indicate the diversity of volunteer experience. In her work on the San Francisco earthquake of 1906 and recent American disasters, Rebecca Solnit emphasizes the ability of local communities to organize their own rescue squads when faced with a democratic state that is either unprepared to respond or, through its response, aggravates the disaster.[55] In a catastrophe such as the tsunami off the coast of Sumatra, Indonesia, in 2004, volunteer aid came in all shapes and sizes. Citizens around the world made cash contributions to the rescue and rebuilding effort, and individuals arrived on the scene to help as well. Throughout the twentieth century, beyond the volunteer efforts of individual citizens, the International Red Cross and Red Crescent, as well as independent NGOs such as Médecins sans Frontières, played important roles in disaster relief.

In the literature, efforts that exist independently of government responses are associated with the development of civil society and the creation of a strong citizenry that can resist or even replace an overbearing state. Despite the apparent ease with which we associate this activity with civil society, the phenomenon remains conceptually difficult to qualify. Civil society itself is a contested term and has a different dynamic depending upon the philosophical inspiration behind the idea – a Lockean version of civil society differs considerably from a Habermasian version, yet both still have supporters today.[56] Whether one focuses on individuals keeping tabs on the government or the bourgeoisie encouraging the development of a free press and pluralistic public sphere, civil society still loosely refers to activities that occur outside a state structure, whether that structure is based on democratic or authoritarian principles. The activity can vary greatly, but most political theorists value the role of volunteer activity, in associational or individual form, because it suggests an active and engaged citizenry. Disasters regularly called forth a massive amount of volunteer activity, yet the political and social significance of volunteer work is not always clear. Sometimes the work of a volunteer and his or her participation in civil society is transient, lasting only as long as the disaster. Citizens organize in moments of disaster and evince characteristics of civil society only to disband once the danger is over. This was evident in the contemporary Russian Federation when fire threatened the population around Moscow. In the summer of 2010, many "volunteers" limited their effort to dropping off clothes at a single point.[57] How does this form of civil society measure up to the work of established associations? The relationship between charitable work and civil society has also been questioned. If volunteering is limited to donating money at the checkout counter or over the internet, does this isolated action qualify the participant for membership in civil society?[58] Finally, there is a moral component to volunteering: If one offers help because one feels it is one's Christian duty to do so, can this help be constitutive of civil society?

When historians write about "state and society,"[59] volunteers are often interpreted as a subset of society. This phenomenon is perhaps most apparent in the history of Imperial Russia because, in this case, it is often easier to separate state and society. In his study of famine in the late nineteenth century, Richard Robbins juxtaposed the efforts of non-state organizations such as the zemstvo and the efforts of the Imperial bureaucracy with regard to coping with the disaster. According to Robbins, the state played a critical role in managing the positive response.[60] Robbins's analysis creates a comparative perspective for disaster response, but it also indicates a critical difference between the Imperial and Soviet eras. In late Imperial times, the boundary between state and society was certainly blurred, but not to the point that the interests of state and society could not be separated.

These difficult questions are further complicated in the authoritarian atmosphere of Imperial Russia and the Soviet Union. In Imperial Russia, subjects of the tsar had much greater opportunities to form independent organizations than did people in the Soviet period. The tsarist state imposed strict parameters on organizational life, had model statutes that volunteer organizations had to adopt, and carefully monitored associational life; yet citizens were free to propose the creation of almost any sort of social organization. Of course, the intentions of the participants can be debated at length, but the spectrum for organizational opportunities was still broader than it was after 1917.[61] The Soviet system continued to refer to a volunteer group as an *obshchestvennaia organizatsiia* (public organization), but the meaning of the expression had changed dramatically since tsarist times. A public organization referred to groups such as the Central Council of Sporting Societies and Organizations or the All-Union Volunteer Society of Booklovers; although one chose to be a member, the organizations themselves were sponsored by the Communist Party. It is for this reason that historians are reluctant to make a link between Soviet volunteer organizations and civil society – a link often taken for granted in other geopolitical contexts.

Unfortunately, this restrictive interpretive position has led scholars to dismiss the Soviet volunteer experience altogether. In a recent work on philanthropy in Russia, the authors give the reader historical background from the Imperial period, skip the Soviet period, and then focus on philanthropy in Russia since the collapse of the Soviet Union. This omission occurs even though the sociological definition of volunteering for the Russian Federation presented in the volume is consistent with the nature of volunteering in the Soviet Union. For example, it refers to any activity conducted in one's free time that helps another person, or any activity that benefits someone else and for which an individual does not receive financial compensation.[62] Disasters called forth an immense number of these activities. While difficult to assess, volunteering in the Soviet Union deserves greater attention.

Although Russian scholars downplay volunteer work in the Soviet Union, historians in Germany and the United States attempt to qualify it. In his study of the militant godless, Daniel Peris comments on the phenomenon of volunteerism in the 1920s. With regard to what he refers to as "single-issue voluntary societies," he spends more time analyzing the benefits of these organizations for the Bolsheviks than he does the benefits that might be associated with joining them.[63] Since the volunteer societies "were as much reflections of Bolshevik political culture as they were conscious agents of change," they did not embody the ideal of those volunteer associations promoted by theorists of civil society. At best, they represented a "mock civil society."[64] Peris is certainly correct to emphasize the abundance of volunteer associations in the 1920s and the limits within which they functioned, but his perspective tells us little about the volunteers themselves.

In a different context, Klaus Gestwa investigates volunteer work at major industrial projects. This differs slightly from what we have addressed so far in that the associational aspect is removed, but it gets to the idea of choice (it is a more philosophical rather than sociological idea of volunteering). In 1956, the Communist Party needed volunteers to help with the construction of the Bratsk Hydroelectric Power Station on the Angara River in Siberia. Very quickly, the authorities received applications from twenty-five thousand volunteers. In his comments on this phenomenon, Gestwa notes that the Komsomol youth who volunteered did not romanticize communism; rather, they romanticized the adventure itself and looked forward to escaping a small apartment in the big city. They wanted to develop a new "feeling of freedom" far out on the taiga.[65] This initiates a discussion of the variety of motives an individual might have for volunteering and challenges the idea that volunteering should be assessed solely according to its ability to establish civil society.

Even more directly, Douglas Weiner evaluates the performance of environmental organizations in the 1960s and the 1970s. To emphasize the broad possibilities of participation, Weiner coins the phrase "a little corner of freedom."[66] His analysis balances three aspects of the volunteer phenomenon. First, the state could actively co-opt an association and make it a mouthpiece for the official view. Second, while this possibility certainly did exist, these organizations could also be politically independent and could exert political pressure, even if they did not threaten to bring down the Soviet state (at least in the 1960s). Weiner indicates how public opposition influenced the execution of grandiose engineering plans. Finally, volunteer organizations allowed individuals a means for at least some sort of creative expression, both in packed meeting halls and in forests and along lakes.[67] This last possibility is closer to the experience of disaster volunteers.

When the All-Russian Society for the Preservation of Historical and Cultural Monuments (*Vserossiiskoe obshchestvo okhrany pamiatnikov istorii i kul'tury* [VOOPIK]) emerged in the 1960s, its membership swelled into the millions, and, as with so many other organizations, the Soviets proudly claimed that the size of the membership reflected the public commitment of Soviet citizens. While much of this membership was coerced and passive, there was a core of volunteers who exerted an influence on state policy. Without contextualizing his analysis within the theoretical frame of civil society, John Dunlap devotes an entire chapter to voluntary societies, demonstrating their political clout.[68] There were all sorts of occasions upon which citizens spontaneously volunteered their time and energy. Volunteer activity came in all shapes and sizes, although it remains difficult to qualify its political nature.

An analysis of the extensive volunteer work undertaken during disasters not only takes a first step towards qualifying volunteer work in the Soviet era but also highlights the diversity of experience that volunteer work made possible. During disasters, the Soviet state encouraged citizens to volunteer, and many did so of their own accord. While political and societal pressures were not absent, disasters allowed citizens to choose how they wished to help. They could send money, work a day for free, travel to the disaster area, house victims, supply food, and so on. In the philosophical sense of the term, they exercised a degree of "free will" in deciding how best to help. Moreover, the state had to develop a number of complex schemes to entice even more volunteers. When a worker from Ukraine was sent to Tashkent, it was not just a matter of buying a train ticket and showing up at a construction site in Uzbekistan. The state developed a complex system of rewards, including salary enhancements, to entice workers to make the trip. Although the reward system can be seen to undermine the propagandistic claims of the Soviet state about the willingness of its citizens to volunteer, it gave subjects a chance to decide their own fate.

The compensatory aspect of volunteer work has to be seen within the context of volunteering in general. We should not dismiss volunteers simply because they received compensation, whether financial or otherwise. That is, volunteer activity should not be perceived solely as an act of altruism – a difficult moral position in a postmodern world in which the volunteer has nothing to gain personally. Volunteer activity in social clubs and public organizations has been associated with social and public prestige as well as with career advancement.[69] Soviet citizens had a mixture of these possibilities. A volunteer was not an unpaid Good Samaritan but, rather, someone who chose the direction of his or her own activities while, at the same time, assisting those in need. If we dismiss Soviet volunteers simply because they received extra pay or the Communist Party had the ability to influence their decision making, we would unjustly eliminate other individual motives (whether these were opposed or faithful to the communist regime).

Disasters were times of great improvisation. While the Soviet state generally had a master plan for all contingencies, and this plan dictated many aspects of the response to disasters, there arose numerous situations that posed unexpected problems and that required spontaneous responses. The extent of improvisation is best seen from the perspective of the Komsomol, the Soviet youth organization that sent out rescue workers. These youths arrived in great numbers, but organizers had a hard time keeping track of their arrival and departure as they were easily distracted by parties, were often immune to ideological lessons, and were highly vulnerable to industrial accidents at reconstruction sites. Needless to say, this resulted in their work being subject to a high degree of instability and irregularity. However, this irregularity was not simply a sign of a Soviet system that did not perform to the standards of its own propaganda machine; rather, it functioned to create spaces for individuals to extend the parameters of their own lives. In architectural terms, improvisation challenged Moscow's master plans. The speed of the rebuilding process and the different tactics of building teams from member republics meant that the reconstruction process did not follow the streets urban planners had carefully drawn on blueprints. And, despite the requirements of authorities in Moscow, Tashkent architectural journals were full of discussions that questioned their plans.[70] These discussions dragged on for years and ensured that, in the 1970s, the reconstruction of a Soviet city was not a neatly planned affair.

Finally, disasters led to a discussion of the relationship between the urban and the rural. Bolshevism had problems with rural areas since October 1917, and, despite Lenin's early concessions, rural areas could hardly expect light treatment at the hands of a party whose ideology was based upon the success of an industrialized society. The relationship between urban area and rural areas is a key theme of Soviet history, and it emerges in the history of disasters as well. For example, large dam projects were celebrated as achievements of Soviet engineering while, at the same time, being human-made disasters resulting in the flooding of traditional Russian villages. In *Poem about the Sea* (*Poema o more*), Alexander Dovzhenko and his wife, Iuliia Solnsteva, dramatically film a story about how villagers had to evacuate their homes to make way for a massive hydroelectric project.[71] The extent of the damage and the problems faced in evacuating ancient villages is hauntingly portrayed in Valentin Rasputin's *Farewell to Matyora* (*Proshchanie s Materoi*).[72]

Whether in the shape of flooding, earthquakes, or radioactive explosions, disasters underscored the continual tensions between rural life and urban life. Urban rebuilding projects had much greater media potential than did the aid efforts that were scattered throughout rural areas. Thus, even though the destruction of a city was extremely expensive for the Soviet state, there was some propagandistic advantage to be gained by, for example, photographing occupants moving into their newly constructed apartments. Aspects of the urban-rural divide were also evident in emigration patterns as many urban evacuees protested their reassignment to rural areas, once again highlighting the element of choice (or lack thereof) presented to residents. It was perhaps the scattered nature of the 1988 Armenian earthquake, which affected both cities and rural areas, that made it difficult for Soviet authorities to categorize. In the thirty-kilometre zone around Chernobyl, the evacuation process was complicated by the fact that both Pripyat, a city of forty-five hundred people, and the tiny villages that dotted the countryside had to be evacuated. Urban and rural residents made separate demands upon an increasingly fragile state.

Globally, disasters expose numerous rifts within various social structures, and they provide researchers from numerous disciplines with the opportunity to analyze their impact on human societies. Bearing in mind the theoretical and interpretive parameters just discussed, we can now turn to specific cases in Soviet history that seem to portray earth, cement, and steel being thrown into the maelstrom.

PART ONE

Disorder in the Orderly Stalinist World

2

The Crimean Peninsula in September 1927 and Ashgabat in October 1948

In the 1920s, the new Soviet authorities had to overcome a number of hurdles before they could solidify the new state. In 1917, the Bolsheviks had successfully put an end to the Imperial government, but by the start of the 1920s they were still fighting a civil war against resilient opponents. Once the civil war ended, social and economic peace did not follow military peace. The Bolsheviks emerged victorious from the civil war and silenced their Menshevik critics, but they were not in a position to impose a full-fledged communist program while the country suffered the aftermath of this war. The revolution had been premised upon Marxist notions of an industrial society, yet industrialization had stalled in the 1920s, when the new Soviet government had to focus on recovering from the civil war. War communism and the widespread nationalization of property yielded to the New Economic Policy (NEP), which promoted small-scale capitalism. When, in 1925, Bukharin told the peasants to enrich themselves, it appeared as though the communist world would be turned upside down.[1] In Fyodor Gladkov's *Cement*, the main characters try to cope with the NEP as they question the direction the revolution has taken.[2] The artistic world was also in flux as artists and architects competed to impose their revolutionary culture on the aesthetic, intellectual, and physical landscape of the Soviet Union.[3]

After Lenin died in 1924, Soviet leadership wrestled with his legacy and struggled to define the Soviet Union on its own terms. Nikolai Bukharin continued to promote the NEP, Leon Trotsky advocated permanent revolution, and Josef Stalin performed a delicate dance between his rivals to ensure his ultimate supremacy.[4] The direction only really became clear after the Shakhty trial in May 1928, when bourgeois engineers were accused of wrecking equipment and jeopardizing the future of the Soviet state. Shortly thereafter, Stalin successfully dismissed his major rivals, initiated the first Five Year Plan, accelerated the tempo of industrialization, and began the brutal process of collectivizing the peasants.

Only months before the Shakhty trial, the Crimean peninsula was rocked by a series of incredibly powerful earthquakes. On 12 September 1927, the first shock hit the region, creating panic among residents and tourists alike.[5] The northern Black Sea region, a holiday destination for NEPmen and workers alike, was transformed into a scene of destruction. Local newspapers had to convince their readers that, despite the rumours, the peninsula was not about to slip into the Black Sea.[6]

Earthquakes in the Crimean peninsula were not uncommon, and even if detailed documentation on the older disasters was lacking, seismologists had no problem listing past tremours. In 1843, in 1855, and in 1859, smaller earthquakes were felt in the region. In the spring of 1872, an earthquake was felt in Yalta, and in 1919, one was registered in Simferopol. More important, only months before the September earthquake discussed here, a strong shock ripped through the entire peninsula. In June 1927, an earthquake rattled windows, shook lamps, and threw objects from shelves.[7] What happened in June was, however, minor in comparison with what happened in September.

Beyond its sheer magnitude, the September earthquake was significant because it ripped through the entire peninsula. Scientists in the Crimean peninsula applied the Rossi-Forel scale to measure the force of the quake. Unlike the Richter scale, which simply measures the force of nature, the Rossi-Forel scale measures the impact of a disaster on the community.[8] For example, in Simferopol, the June earthquake did not exceed level 5, a level at which individuals feel the earthquake, a few objects move, but no real harm is done.[9] In September, the magnitude in coastal cities such as Yalta, Balaklava, and Sevastopol was around level 9 – partial or total destruction of buildings. Simferopol, towards the centre of the peninsula, did not suffer as much, but it registered level 7, two notches higher than what it had registered in June, and thus saw damage to buildings.[10]

The coastal cities were the first to notice shifting ground. Shortly after midnight on 12 September, Alushta, then Yalta and Sevastopol, registered shocks before they spread inland; since Alushta came first, seismologists estimated the epicentre was about twenty-five to thirty kilometres off its shore. The earthquake did not have its epicentre in the middle of a single city, and its "character" changed depending upon geographic, geological, and cultural peculiarities. Perhaps Yalta suffered the most. Numerous buildings from before the Great War had been poorly constructed as owners wanted to take full advantage of those travelling to the spas. Moreover, a number of these spas were built on hilly and unstable terrain.[11] In Alupka, on the outskirts of Yalta, a mosque lost its entire eastern wall. Since Alupka sits at the foot of a mountain, it was particularly susceptible to landslides. In fact, the earthquake in June had already rumbled the slopes and loosened the terrain.[12] Next door to Alupka, Simeiz miraculously suffered very little.[13] Damage varied from place to place within the peninsula, thus making it extremely difficult to coordinate relief efforts and to determine where help was needed the most.

The timing of the earthquake was precipitous as the organization and administration of the Soviet Union was in flux. Although there had been disasters, such as the famine during the civil war, the Soviet state had no set plan for dealing with disasters. This was not a bureaucratic oversight; rather, it reflected a young state still finding its way. Thus, the response was much more haphazard than was the case in later years. When earthquakes struck Ashgabat in 1948 and Tashkent in 1966, Moscow immediately took control of the situation. In 1927, the Soviet state left much of the work to the Russian Soviet Federative Socialist Republic, since the Crimean Autonomous Soviet Socialist Republic (Crimean ASSR) fell under its jurisdiction (only after the Second World War was the Crimean ASSR dissolved and only under Khrushchev did it enter the jurisdiction of Ukraine).[14] In its turn, the RSFSR was willing to pass responsibility on to public organizations such as the Red Cross and to encourage private fundraisers to alleviate a financial burden it could not face. The Crimean earthquake, then, serves to answer important questions about different political and social layers at a time of crisis and to establish a comparative perspective when considering later disasters in the Soviet Union. The Ashgabat earthquake occurred towards the end of the Stalinist USSR, but the response was vastly different from 1927 on the southern periphery of the RSFSR.

Without a centralized response, the rescue operation after the earthquake called upon a variety of agencies and actors. With its unwieldy name, the Committee to Help with Struggle of the Aftermath of the Crimean Earthquake, located within the Ministry of Health within the RSFSR, became the main state organ responsible for coordinating the response and petitioning for funds. Administratively, it was below the Soviet ministries and above the ministries of the Crimean Autonomous Republic, thus ensuring an administration striven with rife and tension. Outside the administrative sphere of the Soviet state, the Soviet Red Cross provided necessary medical aid to victims of the earthquake. In 1927, it enjoyed a considerable amount of freedom, and thus its activities may be juxtaposed with theories of civil society to judge both the political and social value of its efforts. The Soviet Red Cross operated during the entire Soviet period, but the Crimean earthquake was the last time it played an independent role until the Armenian earthquake in 1988. The scientific community, which terrified residents with its predictions, soothed them with its corrections, raised money with its public lectures, and also influenced the outcome of the relief effort. This activity in the Crimean peninsula foreshadowed the public role of scientists after the Chernobyl catastrophe in April 1986, when Crimean scientists protested the expansion of Soviet nuclear energy. Finally, the unique position of the Crimean peninsula as the sanatorium for the entire Soviet Union affected the relief effort as local authorities invented arguments to highlight the critical importance of saving their own region from natural destruction. This strategy would be repeated in later years as well.

While the Crimean peninsula was just recovering from the earthquake when Stalin effectively took sole control of the Soviet Union, at the time of the Ashgabat earthquake in 1948 he had been guiding the country for two decades. The people who had supported the NEP had been banished from memory, kulaks had been deported to Siberia or physically liquidated, the Soviet Union had become an industrial power pushing the creation of massive new cities such as Magnitogorsk, and millions of Soviet citizens had been sent to remote penal colonies spread throughout the harshest regions of the country. In addition to these hardships, there was the German invasion of the Soviet Union in 1941. Stalin was unprepared for battle, millions of lives were lost, and over the course of four years the physical infrastructure of Soviet cities in the USSR's western regions was reduced to rubble. Although Soviet citizens defeated Nazi Germany, once the guns were quiet they had to focus on rebuilding shattered cities and burned out villages. Only three years after Germany's unconditional surrender and only one year before the new superpower tested its first atomic weapon, the Ashgabat earthquake tested the forces of a Soviet state still adjusting to its new international position.

After the earthquake in Ashgabat, the highly centralized Soviet state was in a position to focus its resources on the relief effort. In the wake of the Crimean earthquake, no central authority expressed interest in taking the lead. Two decades later, the Stalinist state orchestrated the response from the very beginning. However, orchestration and effectiveness are not synonymous; despite its attempts, the Soviet state never developed a full-scale relief plan. While it issued decrees and mandated parameters for the reconstruction of the city, it left much of the relief effort to the authorities in Turkmenistan. This aspect of the Stalinist response sheds light on the ability and willingness of the authoritarian state to control and monitor activity on the periphery of the USSR.

Two identical geological phenomena struck the Soviet Union two decades apart. Each tragedy exposed various layers of Soviet society to challenges – challenges that were treated in unique ways. While the response in the Crimean peninsula was taken care of by the RSFSR, after the Second World War, the Stalinist government had to decide how to invoke the concept of the friendship of peoples to best effect. With both earthquakes striking the periphery of Soviet territory, the responses to them highlight the changing dynamic of centre-periphery relations. A comparative perspective is also critical for understanding the nature of volunteering. Volunteers stepped forward in 1927 but were largely absent in 1948. Finally, the movement of peoples also played a role in the disasters. In the aftermath of tragedy, these changes highlight the shifting priorities of the Soviet state and the values of the citizens in the diverse ethnic areas of the USSR.

In early September 1927, the Crimean peninsula was still full of vacationers who had arrived from Moscow and other major cities. They may have been holidaying on the shores of the Black Sea or recovering in a sanatorium when they felt the earth tremble violently below their feet. One vacationer wrote about how the place transformed from being a vacationer's paradise into being a spot where children aged prematurely. The remaining eleven days of people's vacations were spent sleeping outside under the cypress trees. When they returned to Moscow from their summer holidays, they were, for the first time in their lives, thrilled to be home.[15]

Despite the Crimean peninsula's geopolitically vulnerable position, near but not adjacent to sites where the French had landed during the Crimean War, it took weeks for Soviet authorities to soothe the nerves of rattled citizens and bring a semblance of order to the region. In later years, it became de rigueur to laud the controlled behaviour of Soviet citizens in the face of natural disasters – behaviour that was seen as the result of a Bolshevik education – but in the 1920s, the panic was public knowledge. In 1926, Amo Bek-nazaryan opened his box-office hit *Namus* with scenes of destruction and panic in the wake of an earthquake.[16] When an actual earthquake struck the Crimean peninsula in 1927, chaos was in the air. The panic was portrayed in popular literature; for example, the heroes of Il'f and Petrov's *Twelve Chairs* grab the eleventh chair just as the Crimean earthquake strikes. This hugely popular story reflects contemporary accounts of the quake.[17] In Evpatoria, rumours spread about an ever-increasing death toll, and the local police, who "for unknown reasons shot randomly in the air," also succumbed to panic.[18] *Krasnyi Krym*, a local Crimean newspaper, begged its readers to remain calm. It published official statements imploring residents to ignore "foolish stories and rumours" about the earthquake, contending that these rumours did not contain a grain of truth.[19] As it happened, the rumour mill was as powerful as the Soviet government.

The Crimean authorities were worried about individuals but they also had their eyes on the long-term economic consequences for tourism in the area. When the Soviet state was on the eve of a great industrialization drive, Crimean authorities were focusing their efforts in an anti-industrial direction. Bucolic sanatoria had to be rebuilt. Unlike the industrial drive, the recovery was planned as a cooperative effort between the RSFSR and anyone who had the time or energy to help. *Krasnyi Krym* was not embarrassed to publish official remarks to the effect that the state simply did not have the resources to combat the devastation on its own. Anatoly Lunacharsky, the commissar of enlightenment, wrote that, "without the help of the Soviet public [*obshchestvennost'*], the Crimea was unlikely to recover rapidly from its wounds." The head of the rescue commission told readers that the government could not do it alone but that, with the public taking the initiative, the Crimea would once again be an inviting resort for Soviet and international revolutionaries.[20]

The responsible commission formed within the Ministry of Health had to develop a strategy for dealing with the losses when no one had money to hand around; in 1927, the Soviet economy was still struggling after the scissors crisis (i.e., when industrial prices rose and agricultural prices sank). Unemployment was high and dissatisfaction with the NEP was growing in party circles.[21] When the RSFSR asked the Soviet government for supplementary assistance, the government reported that it had no extra money lying around and that the RSFSR's budget gave it the capacity to top off the aid.[22] For their part, representatives of the Crimean Republic pressured the RSFSR for more funds; in response, the RSFSR accused it of exaggerating the destruction in order to finance new building projects in the Crimean peninsula. RSFSR also accused Crimeans of asking for money "to construct homes which had previously not existed." When Crimeans spoke about recovering from the earthquake, they were really talking about transforming the economy of the peninsula.[23] In discussions with Crimean officials, the RSFSR kept reminding them that the state could not cover all their costs. When the Volga region and the Far East experienced flooding, the state turned down requests to provide complete compensation to peasants and *meshchane* (poorer urban residents).[24]

Officials who had visited the region and spoken with peasants wanted to combat the spreading rumour that the state had the resources to rebuild their homes.[25] Instead of rushing to build new homes and redesign cities, committee members were more interested in resuscitating as many old buildings as possible. The transportation of materials across great distances was always a costly endeavour after a natural disaster, and, in 1927, the Crimea had scarce supplies of iron and cement and no money to have them delivered from other republics.[26] Even the thought of investing in the construction of expensive "antiseismological buildings" was considered a task for the future.[27] The RSFSR was also unwilling to rethink insurance rules related to natural disasters. It did not want *Gosstrakh*, the state insurance trust, to be forced to pay out premiums for buildings destroyed in earthquakes, although it did agree that *Gosstrakh* could offer compensation in specific instances.[28]

In their turn, Crimean officials made it clear that they did not want complete compensation. Stalin only pronounced the liquidation of the kulaks as a class in December 1929, but already in 1927 Crimean officials saw no reason to give wealthier peasants aid money. They agreed that they did not have a responsibility to help private owners.[29] The money was designated for the *bedniaki*, or poorer peasants.[30] To ease the burden on the RSFSR, the Crimeans suggested a five-year aid plan and a slow but sure reconstruction.[31] The sanatoria along the coast, which had suffered extensive damage, were a main concern. If they were not repaired, they would not generate revenue; and if they did not generate revenue, there would be no money for repairs.[32] The RSFSR was only willing to offer assistance to select sanatoria (primarily those that were on the state budget roll). Thus many group appeals for reconstruction money for sanatoria, such as one from the *profsoiuz* (trade union), were turned down.[33] In general, Crimean officials complained about the "miserly" sums that were being offered for an earthquake that was estimated to have caused 32 million rubles' worth of damages.[34]

Despite all the haggling, the Crimea received financial aid from the RSFSR in the form of cash and credit. The aid package did not cover the damage, but long-term loans were earmarked for the "poorest" peasants, the sanatoria received some funds, and money was allotted to the reconstruction of the Nikitskii Botanical Gardens.[35] Not all the funds, however, came from the treasury of the RSFSR. Many commentators believed the remaining republics had a responsibility to the Crimean peninsula not because of the "friendship between peoples," a political idea that was only introduced in the middle of the 1930s, but because everyone used the area as a holiday resort.[36] The Crimeans received financial aid from other republics, although this was neither systematic nor coordinated with Moscow. This aid was not significant enough to merit being individualized as a budget item in the recovery plan; however, *Krasnyi Krym* reported when Dagestan sent building materials or Belarus sent a modest amount of money.[37] Since the state emphasized its unwillingness to cover all costs, the public had to find creative ways to raise money. In Saratov, advertisements were placed in the press and pamphlets distributed around town to raise awareness; the local Red Cross spread the word, while movies and theatrical pieces presented in theatres and workers' clubs raised more money.[38] The head of the Moscow Operetta Theatre suggested that theatres raise money through "cheery intermissions" in which renowned actors would perform solo acts in the foyers.[39] Years later, the Moscow Operetta Theatre took an active role in raising spirits after the earthquake in Tashkent.[40] Russian officials did, however, turn down an application from Crimeans to organize a series of fundraising concerts across the RSFSR.[41] Too much public activity was as undesirable as was too little.

In other cases, independent donations arrived from smaller organizations around the Soviet Union. A leprosarium contributed almost seven rubles and church councils offered almost sixty. Seventh Day Adventists gave one hundred rubles.[42] The Perm-Komiak region in the Urals understood that it was donating a "meagre" amount, but it was coming from a poor national region that itself had just suffered a bad harvest. Since peasants from the region had taken a cure in the Crimean peninsula in recent years, they hoped the peninsula would quickly regain its significance as an All-Union sanatorium.[43] Individuals also had creative suggestions for raising money. One person suggested raising money by selling before-and-after picture postcards of the Crimean peninsula, and another urged Muscovites to rid their closets of unnecessary clothes and send them south, where residents risked freezing in the months to come.[44] The All-Ukrainian Committee for Assistance to the Crimean Peninsula conveniently noticed class distinctions in donation patterns – the *profsouizy* in Kharkiv were giving more generously than were the merchants.[45] The available statistical evidence does not, however, warrant this claim across the Soviet Union.

Citizens of the Soviet Union did not mobilize their entire resource structure or make great sacrifices for the Crimean peninsula, but help did trickle in. The bulk of philanthropy came through the collection of donations rather than through volunteer work. The strategies for helping citizens re-emerged years later in Tashkent, Chernobyl, and Armenia. Published in newspapers around the Soviet Union, the contributions created a feeling of community and contributors recognized the all-union importance of the Crimean peninsula, but it would be an exaggeration to suggest the earthquake created one of those bonding moments so necessary to the formation of an imagined or geographically distant community.

The scattered mobilization of resources was accompanied by a more important mobilization – that of people leaving the area. Tourists fled the area en masse, but they did have a place to which they could return. Life for other evacuees was more problematic because no one had developed an evacuation plan. The All-Ukrainian Committee created to help raise funds specifically stated that it was not offering help to individual evacuees: all of the funds it collected were headed to the Crimean peninsula.[46] Officials understood that masses of people were leaving the area but they were less concerned with individual fates than they were with the demographic shifts taking place in the area.[47] The earthquake had occurred in turbulent demographic times. The Soviets had already started to move poor Jewish peasants from their traditional homes in Ukraine and Belarus and had resettled them (as well as some Ukrainians and Belarusians) on farms in the peninsula.[48] Against considerable local opposition, the state hoped to quell Zionism and to provide a counterbalance to the rising nationalism of indigenous populations.[49] The arrival of the Jewish population was controversial when plans were in the works to resettle Orthodox peasants to the steppes.[50] Rumours spread that the earthquake was a symbol of God's anger at the Bolsheviks for resettling Jews in the Crimea.[51] This controversy was not purely religious or ethnic: the sanatoria on the southern shores also argued with peasants about land distribution.[52] The earthquake developed into a convenient opportunity to remove specific populations from the southern shores of the Crimea.

The suggestion that God was angry over a Bolshevik misdeed was not limited to the arrival of the Jewish population as the natural disaster increased the influence of religious authorities in general – a worrisome trend to a Communist Party struggling to dampen peasants' religious beliefs and to instill the atheist values of scientific Marxism.[53] Officials were disquieted by the competition they had from both Orthodox and Muslim religious figures. Priests and "anti-Soviet characters" spread rumours about the end of the world, the peninsula slipping into the sea, and the eruption of volcanoes. Russian women sought permission to organize Christian processions and public prayers, while Tatar communities collected funds for prayer and sacrifice, a phenomenon that also followed the Tashkent earthquake in 1966.[54] Tatar women were reading the Koran.[55] An engineer told the Muslim community he could repair a teetering mosque for six hundred rubles if the Bolsheviks did not forbid it. The Communist Party took issue with this because the engineer had spoken out against the Bolsheviks who thought that it would be best to destroy the mosque.[56]

The spread of rumours was worrisome, but these did not all originate in the minds of religious thinkers. The powerful rumour about the Crimean peninsula's sinking into the Black Sea gained traction because scientists had written about the possibility and had published this view in *Pravda*. Although the catastrophe was only envisioned within the parameters of geological time (about one hundred thousand years), the idea resulted in a wave of panic through the population.[57] Every effort was made to correct misunderstandings; however, according to official reports, the damage had already been done. Even promises that Bolsheviks could storm any fortress had little effect.[58]

The persistence of this rumour is difficult to comprehend, in part, because sources don't explain individual beliefs. Did the rumour spread because the message was delivered through the voice of scientific authority? Did the message spread because its meaning was attached to the social position and credibility of the speaker? Or did the rumour gain strength because it was published in the most important central newspaper? With respect to the first two questions, it would appear that the rumour quickly became detached from the credibility of the speaker as scientists had little seismological authority in the area. Because, until the earthquake, it had not been considered a dangerous area, no seismological stations were in operation on the Crimean peninsula.[59] Scientific committees and geological expeditions were only formed after the destruction had occurred.[60] Scientists responded with a collection of essays in which they explained a number of basic seismological issues, such as why earthquakes happen and why the Crimea would not slip into the sea anytime soon. They issued an article on the history of earthquakes in the peninsula, including a reference to Herodotus, who in Book IV of his *Histories* notes that Scythians perceived earthquakes as miracles.[61] Most likely, this miraculous explanation was easily incorporated into existing religious beliefs and thus persisted.

While scientists were penning their opinions on the earthquake, the Red Cross was providing massive relief throughout the peninsula. In the late 1920s, the Red Cross still enjoyed a degree of independence and could even afford to discuss the extent to which the military should be involved and the degree to which the state should participate in its operation; such discussions would soon be moot. Members of the Red Cross understood that their organization was not an NGO, but they were concerned to protect it from military interference (an issue common to many of these national organizations).[62] After the earthquake, the Red Cross was the single largest independent rescue operator. The Russian Red Cross organized mobile (*peredvizhnaia*) sanitary stations that toured affected areas and dispatched brigades to disinfect regions that were at risk of the spread of disease.[63] State officials were worried about epidemics. Residents who narrowly escaped death feared living in the second storeys of their homes. They moved to the first floor, where they shared space with their animals; this created an infection-prone and potentially more devastating environment than the one directly created by the earthquake.[64] The Russian Red Cross sent its teams to contain disease and also distributed brochures (in both Russian and Tatar) to encourage proper hygienic practices. Finally, the Russian Red Cross mobilized its organizational base to raise funds throughout the RSFSR.[65] It would have to wait until the Armenian earthquake in 1988 before it would again play such an important public role.

As a public problem, the earthquake became a minor issue after the introduction of the first Five Year Plan in the spring of 1929 and the start of the accelerated industrialization program. Since the earthquake occurred just prior to rapid centralization, the rescue response was somewhat haphazard. The Russian Red Cross acted on its own, the RSFSR did not see eye to eye with the Crimean authorities, republics donated as they chose, and scientists lacked the authority to control public opinion. This situation changed with the introduction of the full Stalinist program, but the state never did take full control of disasters. After an earthquake in 1938 in Kyrgyzstan, costs for the relief effort came from the local budget.[66] A decade after this earthquake, the Stalinist state was still unsure how to handle disasters. In Ashgabat in 1948, it usurped the final say of the member republic, but it lacked a contingency plan to cope with a phenomenon that was a regular feature of life along the southern periphery of the empire.

When tragedy struck the Crimean shoreline, the ramifications were primarily domestic. In contrast, the city of Ashgabat was destroyed shortly after the peace agreements made in 1945 were starting to come asunder. Germany's division into four separate spheres had been established as a temporary measure, but growing tensions between the Soviets and the Western powers were hardening the borders. In July 1947, in *Foreign Affairs*, George Kennan published "The Sources of Soviet Conduct," in which he advocates containment, and in June 1948, the Marshall Plan, which was designed to offer assistance and to spread American values, went into operation. Within months of the activation of the Marshall Plan, the Western powers announced a new currency, the Deutsche mark, for the Western zones. Days thereafter the Soviets introduced the Ostmark and isolated the Western sections of Berlin from the rest of Western Europe, closing transportation routes to the German capital. Without the provision of supplies, Western residents in Berlin faced a dire future. In early July, the Americans and the British challenged the Soviets with the airlift of supplies into Berlin, an airlift that continued until May 1949, when the Soviets lifted the blockade. Behind the scenes, Soviet scientists were close to developing an atomic bomb and eliminating a critical American military advantage.[67] When the earth trembled, one author thought Ashgabat had become the victim of an atomic bomb.[68]

The new superpower was preoccupied with these global issues and the reconstruction of cities at home, so the resources it had at its disposal for the recovery of Ashgabat were constrained. Nevertheless, the response involved more central organization than had been the case in the Crimean peninsula: the Stalinist bureaucracy oversaw the rescue effort, although local officials had plenty of room to act on their own. The earthquake occurred before urban planning (and not just urban reconstruction) had become accepted policy, so Ashgabat did not receive the same treatment as did Tashkent in 1966.[69] Without strict planning principles, the reconstruction process was much more haphazard than it was in later years. The disaster was shrouded in secrecy at the international level and received moderate coverage in *Pravda*, but local newspapers offered readers extensive and critical information on the response. To be sure, Stalin and the Communist Party could not be blamed, but the coverage clearly revealed a dynamic that left room for improvisation on the part of local circles. In 1948, the response to the Ashgabat earthquake also offers insights into policies that had yet to fully mature. The slogan "the friendship of peoples" appeared in newspaper publications but was only applied to disaster relief; it had to wait until Tashkent in 1966 for its full realization. In fact, the friendship of peoples ended up being more important in Brezhnevite memories than it had been in Stalinist practice. Under Gorbachev, the memories of the Ashgabat earthquake shifted once again, highlighting the unsteady attitudes of the late 1940s.

Much like the Crimean peninsula, Ashgabat was highly susceptible to earthquakes. Between 1893 and 1950, twenty-five significant earthquakes had been registered in the city, and an earthquake in 1929 caused significant damage. Yet the Ashgabat earthquake of 1948 was by far the most devastating in the history of Turkmenistan. Without any forewarning, in the early morning of 6 October, a ten-second shock wave spread through the city. The force of the earthquake was lightly registered in Moscow, about twenty-five hundred kilometres away, and spread across the border into Iran. Although the exact number of fatalities remains a secret of the Stalinist years, safe estimates range in the tens of thousands in a city with a population of just over 100,000. Many people had to be dug out of the rubble, emerging either as survivors or corpses.[70] The damage to the physical plant of the city was extreme, with aerial photographs validating the comparison with a carpet-bombing campaign. Photographs from street level show cultural institutions such as theatres, schools, and the premises of the Academy of Sciences in ruins.[71] It is important to remember that the accessible imagery was sanitized, and this is why there do not seem to be any existing photographs of corpses lying in the street (something that was reported in textual sources). As discussed in a later chapter, this phenomenon occurred in film as well. Still, such visual imagery, no matter how selective, is better than nothing since very few basic descriptions of the immediate aftermath remain.

The most thorough report comes in the form of a memoir written by D.V. Nalivkin, a geologist and member of the Soviet Academy of Sciences. By chance, Nalivkin had been visiting Ashgabat on business and was talking with party officials in the wee hours of the morning when the building started to shake. After the trembling stopped, these high-ranking Soviet authorities ran out into the night to find a destroyed city. Buildings were damaged, telephones did not work, the telegraph was broken, and, in the moments immediately after the earthquake, the capital of this Soviet republic was isolated. A party member who had been with Nalivkin had already received word that he had lost his family.[72]

Nalivkin reported on the moaning and groaning – something that cannot be heard in photographs. His memoirs provide chilling descriptions of the casualties and the "small groups of dirty clothes," a euphemism for the dead who lay among the living but to whom "no one paid attention." There were many such groups throughout the city. No wonder residents were in shock. Nalivkin came across one half-dressed woman walking in the middle of the road, moaning and pulling at her hair.[73] Given the lack of accounts, these memoirs offer the best sense of what it was like before the more organized rescue efforts began.

Since Nalivkin was with high-ranking Soviet officials when the earthquake occurred, he not only reported on their actions but also saw good in what they did. They were immediately responsive to the needs of citizens and were looked upon with respect as it was believed they could address those needs. In this version, Nalivkin sees the Communist Party as the innocent victim of natural forces. Of course, as a visitor to the city, Nalivkin was an outsider looking in and could not have been expected to understand the complex internal dynamics that complicated and conditioned the response. Thus, his narrative turns away from being a traveller's account and begins with the local information available to residents.

Local newspapers did not report the event as the printing presses had been destroyed, so it was *Pravda*, located in Moscow, that provided immediate coverage.[74] A very awkward formula was evident in the reporting: injuries were all right to report, foreign death tolls were permitted, and the paper mentioned important local communists who had not survived the tragedy. However, printing a total death toll was out of the question. When *Pravda* proudly reported the rescue efforts, readers could gauge the extent of the tragedy by reading about the number of injured who had been flown out of Ashgabat (six thousand) or the number of children without parents (six hundred) who had been transported to other cities.[75] Strangely enough, *Pravda* did not estimate the number of deaths in Ashgabat, but it did give estimates for an earthquake in the Iranian city of Meshed, which it falsely treated as a separate geological event.[76] Finally, *Pravda* reported the names of deceased ministerial officials to reassure readers that all the necessary posts had been filled.[77] Despite all the clues, the Soviets continued to downplay the death toll, which has been placed in the tens of thousands – a number much greater than the handful reported to have perished in Tashkent in 1966.[78] In Moscow, the outpouring of articles that accompanied the Tashkent earthquake was almost entirely absent for Ashgabat. Central newspapers such as *Pravda* soon forgot about the earthquake, however, and left the reporting to local media organs, which were quickly back on their feet.

Certain factors conditioned the initial reporting of the Ashgabat event. The Stalinist government was not interested in revealing possible weaknesses at such a critical time. In contrast to Tashkent in 1966, Ashgabat was not a showcase city that had just been in the international spotlight; rather, it was a relatively unimportant city on the southern periphery of the Soviet empire. Although Ashgabat was much closer to an international border than was Tashkent, being only fifty kilometres from Iran, its southern border was less critical to current Soviet interests. When the *New York Times* first reported the tremour, it said that damage had occurred in the large Iranian city of Meshed (or Mashhad), 270 kilometres to the south of Ashgabat.[79] The reporting from New York testified to the interesting geological fact that earthquakes transcend human divisions. Subsequent Soviet reporting omitted the effects of the earthquake in Iran, treating the recovery effort as a purely domestic issue. Years later, a Soviet author proudly wrote that Ashgabat had been put back on its feet without any help from foreign governments.[80]

The response to the earthquake can be divided into two phases. In the first phase, the days immediately following the tremour, Soviet authorities tried to save lives and prevent panic. Crews worked through rubble, doctors were flown in from around the USSR, and a tent city was established in the centre of town. In the second and longer phase, the Soviets dealt with the reconstruction of new neighbourhoods and long-term architectural planning for the city. This phase required more active involvement from state authorities and highlighted the limits of their influence once the situation had calmed down.

The reports written immediately after the earthquake were harrowing. The local *profsoiuz* commented on central squares and streets filled with injured and dead citizens. The "decaying corpses" lying on the city streets were emitting horrible smells.[81] The Soviets were proud of the ability of its citizens to maintain calm in moments of great crisis. But in Ashgabat, reports immediately emerged of uncontrolled marauding and banditry. Alongside the rescue operation, "extraordinary measures" had been taken to stop looting: looters were "shot immediately."[82] Stalin's solution to the problem of looting differed dramatically from Brezhnev's: twenty years later, in Tashkent, Brezhnev saw that looters and speculators merely received short jail sentences.

Threats of looting also required that citizens be capable of a certain degree of self-defence. D.V. Nalivkin notes in his memoirs that the walls of a prison collapsed, releasing two gangs who quickly armed themselves and began looting. Residents of the city listened in horror to a two-hour gun battle between the police and these bandits. In response to such dangers, residents organized an armed neighbourhood watch, which was instructed to shoot criminals on the spot. When Nalivkin arrived at the Academy of Sciences the next day, many of his colleagues were armed.[83] This trigger-happy justice was not simply the function of Stalinist brutality; rather, it was the result of having to face a situation in which the new superpower could not guarantee law and order.

While citizens protected themselves, Soviet authorities pooled their resources. Relief came in different forms. With the rail connections broken and thousands of railway workers unaccounted for, the state had to find alternate means of transportation.[84] Soon planes were arriving in Ashgabat with medical supplies, and victims were evacuated to safe cities. These airplanes arrived from nearby cities such as Tbilisi in Georgia, Baku in Azerbaijan, and Tashkent, a little further away in Uzbekistan.[85] Doctors arrived from Moscow and other republican capitals to transform Karl Marx Square, with its dais for festive occasions, into an open-air hospital. Finding medication and supplies for the medical staff was complicated because the apothecaries were now under tons of rubble.[86] In Moscow, Muscovites collected blood, thousands of shoes arrived from Leningrad, and potatoes were sent from another part of the country.[87] Building materials such as wood were also sent to the devastated city.[88] The Red Army sent soldiers who cleaned up rubble and extracted bodies from ruined buildings.[89]

In late Stalinist times, this assistance was coerced from around the Soviet Union and then promoted in local newspapers. Not surprisingly, it was advertised as stemming from the friendship of peoples. *Turkmenskaia iskra* lauded the assistance that poured in – "only the Soviet people, raised by the Bolshevik Party in the spirit of the friendship of peoples," could overcome such adversity.[90] In this happy family of nations, the Russians were considered to be the "older brothers."[91] Of course, praise also went to Joseph Stalin, "our natural [*rodnoi*] father," who personally organized this widespread assistance.[92]

At the same time, the implications of this friendship differed considerably from what transpired after the Crimean earthquake and what would later transpire in Tashkent. In the Crimean peninsula, the RSFSR had little power to force participation from other republics, thus inter-republican assistance was marginal, even though members of the All-Russian Central Executive Committee were hoping for help from other republics.[93] In Ashgabat, assistance could be forced, but it was neither as extensive nor as systematized as it was later. The bulk of the assistance came in the form of materials being delivered rather than in the form of thousands of workers arriving from all corners of the Soviet Union. The in-migration that was such an important component of the Tashkent earthquake was lacking. The death toll from the earthquake, not an influx of outside workers, radically changed the demographic profile of Ashgabat.

Furthermore, assistance was not equally distributed between the republics. When Moscow issued a decree concerning the reconstruction of Ashgabat, it specifically mentioned bringing in additional workers from Uzbekistan, Kazakhstan, and the region of Chkalov (now Orenburg, which has a large Muslim population) in the southern part of the Russian Federation.[94] *Turkmenskaia iskra* published an extensive profile on the workers from Uzbekistan, showing photographs of their efforts.[95] Although the Muscovites and Leningradites worked on architectural plans for the new city, the manual labour came from Central Asia. Many republics went entirely unnoticed.[96] This was a far cry from what happened in 1966, when thousands upon thousands of workers from all union republics headed to Tashkent on trains.

Turkmenskaia iskra celebrated the efforts of the Uzbek workers in the summer of 1949, but the tone of the newspaper had changed since the earthquake. The confidence associated with the recovery process yielded to frustration over the reconstruction. Alongside articles that claimed that Ashgabat would become more beautiful than ever were stories about corruption and administrative incompetence.[97] A library had received land upon which to build, only to discover that city council had changed its mind and revoked the land grant. Months later, the library was still without a piece of land. In another instance, bricks had been delivered for the construction of a health centre but were then ordered removed. In yet another, a local architect had put a brick wall around his new home even though brick walls had not been part of the street profile before the earthquake. Residents also found themselves without land because they had failed to fill out the proper forms.[98]

At a meeting held ten months after the earthquake, numerous complaints were raised publicly. One commentator grumbled that the building was being done slowly and poorly. State materials were being wasted, and no attention was being paid to the erection of model homes. Someone else said that the building was being done without a general plan and that, as a result, the new homes had windows that could not be opened and doors that could not be shut.[99] The Stakhanovites had their construction pace slowed because they received parts for homes that were of a different type than those being built.[100] The complaints in the newspaper continued well into 1950 as the construction companies were subjected to public scorn. Ashkhabadproekt "forgot about existing standards and technical conditions."[101] Two years after the earthquake, quality control was still lacking on construction sites as inspectors rarely showed up to review the work.[102]

These commentaries fit within the boundaries of communist self-criticism, but they were significant at another level. The willingness of the central bureaucracy to permit the publication of such scathing articles speaks to indifference in Moscow. Stalin did issue construction guidelines for the city, wanted to minimize the construction of tall buildings (in sharp contrast to Brezhnev, who wanted to construct tall buildings on seismologically active ground), and raised the seismological coefficient of Ashgabat to ensure greater safety.[103] The insistence on small buildings was strictly a safety measure because it did not correspond with general Soviet architectural practice; only a year before the tremour, the foundations had been laid for Moscow's renowned high rises.[104] But Moscow did not have the desire, time, or willpower to intervene architecturally or otherwise, and this attitude reflected itself throughout the reconstruction of Ashgabat. Furthermore, the newspaper articles say something about the construction of Soviet memory under different leaders. Histories of the earthquake published in the Brezhnev years quietly omit the shortcomings of the reconstruction process, even though the newspapers in Stalinist times had belonged to the public domain.[105]

The official reconstruction was inadequate, but the state did not have a monopoly on construction as individual homeowners attempted to restore their own homes. This process was every bit as haphazard as that carried out by the state, and it guaranteed that the city would not be reconstructed according to a general plan determined by Muscovite architects. Since city council was slow in responding to questions from homeowners, they had to find their own way.[106] When they did, they paid scant attention to norms and, thus, were threatened with having their homes taken down.[107] Homeowners did receive insurance payments to help them rebuild private property, but this process was also opaque.[108] Ashgabat was transformed into a "build-your-own" city.[109] Since much of the building was done in neighbourhoods, the work became part of a *khashar*, or Central Asian style barn-raiser. *Turkmenskaia iskra* co-opted the term to refer to group work on state projects, but it can also refer to spontaneous projects carried out to aid the community.[110] The term *khashar* became very popular in conjunction with the Tashkent earthquake, where it was again co-opted by the state.

The alternative to permanent homes was the construction of "temporary" homes to provide desperately needed housing while individuals waited to move into new dwellings. Yet the reconstruction proceeded so slowly that many people never left these *vremianki*, as they came to be known. They had been built with construction scraps left

2.1 New "standard" home on Tashkent Street. Published in *Turkmenskaia iskra*, 9 March 1949.

behind from the earthquake and were so numerous it became too expensive to replace them.[111] In a letter written to *Vechernii Ashkhabad* within the context of the quadridecadal commemoration of the earthquake, the author noted that people were still living in these barrack-style homes. Survivors of the earthquake were stuck in these buildings, while newcomers to the city received new apartments.[112] Decades later, the city still bore the marks of a poorly organized recovery effort.

We find a similar situation with two other organizations that were supposed to play an important role. The Komsomol, the Soviet youth league, was by and large absent in Ashgabat. The heroic deeds of its members went unpublished in newspapers, but their failure to show up at worksites was noticed, and the lack of qualified young workers was openly criticized.[113] The Red Cross, such a critical player in the Crimean earthquake, struggled to find its proper role. Since its organization had changed in the 1930s to accommodate Stalinist centralization, it had eliminated commercial and economic activities to focus on sanitary work.[114]

Turkmenistan had an affiliate, the Red Crescent, which was based in Ashgabat in 1926 and has been active ever since.[115] After the Great Patriotic War, the organization looked after veterans and orphans, offered educational classes in schools, and helped to prevent the spread of diseases (as a result of the war).[116] On the eve of the earthquake, the Red Crescent undertook numerous charitable acts, but it had growing debts because it did not successfully collect membership fees, had not been able to attract Turkmen to its councils, and was still struggling to connect with the masses.[117]

These problems should not have kept an established organization from providing effective aid during the earthquake. The Red Crescent in Turkmenistan received cash and clothing from other republics, yet its relief effort was minimal. In its meetings, it was more concerned with attracting new members, making sure that membership dues were paid, and fulfilling the norms for socialist competitions than it was with providing aid.[118] To the Red Crescent the tragedy of the earthquake was that it had lowered membership, not that it had destroyed homes. To be sure, the organization certainly offered assistance, but, at times, this assistance only revealed further problems with the relief effort. In *Turkmenskaia iskra*, a photograph proudly presents children who are being evacuated to the Artek pioneer camp on the Crimean peninsula.[119] At one of its regular meetings, the Red Crescent decided that one of its main tasks would be to help parents locate children who had been evacuated from Ashgabat and sent to Tashkent, Baku, and other areas (apparently, parents did not know where their children were). The Red Crescent proposed collecting a list of children's names from these cities and posting it at important sites throughout Ashgabat.[120] The concern with this task hints at the careless manner in which these children had been evacuated. The children were first symbols to promote the friendship of peoples and only second were they the sons and daughters of Ashgabatites.

The evacuation of children in such circumstances should not be considered unique. Only years before the earthquake, thousands of children had been evacuated throughout Europe to escape the Second World War. In England, the evacuation of children was associated with patriotism.[121] During the war, the large evacuation of children was an enormous challenge, and British reports contemplated whether the exercise had failed. Welsh families resented the urban influx, and the working class had to bear part of the financial burden.[122] While the British press discussed the difficulties of evacuating children, no such documentary evidence exists for the fate of the children evacuated from Ashgabat. Only extensive oral histories will be able to fill this gap.

Unfortunately, the voices of Ashgabat were silenced throughout the Brezhnev period (when a few stereotypical books and Karelin's novel were published). It was only during perestroika and in the aftermath of the Armenian earthquake that the first critical commentaries appeared. Titles such as "The Secret of 1948" and "The Need for Truth" questioned the death toll but did not reveal personal stories about the tragedy.[123] In 1998, fifty years after the earthquake and seven years after Turkmenistan became an independent state, there appeared the first article that condemned Soviet actions. Kakamurat Ballyev argued that Moscow had only been protecting its own interests and had sent a bunch of thieves to prosper from the sorrow of others. Muscovites were more interested in the jewels of Turkmen women than in providing aid, and this thirst for treasure delayed assistance to people who might otherwise have been saved.[124] In the same issue, *Neitral'nyi Turkmenistan* published a letter from the independent republic of Uzbekistan, in which the writer remembered both the help that Uzbekistan had given in 1948 and the help Turkmenistan had offered Tashkent in 1966. The phrase "the friendship of peoples" had taken on new dimensions, even as other authors continued to defend the Soviet storyline. Anatolii Bial'kin reprinted excerpts from former Soviet papers to highlight instances of the friendship of peoples, though doing so shed no new light on the tragedy.[125] In Ashgabat, the catastrophe had become contemporary history in the spirit celebrated by Henry Rousso: the past was alive in the present as much as the present was alive in the past.[126]

Ashgabat was eventually rebuilt but not because of the earthquake; only in July 1958 did the Soviets finally approve a general plan to accommodate the socialist vision of the time.[127] The new city tried to pave over the chaos left by the fall of 1948. This chaos was not, it should be remembered, unique to Ashgabat as the response in the Crimean peninsula had its shortcomings as well. This common lack of preparedness should not obscure fundamental differences between 1927 and 1948, not all of which were the function of a maturing Stalinist state. In Ashgabat, the Soviet state took public administrative control over the rescue effort, whereas in the Crimean peninsula, the RSFSR saw it through. This was true even though the actual recovery effort in Ashgabat was left to Turkmen officials.

The nature of volunteering and associational help had also changed. As a holiday and sanatoria area, the Black Sea coast appealed to people throughout the RSFSR, and so associations were able to raise funds in faraway cities. These volunteer donations were more difficult to collect in a Central Asian city such as Ashgabat, where the rescue efforts of associations were greatly reduced. It was not just the Red Crescent that found itself marginalized but also theatre groups and book publishers. The centralization that occurred in 1948 militated against any dynamic associational response, even if the ultimate contribution of these associations was difficult to judge. At the local level, the media landscape was similar, with published reports openly criticizing these shortcomings. It was only after the Tashkent earthquake in 1966 that the Communist Party figured out how to turn a natural tragedy into a public relations triumph.

Both the Crimean and Ashgabat earthquakes were quickly relegated to the dark corners of memory, and the Communist Party showed no interest in learning from them or in understanding what they signified for the local populations. In the Crimean peninsula in 1927 and in Ashgabat in 1948, the response was as spontaneous as was the natural disaster itself. Only the Brezhnevite government envisioned responding to a natural disaster on a grand scale, recognizing that rebuilding Tashkent was akin to re-energizing the communist message.

PART TWO

The Mobilization of Soviet Society under Brezhnev

3

April 1966: Tashkent in the News

In the first week of 1966, the capital of Uzbekistan became the home of intense diplomatic discussions between the leaders of Pakistan and India. Aleksei N. Kosygin, the premier of the Soviet Union, had invited President Mohammad Ayub Khan of Pakistan and Prime Minister Lal Bahadur Shastri of India to resolve their conflict over disputed territory in the Kashmir region. The Soviets were taking steps to increase their involvement in South Asian diplomacy. To this end, Soviet officials made extensive preparations to ensure equal treatment of the esteemed guests. Indeed, Soviet efforts at neutral diplomacy reached comical proportions.[1] Upon arrival, both leaders were escorted to country villas that were almost identical in size. When Kosygin made a courtesy call to the two leaders, he spent exactly seventy-five minutes with each one.[2]

The city of Tashkent had been specially chosen because it offered both leaders an air of familiarity. President Ayub attended prayers at the Barak-Khan mosque in the heart of the town, and "the mud huts of the old city" offered a reminder of the Indian subcontinent.[3] If Tashkent was close to home for Pakistanis and Indians, for Western journalists it was a glimpse into an unknown part of the Soviet Union. Soviet authorities wanted the city to shine in the eyes of its visitors. Western reporters questioned Soviet motives for hosting the Tashkent conference and made disparaging remarks, but many were suitably impressed with the city. The French correspondent for *Le Monde* commented that the city of Tamerlane had been replaced with new, modern earthquake-proof buildings![4]

No preparations could completely smooth the diplomatic strains, and the lines of cheering Uzbek citizens that welcomed the foreign delegations could not eliminate tensions between the two South Asian nations. The conference did not resolve the Kashmir problem. Its results were met with protests in Pakistan, and the death of Prime Minister Shastri on 11 January, hours after he had signed the agreement, cast a pall over the proceedings. These shortcomings notwithstanding, the city had developed an international presence that was important for Soviet officials to cultivate. In the minds of international observers, Tashkent had established itself as the capital of Central Asia. Thus, because Tashkent now had an international face that went beyond simplistic Orientalist images of a traditional Central Asian city, Soviet officials hailed the conference as a success.

Unfortunately, the face of the city was soon scarred, and the places the Pakistani and Indian leaders had visited were reduced to or surrounded by rubble. In the early morning of 26 April, a massive earthquake, whose epicentre was right below the centre of town, struck the city. Within seconds, tens of thousands of Tashkentites lost their dwellings. This time people flooded the streets not to welcome foreign dignitaries but to save themselves from the crumbling structures of their former homes. City streets were turned into camps, and people found creative ways to establish temporary housing. Wherever possible, families were housed in schools, public buildings, and student dorms.[5] Soviet officials could not continue to celebrate the capital of Central Asia until they had saved its citizens and rebuilt it to the point at which it was again possible to herald its glories.

Like so many other places in Central Asia, Tashkent had a long history with earthquakes. In 1868, an earthquake destroyed the governor's home, and the city was threatened again in 1886, 1924, and 1946; the phenomenon was familiar in its larger forms as well as in its smaller and less threatening variants.[6] The earthquake of 1966, about three or four kilometres below the centre of town, registered a level 9 force (or about 5.3 on the Richter scale).[7] In terms of sheer power, the earthquake was not one of the greatest seismological events. It did, however, have enormous strength at the surface, where it reached an 8 on the Richter scale. The damage was concentrated in the centre of town. On the outskirts, the impact was milder, in part because the vertical vector of the earthquake was much more significant than was the horizontal vector. Valentin Ulomov, the chief seismologist at the time, recounts a meeting with Brezhnev the day after the earthquake. They were downtown, on the seventh floor of the Communist Party building, discussing rescue efforts when they heard loud screaming from outside. Brezhnev immediately asked whether there had been an aftershock. Ulomov responded that the screams seemed to be coming from the soccer stadium (as the stadium was outside the centre of town, it had not been seriously affected and it was decided to continue with the game).[8] Although Brezhnev was relieved by news of cheering crowds, shortly thereafter an aftershock did move the building. There would be aftershocks for months to come.

The Soviet leadership was in Tashkent almost immediately, but, in the interim, Ulomov became the city's soothsayer. A respected scientist at the seismological station, he seemed to be the only one who knew what was going on. As Vasilii Peskov wrote: "Two weeks ago, no one knew he existed. He sat with 10 of his associates in a tiny building measuring the vibration of the earth's crust … And if the tiny building with the sign 'Seismo station' were to vanish suddenly, the city would not immediately notice its loss. Yet all at once Valentin Ulomov became the most wanted person in Tashkent." Ulomov appeared on television to explain to residents what had happened, and he was the one to tell them whether it was all right to go to sleep.[9]

Fortunately, the death toll was minimal, and even the number of injured was in the low thousands. These are surprising numbers when one considers that, when the earth moved in the early morning, almost everyone was still at home and thus susceptible to falling masonry.[10] Buildings fell into rubble and the damage in the city was extensive. While no statistics can be entirely free from doubt, and Soviet statistics are notoriously difficult to corroborate, general numbers are of assistance. The city lost about one-third of its living space (about 2 million square metres), about ninety-five thousand apartments were thrown into disarray, over 180 educational institutions were rendered useless, and tens of thousands of residents were immediately made homeless, the streets in the centre of town becoming filled with people.[11] The situation was extremely precarious, but one should not conclude that things were out of control. Ravshan Nazarov, a scholar in Uzbekistan today, reported that he was born on that day.[12]

Soviet officials understood the importance of Tashkent and, in contrast to Ashgabat, publicized the involvement of party leadership. The earthquake was immediately reported in major media outlets, and, within a day of the tragedy, Brezhnev and Kosygin arrived in the city.[13] Kosygin was already well known in Tashkent, and Brezhnev, who weeks before had been named general secretary at the Twenty-Third

Party Congress, had a golden opportunity to enhance his image.[14] They arrived in a devastated city, though luckily few people had died. To lift people's spirits, Brezhnev gave a speech to local officials in which he guaranteed the reconstruction of the city in the shortest time possible.[15] The situation was complicated by the aftershocks, which continued to be troublesome throughout the summer of 1966. On 10 May, yet another tremour shook the confidence of inhabitants.[16]

Despite all the difficulties, the Soviets prided themselves on major construction projects and delighted in watching major structures emerge from the earth: the first Russian version of the "Internationale" contained the lines "we will build our new world." This attitude had failed to materialize in Ashgabat; however, in 1966, the Communist Party wanted an organized and efficient recovery that mobilized resources from throughout the USSR. For this reason, the Communist Party, under the guidance of I.T. Novikov, deputy chairman of the Council of Ministers, established a committee to deal with the "liquidation of the aftermath of the earthquake."[17] From the outset, officials were sensitive about the terms used to describe the tragedy. In a document from the Council of Ministers, a heading that referred to providing aid to the population of "Tashkent, which had suffered due to the earthquake" was altered: the line "suffered due to the earthquake" was omitted, and the title now spoke of helping residents with "the liquidation of the consequences of the natural disaster."[18] "Liquidation" had a Stalinist connotation dating back to the late 1920s, when the Soviet government set out to "liquidate the kulaks as a class." The term "liquidation" evoked the ability of the Communist Party to implement special measures to achieve a difficult task. With the goals of the committee established, Brezhnev left the city with the comfortable feeling that the Communist Party had guaranteed a safe future for the capital of Uzbekistan and Central Asia.

But the reconstruction of the city was a much more complex affair than had been anticipated. First, the Soviet bureaucracy had to organize a major media blitz to rally citizens around the tragedy (this was not a secretive affair, like the Chinese response to the Tangshan earthquake in 1976).[19] Despite careful publishing laws, which limited news on catastrophes, the earthquake developed a major news presence.[20] The selective distribution of information came immediately after the earthquake, yet, like the construction itself, it lasted for years. Six years after the tragedy, a celebratory article was published in *Novyi mir*.[21] Exploring the manner in which the Soviet state told the story of this earthquake establishes a backdrop for understanding the process of recovery, and this, in turn, leads us into the next chapter, which discusses the actual reconstruction of Tashkent.

The Brezhnev years have been portrayed either, in the early years, as a neo-totalitarian reaction to the Khrushchev era, in which the firm hand of the state guided the lives of individuals, or, in the later years, as a time of stagnation when a gerontocracy failed to address growing economic and social problems. The story of the Tashkent earthquake suggests an alternative interpretation. The reconstruction of the city established all sorts of new openings for individuals. Moreover, since the reconstruction was such a long, drawn out process, the city never really settled down. The Soviet economy may have been stumbling, but Tashkent continued to grow, first in the news and then, as we see in the next chapter, in the streets of the city.

TASHKENT IN THE NEWS

National media outlets such as *Pravda* immediately seized upon the disaster, reporting the arrival of Kosygin and Brezhnev in Tashkent and the basic parameters of the catastrophe.[22] As was to be expected, certain themes reappeared in all publications. Newspapers emphasized the speed with which the city was to be rebuilt, the help that was flowing in from all corners of the USSR, the calmness in the city, and the critical role that the friendship of peoples was playing in the response. The continued references to calm was a strategy not only to limit panic but also to remind readers that calm citizens had a duty to help with the reconstruction. Such strategies were not unique to the Soviet Union: a similar strategy was used in the American context to motivate the working class to resume work and to distinguish between the response of white and black Americans after the Charleston earthquake of 1886.[23] Each publication addressed these issues on its own terms and placed them within a context familiar to its constituency.

Pravda Vostoka, or *Pravda of the East*, published in Tashkent, was the main source of local information. On 27 April 1927, as part of its efforts to inform readers about the friendship between member republics, *Pravda Vostoka* reported about elections in the USSR, the arrival of Brezhnev and Kosygin, and the presentation of Belarusian literature and art in Uzbekistan.[24] Of course, for years, this newspaper provided the most extensive coverage of the earthquake. It also report-

ДРУЖЕСКАЯ ПОМОЩЬ ТАШКЕНТУ

«Мы чувствуем локоть друг друга» — эти слова из популярной песни стали для жителей Ташкента особенно близки и понятны теперь, когда вся страна пришла на помощь пострадавшему от землетрясения городу. Вся страна! Любой дом, что строится сейчас в столице Узбекистана, можно по праву назвать домом дружбы народов социалистических республик. Тысячи домов дружбы скоро поднимутся на улицах древнего города, а пока сюда продолжают прибывать грузы.

НА СНИМКЕ внизу вы видите момент отъезда в Ташкент большого отряда строителей южных областей Украины — Одесской, Николаевской, Херсонской и Крымской. Вместе с ними отправлен железнодорожный состав с инструментами и строительной техникой.

А здесь вы видите погрузочную площадку Тюменского завода строительных машин. Отсюда каждый день отправляются поезда с новой техникой для ташкентцев.

Фото А. ФАТЕЕВА и Н. САПОЖКОВА

3.1 Construction workers arrive from southern Ukraine. Published in *Stroitel'naia gazeta*, 20 May 1966.

ed about other tragedies but in a muted fashion. Towards the end of June, the Isfairam-Sai River in the northeastern part of Uzbekistan flooded, and the local meteorological station measured the highest water levels in fifty years.[25] *Pravda Vostoka* mentioned the heroic rescue efforts and the help required of three thousand families, but it soon dropped the story.[26] There was a distinct lack of news despite internal reports that indicated that more people died during this flood than during the earthquake in Tashkent.[27]

Pravda Vostoka reiterated standard themes, but it also served a number of diverse functions. First, it indicated the extent to which media outlets had been mobilized. The newspaper published a letter in which tourists from the city of Perm in the Urals wrote that they had heard about the earthquake on the local radio.[28] At the same time, it reported that the Tashkent telecentre aired a news conference in which city leaders from the Fergana region promised their help to the residents of Tashkent.[29] Second, *Pravda Vostoka* understood the specific needs of residents in Tashkent and was honest in its discussion of a number of topics. In what was otherwise a positive assessment of the situation, one journalist wrote that the celebrations of ethnic culture, such as the recently completed Belarusian decade of literature and art, had lost their "emotional" intensity and had become empty "rituals." Numerous people had already "grumbled" that all the speakers at these events were "banal." The decade of literature and arts had "finished making a noise" and had receded into the past. Only the earthquake could transform this friendship and turn pretty words into effective deeds.[30]

Although Soviet newspapers preferred to report about orderliness, *Pravda Vostoka* had to report on disorder and encourage residents to help the police: "now every Tashkentite must, as never before, be fully aware, disciplined [and] guarded against absurd rumours" and, in this way, "support exemplary public order." This appeal came in conjunction with the case of a citizen who had been attacked at a tram stop, where four thieves had stolen his watch, money, and various articles of clothing. Furthermore, the police had to deal with drunkenness and its effect on general order.[31] At the end of May, the public prosecutor of the city of Tashkent told citizens that "not a single lawbreaker" could hope for leniency from the courts; rather, troublemakers could expect "stern punishment." Two shopkeepers who had shifted scales in their favour by fifteen grams had been punished accordingly.[32] Despite reports of a quiet environment, this last article indicated that, over a month after the earthquake, apprehension about crime persisted in the city. In July, the newspaper warned its readers about market speculators and suggested that laws were not tough enough. If speculators were punished, they simply paid a fine or sat out their ten-day sentence and then reappeared to tackle another market.[33] Asserting control in these circumstances was difficult as the state was having a hard time filling markets with its own goods.

Speculation was not unique to the Tashkent earthquake, nor was the inability of the state to provide needed goods.[34] Yet this speculation had an added dimension that *Pravda Vostoka* failed to mention while it highlighted the friendship of peoples. Speculators were associated with the republics in the Caucasus and were clearly identified as those selling fruit for three times the normal price.[35] This grievance paralleled complaints in Ukraine, and this gave speculation an ethnic dimension. In December 1966, workers from Zhdanov wrote Kosygin in Moscow and asked: "Who in the republic of Georgia does useful public work?" These speculators had "entrenched" themselves in local markets and were probably roaming the entire USSR.[36] Speculation in Tashkent and elsewhere was as much an ethnic as an economic problem, and this called into question other articles associated with the idea of multi-ethnic friendship.

Pravda Vostoka also addressed insurance concerns, which kept popping up among citizens who owned their own property. Within days of the tremour, authorities received over six thousand requests from homeowners seeking compensation.[37] In Tashkent, over 115,000 homes were in the private sector and at least half of these suffered, in one way or another, from the earthquake. By 1 June, over fifty-five thousand requests had been assessed. The representative of *Gosstrakh* encouraged citizens to collect their insurance to repair or reconstruct homes. But the report made it clear that, pursuant to the general plan, homes were going to be bulldozed to make way for the new city: urban planning had little tolerance for the maze of houses in the old town.[38] What represented a large insurance expense was an architectural convenience.

The local details were understandably absent in central newspapers, which were more likely to employ catch phrases. *Stroitel'naia gazeta* (*Construction News*), ran regular articles about the earthquake for at least a year. Words such as "brotherhood," "heroism," and "friendship" and militaristic expressions such as "at the front" and "behind the lines" told readers about the massive progress being made in Tashkent; the mood was typically upbeat as people were trying to build a new world.[39] Articles applauded Ukrainians, Latvians, and others who were getting on trains to help with the construction, but they also mentioned the shortcomings of the construction process.[40] In 1967, *Stroitel'naia gazeta* permitted a local member of the Uzbekistan Union of Architects to warn against over-hasty decisions that could destroy the historical (pre-revolutionary and socialist) heritage of the city. K. Kriukov notes that, despite the planning efforts of architects, many buildings had been destroyed for no reason whatsoever: "your heart aches when you see blocks of concrete and detritus at the site of the former movie theater 'Vatan' … This interesting building, erected from 1937–1940 … was not destroyed by an earthquake."[41] Further, *remont* (repair) had become a code word for tearing a building down. Although *Stroitel'naia gazeta* only touched upon this issue, debates raged among architects in the Uzbek capital, many of whom were more concerned with pre-revolutionary structures than they were with movie theatres built during the Stalinist period.

Literaturnaia gazeta, the publishing organ of the Union of Soviet Writers, fit the earthquake into themes it had been emphasizing all year. In January 1966, the city of Tashkent had been featured in conjunction with the Tashkent conference, and, later that month, an article looked at Uzbek efforts to translate more Russian titles and to strengthen ties between the peoples of the USSR.[42] The newspaper ran a series of portraits of Soviet cities, which included nearby Alma-Ata and a description of the problems this ancient city had with flooding until the Russians built a new settlement.[43] After the Tashkent earthquake, the paper turned its attention to human interest stories and efforts to help the children of writers in Uzbekistan. In a nod to the onset of consumerist culture in the Brezhnev years, one observer noted that some Tashkentites "dragged their most valuable goods out on to the street: televisions, refrigerators, shelves with books on them."[44] This may be compared with stories of Japanese citizens, who, in 1964, left their homes with transistor radios, food, clothes, and important papers.[45] The story exaggerated the availability of these items (even if there were already 30 million TV sets in the Soviet Union by 1968) but enumerated what were considered to be treasured goods.[46] Later in June, the paper ran a story about a boarding house near Moscow that was established to help children of writers spend the summer away from Tashkent. Some of the children of Tashkent were also evacuated to the Black Sea to work at a pioneer camp.[47] The gesture was noble but simply repeated the traditional practice of taking children to safety in the countryside (see below). As presented in Kaiumov's film, the departure of children was a traumatic moment for parents.[48]

Details of the earthquake were made available to American audiences through *Soviet Life*, a cultural journal issued by the Soviet government. Vasilii Peskov, a correspondent for *Komsomol'skaia pravda*, emphasized how the quake united Tashkent residents in a time of need, giving them the strength to return to normal life: "Everything is operating. The theatres are giving regular performances. All the big league soccer matches are being played. The May Day demonstration attracted an unusually large crowd."[49] The Soviets certainly did not want to hint at internal weakness. Peskov wrote about two newlyweds who insisted that their wedding go on (a wedding story would again be used in the context of Chernobyl, but the reaction to this story was entirely different). Furthermore, American audiences learned about the cooperation between and among the member republics. In fact, the groom in the above story had a Central Asian name, whereas the bride had a Slavic name.

The domestic media response to the earthquake was by no means accidental. Following decisions made in the Council of Ministers, party officials ordered media outlets to promote information about the disaster. In its "project" to rebuild Tashkent, the Council of Ministers required "central and republican newspapers, journals, radio and television outlets to systematically report about the course of the restoration and construction of the city of Tashkent."[50] This concern with Tashkent can be juxtaposed with the response to another catastrophe that occurred at about the same time. On 28 April 1966, two days after Tashkent, an explosion in a Ukrainian mine killed twenty-four people and injured four others.[51] The mining incident was much more isolated than was the earthquake, but one might expect its local dimension to garner more attention since the suffering was closer to home. A commission conducted an exhaustive study, including extensive interviews with surviving miners, but the tragedy had no public media resonance even as Ukrainian newspapers were beginning to respond to the events in Tashkent. *Komsomolets Donbassa* ignored the mining accident altogether, reprinted a short TASS (Telegraph Agency of the Soviet Union) report about progress in Tashkent, and soon thereafter continued to publish laudatory stories about local miners.[52] The Ukrainian-language paper *Radians'ka Donechchina* immediately reported the Tashkent earthquake, and, two days after the mining explosion, published a tiny article in the bottom right-hand corner of one of its pages expressing sympathy (the top of the same page covered the arrival of Brezhnev and Kosygin in Tashkent.)[53] The article noted that miners had died, but it did not state how many.

The media response to each tragedy may be explained by their respective political circumstances: the Soviets could not be held responsible for the earth shaking, but they could be held responsible for the poor quality of mines. Aside from this, the death toll also played a roll. The minute death toll in Tashkent meant that authorities did not have to worry about extensive funerals and the provocative atmosphere that such occasions encouraged.[54] The Communist Party often sent officials to supervise these events in order to prevent untoward incidents.[55] In 1957, after a mining accident in Ukraine, the mourners discovered that the body of the deceased had been tossed into a coffin that was too short for him. With rumours spreading, officials could not prevent the coffin from being opened. When the truth was revealed, the women wanted to "beat up" the two party officials who attended the funeral, and, later that day, the men caught up with the mine manager, took him to the residence where the deceased was lying, and "started to beat him up." Only the police could wrest the manager from the workers' hands and prevent further injury.[56] Ultimately, the funeral was postponed to a later day, when the body was treated respectfully, and meetings were held to clear the air. At these meetings, it became clear that this was not the first time that a corpse had been mistreated.[57] The Communist Party was confident it could rebuild a city, but it was less confident it could adequately respond to incidents at funerals.

While one might expect that this uncertainty led to policies that reduced the publication of information about tragedies, not all officials believed this helped the communist cause. Dmitrii P. Goriunov, the director general of TASS, wrote to the Central Committee in March 1966 complaining that his agency was unable to properly report these tragedies because publication laws forbade information about "human casualties, catastrophes, crashes, major accidents," and other incidents.[58] In February of the same year, a Soviet plane had crashed at Sheremetyevo aerodrome but TASS was unable to report it. Goriunov suggested that, had TASS provided prompt reporting, "foreign correspondents [*inkor*] would not have been able to disseminate unproven rumours [and] exaggerate the losses of the catastrophe." He wondered if it would not be better if "Muscovites received news of the catastrophe from Soviet print and radio sources rather than from programs on foreign radio stations."[59] In 1963, a plane made an emergency landing on the Neva River in Leningrad, but, because of the "courageous" crew and "excellent organization" of the rescue squad, no one was injured. Despite the positive outcome of a tricky situation and the fact that this happened in broad daylight, before the "eyes" of Leningradites, Glavlit and Aeroflot forbade TASS to publicize the incident. Only "two months later" did *Pravda* report the water landing (in a 1974 Eldar Riazanov comedy, an Aeroflot plane makes an emergency landing on a highway, where it slows down and waits for pedestrians at a zebra crossing; only in 1979 did Soviet filmmakers dare shoot a fictional film about Aeroflot pilots who dramatically prevented their plane from crashing).[60] In 1961, TASS had been forbidden to report on the tragic flooding after a dam broke in the Kurenivka suburb of Kyiv.[61] Goriunov wanted changes to the publication regulations so that TASS could better inform citizens about accidents and natural calamities.[62] Goriunov's appeal was not isolated. Since the late 1950s, Soviet broadcasting was continually being analyzed for improvement and criticized for inadequacies. The authorities were aware they had to raise their broadcasting level to compete with foreign broadcasters and address the number of "fake-sounding reports" that reached listeners' ears.[63]

Although noteworthy rescues were absent in newspapers, fictional accounts did have rescue themes, if on a less grand scale. Vasilii Shukshin, a village prose author, wrote and filmed a story about a young driver in the Altai mountains. Pashka, the hero of *There Is Such a Lad* (*Zhivet takoi paren'*), prevents an industrial-scale tragedy at a fuel-tanking station.[64] When he hears workers scream "fire!," he jumps on a burning truck laden with fuel and drives it into a river away from harm. The next day, at the hospital, a young reporter arrives to interview the hero as she is preparing a piece for the local newspaper.

Unfortunately, Goriunov's appeal did not resonate in the case of Tashkent, where reporting was more about the reconstruction of the city and less about rescue efforts.[65] *Pravda Vostoka*'s mention of the Fergana flooding fits the traditional mould:[66] the reporting expressed sympathy but did not mention that thirty-eight people had perished and that thirty-seven people were missing, with no news of their whereabouts.[67] At about the same time, the Soviets were in the middle of building the Charvak Hydroelectric Power Plant in northern Uzbekistan. In December 1966, plans were being made to evacuate homeowners before the area was flooded to create the reservoir. Of course, these preventive measures and forced evacuations were not newsworthy either.[68]

In June 1966, the Enisei River in Siberia reached levels unseen since 1902. The city of Krasnoyarsk became the site of a major rescue operation. More than fifty-two thousand people were evacuated from flooded areas and housed in schools and administrative buildings.[69] Eighty-six industrial buildings had been flooded, and over thirty-six thousand evacuees were without shelter.[70] Despite the magnitude of the rescue operation, the flooding had little presence in the media. This reluctance to report on flooding might well be associated with the fact that floods generally led to great loss of life through drowning, illness, and famine.[71] *Pravda* preferred to report on French president de Gaulle's visit to Siberia.[72] In later years, reporting on tragedies continued to be equally selective.

The desire to control the media cannot be considered a uniquely Soviet and/or authoritarian phenomenon. The centralization of media made control easier, but media outlets in the United States were equally interested in steering thoughts about calamities. In his research on the 1906 San Francisco earthquake, Ted Steinberg shows how railway companies were intent on shifting the focus away from the earthquake and onto the fires that resulted thereafter. If one trusted the reports of the Southern Pacific Railway Company, "one would never have believed that a quake measuring M 7.7, among the most powerful in the history of North America, had occurred." Because they did not want to discourage capital investment in the state, newspapers played down the seismic qualities of the region.[73] Some took another tack and ignored the earthquake altogether. An editorial in the *San Francisco Call* made its own suggestion: "The whole world is familiar with our calamity, but is it necessary to harp on the subject after it is all over? Why not forget it as soon as possible … If we want to frighten people away from us this is about as good a way as any other."[74] Silencing the San Francisco earthquake helped capitalists just as silencing the Ashgabat earthquake helped Stalinist communists. For its part, the Tashkent earthquake was celebrated because doing so aided the communists in power at the time. In both American and Soviet cases, the depiction of a natural disaster was determined by how it benefited those in power.

Internationally, newspapers reported the earthquake, but, after January 1966, any enthusiasm for the city of Tashkent had dissipated. In Paris, *Le Monde* admitted that the Soviet media were more open than they had been during the Ashgabat earthquake of 1948, when Westerners only discovered years later that the city had been rebuilt; however, this did not mean Western journalists could freely report about the Tashkent earthquake.[75] In January 1966, a *Le Monde* correspondent lauded the treatment of Western journalists in Tashkent; however, at the same time, *Le Monde* published a news agency feed that noted that foreign journalists were not allowed in the city and so could not adequately report the events. The French newspaper was suspicious of Soviet reports emanating from the city but did agree that life in Tashkent had returned to normal. A delegation of the French General Confederation of Labour (Confédération générale du travail) pressed on with its visits of factories in the city.[76]

While newspapers printed the daily news, film crews were taking footage of the city. Film always played a strong propagandistic role in the Soviet Union, and here was an opportunity not to be missed. *Tashkent, Earthquake*, a film mentioned above, created a dramatic visual and aural perspective on the reconstruction efforts.[77] The narrator comments that no scenes of the actual earthquake were available because such an event could not have been foreseen. Instead, the film balances the tragic (scenes of nurses, stretchers, mothers crying, and a funeral procession) with the hopeful (interviews with students on construction sites, people receiving keys to their new apartments, trains arriving with help from other republics, and a half-dressed woman working in the summer heat). As a documentary, it constructs an image of Soviet people overcoming adversity.

Unfortunately, it has not been possible to uncover production information about Kaiumov's film. It is worth noting, however, that producing informational films about disasters was not uncontroversial. In 1970, an earthquake struck Dagestan and caused damage to thousands of homes. The insurance arm of the Russian republic had asked a Dagestani film studio to create a documentary about the events. Problems began even with the title of the film. The director of the studio received a letter from the authorities suggesting that he and his team had "forgotten" who had ordered the film: they had been contracted to satisfy the work order of the ministry. The authorities in Moscow were upset that the studio had changed the name of the film from "The Helping Hand" (*Ruka pomoshchi*) to "Help Is Needed" (*Trebuetsia pomoshch'*). The original title underscored state assistance, whereas the new title suggested that "help had not been given." The director was also asked why the film showed people smiling when a tragedy had just occurred.[78] The author of the original script complained to the film studio as well. The film was supposed to have an ideological role that emphasized the roles of the party and the insurance agents, who took care of people in the disaster's aftermath.[79] The original script imagined the camera "entering" a newly constructed home and interviewing the "man of the house," who had just received help from the insurers.[80] The final fate of this film is unknown, but the local directors did have the courage to resist ideological pressure from above.

Beyond films, the earthquake developed a lasting presence in short stories and monographs. Vasilii Peskov, whose story about Tashkent had appeared in *Soviet Life*, republished it three years later in a collection of essays.[81] Peskov took planes and helicopters around the Soviet

Union, offering the reader a panoramic view of the Soviet state. The earthquake became part of a tourist narrative that included a trip to Lev Tolstoy's *Iasnaia poliana* and the "quiet" Don; urban destruction, albeit accompanied by stories about heroic efforts at reconstruction, was placed alongside natural beauty.[82] In this travelogue, a serene nature neutralizes the destructive force of the earthquake.

In 1970, Nikolai Kornilov published his "Tashkent diary," in which he emphasizes the friendship of peoples.[83] In the same year, the Uzbek Union of Architects issued a brochure that framed the earthquake within a longer historical perspective. In line with censorship procedures, when discussing the earthquake of 1966, the brochure gave exact figures on the amount of living space that had been destroyed, but it ignored the human toll of the tragedy.[84] A decade after the event, T. Chikhov and V. Zhuravlev penned another short book that commemorated the efforts of Soviet soldiers who had helped with the reconstruction of the new suburb (*gorod-sputnik*) Sergeli.[85] Soldiers always played a major role in responses to disasters.

Alongside these common themes, two publications advanced a more novel concept. In 1970, a press in Tula published *Velikii khashar* (*Great khashar*) and, in 1972, *Novyi mir* published an article entitled "Tashkentskii khashar" (Tashkent khashar).[86] *Khashar* is an Uzbek word, and its nearest equivalent in the English language might be "civil society," although it is probably closer to Ferdinand Tönnies concept of *Gemeinschaft*, which refers to the small local community (as opposed to the concept of *Gesellschaft*, which refers to the larger society).[87] Soviet authors provided their Russian readers with their own explanation of the Uzbek phenomenon. In *Novyi mir*, Matchanov defines *khashar* as follows: "It is an excellent folk custom: fellow villagers, neighbours come together to help someone build a house, plant a garden."[88] Orekhov defines *khashar* in a similar manner but explicitly extends the definition. A khashar was usually called to help the people close to you: neighbours, brothers, and sisters. Here the term *khashar* is not limited to communal construction projects in the *makhalla*, or *kishlak*; here a proper Uzbek khashar includes "the Farkhadskaia hydroelectric station, [and] thousands of kilometers of roads." Even the construction of the Fergana Canal, "built by 160,000 people," was considered a khashar. Orekhov wanted all major Soviet engineering projects to be considered khashars.[89]

The introduction and transformation of the concept of khashar had numerous goals. Authors wanted to find a balance between a volunteer who freely gave her/his help and the person who participated in a khashar because doing so was part of social custom, or what Bourdieu might call the Habitus, or the field of social actions that are taken as self-evident. Looked at as a social custom, participation in a khashar did not necessarily suggest freedom of choice; however, Matchanov included letters from people who did freely choose to volunteer in the reconstruction.[90] Duty and choice combined to encourage one family to offer a spare room to children in Tashkent.[91] The khashar, then, was not just about building physical structures but also about providing humanitarian aid. Newspapers also made standard references to the friendship of peoples, which included discussing how members of all nationalities participated in an ancient and traditional Uzbek ritual (for anyone who participated in the khashar was participating in the history of the Uzbek people). At the same time, the inspiration behind such cooperation pre-dated the October revolution of 1917. The communal values of the khashar overlapped with the values of communism. Marxist-Leninist ideology, however, played a diminished role in these newspaper articles as the emphasis on the khashar stressed local custom.

The merger of ideas was made possible because authors co-opt the concept khashar to benefit the state. The original idea of helping a community member was transformed into the idea of helping a member of the state. Because Matchanov was in the Presidium of the Supreme Soviet in Uzbekistan his advocacy of the khashar linked it to the state. The separation between the community and the state, so essential to many (but not all) theories of civil society, was lost.[92] In essence, the khashar suffered the same fate as did the *obshchestvennaia organizatsiia*. What had once referred to a public activity now referred to the activities of the state.

Over time, the attitude towards the Tashkent earthquake remained consistent, even though its details faded from memory. In 1976, the Uzbek republic built a museum in Tashkent with an accompanying "monumental-sculptural complex" to commemorate the friendship of peoples. Symbolically, the stones for the monument came from Ukraine. *Pravda Vostoka* reported the opening ceremonies and paid homage to the efforts of the Muscovites, Leningradites, and others who came to help in Tashkent.[93] After that, public reporting on the earthquake subsided. In April 1986, the newspaper did not commemorate the earthquake, and by late May 1986, Chernobyl made the present more imperative than the past.

It is difficult to explain why, over the years, the media ceased commemorating the Tashkent earthquake. Certainly, changes in leadership in Moscow and in Tashkent influenced decisions, and the onset of perestroika in the mid-1980s also shifted geopolitical dynamics throughout the Soviet Union.[94] In 1985, the earthquake appeared for a few minutes in a cinematic love story in which the father of a young woman forbade her to marry her beloved Timur because he came from a lower social stratum. The director used documentary footage of the Tashkent earthquake to dramatize destruction. In one scene, the male protagonist is carrying bricks at a construction site when two thugs on motorcycles approach him. They threaten him and tell him to keep his distance from their boss's daughter. This scene hints that criminal elements may have been involved during the reconstruction process, though the scene ends happily enough, with the lovers kissing. The final sequence on the earthquake contrasts a scene of a bulldozer destroying an old home with a scene of a dislocated family moving into a brand new apartment building.[95] Twenty years later, the creation of living space still maintained a dominant place in the earthquake narrative.

The most recent film on the Tashkent earthquake, *The Capital of Friendship and Warmth* (*Stolitsa druzhby i tepla*), was produced in 2011 in the authoritarian atmosphere of post-Soviet Uzbekistan, and it reiterates themes of friendship, courage, calm, and the rapid reconstruction of the city.[96] Towards the end of the film, the camera focuses on the monument to the earthquake, which was built in 1976 and displays the exaggerated human figures typical for artistic endeavours during that period in the USSR. In one section, the designers had etched into a block of stone a clock face with a symbolic fracture down the middle. The clock had no mechanical components, and its hands were set between 5:20 a.m. and 5:25 a.m., the time of the first shock. Significantly, this was local, not Moscow, time. Because the hands could not move, time was frozen at this moment. This visual clip closely follows a theme popular since 1966, in which authors started their stories by citing the exact time of the earthquake.[97]

Disasters are not always referred to in exact times. Americans speak about 9/11 as a day, though the first plane struck the World Trade Center at a time measured on watches, not calendars. A reference to a day is not the same as a reference to a certain time: the former does not require a mechanical measuring device (you can just watch the sun rise and then set), whereas the latter does. The imagery of the earthquake contains numerous visual references to mechanical clocks, and it is made clear to the viewer that they are no longer functioning. The mechanical enunciation of time was important because this was something the state could control.

The visual record of the earthquake preserved in Soviet and post-Soviet texts and films indicates that time stopped with the earthquake. Interestingly enough, time is measured in these stories by clocks rather than by watches. Perhaps this is because clocks are public devices whereas wristwatches are a more private way of measuring time. Users synchronize their watches however they wish, whereas the state determines public time.[98] In an accident in Kyiv in 1967, a bus sank to the bottom of the Dnepr River. The autopsies paid careful attention to the victims' wristwatches, and many were slightly off the official time given to mark the catastrophe.[99] In Tashkent, wristwatches kept on ticking, and therefore time did not stop – except for those who, for storytelling purposes, wanted it to.

In *Time, Forward!* (*Vremia, vpered!*), the novelist Valentin Kataev accelerates the pace of Stalinist industrialization to reflect the Soviet desire to accelerate time. So why the fascination with stopping time in 1966? At one level, the emphasis on a specific moment frozen in time gives the event a military character in tune with an invasion or the dropping of a bomb. But it also suggests a brand new beginning – the birth date of the new Tashkent. Time was momentarily suspended only in order to build pressure before being released into the future. The images of clocks allowed the authorities to slow time down before speeding it up again with the flurry of accelerated activity that marked the reconstruction process. The stopping of time functioned to make the reconstruction look that much faster.

The emphasis on time in the coverage of the Tashkent earthquake far exceeds what occurred in the coverage of the Ashgabat earthquake. This should not come as a surprise since Ashgabat, unlike Tashkent, did not become a major news event, either in the immediate aftermath of the tragedy or years later. In Tashkent, for years the earthquake resonated throughout the USSR, and its presence was touted in diverse media. The story did fade when its propaganda value subsided, but in the critical years of reconstruction everyone, in various ways, came to know of Tashkent. At the national level, readers learned about the massive reconstruction efforts and read about opportunities to volunteer, physically or financially, to aid citizens in Tashkent. At the local level, *Pravda Vostoka* reported serious shortcomings and gave assessments of crime and other dangers that follow upon disasters. The press was not free, but it was quite frank.

Of course, the official media provided one way to understand the response to the Tashkent earthquake. Walking the city streets provided another way. Architects toured Tashkent to determine new design schemes, construction workers tanked up their bulldozers and put up their cranes, and students did their best to guard streets and clear rubble. While the media were willing to recognize the shortcomings of these efforts, readers were left wanting details regarding the diversity and complexity of ground-level experience. Too much information about architectural debates and student carousing would have sullied the triumphalism that the USSR wanted the media to display. Yet the story of the Tashkent earthquake is incomplete without these details.

4

April 1966: Tashkent in the Streets

By 1966, the Soviets already had experience with major urban reconstruction projects. In the more creative atmosphere of the 1920s, constructivist architects combined innovative building plans with revolutionary values to make their impact in the new communist capital, though mostly at the level of individual buildings.[1] After the end of the New Economic Policy and the drive to industrialization at the end of the decade, urban changes became even bolder. In the Urals, foreign and domestic architectural planners designed Magnitogorsk, a great industrial city built from scratch.[2] Moscow had a new subway built and experienced such heavy construction that, in 1960, a leading urban planner stated: "Work was currently being done on a new Moscow 20-year plan."[3] By 1960, Leningrad and Kyiv also had subways snaking under city streets.[4] More urgency filled the air in 1966 in Tashkent, but the architectural and construction process was business as usual.

The architectural discussions in Moscow and Tashkent, the relocation of Tashkentites to the other side of the empire, and the arrival of tens of thousands of construction workers all brought their respective organizational challenges. Much has been written about Soviet architecture and even the architecture of Tashkent in the Imperial period, but most analyses stop before the Brezhnev period.[5] Yet the most active architectural period in Tashkent came at the moment Brezhnev and Kosygin adopted leadership roles. Soviet architects had already planned to rebuild Tashkent and transform a tsarist city into a socialist metropolis, yet everything remained in the planning stage until the earthquake, which, ironically, made their task that much easier. But if the earthquake provided a tabula rasa, it did not determine the style of the new city. This new Soviet city was constructed according to Western principles, and, as will become clear, bore no little resemblance to Levittown, New York, where American suburbia first emerged.[6] After looking west, the architects looked east to consider the future of the *makhalla*, the old administrative and cultural centre of the Uzbek city. At a time when Soviet citizens were becoming more concerned with their pre-Soviet architectural heritage, the attention to the *makhalla* was part of a larger Soviet movement.[7] Architects from Uzbekistan were particularly active in discussing this question, suggesting a degree of regional autonomy in local architectural journals.

While architects discussed thoroughfares and housing projects, construction workers were breaking ground for new building projects. The construction process engaged thousands of Ukrainians, Russians, and Latvians who arrived on trains from their respective republics as well as local workers. These workers came bearing the message inherent in the idea expressed in the phrase "the friendship of peoples." Cheering crowds welcomed these saviours as they descended from the wagons at the Tashkent station. The arrival of the trains replayed a traditional colonial moment in that a Central Asian population had to await help from Russians and other Western "brothers." A close study of migrant workers and the dilemmas they faced highlights the prejudice that often lay just below the surface of any given display of the friendship of peoples. Ukrainian and Russian work crews complained bitterly about the lack of preparedness of their friends in Tashkent. The Uzbeks were worried that the arriving builders had no experience with construction in seismologically sensitive zones. The shortcomings encountered at construction sites led to extensive exchanges between Moscow and Tashkent as well as between Kyiv and Tashkent as regional authorities expressed the limits of the help they were willing to offer.

The Komsomol had a critical role to play in the building process. Writers lauded its efforts at maintaining order in the streets immediately after the earthquake, when authorities were concerned with panicky and marauding citizens.[8] Despite the public accolades, the actions of the Komsomol were interesting for the confusion and befuddlement that characterized them. In the minutes of its meetings, the historian discovers leaders who had a hard time keeping track of disinterested members. The story of the *Komsomoltsy* quickly departs from an official narrative and becomes more like a story about youths exploring a new city and themselves, thus indicating the limits of authoritarian control on the margins of regular experience. The problems of the Komsomol were, in part, dictated by the difficulties of adjusting to the foreign environment of Uzbekistan. The *Komsomoltsy* had travelled a great distance to Uzbekistan, and it should not be surprising that, as a result, communication problems emerged.

But the construction workers and the Komsomol were not the only voyagers. The Communist Party organized a massive evacuation of families from Tashkent. Some families were relocated to areas in Uzbekistan, while others were sent as far away as Ukraine. Pioneer camps and sanatoria were transformed into "evacuee hotels," a role they played whenever disaster struck. The evacuation procedure was carefully orchestrated by decrees from Moscow, which neatly calculated the number of evacuees ascribed to each province. Despite the orderly columns, the evacuation process brought new headaches as the evacuees complained bitterly about their relocation.

The construction plans and urban attitudes before the earthquake reveal early thoughts about reconstruction. The earthquake made planning discussions a more public affair since architects wrote about their visions for the city, indicating their attitudes towards construction materials, street design, and cultural monuments. In the 1920s, Fedor Gladkov lauded cement as a building material and used it metaphorically to suggest that the working class was the foundation of society. Gleb Chumalov, the main protagonist in Gladkov's novel, tells his listeners: "With cement we're going to have a great building-up of the Republic. We are cement, Comrades: the working class."[9] In the 1950s and 1960s, cement was no longer just a sturdy building material with metaphorical possibilities but a plastic substance with aesthetic capabilities; urban planners in Tashkent discussed its architectural and aesthetic merits as being in line with broader European trends.[10] Although Tashkent was thousands of kilometres behind the Iron Curtain, the ideas bandied about included influences from Moscow and from Western Europe.

In 1964, A. Mukhamedshin published an article entitled "Tashkent Tomorrow." Photos in the article contrasted the old Tashkent with a model of the general plan for reconstruction.[11] In the past, he saw "endlessly interwoven, cramped, stuffy, little streets, dense adobe fences and dust, dust." The city would not remain this way, however, because "ancient Tashkent" was to become "unrecognizable" and to be transformed into a massive and modern "city-garden."[12] These thoughts came in conjunction with a 1964 architectural competition to develop a new general plan for Tashkent.[13] Nineteen sixty-four was also the year in which experts studied the development of public transportation in the city and first suggested that a subway system was as viable an option as was expanding existing bus routes.[14]

Planners had discussed the seismological profile of the city, and one architect wondered whether Tashkent was not in fact too safe. I.N. Burshtein argued that many people exaggerated the seismic danger in Tashkent. According to his statistics, no earthquake larger than five had been measured between 1953 and 1958 and, in the last fifty years, no earthquake larger than seven had been registered (the exact scale is unclear in this article but it reflects the values in the MSK-64 scale mentioned by Ulomov; five would cause a strong shaking in a building and seven would cause objects to fall from shelves and damage older buildings. A nine causes general panic).[15] Because the danger was exaggerated, construction costs were inflated and the placing of buildings became more difficult.[16] Burshtein was tragically wrong, but, fortunately, there is no evidence that anyone took his advice.

In January 1966, just months before the earthquake, officials in Uzbekistan wrote to Moscow stating that there was a desperate need to reconstruct Tashkent. R. Kurbanov mentioned that many residents were without running water, and he asked central officials to anticipate added expenditures for building projects.[17] It made him uneasy that the one-storey structures in the middle of town did not satisfy "elementary domestic [and] sanitary … norms." The lifespan of "earthquake-prone" homes from the pre-revolutionary period was long past. The time had come for the "reconstruction of the centre, and the main routes and squares of the city."[18] Political officials and architects were pushing to change the look of Tashkent. In this regard, the earthquake was opportune, offering nature's assistance in preparing the ground for future construction.[19] Indeed, shortly after the earthquake, one commentator asserted that bulldozers were completing "nature's work."[20]

Plans to rebuild the city already existed, but now that construction crews were arriving from around the Soviet Union, pressing technical and aesthetic questions were raised. How does one find a proper balance between the old single-storey homes and the modern demand for multiple-storey homes? How could one preserve the historical heritage of the city without promoting the cultural isolation of the *makhalla*? How could one take advantage of the plastic properties of concrete without building a monotonous city? The general reader had access to these questions in *Pravda Vostoka*, while specialists read the *Architectural Journal of Uzbekistan* (*Stroitel'stvo i arkhitektura Uzbekistana*) for details on divergent opinions.

In keeping with the global spirit of the times, architects in Uzbekistan wanted graceful skyscrapers built to withstand the destructive force of regular tremours. This had aspects of Soviet monumentalism, but city planners wanted to contain urban sprawl as Soviet cities had grown exponentially since the 1920s: by 1960, there were as many urban as rural dwellers in the Soviet Union.[21] If planners reduced the number of multi-storey buildings, the "territory of the city" would expand by a couple of thousand square kilometres and the diameter of the city would increase by about thirty to thirty-five kilometres.[22] Subsequently, commuters in the city would lose time getting to and fro. To avoid this, one author envisioned one- or two-storey buildings providing less than 10 per cent of the housing. But skyscrapers were not accepted without discussion. Z.N. Chebotareva wrote in "defence" of single-storey homes and insisted that they did not deserve the epithets "feudal" or "reactionary." Tashkent had to experiment with individual apartments and gardens. Drawing from Western architectural models, Chebotareva argued that these homes had been successfully implemented in places such as England and the Federal Republic of Germany.[23]

Writing in 1974, Chebotareva's comments were part of a broader discussion, already apparent in 1966. A new awareness of cultural heritage had emerged and architects showed greater sensitivity to the cultural reconstruction of old towns. If previous generations had shown little respect for cultural heritage, this was no longer the case: "we have passed that phase of nihilism" when great pieces of art, such as the majority of the Sheikhantaur ensemble in Tashkent "disappeared from the face of the earth."[24] Mistakes had already been made in Bukhara and Samarkand, two cultural gems, so planners had to be careful not to repeat these in Tashkent. In Bukhara, old and unnecessary buildings had been removed to isolate heritage buildings, thus creating unnatural islands of green space around architectural monuments. To avoid this, the Tashkent general plan proposed an "organic blending" between the old and the new parts of the city.[25]

The benefits of the older architecture were becoming more evident as it could be used to encourage tourism and foreign relations. O.A. Shvidkovskii marvelled at how Florence and Venice were able to transform their architectural heritage into income from tourists.[26]

Pravda Vostoka published a photograph of foreign diplomats standing in front of monuments in Bukhara and Samarkand. The caption told readers that the monuments made an "indelible impression" on the diplomats.[27] The photograph promoted the preservation of these buildings, but it still bore the burden of an unresolved tension – preserving individual buildings was less politically problematic than was preserving (or destroying) whole sections of the old town. About one month later, *Pravda Vostoka* proudly presented its readers with a photograph depicting a construction scene on New Arbat Avenue in Moscow, the controversial street that ripped through whole sections of the old town.[28]

In his address to the Union of Architects of Uzbekistan, Shvidkovskii spoke about the reconstruction of ancient towns.[29] He presented the problem as a global one and included humorous cartoons from abroad to illustrate his point. In one cartoon, English motorists stop their car in the middle of a highway overpass. One passenger says to the other: "We have arrived in the centre of Winkelshem." On the ground below a maze of elevated highways is a steeple and a little town core. These international cartoons stress the point that, despite modern technologies, "there was no need to destroy valuable fragments of ancient cities" in an effort to modernize them.[30] Moreover, one simply could not "reconstruct different cities" with "one and the same architectural method." Ukrainian, Caucasian, and Central Asian architectural traditions were all very different from one another.

With the city still in shambles, Shvidkovskii was deeply worried about the preservation of Tashkent and, in an international context, raised his voice against wanton Soviet building techniques. But the comic illustrations that accompanied his points indicate that people were visiting rather than living in the old town. The British motorists wanted a glimpse of old Winkelshem, but they gave no indication that they wanted to buy a home there. His other illustrations show tourists with binoculars gazing at heritage sites or even at St Basil's Cathedral on Red Square. Although his concerns did nothing to save the *makhalla*, they did foreshadow a style of living in American cities – the flight from the centre to the suburbs. Years later, Uzbek architects commented upon this phenomenon.

By 1971, the Uzbek architectural journal was reporting on the restoration and preservation of cultural monuments. Unfortunately, the news was sobering as Uzbekistan had yet to find a way to properly preserve the historical core of its cities. Only in 1971 were the older

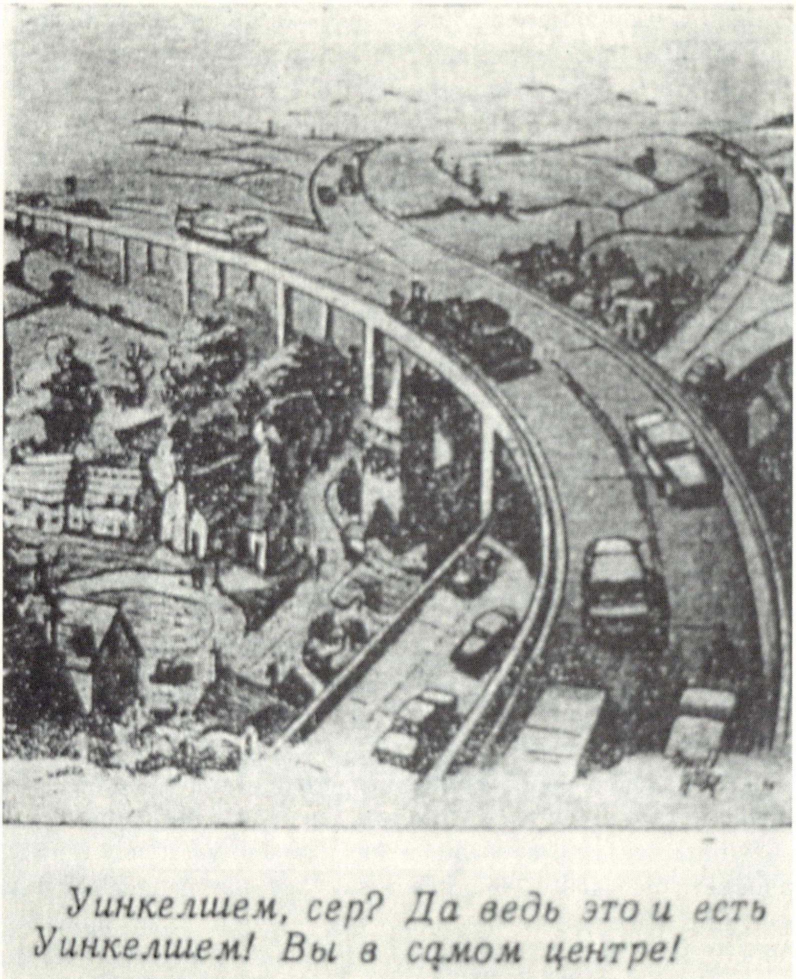

4.1 "Winkelshem, sir? Why, it is Winkelshem! You are right in the centre!" O.A. Shvidkovskii, "Puti rekonstruktsii drevnikh gorodov," *Stroitel'stvo i arkhitektura Uzbekistana* 10 (1968): 21.

parts of Tashkent being evaluated in terms of their architectural value, and, in many cases, this was already too late.[31] Nevertheless, there was ample opposition to the roughshod use of bulldozers, the erection of concrete blocks, and the turning of the crooked streets of the ancient *makhalla* into green space.

The attitude towards the rebuilding process in Tashkent paralleled trends in Moscow. In the 1960s, Russian nationalism was slowly becoming visible through a thick haze of ideology. Village prose authors, or *derevenshchiki*, were writing about traditional Russian villages, and in June 1966, VOOPIK, the All-Russian Society for the Preservation of Historical and Cultural Monuments, held its inaugural meeting.[32] VOOPIK was formed because citizens had become concerned about neglected churches, museums, and pre- and post-revolutionary historical artefacts. Angry VOOPIK members either spoke at meetings or wrote in to express their displeasure. Often this displeasure was aimed at architects who promised they were changing their ways.[33] In these discussions, there was intense tension between the architects and the members of VOOPIK.[34] Soviet film satirized this tension. In the comedy *The Guardian* (*Opekun*), the two central male protagonists try to prevent the destruction of an old man's home by arguing that Pugachev had spent a night there in the eighteenth century. The scene, set in an official's office, shows a model of a new Soviet city plan with a little wooden hut in the middle.[35]

In proper Soviet fashion, VOOPIK received letters from its members. One writer complained that a "marvelous, wooden house from Petrine times" was being destroyed to make way for the construction of New Bashilovka Street in Moscow.[36] In 1969, a more acerbic writer compared the deterioration of the monuments to the Nazi destruction of Russian culture: "There was no need for contemporary Western fascists to physically destroy the Slavs as a nation" since this was already happening "on the spot [*na mestakh*]" with the removal of culturally significant buildings and the erection of skyscrapers.[37] These letters had a sense of urgency as activists were anticipating "general plans" and the "reconstruction" of the urban core in their own cities. In Penza, the anticipated "reconstruction of the central part of the city" made all these "issues" more pressing.[38]

These discussions dealt with the attempt to physically position buildings so as to blend old and new external styles. In addition, activists mentioned building materials and, in particular, were shocked at the use of cement. At the first VOOPIK meeting in 1966, a speaker was met with applause when he demanded that the controversial Rossiia Hotel under construction adjacent to Red Square be a Russian hotel and not just a "concrete and iron cube."[39] In 1971 in Tashkent, an architect reviewed the newly constructed Blue Domes Café (*Golubye kupola*) on Lenin Boulevard. Among other criticisms aimed at this attempt to mix old and new styles, the reviewer was unimpressed with the use of "iron and concrete" in the construction of the cupolas as this made them look "artificial."[40] This reviewer may be seen either (1) as a strong-willed person whose opposition to concrete symbolizes his opposition to the grandiose building plans of the Soviet state or (2) as a conservative who is unwilling to see architects introduce new building materials into their repertoire.

Seen in an international perspective, the above reviewer would fall into the second category. In the 1950s and 1960s, in rebelling against the sleek glass buildings that had become part of the modern skyline, architects in the West had started to embrace the raw qualities of concrete. Advocates of what became known as the New Brutalism, or just Brutalism, wanted passersby to see and feel the power of concrete. In 1969, the American historian of architecture Marcus Whiffen wrote of Brutalism: "Concrete is the favorite material; it is always left exposed."[41] It would be a huge stretch to say that Soviet architects in Tashkent were members of the Brutalist school, but their arguments in favour of concrete have to be seen within the changing landscape of American and European architectural principles. While Fedor Gladkov writes about цемент (cement), these architects (and their detractors) refer to бетон, or *béton*, the French word for concrete. Historians write about the influence of Western radio on Soviet listeners in the 1960s, but Western architectural techniques also made a strong impression on Soviet residents.[42] When concrete was discussed in Tashkent, it was as more than just a building material.

The French connection to the building of Tashkent was not accidental as a French firm had been contracted to build a factory to produce prefabricated pieces so as to accelerate the erection of housing projects. Although France was a Western power it steered a sufficiently independent course, and the Soviets could justify borrowing its expertise.[43] In the 1950s, Raymond Camus had already promoted the rapid construction of housing in the region of Paris, and now his factory had been called upon to do the same in the Soviet Union.[44] In Tashkent, this contract was not uncontroversial as its opponents argued that the Soviet industrial base could complete the task on its own. *Minstroidormash*, the ministry responsible for construction projects, objected that the French equipment required too much manual labour and that it "significantly lagged behind domestic equipment." Moreover, the ministry stated it was "in principle mistaken" to order this equipment without allowing Soviet specialists to examine it.[45] These objections did not have enough force to sway general opinion, and the contract was approved. Among its other benefits, the purchase of the equipment allowed the Soviets to familiarize themselves with the best "contemporary techniques" from abroad.[46] In this way, it transpired that the building blocks for these massive apartment buildings were a Parisian import.

Talk of prefabricated housing developments would seem to undermine the idea that architects were experimenting with concrete rather than just using it as a convenient material to build lots of apartments very quickly. At an all-union level, the Soviets were aware that their mass housing had its deficiencies, and just before the earthquake *Soviet Life* employed the word "monotony" to describe some Soviet neighbourhoods.[47] In Tashkent, architects understood that, despite the masses of prefabricated housing, space existed for aesthetic experiments that bore traces from the other side of the Iron Curtain.

G.I. Korobovtsev recognized the positive attributes of providing housing but criticized the tendency for all housing to look the same. When he contemplated the future of the old town in Tashkent, he quoted Frank Lloyd Wright to the effect that mechanization must serve the creative will of the architect; as long as architects serve mechanization, there will be no great architecture.[48] The "brotherly republics" were helping, but they were erecting endlessly repetitive street scenes, similar to those in other cities in the USSR.[49] Korobovtsev envisioned more plasticity in the structures and drew on Western ideas to explain his goals. He quoted the Frenchman Michel Ragon, an advocate of the plasticity of concrete: "We ignore all the forms which concrete can adopt as a plastic mass" and therefore we build straight-lined boxes.[50] Korobovstev argued that two-storey buildings could not solve the housing problem, advocated the use of concrete in the construction of multi-storey buildings, but did not want a monotonous urbanscape. To this end, he promoted the idea of *blok-fraktsiia*, a method whose purpose is to provide more angularity to housing within the limitations of prefabricated design. While the plans for his *blok-fraktsiia* might strike the contemporary viewer as amounting to only minor adjustments to a monotonous theme, he did mention foreign architecture that satisfied his requirements. His article includes an approving photograph of Habitat '67, the pavilion designed by Moshe Safdie for Expo '67 in Montreal. Habitat '67 was built with interconnected and prefabricated concrete structures yet provided extensive individual living space in a dense urban environment.[51] The urgency to provide housing overwhelmed more creative proposals, but the plastic properties of cement did become visible in Tashkent (e.g., in the Blue Domes Café mentioned above).[52]

In contrast to some architects, Korobovtsev thought of the centre of town as active living space: "The best features of the 'old' town, created over the course of centuries with folk wisdom … must be revived."[53] He appreciated the natural flow, the channels, of the old town. Even though a single principle guided the usage of space (*prostranstvo*) in the old town, this space was multifaceted. Moreover, it was impossible to get lost in the old town since the ever-growing arteries gradually guided you towards important landmarks as well as to "the market square, an ancient muslim school and the mosque."[54] His photographs of the old town emphasize this point. Below a photograph of a curved street upon which we see old two-storied homes and three pedestrians, a subtitle reads: "There is still time to stroll through the narrow, curved streets, peek into shady courtyards, and fall in love with the amazing carvings on doors and wisdom of simple architecture."[55]

After the collapse of the Soviet Union, architects wrote about the tragic loss of these carved doors during the reconstruction of Tashkent. At the time, however, this was not the dominant view. *Pravda Vostoka* published a series of "before-and-after" photographs of various streets. In one shot, the before photo shows a one-storey building with a wagon in front of it, whereas the after shot depicts a multi-storey building with a car in front of it.[56] Korobtsev would have appreciated the multistorey building and the need for urban renewal, but he was not ready to dismiss the positive attributes of the old town.

In his title and throughout his article, Korobovtsev almost always refers to the old town in quotation marks – *"staryi" gorod*. The quotation marks put "old" in a unique voice and add a layer of meaning to a rather commonplace adjective. In the early 1970s, this added layer referred to the *makhalla*, a word that only appears once in Korobovtsev's lengthy two-part article. The makhalla, or the traditional Uzbek community, was at the focal point of the debate about the centre of town. To architects who envisioned rational grid patterns bisected by immense thoroughfares it was a remnant of an unenlightened past, and the photos in *Pravda Vostoka* contributed to this view. To supporters of national traditions, however, the makhalla represented a clever local manner of urban administration and a rational use of urban space.

When we pause to consider the makhalla (a form of communal organization that had an average population of three to four thousand) in Korobovotsev's overall scheme, an interesting paradox emerges.[57] Between his photos showing off the ancient streets of Tashkent and the quotations he borrows from Western architects such as Frank Lloyd Wright and Le Corbusier, the Soviet city almost disappears.[58] This is a slight overstatement, but the Soviet city was squeezed between two visions, one from the West and one from the East. The Western emphasis represented a return to another era in Soviet architecture. Both Wright and Le Corbusier had been discussed in the 1920s, until Stalin steered architectural innovation in another direction.[59] In the Brezhnev era, the Soviets had a tendency to draw extensively from Western architecture: the parallels between the Kalinin Prospekt and Le Corbusier's Ville Radieuse had already gained attention.[60] And from Uzbekistan, architects such as Korobovstev thought deeply about incorporating aspects of the makhalla into modern design. Ultimately, the limitations of Soviet building materials and techniques determined the new skyline, but Korobovstev wanted to superimpose Western and Uzbek principles of design onto these materials.[61] It was only partly true that "Tashkent [was] becoming still more Soviet contemporary in appearance."[62]

Discussions of the makhalla were not unique to Tashkent, nor did they start with the 1966 earthquake. In 1965, the popular Soviet journal *Science and Religion* provided its readers with information about the makhalla and reported on the progress that had been made in introducing communist ideas into these small communities. One author visited a small makhalla in Tashkent and talked with a handful of its five hundred residents. The visitor noted that most followers of Islam were relatively uncultured and possessed a "primitive and vague conception of religion."[63] This did not mean that the makhalla was a religious hotbed; indeed, only a minority of the residents regularly performed religious rites.[64] Yet "it was no secret" that communists in the makhalla did little to spread scientific-atheistic attitudes to residents who were still very traditional and God-fearing.[65] This visitor was more concerned with people than with buildings; nevertheless, he made two interesting architectural comments. He noted that most residents lived in individual homes with their own gardens and that this physical layout contributed to an increase in religiosity. Moreover, the isolation of the makhalla meant that its ethnic composition was quite uniform, whereas in new modern buildings residents lived in mixed communities and thus were more exposed to Soviet values.[66] This theme was pursued less than a year later when another contributor emphasized that the makhalla was a "secluded" community that preserved "archaic" forms of life. Although residents of the makhalla had been resettled in new buildings, they continued to perform ancient rituals.[67]

These Soviet views were published in a USSR-wide journal based in Moscow. Regional reporting was much more sympathetic to the makhalla than was reporting from the centre, even though the need for change was almost universally accepted. Architects in Tashkent had already developed plans to move residents of the makhalla into new buildings before the earthquake, but public support for this sort of community organization went beyond the urban layout.[68] Not everyone saw the makhalla as an isolated community; rather, it acted as a strong administrative centre that "supplemented" the efforts of the Soviet state and formed "the base of collective living and the cohesiveness of the population" for collective decision making. Its economic character had changed over the years, but its communal character, which was in tune with communist values, had not. The makhalla offered educational services, prodded residents to attend local khashars, and even offered certain medical services.[69] In rebuilding Tashkent, one could not ignore the makhalla's ability to encourage "public interaction and independent self-service [*samodeiatel'nnoe obsluzhivanie*]" based on the principle of volunteering.[70]

From an international perspective, the concern about the fate of the makhalla was not unusual. In the West, images persisted of the archaic and threatening nature of old Muslim towns. In the 1930s, Le Corbusier drew up plans to redevelop Algiers that involved separating old from new.[71] In the same decade, in *Pépé le Moko* Jean Gabin starred as a criminal able to hide from French police in the tangled web of the Casbah in Algiers. This story has a parallel in Uzbekistan. After the collapse of the Soviet Union, an inhabitant of Tashkent relayed a story told by his mother about a "secret" tunnel that connected a streetside mausoleum to the Khazrati Imam mosque.[72] In 1966, Gillo Pontecorvo directed *The Battle of Algiers* and depicted the French authorities struggling to contain a revolutionary movement in the old town. Ultimately, they decided to employ explosives and blow members of the resistance out of their hiding places. The Soviets had scarce need for explosives, but they did make extensive use of bulldozers and military tanks that had been converted into bulldozers. Architects were unable to prevent much of the destruction, yet there was ample opposition to the plan and local architects made their concerns public. Ironically, the destruction of the old town drew no small inspiration from Western architects. In 1991, architects heavily criticized the building projects of the late 1960s and noted that the style being used had been "selected from foreign experience, as valuable for Soviet architecture."[73] Further, "maybe it sounds strange (*neobychno*)," but Soviet architecture did not "escape global processes" that moved humanity to attempt to master the natural environment. The ideology behind the buildings was not specifically communist but, rather, was representative of a "rigid pragmatism" that served the interests of citizens who believed they were creating a new society.[74]

In the discussions presented so far, the criticism involves the centre of town: How could architects aesthetically merge modern cement buildings with the few remaining historical structures? The general plan, approved in 1967, presented a vision for the entire city, a vision that was not without Western ideals. The planners had a dream for the suburbs, but getting the population out of the centre and into those developing suburbs had a number of associated problems.

The general plan was applicable not just to Tashkent but to the whole Soviet Union. While architects such as Korobovtsev presented alternatives, the general plan promoted common Soviet urban practices – wide avenues, main squares with statues surrounded by monumental buildings, and the incorporation of extended green space. If the streets were as wide as possible, the buildings were as tall as possible: the expression "multi-storey Tashkent" found its way into the press.[75] The challenge, particular to Tashkent and other cities in Central Asia, was constructing tall buildings that could withstand the force of an earthquake. The Soviets saw this as a challenge for Soviet engineering.

The general plan was implemented in record speed, and only decades later did architects write about its consequences. Korobovtsev, who had been an advocate of tall buildings and dense populations in the early 1970s, wrote that the centre of Tashkent had been filled with too many public buildings, thus decreasing its population density.[76] Since the population of the city increased over this time period, it was clear that residents had gravitated towards the suburbs on the periphery, thus recreating the circulation problems the larger arteries were designed to avoid.

In this discussion of architecture, the focus on the makhalla and Western-inspired design has pushed the construction process to the periphery. The emphasis on architects may give the mistaken impression that the buildings just popped up, much like mushrooms in a rainy Russian forest, once the architects gave the go-ahead. Yet, beyond the smiling faces of Ukrainian workers arriving at the train station and student brigades posing in industrious ways, an incredibly complex building process was under way. The communists had to organize and synchronize tens of thousands of workers, many of whom had little experience and were not familiar with Tashkent. This building process requires further exploration.

THE POLITICS OF RECONSTRUCTION IN TASHKENT

The official story of the reconstruction has been told many times: an earthquake struck the Central Asian city of Tashkent, Brezhnev arrived and promised to rebuild it, soon thereafter trains arrived with construction workers from around the empire, buildings were constructed with brotherly care, and then dislocated residents moved into brand new modern apartments. Reducing Soviet propaganda to an appropriate size has a long history, so it should come as absolutely no surprise that the construction process was not as glamorous as one might have hoped. Beyond demystifying the workers' achievements, the construction process revealed important dynamics in Soviet society: disagreements with levels of government in the various republics, the nature of the "volunteer" status of the workers, the indifference of student brigades to their ideological mission, and the deadly dangers of the construction process.

When architects observed the rebuilding process, they were struck by the lack of coordination between various republican construction trusts working on neighbouring tracts. Each republic was doing its own thing without paying proper attention to the larger architectural scheme. "Opposite sides of the street" lacked architectural coordination, builders had not paid attention to the orientation of the buildings in a sun-drenched city, and the "unsuccessful placement" of buildings designed for children resulted in exits that led onto streets and thoroughfares. Additionally, the poor quality of materials was negatively affecting the quality of construction.[77]

Republics continually complained about having to supply building materials, whose quantities had been determined in Soviet ministries. Within months of the earthquake, the RSFSR was reporting to central authorities that, "despite its limited resources," it had managed to deliver bricks to Uzbekistan but had struggled to send materials to other areas within the Russian republic that had suffered from natural disasters.[78] A massive earthquake had struck Dagestan only days before the one in Tashkent, and thousands of homes had been destroyed.[79] Moreover, because of the distances, the RSFSR did not plan to send crushed brick to Uzbekistan.[80] The RSFSR was standing up to the USSR-level authorities above it, but it also had to coerce regional authorities. Officials in Orenburg, Perm, and Tatarstan expressed their opposition to supplying extra bricks. Ultimately, they were forced to do so.[81]

Moscow, which had sent its own crew, stressed the limitations on its contributions and noted that it was paying to help Tashkent with funds that otherwise were earmarked for capital improvements in Moscow. The city had reduced its capacity to build living space and was unable to satisfy Muscovites who needed to be resettled from "basements, barracks and decrepit homes." Moreover, it was unable to help residents on waiting lists.[82] Nor was Moscow the only city concerned about how resources were being concentrated in Tashkent. The city of Gulistan, a regional Uzbek centre about one hundred kilometres south of Tashkent, complained that most "material-technical resources were bound for the construction of Tashkent," leaving Gulistan in a less than desirable state.[83]

Officials in Kyiv worried about costs. The heightened seismological requirements created additional expenses, so Ukrainian officials conducted cost analyses comparing the cost of building in Tashkent with the cost of building in Kyiv, and they found that the former was significantly more expensive. Further, the calculations considered the added transportation costs of sending workers to Tashkent and replacing them when the time came for the first shift to return home.[84] Ukrainians could appeal to central authorities in Moscow but few funds were available there, so instead they developed creative ways to save.[85] Despite the ideological call to construct tall buildings, costs were prohibitive; therefore Ukrainians built many four-storey rather than nine-storey buildings. They changed construction materials; for example, they used cement instead of ceramic tiles for balconies. They even went so far as to reduce the number of balconies in four-storey homes, a serious measure in a city with intense summer heat.[86]

Beyond these subtle cost-cutting measures, Ukrainians simply turned down requests from their "brothers" in Uzbekistan. About a year after the earthquake, officials in Uzbekistan asked Kyiv to supply more qualified technical and engineering staff to Tashkent. The

Ukrainians noted that sixty specialists had already been sent to Tashkent and that, of these, twenty-nine, "for one reason or another," had left the city. Since Ukraine had already supplied "significant help" and had fulfilled its "obligation," it declined the request to send additional technical personnel.[87]

While Ukraine suggested it had given enough help, Uzbek officials argued the opposite. They contended that they had been sent too many unqualified and young workers and that the administrative apparatus had to be increased (a request that was partially granted).[88] More administrators were asked for the town of Sergeli, but again this request was only partially fulfilled.[89] The electro-technical institute in Tashkent had wanted to build housing, but, until the earthquake, it had been impossible to get a piece of land. After the earthquake, a tract of land had been cleared right next to the institute, so conditions were ideal for erecting housing. Unfortunately, the institute discovered that the RSFSR, and not Tashkent, was responsible for building on the tract, and therefore it petitioned the Soviet Council of Ministers in Moscow to help it with the acquisition of land.[90] The outcome of this petition is unclear, but, regardless, it indicates tensions in the reconstruction process.

Republics protected their own spheres of interest and asserted themselves by reducing their levels of commitment. The USSR could exert its own pressure, but it had no choice but to listen to regional governments when they said they had only limited supplies; the Kremlin did not want to build lower structures, but it was forced to do so once the numbers came rolling in from the republics. The Russian and Ukrainian construction trusts could not demand *more* money from the Kremlin, but they could deliver *fewer* floors and lower-quality materials to Tashkent. The reconstruction process recalls the supply problems associated with the target numbers of the five-year plans, though the suppliers were the republics and not individual factories.[91]

The centre was well informed of these problems as it had conducted probes and sent officials to survey the situation. Since materials were imported from far way, the authorities had a near impossible time coordinating who brought what and when; thousands of train cars idled because Tashkent lacked the ability to unload them.[92] Officials would have preferred that building materials such as bricks had emanated from Tashkent.[93] Local newspapers printed photographs of smiling workers arriving from Ukraine, but they did not print photographs of individual workers leaving Tashkent because their term had ended. An official report noted that, by the spring of 1967, "practically the entire working personnel" of the construction crews from the republics had been "completely replaced."[94] The high attrition rate made it significantly more difficult to guarantee the presence of skilled workers and added extensive travel costs to the budget.[95] Moreover, trains arrived carrying people who did not have the "appropriate" skills.[96] Consequently, the state had to find ways to reduce costs. The most practical was to shrink the height of the buildings, but they also discussed reducing the widths of *magistrali*, or major roads.[97]

The Kremlin targeted specific republics. Each republic had been assigned to build a certain square footage of living space, but many were not pulling their weight. The practice of assigning neat numbers to represent housing was already controversial, but here the Kremlin highlighted the inadequacies of republican construction crews.[98] By September 1966, the Tadjik republic, which was supposed to construct five buildings (eight thousand square metres of living space), had only begun to lay the foundation on one of them.[99] By early 1967, only six of the republics had actually fulfilled their quotas; the other eight were behind.[100] The Russian republic lagged behind, but it later complained that the norms for measuring the construction of living space had been altered to its disadvantage.[101] This offers a stark contrast to the words of the American sympathizer, Mike Davidow, who wrote: "Tashkent provides a peek into the future *when the brotherhood of man masters nature*." And further: "[Tashkent] *is the living symbol of the brotherhood of Soviet cities.*"[102] Much of the construction took place in the suburbs. The two main suburbs were Chilanzar, about ten kilometres from the centre of Tashkent, and Sergeli, about twenty kilometres from the centre. The Chilanzar project had been started before the earthquake; thus, the earthquake did not change procedure, but it did allow the state to transform a local and mundane construction project into an urgent story about help and multi-ethnic compassion. The Sergeli project was under the auspices of the army, not national building crews. With army-like efficiency, the bulldozers arrived in May 1966, and by October residents were already moving into their new homes.[103] Journalists promoted the heroics of the military in providing aid in crisis situations and celebrated their efforts with photographs such as the one depicting the laying of the first "foundation stone" in Sergeli.[104]

The visual material was designed to promote the unique ability of the communist state to recover from disaster, yet the most interesting shots were the panoramas of the suburb. Soviet photographers and filmmakers made extensive use of panoramas because doing so enabled them to depict a wide sweep of cranes filling the length of the horizon. In Sergeli, the panorama shots showed a completed town. Surprisingly, the town could easily have been mistaken for an American suburb: images showed rows of two-storey apartment buildings placed on tract land, arranged in a grid pattern.[105] The apartment buildings in the images were not typical of the American experience, but *Pravda Vostoka* published an elegant photo spread of Sergeli that highlights rows and rows of single-family homes that were much like those that, at the time, would be found in Levittown, Pennsylvania. Although Soviet authorities used the earthquake as an excuse to relocate single-home-dwellers into large apartment complexes, they did make allowances for the continued use of individual properties; not everyone had to live in a nine-storey building.[106]

The last words on the planning and construction process are concerned with where the earthquake began – underground. Even before the earthquake, Uzbek officials wanted a subway because, as the first "in the history of Asian countries," it would have enormous "social and political meaning."[107] The tremour expedited the fulfilment of this wish. At the end of 1968, during the heart of the rebuilding process, a state commission studying the feasibility of a subway in Tashkent made its final report. It approved the plan and recognized that a subway in Tashkent was a necessity.[108] The population was expected to grow, and the "resettlement" of residents from the central zones of the city to Chilanzar was changing the dynamic of traffic flow. With a larger suburban population, the city was experiencing a significant rise in "peak [*pik*] passenger flows for longer distances" because the "settlers" (*pereselentsy*) in these peripheral neighbourhoods still worked in the centre of town.[109] Moreover, the members of the commission were expecting a steep rise in car traffic, with cars being expected to share space with trams on major roads.[110] Construction was soon under way, and equipment arrived from other republics in the Soviet Union, although in 1977 supply problems forced officials in Tashkent to write to their counterparts in Kyiv to complain that insufficient quantities of cable were being delivered (the Ukrainian company responsible had been forced to redirect the supplies somewhere else).[111] Nevertheless, the Metropolitan was completed in 1977, and soon millions of suburbanites rode the subway to work. The planning and construction of this subway had proceeded in parallel with the reconstruction of Tashkent.

4.2 Sergeli, published in *Pravda Vostoka*, 23 October 1966, no. 243.

Before turning to the social aspects of the reconstruction process, two inanimate objects deserve a few words of their own. Functionally, the bulldozer just cleared rubble, but it was also of varied symbolic value. To those who worried about the heritage of the old town, it became a symbol of wanton destruction;[112] more often, however, it was a symbol of Soviet strength and even of atheism.[113] Many bulldozers were former tanks that had had their cannons removed, thus displaying the flexibility and strength of the Soviet army. The bulldozer was present in a religious context as a modernizing force that wiped out old buildings and old beliefs. The "roar" of the bulldozer was a transformational sound in an old neighbourhood.[114] Throughout this period, cranes filled the city's skyline, conveying the impression of a bustling economy, regardless of what was happening on the ground.

SOCIAL ASPECTS OF THE RECONSTRUCTION

The mise en scène of state plans may have been at the centre of everyone's attention, but it was only part of the process. At meetings, workers complained about shortages and dangerous working conditions. People from the outside were arriving only to leave again, families from Tashkent left forever, some left only to come back, and children headed for summer camps. In this atmosphere, individuals had the opportunity to adopt new roles, shed their ideological smiles, speak a little louder, and take advantage of the freedoms linked to such disorganization. Many were dissatisfied with, or even uninterested in, making Tashkent the "most beautiful city in the country." The complaints of workers, the social habits of students, the role of scientists, and a general shifting of values added a critical social dimension, one that often fell outside party control, to the story of the rebuilding of Tashkent.

In general, two forms of complaints emerged in association with the reconstruction. Contributors wrote about supply problems and inefficiencies at construction sites. *Stroitel'naia gazeta* pointed out that the earthquake was not "guilty" of everything. At one worksite, finishers (*otdelochniki*) would be employed to pick up garbage and wash floors, while at another site construction would be slowed down because of a dearth of finishers.[115] The local trade unions issued vocal criticisms at meetings attended by representatives of member republics. A local speaker was embarrassed that construction crews from other republics did not have sufficient food. For two days, a Ukrainian team drank water instead of milk.[116] Another member said it was time to stop talking about the food supply problem and time to start solving it: "but it was not being solved." Further, workers were living in "unsafe" (*avariinye*) apartments.[117] Union members were dissatisfied with the absence of certain types of buildings. Chilanzar did not have one palace of culture (*Dvorets kul'tury*), and in Sergeli "not a single cultural institution, except for a movie theatre" had been built for the twenty-five thousand people who were to live there.[118] Much of this was standard communist self-criticism, but much of it went well beyond the confines of ideological belief.

The most pressing question, though only briefly discussed, was the danger of working at a construction site. The work conditions were "alarming."[119] In the first eight months of 1966, at work sites and enterprises connected with construction, ten accidents had fatal outcomes. In other words, the fatality rate associated with rebuilding the city was about the same as the fatality rate associated with the earthquake.[120] These accidents worried the trade unions and were of continual concern to the student brigades in Tashkent and elsewhere.

Industrial accidents were not unusual in the Soviet Union, where workers rushed to fulfill projected norms, so these complaints were not particular to Tashkent. Not all accidents, however, had the same causes. Carelessness was an obvious issue, such as in 1967 when a bus driver leaving L'viv transported flammable material: the material caught fire en route and seven passengers died. The bus driver admitted taking a sum of money for the flammable cargo, so this accident was, in part, caused by his desire for financial gain.[121] Bus accidents also occurred because employees had a financial interest in arriving on time; they did not receive extra money from passengers but, rather, extra salary from the state. On 25 April 1967, almost exactly a year after the earthquake in Tashkent, a bus in Kyiv skidded off a bridge and sank to the bottom of the Dnepr River, killing at least twenty-three passengers.[122] The bus driver was accused of recklessness, but the commission doing the investigation pointed out that bus drivers sped so they would not lose their bonus by failing to arrive on schedule.[123] In the congested streets of Kyiv, it was nearly impossible to keep to schedule, so accidents were endemic (in 1965, a bus carrying passengers veered on the same bridge, and half the bus hung over the river).[124]

Commissions took care to investigate accidents, and Soviet citizens raised their voices when dissatisfied. In Tashkent, angry voices were raised at trade union meetings, but it is difficult to determine the extent to which these individuals protested. Thus, a 1975 example from Ukraine will have to suffice to indicate the disruptive potential of a lack of attention to safety at the workplace. A bus carrying workers into the countryside to help with the sugar beet harvest crashed, injuring at least sixteen people.[125] The workers demanded to know who was responsible for the accident, what had been done to help the injured, and so on. When no immediate response was forthcoming, a "spontaneous" (*stikhiinaia*) conversation emerged between one hundred of the workers in the courtyard of the factory. These workers were soon joined by others. Ultimately, the problem was resolved by a meeting involving five hundred employees in a movie theatre.[126] Clearly, these accidents had great political potential, and workers did not hesitate to raise concerns and objections, even in a threatening manner.

In Tashkent, the situation was complicated by the fact that so many workers had arrived from afar and therefore had different expectations about what awaited them. These workers were officially referred to as a volunteers, though it was not quite clear what this meant: the word "volunteer" was awkward because the Soviet Union had coercive tendencies and, more often than not, ordered rather than asked its citizens to perform tasks. Moreover, with the reconstruction of Tashkent, the state simply could not run the risk of not having anyone show up. Yet discounting the notion of volunteering would be foolish as a closer looks reveals that individual Soviet citizens had choices to make. Whether an individual felt an inner moral duty to help, wanted to gain additional wages, or simply travelled to Tashkent because adventure called, he or she was making a choice.

Sardor Iskhakov, the director of *The Capital of Friendship and Warmth* (2011), interviewed two elderly gentlemen who, as young men, decided to help with the reconstruction of Tashkent. Nikolai Savenko, a builder from Leningrad, left his wife and child behind to travel to Tashkent. Looking back, he told the camera: "When I heard what happened … I immediately had the desire to go to Tashkent. In Leningrad, I had a good job, a nice apartment in a prestigious neighbourhood but … I did not have a choice because my soul called me to Tashkent."[127] Originally, Savenko planned a two-year stay in Tashkent, after which he planned to return to Leningrad. Things changed, however. In 1968, "[he] got married and stayed forever."[128] Savenko's words give every indication that he volunteered for the project; no one physically coerced him to go to Tashkent or to remarry there and leave his first family.

Savenko mentions internal compulsion: deep in his soul he felt the need to go. The content of the soul can be debated since Savenko does not make clear whether his soul was Soviet, Kantian, Wittgensteinian, or something altogether different. Based on his few words, historians won't decode his soul; however, he did offer slight hints. For example, he did not attach his decision to leave to explicit Soviet values or to a preferred ideological discourse; rather, his words evoke the general moral precept that a friend in need is a friend indeed.

Similarly, Vasilii Karpenko, an engineer from Moscow, explained that he had read A.S. Neverov's *Tashkent: City of Bread* (*Tashkent: Gorod khlebnyi*) and became fascinated with the city. The earthquake provided him with the perfect opportunity to visit the city of his dreams, the city that became his second home.[129] In Neverov's book, a youth travels to Tashkent to escape the famine in the central regions of Russia and to enjoy the plentiful harvest in Tashkent, planning to return home laden with bounty. In 1966, the roles were reversed, and Karpenko brought Tashkent his bread – that is, his labour. The interviews in this recent film were designed to accentuate traditional aspects of the Soviet response to the earthquake, but they also indicate choices made when people decided to travel to and from Tashkent.

As a moral term, "volunteer" has a positive connotation, defining someone who independently arrives at the decision to sacrifice her own time to assist others. Thus, a construction worker whose soul takes him to Tashkent is a volunteer, even though some readers might question the strength of his moral commitment to his family in Leningrad. However, volunteering can be seen in a philosophical sense, whereby it reflects an independent choice rather than a moral quality.

If both Savenko and Karpenko volunteered to stay in Tashkent, others volunteered to leave. While volunteering is often considered to indicate the positive choice of contributing to a project, one should not forget that there were many cases of people choosing to leave. The general attrition rate has already been mentioned, but this does not tell us why people left. No statistics completely explain all the departures, but some documents indicate that many engineers simply left. The Russian republic noted that, from a group of thirty-three specialists from Moscow, sixteen returned home for a variety of reasons. Some left for health reasons, others left because of family issues, at least one refused to work in Tashkent, others left of their own free will, and still others were fired.[130]

No doubt, many volunteered to stay because doing so offered financial remuneration. The Soviets continually referred to the thousands of arriving workers as volunteers, yet these workers received lucrative compensation for making the trip to Tashkent. This practice was certainly not unique to dealing with the aftermath of earthquakes: historians have shown how the Soviet government enticed workers to other major building projects, thus undermining the state's claims regarding volunteers (*dobrovol'tsy*).[131] In Tashkent, the state took great care to define the privileges (*l'goty*) of its reconstruction plan. In some cases, a worker received 50 per cent on top of his or her base salary.[132] Two decades later, when workers were rushed to Chernobyl, these privileges became so complicated that authorities had to issue special brochures explaining the conditions under which they were to be received.[133]

Since workers were temporarily leaving a life behind them, much of the added income they expected was calculated to cover the costs of keeping a family back home: it did not represent an expected windfall. The supplemental cost of going to Tashkent casts doubt on the state's usage of the term "volunteer." The state understood that if it did not provide sufficient compensation, it might not get sufficient personnel as workers could choose to go, not to go, or, having gone, to return. Still, while the state's usage of the term was questionable, from the perspective of an individual worker, the decision to accept the privileges and travel to Tashkent was, indeed, voluntary.

Workers with families had to think twice before making the commitment to go to Tashkent; perhaps Savenko was leaving a difficult situation when he left Leningrad. These family matters remain clouded, but information does exist on the youths who arrived in Tashkent.

From the very beginning, the Komsomol had participated in patrolling the city, and soon they pitched in with the reconstruction effort. *Komsomolets Uzbekistana* presented photographs of local students from the textile and polytechnical institute clearing rubble and letters from youths in distant regions offering assistances.[134] A Komsomol member from Baku "wanted to travel to Tashkent to help with the reconstruction. [He] specialize[d] as a metal-worker, pipelinist and bulldozer driver."[135] This clear reference to his skills creates the mistaken impression that everyone who arrived had the appropriate expertise for the task at hand. In fact, Komsomol efforts added confusion to the construction process.

Ideally, young communists from around the Soviet Union were to arrive in Uzbekistan, build a new city from ashes, and become more enlightened communists in the process. Official documents and meetings outline the parameters of the educational experience, but rarely, if ever, did the day-to-day rhythm of youth correspond to items neatly penned into agendas. In contrast to the late 1920s, when the Komsomol were energetic workers and propagandists at the Dneprostroi power plant, this focus was now lost.[136] At meetings, leaders were as concerned with alcohol consumption as they were with construction numbers. The trends depicted below were not unique to Tashkent and can be considered part and parcel of the Komsomol experience.

The story told around the earthquake was designed to convey the idea of a supreme concentration of forces: the Komsomol heralded its activities in Tashkent and the arrivals of brigades from afar. In 1966, however, Ukrainian brigades were sent all over the USSR. They went to industrial sites within Ukraine, to Siberian cities, and to Tashkent, the latter receiving only a small portion of the students. The Kharkivs'kii Komsomol reported sending three times more youth to help with the flooding in Krasnoyarsk than it did to help with reconstruction in Tashkent; it sent five times as many youths to a chemical plant in Irkutsk. The Dnepropetrovsk Komsomol sent as many people to Krasnoyarsk as it did to Tashkent.[137] Of course, this suggests not only that efforts were not concentrated in Tashkent but also that youths were travelling all over the place.

Although Komsomol labours in Tashkent appeared no different than they did elsewhere in the USSR, in Tashkent they were couched in glorious rhetoric. At a speech given in 1968 to commemorate the fiftieth anniversary of the Komsomol, the speaker said that every generation had its "romantics and enthusiasts," but that if this generation looked back with envy at those who stormed the Winter Palace in 1917, then future generations would look back with envy at the "heroic deeds" of those who arrived in Tashkent.[138] These bold words exaggerated the uniqueness of the Komsomol's role within the greater scheme of youth brigades and paid little attention to the issues that had been discussed at meetings.

The problems started at the outset. At a meeting of the Ukrainian Komsomol construction brigades in the summer of 1966, attended by 197 delegates, the opening speaker mentioned problems with quality control, the lack of political-educational work, and serious personnel problems: "it is no secret that booze-ups and fights" occurred in the Komsomol living quarters. Further, on the day when everybody received their paycheques, the cafeteria was transformed into a "tavern."[139] This cafeteria-as-tavern phenomenon did not stop. Months later, the Komsomol reported "systematic drinking of alcoholic beverages" in the cafeterias.[140] Beyond the problems with alcohol were the arrests. In the first three months of the Komsomol's arrival, twenty-nine people had been arrested and eleven had been given sentences from seven to fifteen days.[141] The speaker summed up the situation with words that have a definite religious tinge: "Let the earth burn beneath the legs of drunkards and hooligans."[142] Shaking earth affected everyone, but burning earth would single out the non-believers.

At the meetings of individual brigades, the real problems were discussed in even more detail and it was explained why, for example, a Komsomol member had been arrested. In 1968, a brigade from Kyiv met to discuss the behaviour of a long-standing Komsomol member who had been accused of manslaughter. In "a drunken state," he had stolen a car and caused an accident (*avariia*) that killed three people. Such behaviour was not "compatible with the heroic works" of the Komsomol. Thirty (of a possible forty-five) attendees voted unanimously to rescind this individual's Komsomol membership and pass the case on to higher authorities.[143] Otherwise, little more was said about it.

This case of manslaughter was extreme, but fights and drunkenness were a popular discussion topic as meetings continually dealt with disciplinary procedures. In the summer of 1967, a drunken Komsomol left his dorm and noticed a fight. He decided to break it up, was himself struck in the process, and then, "without thinking about the circumstances," he punched one of the combatants in the face. Theft also occurred within the travelling brigades.[144] Drunkenness was worrisome because it led to absenteeism at the workplace, a common phenomenon in the Soviet Union.[145]

Unruly behaviour that resulted in tragic outcomes was not unique to Tashkent and is perhaps not atypical of youths living in unfamiliar environments. In 1971, the leader of a student construction brigade working in Ukraine decided to break the rules and drive a tractor at night. The leader and his friends wanted to attend a dance and visit women in a neighbouring village five kilometres away. The youths arrived successfully, parked the tractor in the bushes, and attended the dance. Problems began when they left the dance. The tractor had absolutely no lighting, and thus, when the leader drove it home he could not see where he was going.[146] He drove the tractor into a deep hollow, killing himself but not his partner. The official report clearly stated that the student had had no right to use the tractor and that his lack of experience with tractors was a contributing factor to the accident.[147] This lack of experience with machinery plagued student brigades in Tashkent and throughout the USSR.[148]

The tragic outcomes of drunkenness and fights on payday have parallels elsewhere. In 1971, in the Kharkiv region, the members of a student brigade received their monthly pay and had the weekend off. A group was sent to a nearby town to buy necessary goods but started drinking and ended up in a fight "with unknown local boys." One youth was separated from the group, and, not knowing the way home, found the railway tracks and asked a crossing guard if he could follow the tracks back to his work camp. The rest of the details are not clear, but, in the wee hours of the morning, a train struck the youth, who was apparently lying across the railbed. The engineer loaded the injured man onto the wagon and brought him to the hospital, but he never regained consciousness.[149]

During the heart of perestroika, Vladimir Shlapentokh researched the social habits of Soviet citizens and proposed that they were not interested in the "stated goals" of groups such as the Komsomol but, rather, used these organizations "as a means to achieve their own purposes."[150] Consequently, Komsomol activities were of little interest to most writers. The magazine *The Youth*, for example, "avoid[ed] practically all subjects related to Komsomol activities." Moreover, "if a writer want[ed] to portray life realistically, he either ignore[d] Komsomol activities or present[ed] it as having little to do with the real interests of youth."[151] This argument has two sides, one more plausible than the other. The cases presented so far give no indication that students had a deep commitment to the stated goals of reconstruction, but this does not mean that they offered nothing worth writing about. Writers probably avoided Komsomol life not because it was boring but because they would not get the spicier accident stories past the censors.

The above incidents were nocturnal, but Komsomol members were just as difficult to control in the daytime. In Tashkent, Komsomol officials had a hard time keeping track of the regional Ukrainian divisions. The team from Dnepropetrovsk "had no accounting, no list of members," and so on. The leader of the brigade had failed to attend a meeting to discuss these problems, and only a few individual members were paying attention to the communist mission.[152] Inside the Kyiv brigade, members were not fulfilling their duties in the spirit of the Komsomol and had to be "forcefully dragged" to meetings.[153] This problem was widespread. The groups from Odessa and L'viv rarely held meetings, and the bookkeeping was in disarray.[154] Because of the high attrition rate throughout the city, Komsomol members who left Tashkent remained on the bookkeeping rolls.[155]

The documents from 1966 give a sense of how confusing it was to keep track of members but do not explain why membership rolls were of such concern. Later stories link confused membership rolls with the corruption typical in the Soviet Union. In 1985, a review of student brigades in Ukraine found that, often, the same individual was listed in different brigades or that a leader had employed the brigades in unsanctioned projects and pocketed the money. In another brigade, the Komandir added his relatives to the rolls, and in Donetsk, the brigade added to its list two residents of the town, who took the occasion to travel to Sakhalin oblast and back.[156] Although not documented, such possibilities would also have been available in Tashkent.

With attendance at meetings being so irregular, it should come as no surprise that the educational and political component of the mission was falling short. In the triumphant atmosphere of the rebuilding process, one might expect youth to be especially enthusiastic about their mission. Yet organizers continually complained that clubs were not meeting and that red corners, designed to promote communist values, were being neglected. Some transgressions were minor, such as when a football player was chastised by being sent from the field and no one showed any interest in discussing the incident afterwards.[157] But most complaints were directed squarely against the failure of clubs to inculcate the necessary communist values. Komsomol officials wanted the "education of the masses" to achieve a certain standard, but the administration said the initiative had to come from the members themselves.[158] They imagined movies, theatres, and trips outside the city, and they wanted the brigades to offer "lectures" on themes of interest to youths.[159] These comments came in early 1967, but in late 1966, active youths had already initiated such programs with little success. A Sunday of performing volunteer work to show solidarity with the people in Vietnam had a poor turnout, and the organizers had to require Komsomol members to show up at the next one.[160] A leader from Kharkiv had spoken with many of his 150 members, but it was impossible to speak with everyone individually. By November 1966, he had yet to hold a meeting because he needed more assistance from the party and had no idea how to hold a Komsomol committee meeting. Finally, too much time was spent at the worksite to worry about attending meetings.[161] In all these cases of ill-discipline and poor attendance, the youths were making choices beyond party control.

It is worth taking a closer look at the planned activities for the Luhansk and Kharkiv Komsomol crews in July 1966. The calendar for July had an activity every single day. These included lectures on drinking habits in hot climates, innovations in cybernetics, and the moral outlook of the Soviet citizen. Sporting events, fishing trips, excursions to sites of historical interest in Tashkent, and trips outside of town were pencilled onto the calendar.[162] For the summer of 1966, the Kharkiv brigade had a list of its own lecture topics that further indicates the challenge organizers faced. Among the themes were "the harm of alcohol," "a girl's honour and pride," and "venereal diseases and their prevention."[163] Sex was a big part of the Komsomol experience in Tashkent.

Abstinence was the best way to prevent the transmission of sexual diseases; however, even if this had been suggested during the lecture, most people would have understood this to be unrealistic. The earthquake occurred contemporaneously with the sexual revolution in the West (it should come as no surprise that the word *секс* [sex] entered the Russian language in 1963).[164] The documented sexual transgressions were mild, but promiscuity filled the air. At the dorms, the women were not shy, and they allowed "the boys to sit with them in their rooms until one in the morning and even later."[165] A member of the Kyiv brigade "attempted to offend [*oskorbit'*] the personal dignity" of another man's wife. The wife had gone to her room to nap when the offender entered and started to "pester" her; she did not, however, "allow" him to "get what he wanted."[166] The man apparently failed in his endeavour and was roundly condemned at a Komosomol meeting. But, of course, a man's visiting a woman's room was not that unusual.

Perhaps the best example of promiscuity comes not from the minutes of a closed meeting but from a movie. Malik Kaiumov's film *Tashkent, Earthquake* has already been mentioned in a number of contexts.[167] The film is generally faithful to the regime's needs, but it contains a scene that wonderfully portrays the potential for sexual promiscuity. The scene begins with an interview with a well-dressed young man who explains his noble reasons for going to Tashkent; however, thereafter follows a sequence that starts with two youths walking arm in arm. This pair walks casually through scenes of construction, implying that love and romance is part of the reconstruction process. In the next sequence, the camera focuses on a woman who is working on a construction site and who, owing to the heat, wears only a bra on her upper body. This suggests a natural progression from walking arm in arm to taking off one's top. Moreover, because the working woman appears to be wearing undergarments rather than a bikini, the visual experience is dynamic rather than static: the revealed bra evokes the act of either undressing (the sex act is about to happen) or dressing (the sex act has already happened) – either way, the act is in progress as opposed to being complete (a bikini top is an outfit in and of itself and is therefore static rather than dynamic). Almost immediately thereafter the camera focuses on a newspaper clipping with the headline "Tashkent Is in the Heat," nominally drawing attention to the high temperature of a summer day. The heat in this scene is clearly more sensual than anything that can be measured on a thermometer, but what is interesting about the director's choice to use a newspaper to express a sexual message is that it recontextualizes the "innocent" message of an official news source. After the newspaper, the lens holds steady on the sweat dripping down the backs of the naked men. The newspaper plays the role of a visual copula linking the bra-wearing woman with the topless men, implicitly proposing a union between the two.

A little later in the film, Kaiumov shoots a wedding ceremony. The separation of the wedding scene from the sensual scenes implies that the reconstruction process comprised two sorts of gender relations: the instinctual and the socially sanctioned. The film offers its viewers choices in terms of sexual conduct and returns the discussion to the unforeseen opportunities that emerged as a result of the earthquake.

To better understand diverse lifestyles in the Soviet Union, historians have looked beyond dissident movements shaped by Muscovite intellectuals and investigated other forms of political activity. The focus on a traditional intellectual elite eliminated, de facto, the voices of ordinary citizens who had little time to write yet still found discrete ways to protest through revolutionary plans of their own. Vladimir Kozlov and his team have published a selection of documents from the Prokuratura (a Soviet government bureau concerned with ensuring administrative legality), which shows how regular people expressed contempt for the regime. Kozlov shifts the focus away from "dissidence," an awkward and foreign term for the Russian speaker. His preferred term is *kramola*, which is translated in English as "sedition."[168] Sedition encompassed acts of popular resistance, such as dropping a provocative pamphlet containing "anti-Soviet expressions" or uttering oral expressions of discontent concerning the regime's foreign or domestic policies.[169] The evidence is taken from the thousands of cases in the Prokuratura that were officially treated as sedition. A disadvantage with this approach is that sedition is defined by the state and not by the people supposedly engaged in it.[170] At the same time, it diversifies historians' understanding of how individuals constructed anti-Soviet views.

Within the available Komsomol documents treating Tashkent, the Prokuratura was rarely involved, and many of the crimes and misdemeanors reported were typical of a youthful, non-ideological rebellion against authority. Although these acts were not as explicitly oppositional as are the examples from the Prokuratura, can drinking and lack of attendance at lectures and educational events be considered sedition? Or was there another shade of grey between sedition and passive acceptance of the regime? A shade of grey that allowed freedom of movement and that disregarded the Komsomol mission statement yet without involving oral or written attacks on the regime? Indeed, it is the latter path that many Komsomol members followed.

Outside the Komsomol, a few citizens did write and complain about the living conditions. In one unsigned letter to Brezhnev, the author claimed that a senior party official responsible for the post-earthquake reconstruction had taken the opportunity to take over and repair a twelve-room "mansion" (*osobniak*), a task that required the attention of ten to twelve construction workers.[171] The Communist

Party in Uzbekistan took appropriate steps and reprimanded the official. This process resembles helpful communist self-criticism, whereby citizens were encouraged to report local administrative abuses.[172]

Beyond receiving this approved criticism, Brezhnev and his entourage came under fire for shortcomings relating to other housing situations. Angry citizens ("we, citizens of Tashkent") who had lost their living quarters were moved from their homes at the epicentre of the earthquake and placed in schools in Chilanzar. One particular group was placed in a school with five hundred people, and young families lived together without any curtains separating them. Local officials "had forgotten about [their] existence" and were completely uninterested in investigating the "nightmarish" conditions in which they lived. They believed that "concern for the Soviet people should be expressed not just in newspapers and radio but should be realized in practice, as Lenin taught."[173] These citizens had moved right after the earthquake and were a small part of a large migration process. Another woman petitioned officials in Moscow in an attempt to solve her living problem. After her apartment had been destroyed she left Tashkent for Barnaul, more than a thousand kilometres away, but was denied housing there. When local officials offered her housing in the countryside, she refused it.[174]

The earthquake caused all sorts of migration patterns, which are difficult to qualify because people went in many directions and had different experiences depending upon which direction they chose. Officially, the distribution of citizens throughout the USSR was part of a display of the friendship of peoples; not only did construction crews arrive in Tashkent from afar, but far away republics welcomed Tashkentites into their communities. A married couple from the Black Sea region wrote to *Pravda Vostoka* inviting people to stay with them. "Having survived the Crimean earthquake in 1927," the couple understood the hardships in Uzbekistan.[175] There is no reason to doubt the sincerity of this philanthropy.

In typical authoritarian fashion, the state determined exactly who went where, and local authorities were to follow this determination. For example, Ukraine had been allotted two thousand families, the round decimal number giving an indication of how much thought the state had given to the problem at a human level.[176] Much like measuring the construction of housing in square metres, families were treated as numbers to be selectively distributed around the USSR. In drawing up these lists, the state wanted to prevent a mass migration to preferred locales. Authorities in Uzbekistan asked if residents could relocate to their relatives in other places. In a letter signed by Kosygin, the response was positive, making it clear that these families could go wherever they wanted *except* "Moscow, Leningrad, the resort locations in the Northern Caucasus and the Crimean Peninsula."[177] This attitude was similar to that in evidence after Chernobyl, when officials were reluctant to let evacuees settle in Kyiv, and after ethnic tensions in Baku and the Armenian earthquake, when Armenians arrived to a reluctant Moscow.

The process of migration was more complicated than the Muscovites had imagined, and there emerged a lengthy correspondence between Kyiv and Tashkent, whose officials were left to solve outstanding issues. Ukrainians had problems receiving families, and Uzbeks were not quite sure who was going. Moreover, the authorities who wrote the migrant numbers on paper did not predict that flesh-and-blood families would protest against certain aspects of the migration process.

When families arrived in Ukraine, it became clear that many travellers had not received approval from the appropriate authorities in Tashkent; Ukrainian officials wrote to Tashkent complaining about these unregistered travellers because they had not planned the resources to take care of them.[178] Ukrainians also had to deal with the false expectations created by Uzbek officials. It would be an exaggeration to say that they wrote of a mythical Ukraine, but they did spread fictitious stories in Tashkent to lighten anxiety. A family arriving in Bakhmach in the Chernihiv region had been told it was a "large, ancient town," but to their eyes it was little more than a large village.[179] The commission told another family that it was to receive an apartment in a regional centre but failed to warn it about having to work on a collective farm. In response to this, Ukrainian officials required Uzbeks to notify the evacuees about working on collective farms.[180] In the Nikolaev region, 80 per cent of migrant families had been allotted to rural areas.

The reluctance to work on collective farms or to live in rural areas was widespread.[181] Evacuees wanted to live in "big cities" because they offered work and cultural opportunities.[182] Evacuees were arriving from the cultural capital of Uzbekistan and they wanted no truck with backwards rural areas in Ukraine: the East was ahead of the West in this narrative. Families who went to the Odessa region complained they had not been told that they would be resettled in rural areas.[183]

Sometimes even certain towns were not acceptable. One woman tried three cities before deciding to return to Tashkent. The first two offers she downright refused, but she agreed to accept an apartment in Donetsk as long as it was in the centre of town. When this wish was not granted, she chose to return home.[184]

Faced with life in the countryside or in poorly constructed housing, evacuees simply refused to accept the state's offer. If an evacuee returned home to Tashkent, the problem for the Ukrainian officials had been solved. In other cases, Ukrainian officials reported that dissatisfied evacuees had left a region without bothering to say where they had gone.[185] Finally, many evacuees rejected the official solution and decided to live with relatives.[186] Evacuees who chose this option were often not registered with Uzbek authorities and were, therefore, part of a spontaneous and disorganized emigration. In many cases, the evacuation of Tashkent could have been a re-emigration back home. After the Second World War, many Jews had not been allowed to "re-evacuate" from Tashkent back to Ukraine.[187] It is quite likely that families who had been evacuated to Tashkent during the Second World War were simply taking advantage of the earthquake to return home.

In addition to families, the migration involved children who were immediately evacuated from Tashkent and sent to pioneer camps in the western parts of the Soviet Union. In disasters, these pioneer camps had pride of place: they were used after the Ashgabat earthquake (when authorities lost track of some children), Chernobyl, and the Armenian earthquake. Kaiumov filmed children departing in trains from Tashkent, their worried mothers crying at the prospect of their loss. Despite the tears, however, these pioneer camps played a pivotal role in disaster relief. They were presented as symbols of purity and safety, far from the areas that had suffered catastrophe.

The experience of the children being sent away was neither uniform nor equal. The Union of Soviet Journalists invited children whose parents worked in the publishing industry to its House of Creativity near Moscow.[188] *Literaturnaia gazeta* wrote about the children who were evacuated to Moscow: fifty-five children of writers from Uzbekistan were placed in a *pansionat*.[189] Other children relaxed on the Black Sea in Georgia, where they not only escaped the earthquake but also met with children from Moscow, St Petersburg, and Tbilisi.[190] Children also went to the Artek pioneer lager in the Crimean peninsula, where they shared Uzbek culture with other children.[191] These trips involved a manageable number of children, but the *profsoiuz*, or trade union, was responsible for sending thousands of children and could not afford their passage to other republics. It had to appeal to various ministries for funding.[192] Whatever financial obstacles stood in their way, the trips had the dual function of propagandizing the friendship of peoples in countryside resorts and allowing children to flee so they could later return to a city of the future.

The Tashkent earthquake caused an incredible movement of people, but not everyone had the chance to leave, and those who remained in campsites or elsewhere had to find ways to cope. One of these ways was to appeal to religion. The Soviet religious figures in Tashkent received condolences from abroad, such as the one from Egypt that stated that "Allah would help all those who suffered from the earthquake."[193] The religious reaction came not just from abroad but also from the streets of Uzbekistan. Officials were worried about an increase in religion and published articles to limit the spread of religious superstitions. They mocked those who saw the earthquake as godly retribution and insisted on nature's indifference towards its victims: when an earthquake hit Morocco in 1960, Muslims and Europeans suffered alike.[194] Yet rumours did spread. At a bus station in Kattakurgan, about 350 kilometres south of Tashkent, an atheist listened to a person who gathered a crowd around him and "preached" (*propovedoval*): "In Tashkent, there was an earthquake. Allah punished non-believers and traitors of Islam."[195] Atheists had to be vigilant, "especially" after a city had suffered a natural disaster.[196]

Historians refer to the rise in religious belief after the Tashkent earthquake. T.S. Saidbaev claims that ritual sacrifices had almost completely disappeared before the earthquake, yet after the earthquake many forgotten religious rites reappeared.[197] However, the extent of religious revival should not be exaggerated as a 1968 report to the Central Committee of the Communist Party indicated that volunteer contributions to mosques in Central Asia had been rising for the last five years – that is, they had been rising well before the earthquake.[198] Although the occurrence of the earthquake encouraged an increased religiosity, this was in an environment within which the social influence of Islam was already on the rise.[199]

CONCLUSION

Already in 1967 articles appeared in *Pravda Vostoka* saying goodbye to work crews from other republics. By the summer of 1967, the Kirgiz and Lithuanians had finished their tasks, while Russians and Ukrainians stayed to celebrate the fiftieth anniversary of the October Revolution in November.[200] The latter two groups departed shortly thereafter, leaving residents to settle into a new Tashkent. They left behind a city with taller buildings, broader streets, shiny suburbs, and the basics for a new subway system. Tashkent never looked the same again.

The Brezhnev government applied existing policies to the resurrection of Tashkent and more or less succeeded in returning law and order to the city. Cranes, bulldozers, student brigades, and receptions at train stations were choreographed to a communist rhythm. The entire reconstruction of the city was conceived as a festival of Soviet values. The Soviets managed to relocate thousands of citizens in record time, even if the quality of the new housing was often suspect. They also mobilized citizens from thousands of kilometres away, even if at a cost that many republics were reluctant to pay. Clear limitations on resources hindered complete control of the earthquake, but even where projects were successful the outcomes were ambiguous. The new Soviet city was supposed to convey Soviet values, but its production materials and architectural inspiration came from the West. The celebration and endless photographs devoted to the satellite-city Sergeli only furthered comparisons with Western urban design. The earthquake was an invitation to bulldoze the old town, but, despite the destruction, the old town remained vibrant, at least until the collapse of the Soviet Union.[201] Tashkent changed accordingly but not completely, and, as much as Soviet authorities wanted the clock to start ticking after 5:23 a.m., the earthquake has a before-and-after story.

The student brigades promoted their accomplishments at the same time as they showed little or no interest in ideological training, caroused about town, and even became involved in petty crimes. Workers came and went according both to their needs and to those of the state; the nature of the turnaround ensured that few people stayed for the entire process. Architects welcomed the challenge of building a new city, but they evinced no evident consensus. Many showed concern about the bulldozing going on around town and seized the moment to present alternate visions for the rebuilding process. The authoritarian state existed alongside individuals who went about pursuing their own dreams.

Understanding the response to the earthquake in Tashkent involves more than just measuring the gap between communist fantasy and urban reality; it must consider the slow progression from Ashgabat (where Stalinist policy was radically different and much less involved than were the policies of other leaders) to Tashkent. During the latter crisis, the word "Ashgabat" rarely, if ever, appears in official documents. Lazar Karelin published *Earthquake*, his novel about Ashgabat, shortly after the Tashkent earthquake, but this was an isolated publication. Somehow the authoritarian state was unwilling to admit that it could learn from previous mistakes and, to this end, attempted to control memory, presenting the earthquake as a function of socialist needs. In the Brezhnev era, this meant forgetting about the natural disaster in Ashgabat and doing everything possible to ensure a lasting memory of the reconstruction of Tashkent.

The earthquake brought to the fore the distinct challenges of a geological phenomenon as well as the social parameters of Soviet existence. The earthquake in Tashkent was by far the largest disruptive force in the 1960s, but other accidents, human-made or otherwise, established niches for alternative behaviour. When a bus carrying workers crashed in 1972, five hundred people met to discuss the incident. A student on a summer brigade died when his tractor slipped into a hollow – the accident was tragic, but it revealed the priorities of students who used state equipment in the service of their own entertainment. Since these accidents did not serve ideological purposes, they rarely made it into the news.

The Tashkent earthquake was neither the beginning nor the end of natural disasters in the Soviet Union, but the Soviets chose to transform it into something that was larger than life. No other natural disaster could compete with the social and political attention placed on Tashkent. When a massive storm struck Odessa in 1975, local newspapers only mentioned it five days after the event, once the danger had passed and residents had already started the clean-up. In internal memos, the authorities in Odessa expressed concern about their reliance on external sources of electricity and grumbled that the city needed a nuclear power plant.[202] In the early 1980s, two significant earthquakes struck Tashkent and the nearby region.[203] They destroyed homes and dislocated residents but never became important media issues. In the social context of the early 1980s, these disasters could not compete with other pressing issues, and thus there was no reason to put Tashkent back in the spotlight.

Of all places, however, Tashkent reappeared in the newspaper *Tribuna energetika* (*Tribune of the Energy Worker*). In October 1988, the newspaper published an article entitled "That 26th of April," which involved an interview both with a student in Tashkent when the earthquake occurred in 1966 and a construction director in Pripyat on 26 April 1986. The interviewer asked readers if they did not perhaps believe in "mysticism."[204] Was there a mystic link between the earthquake in Tashkent and the explosion at Chernobyl? Or was it the same Communist Party, now standing on terra firma in Moscow, that applied the same methods to both tragedies?

INTERLUDE

Visualizing Soviet Disasters from 1945 to 1986

In the preceding chapters, brief references have been made to films – documentary and narrative – in order to demonstrate the influence of disasters within a broad spectrum. While these visual references are important throughout, they are isolated phenomena embedded within an analysis based on textual sources. The time has now come for a visual interlude in which textual sources cede their dominant position: this interlude revisits familiar empirical and historical ground but explores the visual sources related to it. As mentioned in the introduction, Soviet historiography has been obsessed with language at the expense of visual analysis.[1] This linguistic turn was designed to overcome a naïve empiricism based on sense data, but the moment is ripe to explore visual sources and add another dimension to the understanding of disasters. The point here is not to get a better idea of what individuals saw but, rather, to understand how cinematographers and their statist sponsors chose to portray disasters.

Visual media have played an important role in the presentation of American disasters, both fictionally and non-fictionally, and the same was true in the Soviet Union. After the Second World War, movie theatre attendance began to rise, and by the early 1970s many Soviet citizens had televisions with which to watch the daily news: Soviet society was becoming more visual. This phenomenon has been studied extensively by cultural and film historians, but the disaster genre has been almost completely ignored.[2] In David Gillespie's excellent introduction to Russian cinema, not a single disaster film is presented to readers.[3] Denise Youngblood offers the field a seminal work on war films, but disaster films are beyond her purview.[4] Films related to disasters, which lack the explosive force of an Eisenstein film, constitute an overlooked genre. While the catastrophe film as a genre entered Soviet filmography in the 1970s, disasters have been the subject of films for decades. In the 1920s, *Namus*, a hugely popular love story, offered its viewers graphic dramatizations of a mid-nineteenth-century Armenian earthquake.[5] Alexander Dovzhenko promoted the necessity of industrial change in his *Poema o more*, posthumously finished by his wife in 1958.[6] The film anticipated (but did not show) the flooding of an entire village to make way for a hydroelectric dam. In the 1970s, Soviet directors and cinematographers presented visions of earthquakes, floods, fires, and even a radioactive experiment gone wrong. Each subsequent visual representation changed the terms according to which viewers understood disaster. In the next chapter, I return to textual analysis, but here I focus on how Soviet directors visually dramatized the tragedies of their cities and citizens.

In general, the two most common disasters encountered in films are earthquakes in the southern periphery of the Soviet Union and flooding almost everywhere else. Filmmakers portray either the results of a natural disaster or disasters caused by large human-made projects; in the second instance, directors had to be careful not to directly attack Soviet projects. Disasters also typically involved airplanes and the possibility of their crashing. These plots gave directors a chance both to highlight Soviet technological advances and to add an international dimension to the depiction of disaster. But while directors could contemplate the consequences of radioactive fallout, other accidents remained out of bounds. Mining disasters, for example, a monthly phenomenon in the industrial areas of Ukraine, could not be depicted as doing so would call into question the party that was the vanguard of the Soviet people. Despite this limitation, filmmakers were free to present all sorts of disasters to the viewing public.

Understanding the visual representation of disasters requires focusing on a number of specific issues. We cannot ignore the portrayal of the state and its role, sometimes larger, sometimes smaller, in the attempts to return a situation to normal. The Soviet Union was certainly a Marxist-Leninist state, but what role did ideology play in these films? Could Marxist-Leninist ideology be surpassed by a desire to emphasize the multinational dimension of the Soviet Union? Keeping this in mind, we should not be lulled by Moscow film reviewers into believing that disasters first made their appearance in the early 1980s. Some of the first depictions of disaster came from the Central Asian republics and Armenia precisely because these areas were so susceptible to earthquakes.

Turkmenfilm, Uzbekfilm, and Kazakhfilm had a role to play in creating films about disasters, even if their productions were nominally documentary and pursued a traditional narrative. Thus, Lazar' Karelin had good reason to centre his novel of the Ashgabat earthquake on characters from the film studio in Ashgabat.[7] In many of these films, the friendship of peoples superseded Marxist-Leninist ideology.

If the first lengthy films on disasters came from the south, by the 1970s directors in northern areas were experimenting with the genre and tiptoeing around dangerous themes. The Brezhnev era has been characterized as stagnant, but the filming of disasters continued to become more creative and more diversified. In 1972, Belarusfil'm produced *Tale of a Night* (*Khronika nochi*) about the hijacking of a plane on its way to Africa, and, in 1975, Mosfil'm produced *When the Earth Shakes* (*Kogda drozhit zemlia*) about an earthquake during the construction of a hydroelectric dam in Dagestan.[8] Whether these films portended technological disaster (such as the possible crash of an airplane) or drew from actual historical disaster (such as the 1970 Dagestan earthquake), they set a precedent for later efforts (such as *Crew* [*Ekipazh*] in 1980).[9] *Ekipazh*, a blockbuster hit at the end of the Brezhnev era, brought together all the elements of disasters. In many ways, the disaster films of the 1970s prepared viewers for perestroika, even if the Pandora's box had yet to be fully opened. The contrast between disaster films of the 1970s and 1980s was not as great as the rupture found in the economic and political spheres.

Moving to and fro between fact and fiction was also very important.[10] Cinematographers and editors of all types of films had a basic script to follow – emphasizing the speed of recovery and the extent to which aid flowed in from all the republics – but the story line changed depending upon the specifics and, to paraphrase a common trope in Soviet society, viewers could see between the frames. The parameters, of course, changed depending upon the type of film. In newsreels and documentaries, fiction crept into the visual as soothing voices and industrious work crews downplayed the dangers. In fictional films, non-fiction crept into the experience when the dangerous situations faced by heroes reminded viewers of the disasters in their own backyards. Viewers could find a disconnect between visual portrayal and real-life circumstances. Paradoxically, the visual representation of disasters offered an escape from other Soviet problems.

At the start of perestroika, film writers in the Soviet Union began to pay greater respect to the disaster genre. These films had been gaining attention since the early 1980s, but only after the arrival of Mikhail Gorbachev and his call for perestroika did a more open discussion of the genre become possible. In the 1987 issue of *The Art of Cinema* (*Iskusstvo kino*), K. Razlogov wrote an extensive review of the new film *Breakthrough* (*Proryv*).[11] He welcomed the genre but still saw major shortcomings in this particular film. Although it daringly exposed the story of a major catastrophe in the Leningrad subway in the early 1970s, the directors still hesitated to ask the bigger questions: Why had the subway been built in such a dangerous area in the first place? And, implicitly, what were the Soviet engineers thinking when they designed it? At an aesthetic and dramatic level, Razlogov suggested the film never really found a balance between the spectacle required in a disaster film and the story of an actual disaster.[12] He was referring to a single film, but, throughout the Soviet years, the tension between spectacle and story was characteristic of the visualization of disaster.

PORTRAYALS OF DISASTER IN THE STALINIST ERA

In the Stalinist era, there was much less visual imagery pertaining to disaster. There were fewer significant natural disasters, film stock was a much more precious commodity, and when disasters did appear on film, they tended to be related to the Second World War or other military adventures. In the latter case, the rules of the game were different because directors were allowed to show corpses.[13] Nevertheless, at least two interesting documentaries emerged. The first has to do with the Crimean earthquake of 1927, technically just before Stalin's time, and the second concerns the representation of the massive earthquake in Ashgabat in 1948.

Although there is quite a bit of textual documentation to help historians understand the Crimean earthquake of 1927, there is almost no filmed documentation of its aftermath.[14] The one exception, a very short silent reel of film, is instructive because it offers a stark contrast to almost all the visual evidence, fiction or non-fiction, that followed. Filmmakers can rarely film an actual earthquake, but they can wander through cities after the fact. In 1927, an unknown cinematographer walked around Yalta and recorded the destruction. The video shows the expected rubble, but it also has two particularly interesting features. In one scene, a subtitle tells literate viewers that individuals were lining up for tickets, and then the cameraperson shows exactly that. The scene suggests that the state was not responsible for the evacuation procedure and that families, many of whom had been on vacation, had to find their own way out of the mess. Another sequence, called "queue for the telegraph," suggests the same thing: individuals had to take it upon themselves to report their circumstances to the outside world.[15] The subtitle at the end of the film suggests that the state will help with the evacuation, but the visuals indicate otherwise. This near complete absence of visualizing the state would never again be repeated in the Soviet era.

In stark contrast, the silent 1948 film on Ashgabat emphasizes the idea that a distant state would rush to save the fallen city. Perhaps familiar with the opening scenes of Leni Riefenstahl's *Triumph of the Will* (1935), the filmmakers show Soviet planes in flight on their way to Ashgabat. While it was not Stalin who emerged from these planes (he did not show any interest in visiting the destroyed city), white-clad Muscovite doctors poured out of them once they landed.[16] This motif fit the idea of the friendship of peoples at two levels: it not only promoted the idea that help was coming from other republics but also the idea that technical and medical expertise flowed from advanced Russian "brothers."

The film set a few standards particular to domestic disasters. First, dead bodies were not permitted to be shown despite the thousands who died, thus promoting an enormous lie. This practice, repeated in many subsequent disaster films, was interesting because it only applied to the domestic situation. When documentary filmmakers went to Skopje in Yugoslavia in 1963, they told viewers about the death toll and showed both a hand that either had been dismembered or was simply the only visible part of a body buried under the rubble. When rescuers carried a stretcher, a blanket covered the victim's entire body.[17] In the scenes in Ashgabat, however, a head always emerged from the blanket, suggesting the victim was not only alive but also about to be given expert medical treatment.

The filmmakers hesitated to show the physical destruction of the city, even if they did so only to create a narrative contrast with its eventual reconstruction. Texts labelled visual panoramas so that viewers understood that the leather factory, the movie theatre, and the Ashgabat Kinostudiia had been completely destroyed.[18] But images of destruction were juxtaposed with images of the future. In one scene, residents welcome the return of electricity as they celebrate a working light bulb:[19] Lenin's electricity had been restored.

Interestingly, the street scenes have a distinctive non-urban feel. Instead of portraying the Soviet industrial city, viewers see a camp-like setting. Tents have been erected in forested groves where the local newspaper has set up shop and families have assembled all their goods.[20] As an alternative to the forested atmosphere, one family is shown, with the contents of their home, on the side of a major street. The images of so many worldly goods on the streets encourages the thought that residents did not have to worry about looting. One frame shows a wall poster that states that it is strictly forbidden to remove anything from within the building, but this is the only suggestion of possible unrest.[21] No visual clues suggest that people's militias had formed to protect goods, as was reported much later on.[22]

In the Stalinist atmosphere, the filmmaker wanted to show that citizens were well-informed. In the little tent city, a wooden sign is pegged onto a tree: "Editorial Board, Turkmenskaia gazeta." This newspaper had been stopped in the immediate aftermath of the earthquake, but, as the visuals indicate, even in the unsettled conditions of a tent city the editors managed to revive this source of important public information. Thereafter, Ashgabatites can be seen eagerly scooping up these broadsheets and reading the articles; the camera zooms in on a headline that reads: "calm and order."[23] But the newspaper does not just herald successes, it actually conveys local frustration in a way that the video does not. In the days after the earthquake, *Turkmenskaia iskra* remained hopeful; however, by the spring of 1949, it published articles suggesting the corruption of architects and the slow pace of the city council.[24] It certainly did not criticize the leadership in Moscow, but local readers, the very people shown poring over the words in the film, received a regional version of events that differed from that received by viewers of the film, wherever they might be. The visual and the textual storylines competed with each other, and at least two "truths" were allowed to circulate publicly.

It is difficult to tell who watched this 1948 film or where it was watched since there are no readily available numbers. Newsreels, however, continued the story and added layers to the initial films while slowly easing out the dramatic images of rubble. The reconstruction of Ashgabat was juxtaposed with other building projects, placing the disaster story within the context of industrial and agricultural achievements as a Soviet society made its way towards socialism. In July 1951, *News of the Day* (*Novosti dnia*) squeezed the earthquake story between news of car production in Minsk, the mechanization of agriculture, and a school graduation. Although this was not always typical, the news showed no damage from the earthquake but, instead, showed pedestrians on sunny streets and engineers in a laboratory where they were developing seismically resistant bricks.[25] In 1964, the newsreel *Around the Soviet Union* (*Po Sovetskomu Soiuzu*) showed short scenes of devastation before it showed the seismic springs in the basement of a new building and explained how these could withstand the shock of an earthquake (a crane is shown dropping a one-ton block of concrete next to the building).[26] In these newsreels, the various filmmakers keep the official story of Ashgabat alive long after it had faded from other media sources.

The Soviet regime sanitized the disaster in Ashgabat by editing the film reels, obfuscating the immediate aftermath of the earthquake. It is interesting to compare this footage with that from the Armenian earthquake of 1988, where the death toll was also in the tens of thousands. In Armenia, cameras rolled and rolled and did not shy away from depicting dead and dust-covered bodies being yanked from the rubble and lowered unceremoniously into coffins.[27] Cars were filmed driving off with coffins in their trunks or on their roofs.[28] All these details were absent in the case of Ashgabat, where the cinematographers showed a Potemkin village in a forested setting.

A common theme throughout this book is the selective treatment of disaster and the hardly surprising emphasis on urban tragedy at the expense of rural tragedy. In most cases, an urban earthquake had greater political potential than, for example, did a rural flood. Visually, this is no less true. In 1950, the film studio in Vladivostok documented the massive flooding in the region with a silent black-and-white film.[29] The aerial shots, a typical feature, showed gridiron-patterned rivers that reached the roofs of wooden homes. The camera did not pan the skyline to show planes coming to the rescue or offer a sequence featuring relief planes landing at an airport; rather, a viewer might see a few villagers paddle down a street or be offered images of maps to indicate how and where the rivers had risen. Except for the very end, when the camera focuses on workers hammering in a post, no state officials appear in the scene. The film does not even hint that the state could do much to improve the situation.

Since the earthquake in Ashgabat was such a major catastrophe, it is perhaps not surprising that it gained so much attention. In fact, it had no rival for a decade, in part because no major disaster occurred during the Khrushchev years. The 1957 nuclear accident in the Urals has been documented in text, but film footage still appears to be either unavailable or simply non-existent.[30] While there were no documentary films, full-length narrative films began to inform readers about the possibility of technological catastrophe. In 1962, Mikhail Romm's *9 Days in One Year* (*9 Dnei odnogo goda*), starring Aleksei Batalov, and the espionage adventure *Flight 713 Is Ready for Boarding* (*713-i prosit posadku*), with Vladimir Vysotskii in an early role, fictionalize dangerous possibilities.[31] These films can only marginally be considered disaster films. Although Romm's lead gets radiation sickness, the story revolves around his battle with love and health, not with the public danger of widespread radiation. *Flight 713* is closer to such later films as *Ekipazh*; however, unlike *Ekipazh*, it does not combine an earthquake with airplane technology but, instead, relates the story of a terrorist plot to hijack a transatlantic flight on a non-Soviet plane and destroy a Soviet delegation. Although the Soviet delegation ultimately fails to board, viewers are treated to dramatic scenes of drugged pilots falling asleep and panicked passengers pursuing their own needs (when, of course, the ideal Soviet citizen would not have panicked but would have acted communally). In the early ages of air travel, a time when few Soviets were flying, the film hints at danger but does not expose technical limitations (the plane functions properly, just not in the absence of a skilled pilot). The film has an ideological component but, being so high in the air and so far over the Atlantic, is distant from the real concerns of Soviet viewers.

Both the above films were made at the end of the thaw period, so directors had some room to manouevre. Nevertheless, a much greater diversification of subjects came after 1964, when Brezhnev took over the reins of the Soviet Union. It is much easier to analyze visual representations of disaster in this period because there are so many variants. Documentary films, which featured Soviet fictions, came out of Tadzhikistan and Uzbekistan, while fictional films, which embodied Soviet reality in fictional characters, came out of Moscow and Leningrad. Moreover, these films were starting to gain the attention of film critics and, in one form or another, to appear in major Soviet film journals.

Although only about fifteen minutes long and black and white, *Heroic Deed on the Zeravshan River* (*Podvig na Zeravshane*) fits the parameters of a disaster film since the film itself was born of accidental circumstances in 1964. While the film crew had been busily filming the documentary *Seven Beauties* (*Sem' krasavits*) in Tadzhikistan, they heard there had been a nearby landslide that had blocked the course of the river and that there was a risk that water would pour into nearby villages.[32]

Although the cinematographers did not capture the landslide itself, they rushed to the scene and filmed the heroic efforts to build a canal and divert the water. The film, by the female director Z. Tuzova, has a dramatic introduction, with credits rolling for the script and other components, suggesting a carefully composed narrative structure.

Heroic Deed on the Zeravshan River was designed around a basic narrative structure in which impending doom was to be averted by the Communist Party, Soviet engineering, and cooperation between the national republics. Near the start of the film, a little plane is shown landing, and I.T. Novikov, the head of the extraordinary commission, confidently discusses the salvage project with his underlings. In contrast to Ashgabat, where the disaster had already happened, in Tadzhikistan the grave consequences were exaggerated to highlight what had been saved. Clips taken from international newspapers indicate that Samarkand was at risk; shots of telephone poles surrounded by water indicate the degree to which water levels were rising. Once the drama of the event is made clear, the film turns to the rescue effort itself. Bulldozers, three abreast in a pseudo-military formation, roll forward to push aside dirt for the divergent canal. The camera rolls when the sun has set, showing bulldozers with headlights continuing their work. Ultimately, the successful construction of the canal stops the rising water. Viewers are then treated to scenes of cheering workers and water rushing into the newly built canal.

The triumphal conquest of nature is hardly surprising as the Soviets had already claimed to tame much larger rivers through their massive dam projects. Of greater interest is the way in which Tuzova added sophistication by superimposing an edited visual plotline onto the disaster. Four years later, this methodology would be taken many steps further with *Tashkent, Earthquake* (*Tashkent, zemletriasenie*), a production of the documentary film studio in Uzbekistan.[33] Articles on this film appear both in *Sovetskii ekran* and in *Sovetskii fil'm*, thus ensuring it was fully exposed to movie goers.[34] A full hour, in colour, and proudly presented at the first International Film Festival of the Countries of Asia and Africa (held in Tashkent in 1968), Malik Kaiumov's film packages the story of a city that had been destroyed two years earlier.

Instead of just letting a camera scan the damage, Kaiumov begins his story two years after the 1966 disaster so that he can show peaceful residents who had recovered from the catastrophe. The film then goes back two years to show a city in ruins. Kaiumov provides plenty of traditional footage – republic construction crews at work, Brezhnev giving a speech – but he also introduces love and sex to add dramatic tension. The little bit on the Ukrainian wedding is harmless, but Kaiumov, as is mentioned in the preceding chapter, also shows a couple walking arm in arm and then the viewer comes upon a young woman worker wearing a bra. Similarly, the filmmaker takes the rare step of showing a funeral procession through a city street, followed by showing women grieving over a mound of dirt.[35] The Soviets were generally averse to even implying the existence of death, but, since the actual death toll in Tashkent was so low, conceding the visual representation of a single coffin was not considered too risky. Nevertheless, the pile of earth and the flowers covering it encourages viewers to think about their own losses, much as the shot of the woman in a bra prompts them to think of sex. Although the film omits the names of almost all these people (except such personalities as the city seismologist), it infuses a human story into the disaster. When the fictional *Ekipazh* appeared in theaters in 1980, the first half focused on the personal lives of the main characters, and only in the second half did these characters deal with disaster. It is difficult to tell whether the director of *Ekipazh* saw *Tashkent, Earthquake*, but Kaiumov's film was the first to weave personal stories into a natural disaster film.

Shortly after *Tashkent, Earthquake*, the disaster film became a genre unto itself in Hollywood. *Airport* (1970), *Earthquake* (1974), and *The Towering Inferno* (1974) were all products of the early 1970s and did not go unnoticed in the Soviet Union.[36] They were generally seen as synonymous with the decadence of the bourgeois world, evidence of Western individualism, and harbingers of the economic doom awaiting the capitalist world.[37] Soviet filmmakers also understood how to satirize the genre and poke fun at Hollywood. In *The Unbelievable Adventures of Italians in Russia* (*Neveroiatnye prikliucheniia ital'iantsev v Rossii*) of 1974, Eldar Riazanov incorporates an emergency landing into the script. The Italians are on their way to Russia when a passenger breaks a window and later gets stuck in it. The Aeroflot pilots land the plane safely on a major road in the middle of the day. When the plane starts to drive down the highway, it stops at a red light to let pedestrians cross.[38] (This scene had an element of risk because, in 1963, Soviet news was not allowed to report a successful emergency landing on the Neva River.)[39] The Soviet film world either treated this genre with disdain or satirized it, but this did not stop it from experimenting with disaster films throughout the 1970s. Directors carefully avoided using the word "disaster" in their titles, but, in mutated form, the genre made it into the Soviet Union.[40]

Before turning to fictional films about disasters produced in the northwestern regions of the Soviet Union, a final documentary example from Central Asia needs to be discussed as it came out in 1973, close on the heels of the first disaster films. Produced by Kazakhfilm, *Medeo – Days and Nights of Courage* (*Medeo – dni i nochi muzhestva*) has all the dramatic elements of the disaster genre as it, once again, tells the story of a landslide and the Soviet race to protect Alma-Aty from sure destruction – all this in a film lasting about twenty minutes.[41] The on-screen title of the film employs stylized letters that American viewers might associate with a horror film or the cover page of a pulp novel. After this title and dramatic music, the story is presented as a race against the clock – the directors sabotage the certainty of a Soviet victory over nature with a storyline that allows doubt to creep in. Maybe nature would win? Although this does not happen, the film shows setbacks – a stream of water breaks through the dam, a rock shield is erected only to be smashed apart by rushing water – before the day is saved.

This storytelling structure reappears in *When the Earth Shakes* (*Kogda drozhit zemlia*), a fictional 1975 film about a hydroelectric dam whose construction is threatened by a rocky outcrop that would come tumbling down should an earthquake dislodge it (a real threat since the story was set in Dagestan, where an earthquake struck in 1970).[42] The basic premise of this film – a natural and technical disaster and impending doom for scores of workers – fits the parameters of a disaster film. In this case, the plot revolves around two officials and their respective approaches to solving the "outcrop" problem. The younger engineer wants to halt work and remove the rock while the elder official believes an earthquake would not jar it and that, therefore, construction should continue. The film features an earthquake and screaming workers fleeing as the earth trembles, but since the earthquake did not dislodge the rock, the aftermath of this disaster is minimal. In contrast to the prototypes of this genre, according to which individuals are in danger through great portions of the film, here the disaster scene comes very late in the film and only lasts a short while. The focus is not the disaster but, rather, the psychological struggle between the young engineer (who wants to suspend construction and blast off the outcrop) and the older official (who does not want to delay construction and trusts that the rock will not move). The film received a lengthy, if critical, review in *Iskusstvo kino*, demonstrating the attention these disaster films were beginning to receive.[43]

When the Earth Shakes has a number of distinguishing features. First, the resolution to the crisis comes as result of doing nothing. Whereas earlier films focus on the ability of the Soviets to move heaven and earth, the elder official in this film, Andrei S. Demidov, advocates leaving the outcrop alone. He knows it will not break off because he has made the correct calculations (*Potomu chto u menia byli raschety*). In this case, the role of Soviet mathematics is to let nature be.[44] No dynamite or bulldozers are called for. The film focuses on the tensions between the two main protagonists, while the state and its grandiose building plans are placed at a measured distance from the main events. Soviet citizens are not supposed to panic, but scenes show workers fleeing as the earth trembles, and one worker abandons everything to save his family. While such actions are not condoned, they do serve to expose the concocted elements of standard documentary films, according to which everyone is always pitching in. Finally, set in the southernmost part of the RSFSR, *When the Earth Shakes* differs from films before it in that it does not explicitly drone on about the friendship of peoples. It does feature at least one Dagestani worker, and it contains a scene in which the worker's father comes to the site to take his son home to a pre-selected bride. The son does not want to leave the construction project, and Demidov explains the importance of the project to the traditional father, who ultimately relents. In the mid-1970s, directors still believed the father's generation had to be convinced of the value of the Soviet project.

At this time, major Soviet directors were producing classics that still resonate today; a film such as *When the Earth Shakes* does not belong in the same aesthetic category (as its reviewers indicated). Nevertheless, these films *were* getting reviewed. In 1978, *Iskusstvo kino* gave ten pages to *Investigative Commission* (*Komissiia po rassledovaniiu*), a film about an accident (not a catastrophe) at a nuclear reactor that appeared in theatres eight years before Chernobyl.[45] Foreshadowing the causes of the Chernobyl catastrophe, an accident occurred after engineers at the plant had conducted tests. In the opening scene of the film, a lead engineer gets a call, announces to his wife that there has been an accident, and rushes to the plant. The accident is brought under control well before a catastrophe, but the film does hint that these Soviet installations are fallible.[46] In his work on Chernobyl, David Marples notes that, already in the 1970s, Soviet scientists were expressing concerns about the quality and safety of these power plants.[47]

For a disaster film, the idea of a radioactive accident was more daring than the subject matter in *When the Earth Shakes*, but, absent the radioactive fallout, the drama in the film was rather tepid. Without the subsequent catastrophe at Chernobyl, this film could easily be passed over since its emphasis is on the bureaucracy and professional staff. The social consequences of radiation being spread over a populated area are ignored and, instead, the directors focus on the bureaucratic attempt to find the guilty party. The commissions responsible for this were called together after mining disasters or major traffic accidents, and they met in order to determine how the particular accident in question happened and what might have been done to avoid it. In this film, then, the viewer sees hardly anything of the nuclear power plant or the actual city and is instead treated to a series of meetings in which plant officials try to defend their own skins. A small group of engineers keeps silent on important information about its experiment, hoping that blame will fall on its opponents. Although the film only shows this collusion within a bureaucratic context and does not explore its potentially fatal consequences, it certainly did not breed confidence in the quality of staff at these installations. Unlike the other disaster films discussed so far, *When the Earth Shakes* has no multi-ethnic component. High physics was Russian subject matter, whereas moving dirt to make way for a diversionary canal could involve all the republics.

The 1978 *Investigative Commission*, which deals with the bureaucracy, may seem a step backwards with respect to the disaster film genre, but it is another example of hesitantly approaching the subject before Soviet directors fully embraced the genre in the spirit of Hollywood. Two years after *Investigative Commission* and still firmly within the Brezhnev era, Aleksandr Mitta released *Crew* (*Ekipazh*), a two-part film that challenged *Moscow Does Not Believe in Tears* (*Moskva slezam ne verit*) at the box office.[48] Soviet critics had mocked the disaster genre, but *Ekipazh* was very well received.[49] After *Ekipazh* came films such as *Alarming Sunday* (*Trevozhnoe voskresen'e*), about a burning ship on the Black Sea; *Express Train 34* (*34-i skoryi*), based on a railway incident from the late 1970s; and *Proryv*, the film mentioned at the start of this chapter.[50] None of the subsequent films matched the popularity of *Ekipazh*, but they continued the genre.[51]

Ekipazh combines personal drama, a natural disaster, and the near destruction of a packed airplane, thus presenting many stories in one. Soviet critics applauded the long character development in the first half of the film because this distinguished it from the shock-and-awe tactics of an American film. Andrei Plakhov, who also reviewed *Investigative Commission*, explicitly compared the similarities of *Ekipazh* and *Airport* only to note that the former "stood in opposition to Western films which depict total fear and the atomization of people in time of need."[52] Even the title – *Ekipazh* – pushes away thoughts of individualism. Plakhov's emphasis need not be taken too seriously since the film has so much in common with the genre the Soviets pretended to despise. Furthermore, the review in *Sovetskii film* featured stills of dramatic fires and near nudity.[53] The film critic was trying to find an acceptable way to embrace a genre that fit the Brezhnevite tendency to produce consumer-oriented goods. Obviously, *When the Earth Shakes* and *Investigative Commission* were not exciting enough, even though the latter was more daring than *Ekipazh* because it suggested human error.

After the viewer learns about the peccadilloes and problems of the main characters, *Ekipazh* tells the story of the team of Soviet pilots that flew to an airport in Africa to rescue Soviet oil refinery workers from an earthquake (thus the director merges elements of *Airport* with elements of *Earthquake*). The pilots arrive to a completely chaotic scene in which flames threaten to engulf the entire airport and all the people near the crumbling airport structure. Among the terrified voices, some English speakers can be faintly heard, promoting the idea that the Soviets will offer international relief. The Aeroflot plane is quickly loaded with grateful passengers, but take off is impeded because the runway has developed a massive crack. In the background, viewers see what looks like another Aeroflot plane attempt to take off, but it hits the crack and explodes. The main protagonists are undaunted and manage to get the plane in the air. Once in the air, they discover a hole in the fuselage, and the crew members get frostbite trying to seal it. Their efforts are not in vain, however, because the pilots, in a vicious storm, managed to bring the plane down safely at the airport in Moscow.

The choice to focus on an airplane in *Ekipazh* is not insignificant. Obviously, the director had a model in *Airport*, but airplanes have had a fundamental role in Soviet disaster films since Ashgabat. In Ashgabat, a fleet of elegant planes arrives to rescue the city, but over the years planes appear in more dramatic roles. In *Flight 713 Is Ready for*

Boarding (1962), the pilots are drugged, and in *Tale of a Night* (1973), a plane heading to Africa is hijacked. Directors are always careful to cast troubled planes as foreign and to emphasize the role of Aeroflot planes in rescue missions. In an archival film on the Ashgabat earthquake, the bus that arrives in town from the airport is clearly marked with the Aeroflot insignia, just in case the viewer might forget how these individuals had arrived.[54] Riazanov employs an Aeroflot plane for the emergency, but it lands on a sunny day, coming down smoothly and calmly along the highway. *Ekipazh* is the first film to show Aeroflot planes in serious danger and the first to show an Aeroflot plane lose half its fuselage. As Boris Berman points out, the public was interested in seeing "the most reliable, the most, most, most [reliable]" airline in the world in such difficult circumstances.[55] The film does not suggest technical defects: it is the natural disaster that causes damage to the fuselage and the pilots perform heroically. Nevertheless, the film is the first to suggest the possibility of a dramatic crash, and this could remind viewers of other air disasters (since there had been many in the Soviet Union). The fictional film cuts through the fictional rhetoric of the non-fictional regime.

The earthquake as a backdrop is no accident either. Although the Soviets were well aware of *The Towering Inferno* and had made good propaganda usage of the Joelma high rise fire in Sao Paolo, Brazil, in 1974, earthquakes were the dominant visual national disaster. Furthermore, an earthquake had advantages that a film about a skyscraper or massive flood did not.[56] In the visual history of earthquakes, Russians were in a hegemonic position, helping the people of lesser republics, whereas this was not the case with seasonal flooding in Russian areas. Ashgabat and Tashkent are in Central Asia, and *Ekipazh* implicitly reminds viewers of Soviet aid to these areas, even though it is set in Africa and has absolutely nothing to do with reconstruction (work crews were being evacuated from the region). Of course, the African component refers to Soviet foreign policy in the 1970s and its assistance in underdeveloped areas. Setting the disaster in a foreign land also meant that showing dead bodies would not be such a novelty. Nevertheless, the scenes of complete panic and helpless Soviet citizens conflict with the Tashkent story about calm people returning to work the very next day. Since the bulk of Soviet earthquakes struck Central Asia, viewers in these areas could easily connect these scenarios with Uzbekistan and Kazakhstan and see behind the competing stories.

Two important events shortly after the release of *Ekipazh* dramatically changed the visual representation of disaster. In 1982, Leonid Brezhnev died and left his successors with a mountain of unsolved problems, and, in 1985, Gorbachev became general secretary and slowly revealed his plans to remake the Soviet economy and Soviet society. Within the environment of perestroika, the visual landscape changed dramatically. After the Chernobyl explosion in 1986, eyewitness filmmakers were almost immediately in the vicinity of the disaster, recording whatever they could. Since radiation is not visible on film, they could not capture the source of the danger, but they could film rescue workers removing debris from the top of the fourth block. As mentioned in chapter 5 (the chapter on Chernobyl), the renowned filmmaker Vladimir Shevchenko died of radiation poisoning.[57] Footage of all aspects of the Chernobyl process, except the internal discussions of the Central Committee, abound. The immediate footage of the earthquake in Armenia was equally dramatic and was taken from all sides. The army filmed and interviewed its soldiers performing heroic deeds, the Red Cross and Red Crescent emphasized the support they were giving, and independent film crews chronicled death, destruction, and the massive discontent of individuals and officials who recognized the Soviet apparatus was grossly unprepared for such a catastrophe.[58] Filmmakers on the scene at the Bashkir train wreck did not shy away from filming the burned and scarred faces of survivors.[59] In the film *Trace* (*Sled*), Armenian filmmakers team up with their counterparts in Yugoslavia to focus on the tragic fate of the Yugoslavian pilots who crashed their planes, and they emphasize the international dimension of the response.[60]

These dramatic scenes from the perestroika era should not lead us to the mistaken conclusion that they came out of nowhere. Since the end of the Second World War, Soviet filmmakers have been slowly adapting and changing the manner in which they present visual aspects of tragedies. In the Stalinist era, it is no surprise that dead bodies and panic were totally washed from the celluloid. If, however, because of the strict censorship the scholar chooses to ignore the story that is told, she risks omitting the contribution of Central Asian directors. These directors played a key role and, from Ashgabat to Tashkent, made substantial technical improvements and dramatic changes to the disaster narrative. Even if Kaiumov awkwardly transforms aspects of a tragedy into a love story, his film *Tashkent, Earthquake* reinforces themes evident in previous chapters: the tragedy was not just an exercise in depicting the fulfilment of communist propaganda but, rather, an opportunity to experience new adventures. The daring sexual scenes helped to determine the agenda items at Komsomol meetings, where they discussed sexually transmitted diseases. This documentary film may present the earthquake as a spectacle, but it also tells true stories about the earthquake, even if it does not mention many real names.

The effective transition from story to spectacle came in the 1970s, when directors at the central studios put greater effort into the disaster genre. *Ekipazh* was said to be the first of its kind, but other films, without aspiring to blockbuster status, paved the way for *Ekipazh*. *When the Earth Shakes*, which came right after the Kazakh film *Medeo – Days and Nights of Courage*, has all the makings of a disaster film, though the pyrotechnics are minimal in comparison to those in *Ekipazh*. *Investigative Commission* goes after a much more daring topic, with radioactivity at the heart of the matter. *Ekipazh*, borrowing from both Soviet and American models, takes the genre a step further and continues to expose Soviet audiences to the possibility of disaster. When Soviet film reviewers said that American audiences could find solace in the idea that the tragic images on the large screen made their own lives more bearable, they could have said the same about their domestic audiences as these grew accustomed to disaster films.

Ironically, the fictional disaster films were preparing audiences for an uncertain future, and directors continued to produce them into the perestroika era. Documentary and fictional film directors still had to be careful, but, as censorship was loosened, they had room to be more daring.[61] However, if filmmakers had come a long way since the late 1940s and changed the rhythm of catastrophe in their films, the same could not be said of the Soviet state. When the fourth reactor blew at Chernobyl, and when the earth trembled in Armenia, the attitude of Soviet officials towards disasters had not evolved. Maybe they had not watched these films for they applied the same methods and templates to these new disasters as they had to the old ones. Unfortunately, the fictional scenario they created for themselves would now face a new reality.

PART THREE

Aging Response Models in Gorbachev's New World

5

April 1986: Chernobyl

On 15 May 1985, a radio station in Kyiv announced that the Kyiv Hydroelectric Dam had burst open and that there was a high risk of catastrophic flooding. The announcement came across the airwaves as follows: "The headquarters of the civil defence of the city of Kyiv is speaking. The headquarters of the civil defence of the city of Kyiv is speaking ... There is a threat of catastrophic flooding. There is a threat of catastrophic flooding ... As a result of the breach of the dam at the Kyiv Hydroelectric Station, there is a risk of short-term flooding along the banks of the Dnepr River ... Citizens! Quickly leave for the unflooded parts of town. Bring with you personal documents, necessary items, and nourishment. As you leave your house, turn off the lights, gas and electric heaters. Maintain order on the road, do not permit fuss or panic and precisely carry out the orders of the organs of the civil defense and of the police."[1] Over a period of four minutes, the radio station provided instructions on how to deal with the catastrophe. From ample experience, Ukrainians knew full well how devastating flooding could be.

Citizens did not, however, flee immediately; instead, over eight hundred callers phoned the radio station to ask whether the report was true. Eleven minutes after the original broadcast, the radio station announced to its listeners that the message had been transmitted in error and was, in fact, a training tape that had mistakenly been broadcast. During a training session for technical employees, the radio operators had forgotten to turn off the appropriate equipment. Despite the broadcast, few people appear to have taken further action, although official reports worried that over a thousand people had stopped working in fourteen factories and thus limited the economic efficiency of the city.[2] Subsequently, the city took measures to improve the first response system.[3]

Kyivans did not have to deal with a leaking dam, but this radio broadcast was still very important. The unwillingness to believe the news as broadcast reflects the Soviet citizens' mistrust of official news sources. Ironically, when something did not happen, they found out immediately, whereas when something did happen, they had to wait to hear about it. The radio incident undermines Soviet claims that they waited to inform residents about the explosion at Chernobyl because they did not want panic to break out in Kyiv.[4] This claim appears suspect when one remembers how few people reacted to the announcement of the imminent flooding of their neighbourhoods (never mind the fact that communist officials prided themselves on the lack of panicky citizens during earthquakes and other disasters). Finally, the calm, even indifferent, reaction to the radio broadcast testified to the regularity of disasters: a flood was not big news. In the years before, Soviet citizens had dealt with numerous shapes and forms of disasters. A nuclear explosion was certainly unprecedented, but it occurred within the contours of experience with prior disasters – for Kyivans and all Soviet citizens.

As Tashkent awoke on the morning of 26 April 1986, older residents probably checked the ground under their feet. Little did they know that, in the western part of the USSR, a nuclear reactor had exploded, sending a massive plume of radioactive material into the air. Unlike Ukrainians, who immediately received news of the earthquake, residents of Tashkent had to wait for weeks to hear about the nuclear explosion and months to learn (or guess) about its consequences. Shortly after the earthquake in 1966, the Soviet Union proudly announced that Tashkent residents were already going about their daily business. On the same day in 1986, Tashkentites went about their daily routines oblivious to the tragedy that had occurred in the entire western part of the Soviet Union. An accident deep in the heart of Central Asia had been news fit for everyone to hear, but an accident in the westernmost part of the empire was quickly hushed up and strictly censored.

The news of the explosion reached officials in Moscow within hours of the incident, but the slow response thereafter has become legendary: strange behaviour when one considers how swiftly the same Communist Party reacted in Tashkent.[5] The Soviet engineers underestimated the strength of the explosion and were initially hesitant to evacuate Pripyat, the town of forty-five thousand that housed the workers of the nuclear power plant.[6] In Pripyat, on 26 April, children were encouraged to go to school until the next day, when an evacuation began in earnest. Only then did waves of buses take residents to Poliske, about fifty kilometres away. In contrast to Brezhnev, who immediately boarded a plane to visit the earthquake area in Tashkent, Gorbachev hesitated to go to Kyiv, choosing to remain in Moscow. Nikolai Ryzhkov, the chair of the Council of Ministers who made the trip to Kyiv on 2 May, wrote that the general secretary preferred to avoid visiting dirty and disorganized disaster sites.[7] Ryzhkov arrived after the May Day celebrations in Kyiv, which had not been cancelled despite the fact that the extent of the disaster was well known. Authorities also allowed an international bike race to take place in Kyiv.

A number of factors contributed to this behaviour. First, earthquakes were a regular feature of life in the Soviet Union, whereas this was the first major nuclear explosion in a heavily populated area and the first one that registered on the radioactive scales of Western power plants.[8] Second, because the radiation eventually spread to and lingered in Western countries, it transcended the borders of the Soviet Union in a way that the Tashkent earthquake did not: the Soviets could not ignore the concerns of the Swedes or the Germans. Third, the explosion did not destroy identifiable living space, burn forests, or flood villages: the danger was invisible, spreading uncontrollably with the dominant winds, and it was difficult for the people who lived in the area to comprehend what had happened. Finally, a nuclear explosion was directly tied to the military supremacy of the Soviet Union, philosophical debates about nuclear weapons, and the question of disarmament.[9] Almost immediately after the explosion, comparisons were being made with Hiroshima and there was much talk of the potential of nuclear energy to wipe out humanity, making areas the size of Belarus uninhabitable.

Despite the apocalyptic possibilities of nuclear explosions, the Chernobyl catastrophe invites comparisons to earlier disasters and the government's response to them. Perestroika and glasnost had changed the nature of political debate in the Soviet Union, thus giving this comparison an added degree of relevance. Was the Brezhnev regime better prepared to deal with disaster than was the Gorbachev regime? How did the nature of volunteer work change in Chernobyl? Which republics answered the call when the state trumpeted the friendship of peoples? Did the political protest have antecedents in previous disasters? How did the anti-nuclear movement benefit from the ability of the particularities of nuclear energy to exert pressure on the state?

Although Chernobyl was at the centre of international attention, the most active voices were in the Crimea, where they were desperately trying to stop the construction of a nuclear power plant. Chernobyl had strong regional importance as local party officials clashed with their counterparts in Kyiv and Moscow. In pushing the boundaries of their own influence, they were expanding the public sphere within the Communist Party. Chernobyl was also of national importance as disasters were employed to undermine the idea of the friendship of peoples, a critical component in the recovery in Tashkent. Here, other questions come to the fore: How did Ukrainian communists take advantage of the disaster to support nationalist tactics? And how did these tactics differ from those in Armenia two years later? These questions frame a discussion that begins with a basic outline of the Chernobyl incident before going on to analyze the nuclear explosion not as a scientific event but, rather, as one piece of a larger puzzle that represents the experiences of individuals in the Marxist-Leninist state.

The Chernobyl incident has been studied extensively but almost always in isolation, both geographically and thematically.[10] Geographically, studies focus on Ukraine; thematically, they focus on the scientific aspects of the explosion. Nikolai Ryzhkov, who went to both Chernobyl and Spitak, briefly mentions his experience in Ukraine and Armenia, but most histories of Chernobyl present it separately from the Armenian earthquake.[11] Even so, there are parallels between the two catastrophes. When the earthquake struck Armenia in late 1988, Soviet citizens were still experiencing radiation from Chernobyl, which continued to spread. Almost comically, Ukrainian construction crews were rushed to help Armenians as Armenian construction crews rushed to help Ukrainians. Did their trains pass somewhere in the night?

Despite isolationist tendencies in the scholarship, major works do hint at issues whose importance is amplified when placed within the broader context of disaster studies. Within months of the incident at Chernobyl Western commentators were penning histories. Although limited by access to sensitive materials and chronological proximity to the explosion, David Marples provides two thorough accounts of the immediate aftermath of the disaster.[12] Because the Chernobyl collection in the Russian State Archive of Contemporary History (*Rossiiskii gosudarstvennyi arkhiv noveishchei istorii* [RGANI]) has subsequently been prepared much like a college reader, with carefully selected and photocopied documents, Marples's source analysis is more helpful. His two books were written before the collapse of the Soviet Union and therefore have a political purpose in that they highlight the incompetencies of the Soviet government. They offer a detailed analysis of the period immediately following the explosion but do not analyze the ongoing trauma of Chernobyl as the Soviet Union teetered to-wards its collapse. Marples briefly places Chernobyl within the context of contemporary accidents in Ukraine, but his focus is squarely on Chernobyl.[13]

The official Soviet literature of the time attempts to draw a parallel between Chernobyl and the significantly less dangerous American incident at Three-Mile Island in 1979. Not surprisingly, it tried to downplay Chernobyl so that the Soviet Union could continue with its ambitious nuclear energy program.[14] Although Valerii Legasov draws a parallel between Chernobyl and Three-Mile Island, a questionable comparison at best, he does not simply toe the party line. He had been the first deputy director of the Institute of Atomic Energy, a respected professor of physics at Moscow State University, and a lead member of the government commission investigating the meltdown. Frustrated by an inability to publish critical information about the disaster, he hung himself in his apartment on the second anniversary of the explosion. His attitude speaks to the complicated position of the scientists involved.

The official response was not surprising, but it was not the only one to emerge. Film directors documented the horrors of workers on the roof of the reactor block who had seconds to get rid of radioactive debris. In *Bells of Chernobyl* (*Kolokol Chernobylia*), Rolan Sergiyenko and his crew filmed scenes within two months of the accident and interviewed villagers facing the effects of radiation. Vladimir Shevchenko, the director of *Chernobyl: A Chronicle of Difficult Weeks* (*Chernobyl: khronika trudnykh nedel'*), died within a year of the explosion after completing footage for a sensitive film that underwent drastic editing.[15] These films provide valuable material for the immediate period after the explosion in the region of Chernobyl. Recent assessments are less ambiguous in their consideration of this incident. Alla Iaroshinskaia documents the crimes of Soviet authorities who refused to recognize that specific areas had been irradiated.[16] Iaroshinskaia's analysis returns to a theme prominent throughout Marples's work – the misdeeds of the Soviet Communist Party. The title of her work, *Crime without Punishment*, emphasizes this point. Discussions about the responsibility of specific Communist Party officials is by no means over (only recently, Nikolai Ryzhkov defended his actions in his autobiography) and will continue to stir emotions for there can be no doubt that massive and avoidable errors were made along the way.

With time, local studies have become more nuanced, without their former ideological restraints; thus, even though Chernobyl continues to be studied in isolation, these offer starting points for further discussion. Works in Ukrainian focus on the Ukrainian Academy of Sciences and its role at a time when Ukraine was evolving into an independent state. These efforts are less concerned with the failure of Soviet science leading up to the explosion than they are with the innovative scientific procedures developed in response to it. Scientists write about meeting the disaster "head on" and "sleeping in their offices" while battling the effects of a nuclear explosion.[17] N.P. Baranovs'ka suggests that the Ukrainian Academy of Sciences did original research on radioecology and radiobiology based on the materials and samples scientists collected in the radioactive zone. In this way a dehumanized zone is transformed into a laboratory to be admired.[18] The scientific works recognize the nuclear tragedy but limit their focus to strictly scientific issues and highlight the achievements of a fledgling nation. Despite their limitations, these works remind the reader to look beyond the physical science and to explore the social role of scientists outside the laboratory. In the Crimean peninsula, scientists adopted an expanded social role, much as had their forebears after the Crimean earthquake in 1927. The social role of scientists requires further exploration.

Over the last decade, Chernobyl's clean-up crews (*likvidatory* in Russian) have made their voices heard in areas across the former Soviet Union. Regional groups have published memorial volumes dedicated to the liquidators who died from radiation-related sicknesses as well as lists of all the individuals who helped at Chernobyl. These books provide us with images of the men and women who left their hometowns and travelled as "volunteers" to Chernobyl.[19] The tone of these works varies, at times accusing the USSR of incompetence, at times lauding the heroic deeds of fallen friends, and at times evincing pride in the innovative Soviet technology that brought the fourth reactor under control. Twenty years after the explosion, and published in a radically different socio-political environment, the content of these commemorative albums is linked to the changing memory of Chernobyl. After the collapse of the Soviet Union, Ashgabatites repositioned their memory of the 1948 earthquake; twenty years after the collapse of the Soviet Union, the 1986 liquidators did the same with their recollection of Chernobyl. Although these are separate topics, they both offer clues to such critical issues as the nature of volunteering and the migration patterns of people who travelled great distances to Ukraine.

This literature on Chernobyl is limited to the disaster, but, when placed within a broader social setting and a long-term analysis of the Soviet treatment of catastrophes, it opens avenues for further exploration. By integrating the concerns of the scientists and first responders with questions that can be asked about all disasters, the story of Chernobyl takes on a wider social significance. Moreover, it becomes part of a long Soviet narrative rather than a recent symbol of Soviet collapse. This long Soviet narrative becomes increasingly apparent throughout the analysis below; however, in order to establish a backdrop to Chernobyl, it is first necessary to discuss the drama of perestroika. Doing so enables us slowly to understand why Brezhnev was more successful in Uzbekistan than Gorbachev was in Ukraine and to see how, in unsettled times, Soviet citizens once again found space to manouevre.

PERESTROIKA AND CHERNOBYL

A central theme in this book is the long temporal context of disasters: an examination of a single disaster must look beyond its immediate circumstances. Chernobyl is no different in this respect as the prehistory of the nuclear industry shows uneven experiences with technological innovation and even with small-scale radioactive leakage. When an actual breakdown did occur, the consequences were more dangerous than those presented in the film *Komissiia po rassledovaniiu*, which only foreshadows what *might* happen. While the history of Soviet nuclear energy is not the focus of the current discussion, a few examples of near misses expose the fragility of Soviet nuclear power in its most formative and expansive years.[20] No national nuclear program has been without its problems, so the comments here are not designed to single out the Soviet Union but, rather, to highlight its own sources of vulnerability.

Difficulties emerged well before the construction of Chernobyl and continued until perestroika. For instance, in 1968 a malfunction in the cooling apparatus at the Beloiarsk nuclear power plant lead to melting in one of the channels.[21] In an earlier work, in which he draws from published Soviet sources, David Marples chronicles social and technological factors from the 1970s and 1980s in which Soviet authorities expressed dismay over the state of nuclear power. While meltdowns did not appear in public sources, Marples could point to any number of shortcomings. In Ukraine, officials complained about an unskilled workforce and power plants that had been built without any accessible transportation networks nearby.[22] In the late 1970s, senior officials worried about the presence of radioactivity throughout the transport network.[23] In 1983, even *Pravda* reported grave problems with the construction at the Volgodonsk reactor vessel plant, a supplier to nuclear power plants.[24] The rush to construct these plants led to random irregularities.

Engineering shortcuts do not necessarily lead to major incidents.[25] In the fall of 1982, however, Chernobyl had its first rupture that led to radiation leaking into the air. Documents from the Ukrainian KGB, which are now available on the internet, indicate that on 9 September 1982, an accident (*avariia*) had occurred in conjunction with a planned retrofit (*kapital'nyi remont*) of the first block.[26] Originally, the reports stated that radiation had not spread on the premises.[27] By 14 September, however, radioactive elements had been released into the air and noticed on the grounds of the power plant.[28] By the end of October, radiation levels were tested in a much larger zone outside the power plant, and the commission found that in a north-northeast direction radiation had spread as far as fourteen kilometres. In the village of Chistogalovka, five kilometres from the power plant, "hot" particles were one hundred times the accepted norm. In fish and crab, however, they found no significant rise in radiation levels.[29] Despite the general rise in radiation levels, the official commission did not think an evacuation was necessary.[30] The entire history of this leak is still poorly known and requires further investigation to understand its impact on policy (if any) as well as the reaction of those who were exposed to it (Chistogalovka was abandoned after the meltdown of 1986). This short excursus, however, adds a temporal context to the cataclysm of 1986. By this time, the Soviets already had some experience with nuclear incidents at Chernobyl, even if these never made the news. As the Soviets gained experience with these unexpected incidents, politics were rapidly changing.

By the mid-1980s, the Soviet Union no longer resembled the state Brezhnev and Kosygin had led in the mid-1960s. By the mid-1960s, the Soviets had recovered from the Second World War, eliminated Stalinist excesses, and expressed confidence in their system as they watched the United States struggle abroad in Vietnam and at home with the Civil Rights Movement. This external confidence was certainly encouraged by building projects in places such as Tashkent, but the unwillingness of an aging Brezhnev regime to analyze real statistics played a role as well. After Brezhnev's death in 1982, confidence quickly waned when the first reality-based analyses were performed.

In April 1983, the economic team of Tatiana Zaslavskaia in Novosibirsk made use of actual statistics to argue that the current economic system had become untenable.[31] Although not yet general secretary, Mikhail Gorbachev was familiar with what became known as the Novosibirsk Report, a report that did not convince everyone but that nevertheless spread troubling news about the economic situation of the USSR. Of course, the economic situation was not the only source of anxiety. After four years, the war in Afghanistan continued to drain the treasury and the economic system had ceased to replenish it. In the West, Solidarity had raised the possibility of revolt in Eastern Europe and highlighted the common bankruptcy of the economies across the Eastern Bloc.

When Gorbachev became general secretary in the spring of 1985, it was already clear that reform was necessary, though no one was yet sure what it would entail. Perestroika had been tentatively announced at the Twenty-Seventh Party Congress in late February and early March 1986, but this announcement stressed the need for change rather than the strict direction that it would take. Thus when the explosion occurred in April 1986, the Soviet Union was still much as it had been in the years preceding it. Almost immediately thereafter perestroika and, subsequently, glasnost pushed the communist state into unforeseen directions. In the summer of 1986, Gorbachev relaxed pressure on the publishing industry, and intellectuals who had previously seen their works censored had more, if still limited, freedom to express their views. In December 1986, the exiled scientist Andrei Sakharov was allowed to return to Moscow. It was only in the years after the explosion that the political system changed radically. Whereas the Tashkent earthquake occurred in relatively stable times, and the Armenian earthquake shook the earth when ethnic tensions had already sparked evacuations, Chernobyl was wedged between two separate epochs in the history of the Soviet Union. The explosion happened in the calm before the storm.

Most details of the explosion have become common knowledge and are available in numerous published sources, so only the basics are mentioned here.[32] During the weekend of 25 and 26 April 1986, the authorities at Chernobyl carried out standard tests on a reactor core that should have been tested long ago.[33] Owing to power surges in the closed-loop system, it became impossible for the test operators to control the rising heat in the reactor core. At around 1:20 a.m., there was an explosion in the fourth reactor block that raised the roof of the reactor hall. Once out of control, a second explosion blew "graphite blocks and fuel channels" through the hole in the roof of that hall. Although the situation could not be stopped, the first reports from the power plant to the Central Committee in Moscow downplayed the extent of the catastrophe. O.N. Makhukhin, first deputy minister of power and electrification in the USSR, informed the Central Committee that the fire had been put out by 3:30 a.m. and that he did not foresee the need for an evacuation of Pripyat.[34] Despite the calming words sent to Moscow, fire crews were already frantically trying to contain the burning reactor while they inhaled the deadly radioactive fumes.[35] Although they managed to put out the flames, they could not prevent the radiation spreading as a massive plume of smoke rose in the air. Within a day, the Forsmark nuclear power plant in Sweden registered unusual radiation levels and became the first Western entity to realize that something had gone wrong somewhere in the Eastern Bloc.

The emergency required the mobilization of mass resources. On 27 April, hundreds of buses arrived from Kyiv to evacuate residents to outside the contaminated zone. While Soviet workers were moved away from apartments, engineers and military personnel dealt with the radiation. The Soviets tried to spray villages to prevent the spread of radiation as engineers discussed the fate of a reactor that continued to burn. The work of the firefighters prevented the catastrophe from spreading to other reactors, but the core of the fourth reactor remained radioactive. In May, the Soviets announced that the reactor would be placed in a sarcophagus made of reinforced concrete that would contain the dangerous remains for "hundreds of years."[36] The elimination of radioactive debris from the roof of the reactor and the construction of the sarcophagus were wrapped in Soviet mythologizing as its speedy completion became a symbol of Soviet ingenuity. When the sarcophagus was completed in October 1986, the political profile of the Soviet had undergone further change.

Chernobyl certainly accelerated the need for reform, but it must be considered within a larger network of socio-political trends. Gorbachev's foreign policy and shifting attitude towards the West situates and explains certain aspects of the response to Chernobyl. Although Gorbachev was welcomed in the West as a refreshing change from the stale suits of the 1970s, his policies were not immediately friendly to Western nations, as is evident in the failure of the Reykjavík summit in the autumn of 1986. The role of foreign help in disaster relief, negligible at Chernobyl and overwhelming in Armenia, reflected the progression of Soviet foreign policy as the USSR reassessed its isolationist tendencies when coping with tragedies. The rising of ethnic tensions in the mid-1980s also influenced the long-term response to Chernobyl. Nationalism, even Russian nationalism, had been brewing since the mid-1960s, and Chernobyl exploded just as cracks were already showing in the friendship of peoples – "friends" ceased to be "friends." By 1987, the first public signs of deep divisions between Armenians and Azerbaijanis had bubbled to the surface in the Nagorno-Karabagh region. In the summer of 1987, the first independence demonstrations were openly held in Riga, the capital of Latvia. Similarly, it slowly became impossible to develop a unified approach to Chernobyl because even the core republics were going their own way as Russia, Ukraine, and Belarus developed individual responses. Finally, in a heady atmosphere in which editors and publishers were pushing, scientists became involved in public debates that targeted individual ministries and urged on larger protest movements. Chernobyl became entangled in an incredibly complex domestic situation, while the Communist Party tried to control the terms of the response.

Despite the disastrous explosion and flummoxed leadership, the immediate response to the catastrophe was not a problem for Soviet authorities. In April 1986, the they did not yet have to face protesting scientists or angry publicists and could treat the explosion as just another large-scale engineering challenge. In what has been called the "accident phase," from the explosion in April to the completion of the sarcophagus at the end of the year, Soviet authorities were dealing with a classic management and engineering problem.[37] Extinguishing the fire at the reactor, evacuating Pripyat, and building the sarcophagus were traditional exercises suited to an authoritarian state – an accident occurs and central organs mobilize incredible resources from thousands of kilometres away, paying little attention to the cost of human life in bringing the situation under control. Soviet authorities have been heavily criticized for delaying the evacuation of Pripyat when they already knew of the explosion; yet once the evacuation did begin it was effective. The construction of the sarcophagus around the exposed reactor core required resources and coordination for which the authoritarian state was well suited. Unfortunately, containing the reactor to limit the effects of radiation was much like imprisoning a dissident with the naïve hope that the samizdat underground would not continue to spread his or her ideas.

The accident phase mobilized Soviet citizens, who were rushed to Chernobyl to perform any number of deadly tasks that almost guaranteed exposure to radiation. Officially, the heroism of Soviet citizens represented their willingness to volunteer in difficult times; volunteer work became another opportunity for the Soviets to reward their citizens by bestowing upon them medals for heroism.[38] A medal has two sides, and so did this heroism. The official rewards fit authoritarian patterns but did not capture the perspective of participants. Importantly, publications of the Ukrainian Academy of Sciences (UAS) and the memory books (*Knigi pamiati*) focus on the accident phase of Chernobyl. In contrast to many response situations, in which survivors of local communities are the first respondents, here the state was the most important first responder as the catastrophe was too large to be handled at the local level.[39]

In 2004, the UAS published the reflections of members who were involved, in one capacity or another, with the Chernobyl explosion. In the new Ukraine, scientists did not have to follow scripted Soviet procedure, so their memories were less a function of Muscovite experience than might have been the case in earlier times.[40] Instead of condemning the response, as has been done internationally for decades, their stories defend the actions of the UAS and highlight the independence of Ukrainian science. As historians of memory emphasize, memory is not a solid phenomenon that yields objective insights into the historical past but, rather, a malleable phenomenon subject to change in the light of new experiences. The memories of Ukrainian scientists should be considered with this in mind, though it is remarkable how a Soviet narrative of grand science continues to underlie the stories they tell.

In the spirit of Soviet storytelling, the scientists recounted the selfless devotion of Soviet colleagues, the integrity of their science, and the losses in their ranks. I.K. Pokhodnia, then vice-president of the UAS, entitled his reminiscences: "Everyone Appreciated the Heroic Work of Our Scientists."[41] The commissions of the academy "quickly gained respect throughout the republic" and coordinated their work with Soviet authorities.[42] Pokhodnia emphasizes the heroic work of restarting the remaining Chernobyl reactors, even though the UAS soon thereafter became a vocal supporter of alternate energy sources. At the end of the summer, engineers discovered deficiencies in the other reactor blocs that had to be fixed. In this heroic tale "even a radioactive background" did not "stop the scientists."[43] The unit was fixed and ready to run.[44] Pokhodnia is not entirely uncritical for he recognizes shortcomings in equipment and procedures, but the desire to promote the UAS pulls his story closer to the Soviet version from 1986 and 1987.

Significantly, the stories of the Ukrainian scientists cover the heroic phase, when the situation required innovative scientific methods to limit radiation, purify water, and solve scientific problems. The scientists are less interested in the evacuation of villages and the villagers who were not evacuated and who complained bitterly about the inability of scientists to solve local problems.

The academicians promoted a variety of heroism that links the individual heroism of the deed to the broader goal of the Soviet state to come to terms with the disaster. This attitude emerges in both Russian- and Ukrainian-language reminiscences. Pokhodnia writes that, when he and his colleagues looked back, they joked that had they always worked with such self-sacrifice they would have been living in communism (*pri kommunizme*) a long time ago.[45] Scientific heroism had classic military undertones as tasks were accomplished in ways that were foreign to "peacetime." Deliveries were made without paperwork, and scientists did not argue among themselves as they strove to complete state-prescribed tasks.[46] Finally, if such an accident were to happen again, post-Soviet Ukraine would lack the resources to fight the tragedy in the spectacular manner of the Soviet Union.[47] Not all scientists expressed their memories so vividly, but the promotion of scientific excellence was inexorably tied with the classic motifs common to Soviet disasters.

The memories of these scientists are presented within the context of an institutional academy, whereas works dedicated to the memories of liquidators, published on a regional basis, promote positive memories while finding a balance between collective (i.e., Soviet) and individual needs. Echoing the memoirs of scientists, testimonials speak to a grandiose engineering accomplishment, whether this means working at a military camp or helping with the construction of the sarcophagus. Two decades later, I.A. Beliaev remembers the cooperation of the member republics and the performance of heroic deeds. He writes about Efim Pavlovich Slavskii, a leader of the Soviet atomic industry, who "was their Stalin" at Chernobyl.[48] Beliaev also believes that, had the accident happened after 1991 and the collapse of the Soviet Union, the situation would have been utterly catastrophic.[49]

In Ukraine and Russia, local activists who have seen the long-term health consequences experienced by liquidators have issued more tempered testimonials. In listing the names and photos of the men and women who arrived in Chernobyl, these collections present the catastrophe in terms of the fates of individuals rather than of the fate of an institution or country.

The regional accounts, twenty years after the event, nevertheless see the accident phase of Chernobyl in terms of a grand Soviet project. The prefaces, written by a local governor or other high-standing member of officialdom, suggest the statist reminiscences of the Soviet years.[50] In Cheliabinsk, the liquidators situate their response within the tragic context of their own experience of a nuclear disaster in 1957, but they still write of the sarcophagus as the "heroic deed of builders."[51] The response was immediate, and "volunteers" were ready to head west; the volunteers from the Urals were "among the first" to start on the construction of the sarcophagus.[52] In Cheliabinsk, they remember the personnel and technical expertise that was supplied. The region of Cheliabinsk developed radio-controlled tractors that could penetrate areas that humans could not.[53] Finally, the heroics of the engineering project are presented in militaristic terms. Regional accounts remember the situation as "war-like."[54] In Nizhnii Tagil, also in the Urals, they invoke the slogan from the Great War of the Fatherland to pay homage to their liquidators: "No one is forgotten and nothing is forgotten."[55] Heroism and militarism remained common denominators among most regional memories. These memories have a twofold importance: (1) they indicate that Chernobyl is an ongoing phenomenon and (2) they keep alive aspects of Soviet disaster response that would be familiar to those who travelled across the union to assist in the reconstruction of Tashkent.

These memories are not blind to the fates of the liquidators. Nevertheless, the accident phase remains remarkably stable in these post-Soviet narratives and quite foreign to the widespread condemnation found in Western sources. Naturally, the response of liquidators from the Urals differed from the response of those who lived in or who were evacuated from the zone. Moreover, attitudes changed after the completion of the sarcophagus, when the extent of the tragedy settled in.

Alongside the incredible efforts to evacuate citizens and contain the reactor were the prolonged consequences of the explosion – consequences that varied depending upon regional and social differences. Although the Crimean peninsula was, for the most part, unaffected by radiation, a nuclear power plant under construction on its northeastern shores became the subject of a growing political movement. Our discussion starts with this movement because it expresses the broad political mobilization of scientists and activists who maintained faith in Soviet science while losing faith in Soviet bureaucracy. Closer to the plant, the recovery effort reflected elements common to other disasters. Children were evacuated to pioneer camps, member republics shipped in workers to build a new settlement for the evacuated Chernobyl employees, the military played a key role, and the Soviet bureaucracy developed a complex pay scale to reward "volunteers" who increasingly risked their lives the closer they got to the reactor core. In addition to these familiar elements of response, central officials had to deal with growing dissatisfaction from local communists who found themselves allied with the perestroika equivalent of a non-governmental organization.

Whereas the Communist Party in Moscow focused on the aftermath of Chernobyl, the disaster itself developed regional dimensions: one region dealt with lingering radiation, while another region mobilized resources to prevent the development of nuclear energy in its backyard. For decades, the USSR in general and Ukraine in particular had been concerned about producing enough energy to satisfy the requirements of a modern industrial state and both were slowly placing a greater emphasis on nuclear energy.[56] Between 1980 and 1985, consumption of nuclear-generated electricity doubled.[57] Throughout Ukraine, nuclear power plants were being constructed or retrofitted just as Chernobyl exploded. In October 1987, the poorly lighted streets of Moscow were a symbol of reliance on nuclear power. There was not enough energy to go around when nuclear power plants were being retrofitted.[58]

The lack of electrical power did not diminish the social power associated with an anti-nuclear movement that protested the construction of nuclear power plants in Ukraine. Protests were staged at nuclear sites around Ukraine, but the most active were in the Crimean peninsula, where a nuclear power plant was already under construction. Activists recognized that the construction of a power plant had potentially disastrous consequences because of the seismological properties of the earth underneath it.[59] When residents experienced the earthquake in 1927, they worried that the peninsula would slip into the sea but not that the entire region would become uninhabitable through radiation. Activists were quiet during the initial building phases of the power plant (construction began in 1975), but after Chernobyl voices were raised about the appalling quality of the buildings.[60] A pitched battle ensued with the beleaguered director of the power plant. In May 1988, during the heart of perestroika, *Krymskii komsomolets* published articles questioning the viability of the power plant, and, by the winter of 1989, the newspaper regularly fought against centralized plans to raise electrical production through the use of nuclear energy.

In May 1988, Simferopol State University held a science symposium to discuss the construction of the Crimean nuclear power plant. Participants disagreed with each other, but almost all of them criticized the preparation prior to construction. Proper seismic tests had not been conducted, despite the area's active seismological profile: twenty-five earthquakes had occurred in the past year alone. Furthermore, commentators emphasized the critical role of the Crimean peninsula in the imagination of Soviet citizens: the region was not just the permanent home to 2 million people but also the holiday destination of 10 million more who travelled there to enjoy a unique ecological environment. With respect to its environmental properties, participants quoted Vladimir Lenin to the effect that the Crimean peninsula was a sanatorium and health spa for all Soviet people. Parallels were drawn between the growth of industry in the region and in the Ukrainian industrial heartland in the Donbass. These commentators wanted to preserve the Crimea (*Krym*) and not develop the Crimbass (*Krymbass*).[61] Many of these arguments would have been familiar to the officials trying to save the peninsula after the earthquake of 1927.

The other side had its say too. Officials associated with the construction of the power plant, who were under the auspices of the Soviet Union's Ministry of Atomic Energy, complained bitterly to the Central Committee of the Ukrainian Communist Party in Kyiv that the press was so biased against the power plant that it had become impossible for them to carry out work (which, even in the best cases, had been just slogging along). In June 1988, officials of the Crimean Atomic Energy Station (AES) wrote to the Central Committee in Moscow and to the Council of Ministers in Moscow and Kyiv about the campaign to close the station down and attempts to spread fear about another Chernobyl. They were particularly concerned that local communist organs were pursuing a policy of "silence," that local newspapers refused to publish the official point of view, and that the workers at the plant were being referred to as "mutants."[62]

A year later, the director of the Crimean AES presented the protests as an attack on the construction workers at the site who, unswayed by the protesters' propaganda, "regarded the reports as the usual attempt of informal organizations to employ any means possible to enflame unhealthy circumstances surrounding the atomic energy plant."[63] The inhabitants of Shchelkino, the workers' settlement nearby, wrote a letter to the first secretary of the Communist Party in Ukraine to complain about the inaccurate reporting and the exaggeration of the seismological conditions. According to this letter, the newspapers had reported that the settlement was in a dangerous seismological zone and that buildings had already been damaged. The damage, however, was an old story and was the result of the poor quality of the buildings rather than the shaking of the earth.[64] The damage may have come as a result of complacent construction crews, but construction problems were endemic.[65] The demands of "extremists" were unsettling the population of Shchelkino, which already had problems with unemployment as work had been effectively halted: with two thousand families waiting for housing, the situation was critical, and therefore a proposed referendum to decide the fate of the power plant was to be avoided at all costs: "the people are not ready for a referendum."[66]

In the same archival file, photographs accompany the above letter, their images depicting aspects of the power plant and having captions (written by a supporter of the power plant) on their flipside. One photograph shows a bus stop near the entrance of the power plant that has been defaced with the following slogan: "The Crimean Atomic Energy Plant is 30 Chernobyls on top of Spitak … Workers, at the price of a global catastrophe, you are receiving apartments and black money."[67] Another photograph depicts three or four women protesting on the side of the road, with the power plant in the back-

5.1 Protest on the side of the road, atomic energy plant visible in the background. The text on the banner reads: "Minatomenergo and foreigners get out of the Crimea! Trust Soviet scientists." The word "scientists" at the end is obscured. TsDAGO, f. 1, op. 32, d. 2583, l. 77.

ground. Their banner reads: "*Minatomenergo* [Ministry of Atomic Energy] and Foreigners. Get out of the Crimea! Trust Soviet scientists." On the back of the photograph, a supporter of the Crimean AES had written: "Believe your eyes and not the reports from the *Krymskii komsomolets*. The real picture of the 'many thousand ... ' picketers with the construction of the Crimean AES in the background."[68] This photograph was taken in August 1989, when massive pressure was mounting against the construction process and appeals to the upper echelons of the Ukrainian Communist Party in Kyiv were becoming increasingly ineffective.

The author of the caption on the reverse side of this photograph was not just dreaming. A vast construction site stands in the background, and the few individuals, who appear to be sweltering under the sun, do not look like an angry revolutionary mob about to storm either barricades or the construction site. These individuals were part of a much larger movement whose aims provide insight into the dynamics of public protest in Ukraine during the glasnost years.

The public activism of scientists in the Crimean peninsula was not a unique phenomenon. After the explosion, the government commissioned a report, but when it came time to submit it not all the participants were willing to sign because it had been rushed. Gennadii Shasharin (a power engineer), Boris Prushinskii (an expert in planning and operating nuclear power plants), and Armen Abagian (a physicist) withheld their names.[69] Vladimir Volkov, a scientific researcher at the Institute of Atomic Energy, wrote Gorbachev after he had been banned from his workplace for resubmitting a copy of the list of reservations he had expressed in the 1970s.[70] Most poignant was the fate of Valerii Legasov, who presented the results of the commission to the International Atomic Energy Agency in Vienna in August 1986. He grew increasingly disenchanted with the official bureaucracy and, as mentioned earlier, took his life on the second anniversary of the Chernobyl disaster. Thus, the protesters were quite correct to distinguish between a Soviet ministry and the work of Soviet scientists and engineers.

The slogan on the banner demonstrates the complexity of the movement. It speaks against a ministry based in Moscow and against foreigners who provided limited aid to Chernobyl (and who, by this time, were flooding into Armenia to assist with the earthquake rescue), yet it supports the scientists whose technology led to the debacle at Chernobyl. In his work on the Soviet intelligentsia, Vladislav Zubok writes: "In the aftermath of the Chernobyl tragedy, there was a public backlash against nuclear scientists ... scientists were now blamed for what they had been admired for just three decades earlier."[71] Although the banner does not identify a specific branch of science, it advances a fundamental trust in the Soviet scientific community, a community that did everything possible to stop the construction of the Crimean plant. One must bear in mind that the construction of the power plant was as much a geological as a nuclear issue.

These protesters were also clearly integrated into the debates that appeared in *Krymskii Komsomolets*. In this newspaper, contributors expressed their resentment that public opinion had not been gathered before deciding to place the plant in the Crimea; in 1989, the women in the above photograph gave voice to this. The photograph was taken once the discussion was well under way, so they already had the support of at least a year's worth of articles. In June 1988, *Krymskii Kom-*

somolets published a mini-questionnaire in which it asked residents to answer five questions about the construction of the AES: it received just over ten thousand answers with over thirty thousand signatures, almost all responses being against construction.[72] In September 1989, the paper ran another article against the power plant, situating a local meeting within broader political issues.[73] It published scores of articles that furthered the spirit of the banner.

The villains in these articles were not scientists (who continued to play a heroic role) but the bureaucracy and, in particular, the *Minatomenergo*. A cartoon from the summer of 1989 shows a bureaucrat from the *Minatomenergo* planting a bomb on the east side of the Crimean peninsula.[74] Singular voices were raised against *atomshchiki*, but faith was placed in the hands of local Soviet scientists who were engaged in a battle with Moscow.[75] In "The Crimean AES on the Scales of Seismologists," a journalist interviews scientists who had participated in a forum whose purpose was to discuss the power plant. He thanks the Crimean scientists for their efforts and welcomes the comments of a member of the UAS who referred to the construction project as a "crime."[76]

Interestingly, in this confrontation with the *Minatomenergo*, the defence of Soviet science comes in strange ways. Seismologists in the region were obviously worried that the plant was being built on unsteady territory, even though talk about the peninsula slipping into the sea was a bit over the top. A seismologist criticized the *Minatomenergo* for playing games when Soviet scientists had already evaluated the seismic properties of the area. Apparently, they dragged out the evaluation process by seeking more data from Western scientists with the hope that residents would be faced with a fait accompli – that is, a finished power plant (once the scientific data had been properly analyzed). As the seismologist noted, the Soviet scientists had the ability to perform tests independently.[77] In this scenario, the bureaucracy was the villain because it, not the people, had ceased to trust its own scientists. The women in the picture above most certainly would have agreed.

Seismology was more important in these discussions than was nuclear science because of the terrain in the Crimea and the recent incident in Armenia, where an atomic power plant had narrowly escaped an earthquake. About a month after the Armenian earthquake, *Krymskii komsomolets* reported that the decision to close the power plant had yet to be made but was imminent.[78] The reporting, however, did not simply focus on the role of public opinion in shutting down the power plant: it also expressed interest in helping the Armenians recover. Here the newspaper resorted to traditional Soviet language – the Crimeans were offering "brotherly help" to a neighbouring republic, mirroring much of the wording associated with Tashkent. Villages wrote about the fruit and vegetables they had collected or the funds they had donated from a day's work. A special correspondent had been sent to provide information about what equipment was needed.[79] Now in the middle of perestroika, the newspaper reflected the transitional mood in the Soviet Union. As it fought bitterly against Soviet policies from Moscow, it easily shifted voices and spoke in the reassuring tones of the Brezhnev period.

The protesters in the photograph belonged to the social and political circle represented in the articles in *Krymskii komsomolets*, but they also shared in the political currents of glasnost. By the summer of 1989, public organizations had emerged throughout the Ukrainian republic. Rukh (Movement), which was first announced in the spring of 1989 and had its founding congress in the fall of the same year, promoted the nationalist ideals of Ukrainians.[80] The Ukrainian Culturological Club had been active since the summer of 1987, and, on 26 April 1988, it organized a demonstration in Kyiv, with slogans such as "No More Chernobyls" and "Turn Ukraine into a Nuclear-Free Ukraine."[81] In late 1987, Green World (Zelenii svit) emerged and, while working together with other Ukrainian associations, concerned itself with the aftermath of Chernobyl and pushed for more state responsibility through vehicles such as referenda.[82] In the autumn of 1988, the human rights association Memorial organized in Ukraine, held its inaugural congress in March 1989, and focused on aspects of Stalinist repression in the area.[83] In May 1988, Ecology and Peace (Ekologiia i mir) was formed to protest the construction of the Crimean AES, and many contributors to *Krymskii komsomolets* were members of this organization.[84]

With so many political options available to the protesters in the photograph, it is difficult to categorize the direction of their dissatisfaction: Were they anti-communists, anti-bureaucrats, anti-Moscow, pro-Kyiv, or all or none of the above? Did they embody the classic Habermasian confrontation between state and society in a shifting public sphere?[85] The photograph will not provide a conclusive answer to these questions, but it pushes the discussion towards unexplored themes. For example, Ekologiia i mir, based in the predominantly

Russian city of Simferopol, could hardly be expected to be a flag bearer of Ukrainian nationalism. On the Crimean peninsula, protesters, unlike Ukrainian nationalists, had little interest in linking the Ukrainian famine of the early 1930s with the Chernobyl catastrophe.[86] Activists on the Crimean peninsula were fully integrated into discussions of Chernobyl, but they did not have a nationalist undercurrent and, therefore, Chernobyl meant something different to them than it did to Ukraine.

Activists in the Crimea may not have been nationalists, but there was a direct overlap between their interests and the interests of the UAS, an academy that bridged the particular interests in the Crimea and the continuing tragedy surrounding the thirty-kilometre zone. As a body of scientists, the UAS did extensive reports on the feasibility of future power plants throughout Ukraine. The UAS had extremely close ties to officials in Kyiv and exercised an enormous influence over Ukrainian energy policy just as Ukraine was moving towards independence. Both the UAS and the Communist Party in Ukraine pointed fingers at Soviet ministries, accusing them of being unable to guarantee safety at these plants.[87] In the winter of 1987, the UAS was already arguing that the economic advantages of nuclear power over thermal energy did not outweigh the potential dangers.[88]

In December 1988, the UAS presented an evaluation to the Central Committee of the Communist Party in Ukraine in which it analyzed the Soviet plan to expand the nuclear energy capacity of the republic until 2005. Not surprisingly, it did not offer its backing. The change of water levels in the Dnepr River was already having a negative effect on fishing and recreation in the area. As an alternative, the report suggested rethinking the entire economic basis of "previous years" to focus on the development of "high-technology, low-energy and ecologically clean" industry, as had been done in the United States, Japan, and West Germany over the last few decades.[89] These comments were a prelude to the more important assertion that nuclear power plants had not been built according to the codes established in the Soviet Union. Just like the Helsinki activists of the 1970s, who demanded that the Soviet Union adhere to its own Constitution, the scientists who wrote this report supported Soviet standards for locating nuclear power plants, but they listed cases in which guidelines had been ignored: the Rovno AES had been built in an active karst zone (karst, which is very unstable, forms when soluble rocks dissolve).[90] The Zaporizhzhia AES had been built too close to a populated settlement, and the Crimean AES was being built in a recreation zone that was not only of all-union significance but also tectonically active. Thus continued construction was "pointless." Finally, the miscalculations of the *Minatomenergo* in Moscow in its selection of construction sites had had a negative effect on local populations.[91]

Communists at the local and republican levels in Ukraine quickly recognized the worsening ecological situation.[92] In June 1989, the Central Committee in Ukraine wrote the Central Committee of the Communist Party of the Soviet Union, supporting the validity of the scientists' concerns and public opinion.[93] The Ukrainian side saw the benefits of increased electrical production but mentioned poor safety records, bad equipment, reactor stoppages, and contamination at waste sites.[94] The continued inability of the *Minatomenergo* to improve circumstances guaranteed the situation would continue to be alarming. It therefore made no sense to the Central Committee to consider increasing the capacity of existing plants, and an "unambiguous" decision had to be made about the "transformation [*pereprofilirovanie*] of the Crimean AES."[95]

A long chain links the women in the photograph to contributors to newspapers to the UAS to the Central Committee of the Communist Party of Ukraine. As a result of Gorbachev's policy of glasnost, public opinion was a much more powerful force than it had been in 1966 and effectively forced the state to stop construction of the Crimean AES, whereas it did not stop the bulldozers in Tashkent. However, public opinion was closely connected to state structures. So often the attack was against specific aspects of the state rather than against the state as a whole. The main villain from the Ukrainian perspective was the *Minatomenergo*. Communist Party members in the Crimea provided silent support for the protesters, and the Central Committee echoed the four women with their slogans, which it might well have written itself. Even in the heart of the crisis, no clear distinction between state and society emerged.

The focus on Crimean activists may appear to be a distraction, given the ongoing tragedy in the northern areas of Ukraine. The picketers and protesters did not have to worry about spreading radiation or eating contaminated foods. For, although Soviet engineers quickly contained the reactor within the sarcophagus, in and around the thirty-kilometre zone residents still had to deal with high radiation levels, relocation procedures, and a Soviet government that insisted on the continued production of energy at Chernobyl and, hence, had to find new housing for workers responsible for operating the three active reactors.

Now that our discussion of the Crimean protests has enabled us to see Chernobyl within a broader perspective, it is time to turn to the continuing tragedy surrounding the reactor and to indicate both where the recovery process displayed the hallmark of procedures dating from Tashkent and where perestroika had introduced new procedural issues. From the relocation of children to pioneer camps to the republican work crews that arrived to build the new workers' town to the increasing anger of local communist officials, the Chernobyl tragedy evoked volunteer and philanthropic efforts from individuals and newly formed organizations while the state was continually forced to renegotiate its position relative to the citizens it pretended to protect.

In Tashkent, the Brezhnev government advertized the efforts to send children to pioneer camps in Moscow and the Black Sea region, and individual republics pitched in to help these children recover emotionally. After Chernobyl, the same process occurred as children were being evacuated to escape potentially dangerous radiation. Thousands upon thousands of children were sent to pioneer camps, where the air was fresh and the trees free of dangerous isotopes.[96] Despite evident similarities between Tashkent and Chernobyl, two aspects of the latter response indicate shifting strategies.

First, the evacuation of children from Tashkent was presented as a fait accompli in the news in so far as they were expected to travel to the Black Sea. After Chernobyl, the evacuation of children was subject to negotiation and to refusal. In May 1986, the republic of Turkmenistan offered "its modest resources" to house 120 children at a children's camp near Ashgabat; there is no evidence the offer was accepted.[97] A month later, the Uzbek Republican Council of Tourism and Travel made an even more modest offer to accept thirty older children for fifteen days in Tashkent. The Ukrainians thanked the council for its generous offer but said they were getting along fine and would be in touch "if necessary."[98] Since the Crimean peninsula was in Ukraine, the bulk of Ukrainian children went to places within the Ukrainian republic and thus the republic did not need additional assistance.

Originally, the distribution of children had been designed to emphasize the friendship of peoples. In 1986, Ukrainians did not accept the friendship of the Central Asian republics, but, by 1990, they looked beyond their borders and designed a plan to send the children of Chernobyl to Cuba. The public goals of the mission had not changed, but now the evacuation of children had an international dimension. Two contributing factors made this possible. The situation in the Soviet republics had become so unstable that it made little sense to send children into areas whose political future was uncertain. By 1990, member republics were on the whole unwilling to accept evacuees in any circumstances. Kirgizia and Tadzhikistan had hundreds of thousands without work and were therefore reluctant to accept evacuees from Azerbaijan.[99] Second, the response in Armenia developed such an international dimension that, after the earthquake there, Soviet authorities began to think internationally about disaster response. This meant not only accepting aid from European and North American NGOs but also promoting communist values across the Atlantic.

Published photographs of weeping children and anxious parents on the eve of departure, reminiscent of Soviet strategies in Tashkent, highlighted a friendship with communist Cuba. However, both publicly and privately, these trips were highly controversial. Within the Komsomol, which was instrumental in organizing the trips, voices were raised against the extravagant plans: Why send children to a distant country that can barely take care of its own children? In 1986, officials had no interest in sending thirty children to Uzbekistan; but, in 1990 and 1991, they sent twenty-two hundred children to Cuba.[100] The volunteer association, the Union of Chernobyl, referred to the project as a form of "adventurism" that satisfied the "sensational goals" of individual bureaucrats and took attention away from more meaningful international cooperation.[101]

From the very beginning, financial issues were of public concern and organizers had to answer questions about the funding of a controversial project. They had to assure the public that the Komsomol was not pursuing political goals and that it had arranged creative ways to finance the trips. Because Ukrainian organizations had no money to pay for flights, the Cubans agreed to provide a chartered aircraft; since the children did not all return at the same time, they received help from Lufthansa and PanAm airlines.[102] These creative solutions were, however, just silent reminders that Cuban aid had its limits. While newspapers printed stories about Fidel Castro greeting the new arrivals, who received packages of tropical fruits, the Komsomol understood that, because of the "real economic situation" in Cuba, it had to offer technical assistance.[103] After an official delegation visited

Cuba in February 1991, it concluded that the Soviets had to provide technical supplies (cars, buses, computers) to their Spanish-speaking socialist comrades.[104]

The controversy had as much to do with the Komsomol as it did with moving children around. The Komsomol represented a youthful force in disaster situations, but it was struggling even more in Chernobyl than it had in Tashkent, where youths were easily distracted from their work and paid scant attention to their ideological education. Right after the Chernobyl explosion, one Komsomol leader ran away and another "shirked his duties."[105] These reactions were not unexpected as the Communist Party already had plenty of statistics that indicated how dangerous brigade work, never mind radioactive brigade work, could be. By the mid-1980s, the Communist Party had recognized that there were severe problems with student brigades. Organizers were manipulating funds, and the accident rate continued to increase owing to a lack of training. In 1985, the number of deadly accidents had risen in at least five republics, and collective drinking bouts were still widespread.[106] By 1987, the Communist Party knew that not enough was being done to ensure safety for youths at the worksite.[107]

These safety concerns were part of a broader problem – the mundane but tragic history of accidents in Ukraine. Chernobyl has gained most of the attention, but Ukrainians were also being killed on dangerous roads. In March 1989, a bus veered off the road in the region of Chernihiv, not far from Chernobyl, killing at least eighteen people.[108] Of course, this accident had no direct relation to what happened in Chernobyl, but such incidents did seep into the subconscious of residents. Later that year, children in a radiated area were put on a bus and sent to pioneer camps to recover. Rumours circulated that the bus was going to flip over, and this, not surprisingly, terrified the children. A Komsomol journalist dismissed the rumours, but the children's fears were obviously not unfounded.[109] The Komsomol had to deal with the safety of children and the safety of its own increasingly wary members.

These limitations notwithstanding, the Komsomol did produce constructive work and did take the time to evaluate its activities. The Ukrainian Komsomol reported that its brigades had built eight hundred rural homesteads and scores of cultural buildings. To the extent that its commitment to post-Chernobyl construction helped the Kyiv region, the brigades it sent to other parts of the country were incomplete.[110] Despite the positive accomplishments of the Komsomol, these brigades were often turned back at worksites. A Tiumen building company refused to accept one brigade because it had women members, and a kolkhoz in Arkhangelsk "categorically refused" to reinvite a brigade after one its members stole from the local population.[111] Brigades from Latvia and Azerbaijan were undisciplined and displayed a "self-seeking mood."[112] Unfortunately, this critical commentary foreshadowed later troubles. When the time came to rebuild Armenia in 1989, a local Komsomol commander struggled to attract youths to aid in this because the slogan "we do not need the Komsomol" (*ne treba nam komsomolu*) was making the rounds in his area.[113] The Komsomol represented a small proportion of the work crews, but its problems were amplified in the larger projects.

Slavutich became the poster child for the building problems that came in the wake of Chernobyl.[114] The Communist Party still envisioned a long future for the Chernobyl power plant, and workers needed a place to live since Pripyat had been evacuated and declared uninhabitable. By September 1986, the site for the new town had been decided upon, though concerns were raised about the radiation levels in the area (comparatively, the site had lower radiation levels than did other nearby areas). Although the site was deemed habitable, extra precautions (such as spraying water on the streets) were recommended.[115] When the construction plans were complete, planners foresaw a population of twenty thousand people in comfortable apartments by 1989. The accelerated tempo of construction caused its own problems as, despite the fledgling promise of perestroika, the party was still using a Five-Year Plan mentality.

Officials wanted to involve member republics in the enterprise and once again emphasized the friendship of peoples. Yet the tone was muted and the approach had been altered. The Central Committee in Moscow now made the invitation selective. Rather than requiring all member republics to make a contribution, only eight republics were asked to contribute.[116] Whereas in Ashgabat the Central Asian republics were critical to the response, they were not asked to help with the construction of Slavutich and they played a much diminished role throughout the recovery of Chernobyl. Their newspapers expressed sympathy and they raised money at schools and at work, but in Slavutich they were absent.[117] This absence meant they escaped blame when it became clear which republics were not filling their quotas.[118] Of course, the inability of the Armenians, Azerbaijanis, and local Ukrainians to complete their task was explained by their respective circumstances.[119]

The construction of Slavutich has parallels with other Soviet building projects and draws a little bit from each. When the work crews arrived from the eight participant republics, they found themselves in the heart of nature. Much like the builders of Magnitogorsk, their job was to transform a piece of nature into a beautiful new Soviet city.[120] Slavutich's role as an urban centre had a heightened importance. In contrast, Ukrainian construction crews took care of transporting villagers from Chernobyl's thirty-kilometre zone and resettling them in new villages, and thus, in this instance, the building process did not have a pan-Soviet flavour. While the external observer of Slavutich may have lamented the monotony of Soviet architectural design, building experts saw a blending of national architectural traditions and an overlap of methods.[121] In Tashkent, despite external appearances to the contrary, commentators welcomed the diversity of construction methods and the aesthetic beauty of a Muscovite touch.[122] This diversity notwithstanding, aerial overviews of Slavutich are strongly reminiscent of those of Sergeli, the satellite city constructed on the perimeter of Tashkent. Slavutich had the standard tall buildings in the downtown core, but it also had sections of detached cottages positioned on grid-like streets; 20 per cent of the city's dwellers were supposed to live in these cottages.[123]

The construction problems in Slavutich were immediately apparent to the public, yet, despite a confused construction process that suggested a weak Soviet state, the local population wanted the project to succeed.[124] *Tribuna energetika*, the voice of workers at the Chernobyl AES, published scathing condemnations of the construction process but did not give up hope that the "so-called city of the future" would be provided to its residents.[125] There were water supply problems, and project managers had ordered the incorrect length of piping, but a contest was announced to name the streets in the new city.[126] Alongside rumours about the suspicious behaviour of Armenians procuring cement for their construction sites were poems dedicated to the efforts of Georgians and Latvians.[127] In September 1988, a journalist wrote about the chaotic process of moving into apartment blocks that were not yet finished but, at the same time, presented an image of a happy young family in a comfortable new apartment.[128] Slavutich was not a tragedy for everyone, despite its difficulties.[129]

A different phenomenon was taking place in rural areas. If Soviet authorities wanted to erect the city of the future for employees of the Chernobyl AES, they really were not sure what they wanted for the peasants who were to be taken from the radioactive zones and resettled. From previous disasters, they had blueprints for urban areas and for small-scale evacuations premised upon an eventual return to former domiciles, but after the explosion, Soviet authorities displayed so little clarity and, indeed, so little interest that new settlements were built upon irradiated territory.[130] Instead of asserting central control, the state told local areas to accommodate evacuees by engaging in their own building projects. This was not a solution, and complex problems filled the void the state had left behind.

Because local communists were struggling to meet the needs of the resettled villagers, these rural projects were not presented as the heroic endeavours of Bolsheviks who could storm any fortress. They communicated with the Central Committee in Kyiv and wrote about their ever-diminishing standing in the community. To reach out to the public, local communists held town hall meetings to discuss the needs of their communities. Villagers complained that, in the evacuation process, housing was assigned to families and little consideration was given to groups of people who wished to resettle in the same place. In Narodich, residents wanted to travel with "work colleagues, family members, or neighbours."[131]

These requests became difficult to satisfy as individual regions were short on supplies and had become stingy about helping other regions. In the immediate aftermath of the catastrophe at Chernobyl, residents wrote letters to the Central Committee in Kyiv, but most of these went to regional communists. In Kyiv, letter writers carped about how they were being treated in other regions of Ukraine.[132] In 1988, the communists in Zhitomir oblast claimed they were not in a position to solve their own problems. They had appealed to other regions but had not received a positive answer.[133] The situation in Zhitomir in 1989 was critical because they were trying to relocate entire villages and neighbourhoods.[134] Communists in Luhansk were unable to complete their buildings and asked for help not from other republics but, rather, from other regions in Ukraine. This problem had already surfaced in the summer of 1986, when evacuees from the Chernobyl region complained that their hosts at the Zaporizhzhia AES were less than welcoming. The evacuees were told they were neither heroes nor exceptional because the Zaporizhzhia region itself was in critical mode. The evacuees were disheartened to learn that, in a city of forty-four thousand, only one resident was willing to offer them living space.[135]

Rather than improving, however, the situation deteriorated five years after the explosion, when regions openly refused assistance to each other. In 1990, the Cherkasy region asked not to be involved in external projects because it was struggling to house evacuees at home.[136] Outright rejections came soon after. In 1991, the Ministry of Construction in Kyiv, which recognized that it did not have sufficient resources to complete the housing projects on its own, reported that regional councils were refusing to continue their support. The Dnepropetrovsk regional council stopped assisting the Kyiv region, and their counterparts in the Kharkiv region ended their help to an area in the Zhitomir region. Officials in Kherson had divided building responsibilities among thirteen different enterprises, most of which never even started any construction.[137] Stubborn refusals came from areas in the southeastern parts of Ukraine – that is, those furthest from the catastrophe and with the largest Russian-speaking populations. If the friendship of peoples was starting to fray, so was the friendship of regions.

Contingent factors influenced these decisions. In the immediate aftermath of the explosion, southern areas were less affected than others and therefore had additional resources. Over time, however, they had to consider local building projects to house individuals who needed medical treatment after having volunteered in Chernobyl. In Donetsk, officials sought money to build an apartment block for liquidators who had been disabled due to their work at Chernobyl. The city council in Donetsk suggested the construction of this apartment block would be a good example of the Communist Party providing "charity to all" in this "complicated political situation."[138]

Yet the growing absenteeism, at both the republican and the regional levels, made such a policy increasingly difficult. Another conspicuous absentee during construction was the military. In Tashkent, the military had been responsible for Sergeli, but, in Slavutich, the construction was left to the eight republics. This is not to say the military played no role in the disaster response: its efforts were focused on the plant site itself and here it influenced all aspects of the recovery. Moreover, the military conscripted volunteers from across the Soviet Union to work in the particularly dangerous radioactive areas.[139] A military man from Uzbekistan knew where he was going when he received a call from the military recruitment office (*voenkomat*).[140] In Staryi Oskol in the western part of the RSFSR, the military appeared one evening at a young man's door and told him to be at the recruitment office the next morning at six. The military did not listen when he tried to explain that his wife and children were away at the moment, thus being denied what could possibly be a last goodbye.[141]

This behaviour may be considered typical for an authoritarian state in which the military enjoys privileged status, but it does not reflect the situation in toto. By 1990, the Ukrainian Central Committee heard grumbling from military personnel who complained that other republics were not releasing soldiers to help.[142] When this information was presented to the Soviet Ministry of Defence, it responded that it could do little because many republics categorically refused to send soldiers to the radioactive zone.[143] The refusal of other republics to send soldiers meant the contingents had to be found locally, thus draining the supply of reserves. As many of the local reserves came from rural areas in Ukraine, this had a negative impact on the rural economy.[144] Although the military had a much different task than did construction workers in Slavutich or in a small Ukrainian town, the fractured response from both republics and regions was similar.

Beyond seeking military assistance, the Communist Party in Kyiv wanted to reduce the time of duty for liquidators and properly regulate remuneration for this work. Complaints had surfaced about the inequity of pay scales as individuals doing the same work received more or less money depending upon the ministry in which they worked. In 1990, the communists had brought this to the attention of the Kremlin; it was the logical outcome of an incredibly complex reward system, which had caused problems in Tashkent as well. Whereas in Tashkent the financial privileges were designed to maintain house and home while a worker was away, in the case of Chernobyl, a whole slew of risk factors had to be taken into consideration. Consequently, no one quite knew what to expect, and dissatisfaction grew in unexpected places because the reward system was impossible to comprehend. When Valerii Legasov admitted, "it is true that they [volunteer workers] were paid high wages," he was only skimming the surface of a complex problem.[145]

Decoding the intricate details of the reward system would only add more confusion to an already difficult story, but the general parameters are worth exploring because they affect our understanding of volunteer work. Between the explosion itself and the collapse of the Soviet Union in 1991, three different situations required special privileges: (1) the salaries of liquidators who endangered their lives, (2) the further care of workers who had completed their task, and (3) compensation to villagers and residents who lived in the contaminated zone. These three situations often overlapped, thus further convoluting a politically precarious situation

The extra cash bonus in the first situation encouraged people to volunteer to go to Chernobyl, while it encouraged those who were conscripted to volunteer for the more dangerous tasks. In 1988, the Communist Party in Kyiv issued a fifteen-page booklet to explain the privilege system to managers working on-site.[146] The booklet was written in a question-and-answer format and outlined the circumstances in which double pay could become triple pay, the length of the work week, and the bonus for working on weekends and holidays (complaints had been made that workers were illegally forced to work on weekends). The structure was complex, but workers knew the financial advantages of volunteering.[147]

If the booklet explained circumstances surrounding pay scales, arguments arose about who was eligible to receive extra pay because each ministry or bureaucratic division treated its workers differently. In 1990 in Kyiv, there were major protests from bus drivers who threatened to strike if they did not receive adequate compensation. Drivers at the Makharovsk Motor Company (*Makharovskoe avtotransportnoe predpriiatie*) were upset after reading a *Pravda* article that reported that drivers on Kyiv's payroll had received pay and a half, whereas they had received nothing even though they had been involved with the evacuation of Pripyat.[148] They demanded financial compensation for work completed. They were less concerned with free health services for affected employees, even though bus companies were generally concerned with health issues.[149] An official from the Sumsk region reported that all liquidators shared the same hospital (*lechebnoe zavedenie*), talked with each other about health issues, and understood how their legal situations differed. This just "aggravated the problem."[150]

Other groups dissatisfied with the pay scales made recommendations of their own. Since the Soviet Union was not without precedent in offering rewards to workers, there were numerous models from which to draw. The Stakhanovites under Stalin received perks, egalitarian wage structures were abandoned in the 1930s, pensions for the spouse of a breadwinner who perished at work depended upon his or her salary, and a worker in the far north received compensation up to and beyond the normal salary.[151] Inhabitants in the district of Olevsk, concerned that their milk still had unacceptable radiation levels three years after the explosion, asked that they receive the same privileges as those who worked in the far north (the comparison could hardly have been comforting to someone working in the far north).[152] This suggestion had also been made at the oblast level, so it was floating around in the minds of local officials.[153] These requests were rejected, but they indicate the continued dissatisfaction with the reimbursement schemes.[154]

Regions made these requests because they could not understand why a liquidator from afar was eligible to receive additional pay but a local liquidator was not. In 1991, Belarusians indicated that "it was no secret" that workers who arrived in the zone received compensation for their risk, yet inhabitants were "often denied" such payments despite spending more time in the zone than anyone else because they lived there.[155] They proposed that geographic space and not human function should determine compensation, which should be calculated according to "the time spent in the Chernobyl disaster zone." Yet, since there was no real sense in which a resident of a contaminated area had actually "volunteered" anything, they were treated differently under the law.[156]

Military metaphors were never far from the surface in Soviet life, but the demand to equate the work done at Chernobyl with the defence of the western frontier in the Second World War was very real. The association "Workers of Chernobyl" argued that it should receive the same privileges, financial and otherwise, as veterans of the Great War of the Fatherland, which the government had apparently promised as early as 1986.[157] Unfortunately, this suggestion caused problems of its own. The Soviet Ministry of Defence was worried that the accumulated privileges of workers could exceed the privileges of war veterans and that, for "unfounded" reasons, these workers would then find themselves in a "better position" than the war veterans. The latter could protest this inequity, and then the pensions of disabled veterans would have to be raised. The ministry could not afford this in the economic landscape of late perestroika.[158]

These heated discussions about compensation or privileges came three to four years after the explosion, when the economic situation throughout the Soviet Union had reached a critical stage, when individuals who thought they had volunteered for a discrete stint were burdened with chronically bad health, and when rural areas were dealing with lingering radiation. In this atmosphere there grew the bitter feeling that the state had abandoned its volunteers.[159]

Of course, the definition of "volunteers" is ambiguous because volunteering combined a genuine concern for fellow citizens with the personal pursuit of fiscal advantages and public awards. The payment schemes belie any purely altruistic aspect of volunteering, but they should not belie the fact that citizens had free choices to make. Many volunteers performed their duties in the spirit of those who went to Tashkent in 1966. They had a vision of travelling great distances to support not just Soviet citizens but also regions in which they or their families had once lived (much like volunteers who went to Tashkent because it had housed evacuees during the Second World War). Nikolai Davydenko had been working in a mine in Norilsk but had family members in Ukraine and became one of the twelve thousand volunteers who went of their own free will to Chernobyl.[160] Davydenko's journey brought a resident from an area deep in the RSFSR to Ukraine and bridged the gap between two republics.

Volunteering was not simply an individual phenomenon as volunteer associations popped up in the middle of the perestroika years. After the collapse of the Soviet Union, the writings of Alexis de Tocqueville inspired historians and sociologists to seek the roots of civil society in volunteer activity and volunteer associations.[161] In this early nineteenth-century variant of civil society, volunteer associations are the best guarantee of maintaining democratic governance and of preventing the modern state from encroaching on the activities of citizens who are actively attempting to solve social and political problems on their own. Because of their efforts to challenge policy making in Moscow, volunteer associations such as Memorial and Ecology and Peace were emblematic of this trend. Memorial's explicit challenges to Soviet ideology and history placed it in a much stronger oppositional role than Ecology and Peace, which shared interests with quite a few statist organizations.

Another volunteer organization that sought to cooperate with the state was Soiuz "Chernobyl." According to its guidelines, it was "a public voluntary association uniting those citizens who had taken part in the liquidation of the consequences of the emergency [*avariia*] at the Chernobyl power plant."[162] Three years after the explosion, the association was formed to protect the interests of workers who were not receiving adequate treatment from the state. It was in an interesting position, however, because those who "volunteered" at Chernobyl could voluntarily become its members. It thus encompassed two levels of volunteering – the often but not always coercive sort promoted by the Communist Party and the less coercive variant that emerged within the accepted boundaries of perestroika and was embodied in these new model volunteer associations.

The atmosphere had become more permissive by 1989, but gaining official recognition for a volunteer organization remained difficult. The momentum to form such organizations was so strong that the Communist Party tried to delay approval of the requisite statutes, a tactic reminiscent of the tsarist regime. The Union of Chernobyl had met in May 1989, yet by December of that year it still complained that its statutes had not been approved by Kyiv.[163] The delays "denied" its members the opportunity to secure medical and social help. The Union of Workers of Chernobyl found itself in a similar position, and its statutes were only approved in May 1990.[164] Its goal was not, however, to promote strikes and "other political actions" that could destabilize society.[165] When miners went on a hunger strike in February 1990, A. Tyshkevich stressed his solidarity with their concerns but pleaded with them to redirect their energies in more productive directions.[166] Much like the statute of the Union of Chernobyl, the statute of the Union of Workers of Chernobyl envisioned close contacts with a state that still had to bear responsibility for, and find solutions to, major issues; within the framework of theories of civil society, these statutes left room for a strong, centralized state. In some cases, these associations pressured the state by cooperating with local state representatives, as was the case when they submitted common complaints to higher authorities.

Because of a general decrease in resources and because of serious concerns about the distribution of the few resources that were available, appeals to the state were becoming less effective. After the Tashkent earthquake in 1966, Gulistan complained about the allocation of resources to the Uzbek capital. With Chernobyl, a similar dynamic evolved as Belarusian commentators believed they were not only the most affected but also the most neglected; the Russians argued that, because they were less affected, they were totally neglected; and the Ukrainians wondered why compensation was better in Belarus than it was at home. And everyone wondered how Moscow would pay for all this. In the western borderlands of the RSFSR, activists were aware of the huge discrepancy between the money already given

Belarus and Ukraine and the funds received in the Briansk region. In neighbouring republics, maps indicating irradiated areas were hung openly on the streets; in the RSFSR, such maps were locked away in safes.[167] In January 1990, the Workers of Chernobyl noted the shortcomings of the Russian project and how it was scarcely at the level of the two other republics.[168] Since 70 per cent of the damage from the explosion had fallen on the Belarusian republic, it financed more building projects than did Ukraine. It rejected proposals for the amalgamation of duties across republics.[169] Criticisms about the distribution of resources also involved republics far from the radiation. According to one critic of the program, the Ukrainian Ministry of Health had been "throwing" resources at Armenia and Azerbaijan.[170]

These concerns were expressed when Gosplan SSSR (the state planning committee for the USSR) convened a commission in 1990 to develop a working plan to handle the consequences of the disaster from 1990 to 1995. The expert commission summoned to provide a general commentary on a draft of the project wrote that Gosplan SSSR was pretending that the road to recovery had progressed admirably, yet it had not developed plans to divide financing among the four bases of authority (the USSR, the RSFSR, Ukraine, and Belarus).[171] This was a difficult issue when the republics were pushing for more ministerial responsibility, which required greater financial resources from Moscow.[172]

Since the Soviet Union had no satisfactory solution, the individual republics stormed ahead with their own programs.[173] Belarus, Ukraine, the RSFSR, and the USSR had been working on laws that dealt with the defence of citizens who had suffered as a result of the Chernobyl catastrophe (originally, the Soviet project began with the word "accident," but this language was unsatisfactory to many).[174] The original Soviet project was problematic because Ukraine and Belarus already had advanced programs and were therefore critical and even suspicious of the Soviet law. Moreover, the plans in Ukraine and Belarus were known in other republics. Although thousands of kilometres from the radiation, officials in Uzbekistan knew what had been done in Belarus and Ukraine, and they wanted a stronger plan from Moscow to compensate for the lack of activity in Uzbekistan.[175] The extra efforts in the western republics made weaknesses in Moscow clear throughout the Soviet state.

The divergent plans from three core republics were inimical to the continued geographical integrity of the Soviet Union as four political interests were pulling in alternate directions.[176] In a letter to the newly elected Supreme Soviet, the highest law-making body in the Soviet Union, the Belarusians complained that the planned Soviet law to elucidate a general recovery plan was not based on the principle of taking responsibility for a crime (*delikt*) but, rather, just looked at the recovery cost and who was responsible for paying it.[177] The region of Gomel insisted that compensation be equal across the board and that it be paid by the Soviet Union and not the republics. If individual republics had the right to add extra privileges, this would only exacerbate a volatile social situation.[178] Ukrainians complained that the Soviet plans for the law did not "clearly" distinguish between the state and the republics with regard to spheres of activity, whereas the Ukrainian draft made absolutely certain to do so. Fundamental differences dug even deeper trenches: the Ukrainian draft foresaw the end of the operation of the power plant, whereas the Soviets envisioned it as an energy producer for the future.[179] Although a concrete project, such as building the sarcophagus around the remnants of the reactor, could be portrayed as a glorious Soviet achievement, little common ground was found in the recovery plans.

Commissions had been convened to make recommendations to overcome problems connected to lingering radiation. The commissions were not, however, the only ones with remedies and recipes. The atmosphere of glasnost had not only encouraged criticisms of party conventions but had also stimulated inventors and hobby scientists to enter the fray. A. Tyshkevich of the Union of Chernobyl wanted officials to "revive deserted villages" in unaffected regions.[180] This proposal is intriguing because so much has been made of Pripyat as an abandoned city that one easily forgets about other abandoned settlements scattered throughout the Soviet Union. To be sure, Pripyat was the largest but it was not unique. As the authors of *The Dead Zone* write, it is rather difficult to imagine how many towns in Russia shared the same fate as Pripyat: Iultin, Khalmer-Iu, and Kadykchan were also abandoned in recent years.[181] Less interested in cities, Tyshkevich advocates a kind of resettling program based on small human settlements. In Ukraine, the Central Committee received a proposal, based on pyschoenergy (*psikhoenergetika*), to reduce radiation with a special device placed upon helicopters.[182] The proposal arrived in the spring of 1990, and, in the spirit of late perestroika, the inventors supplied a business contract to be signed in case the Central Committee wanted to proceed. A member of the UAS reviewed the proposal and found no scientific basis for accepting it.[183]

Chernobyl was being discussed in the Supreme Soviet, but the Soviet Union still had no formal procedure for treating catastrophic emergencies. With each emergency, it convened its leading lights to solve the problem, but it lacked a bureaucratic arm with which to tackle the problem systematically. After the earthquake in Armenia in December 1988 and the gas explosion that killed hundreds of train passengers in Bashkiriia in June 1989, Muscovite authorities realized that these disasters were neither isolated nor infrequent. To coordinate the response, in 1989 the Soviets created a commission for extraordinary situations that later became known as the Ministry of Extraordinary Situations in the Russian Federation.[184] Shortly after its formation, the commission canvassed all Soviet republics and asked them to submit information about their major concerns. The responses were not unexpected: the Central Asian republics worried about earthquakes and the western republics worried about radiation and the future of nuclear power plants. In Uzbekistan, earthquakes had the potential to inflict "massive damage" on the civil and industrial infrastructure. In listing technical problems, Uzbekistan needed to improve building norms to ensure better safety and study the relationship between large water reservoirs and seismological activity. The situation had positive elements since it recognized progress in treating catastrophes in large cities (based on the example of the Tashkent earthquake in 1966) and seismological improvements made to the subway.[185] In Kazakhstan, earthquakes and avalanches were paired with emergencies at industrial sites.[186] In Belarus, beyond the danger of radiation, they had to consider train crashes as well as emergencies at chemical plants and gas pipelines.[187]

The belated decision to form such a commission indicated that the Communist Party finally recognized that previous efforts at combating disasters had been insufficient. The Soviet Union already had a civil defence (*Grazhdanskaia oborona*) whose task was to prepare civilians for extreme situations such as being subject to an attack using weapons of mass destruction.[188] The specific role of the civil defence was not entirely clear, although it did work with ministries such as the Ministry of Defence and it was active during natural disasters (it considered forest fires, floods, and earthquakes to be within its sphere of influence).[189] Clearly, however, the creation of the commission to treat extraordinary situations indicates that the civil defence was not sufficient and that, in dangerous situations, the Communist Party needed a more responsive managerial body. The Ministry of Extraordinary Situations did not replace civil defence, but it did offer a higher level of coordination and centralized response. Whereas an ad hoc committee led by I.T. Novikov immediately led the response in Tashkent, the Ministry of Extraordinary Situations tried to remove the spontaneity from the response to spontaneous disasters. The commission never had time to prove itself as the dissolution of the Soviet Union was just over the horizon, but its Russian variant played a critical, if highly criticized, role during the fires around Moscow in the summer of 2010.

In its attempt to reduce the haphazardness of the response, the Soviet state sought to incorporate an essentially disorderly natural phenomenon into an orderly bureaucracy. The move was supposed to reduce variables in citizens' lives and impose constraints on spontaneity. Outwardly this implied controlling events that transpired in both physical space and time. Thus, the Commission on Extraordinary Situations had a mandate to accelerate or decelerate events, depending upon the circumstances. Despite a central desire to order time, Chernobyl presented new challenges for, more often than not, time was not being measured on familiar clocks.

Time has always played an important role in the perception of accidents and disasters. In Ashgabat, the clock recording the exact time of the earthquake was significant, but the lived time of survivors was suppressed until, almost half a century later, perestroika allowed recollections to surface. In Tashkent, 5:23 a.m. became an iconic moment, frozen in photographs of clocks and repeated in accounts throughout the years. "Five twenty-three," an awkward noun, was not just a physical marker relative to human clocks but also a symbolic marker signifying the birth of a new city. At Chernobyl, time was and is no less important. On its website, the Chernobyl Union of Ukraine presents the time of the explosion down to the very second at which it occurred – 1:23:42.[190] Time, however, is not just a measurement but a series of relations.

Advocates of *Begriffsgeschichte* (the history of concepts) have encouraged historians to see descriptive terms within a broad social, cultural, and temporal frame.[191] A geographic term such as "Tashkent" is not just a place marker of geographic space, a convenient shorthand to denote a piece of land in Central Asia, but a holder of cultural imagery for those who employ it. In its turn, Chernobyl quickly became "a symbol that transcended the case of Chernobyl."[192] And if the name of a city can absorb all sorts of related imagery, it can also contain perceptions of time. In this regard, the words "Tashkent" and "Chernobyl" absorbed time in very different ways. After the earthquake, the word "Tashkent" became associated with rebirth and immanent resurrection, but it did not radically shift the measurement of time. The city moved forward with regular clocks and watches marking its reconstruction. In Tashkent, time could be easily visualized by showing clocks that stood still after the shock. This was not the case for Chernobyl.

Chernobyl embodied another time, a more haunting time, one that could not be easily measured. Radioactive elements were to last for generations and, with regard to certain isotopes, even for millions of years. The passage of time, normally marked by the rotation of seasons and the rites of life, had changed. In the region, scientists told residents that the body of a deceased individual who had inhaled hot radioactive particles would remain radioactive for "hundreds or thousands" of years. If the body were disinterred years later, anyone who inhaled the particles might die – the person may have died prematurely, but the lifespan of her or his body had been extended indefinitely.[193] Scientific time could measure the exact half-lives of specific isotopes, but, for residents, this was not a meaningful measurement as they had difficulty understanding how specific elements in a human body could transcend spiritual and even secular time.

Frédérick Lemarchand points out the ambiguous nature of time stored in objects in a post-Soviet museum in Minsk, Belarus. Cultural artefacts taken from the radiated zone were purified of radiation and then put on display for museum visitors.[194] The temporal context of the artifacts was thus thrown in doubt. They had been made in a pre-Soviet era, yet, because they were clearly identified as coming from the radiated zone, they belonged to the very near past. The exhibits therefore reflected time within two unique cultural frameworks that were nearly impossible to reconcile. Moreover, the extraction of the radiation could also be seen as the extraction of time. These artefacts will enjoy a future different from that of identical treasures left in the zone, which are still subject to the scientific time of a half-life. The objects in the museum were thus emptied of a critical component of historical time.

Historical time had always been important to the Communist Party. Time was an empirical entity that could be nudged, pushed, and accelerated into a radiant future: it had hands and arms that could be moved like those of a puppet as long as the Communist Party pulled the strings. Chernobyl certainly demonstrated the limits of party control, but it also threw time into the maelstrom. Time no longer had a specific direction, and if the time axis slipped from Communist Party control, the spatial axis could not be far behind. The puppet's strings had snapped. In fact, because it was no longer subject to control, time became meaningless.

During much of the response at Chernobyl, it almost appeared as though time actually had stood still. The catastrophe came very early during perestroika, but the regime approached it with the same tools as had its predecessors; in fact, in many ways, it was slower than its predecessors and less agile in manipulating the situation. After Tashkent, Brezhnev and his advisors orchestrated a media response that went well beyond the traditional Soviet silence. The strict laws about reporting on catastrophes were not broken, but energetic officials in Moscow and Tashkent prepared what might be considered a creative press release. After Chernobyl, there was no middle ground. At the beginning, the Gorbachev government said almost nothing and imposed the faceless silence for which the Soviets had become renowned. Time changed nothing until an overwhelmingly disgruntled public broke down the barricades and insisted on talking about the disaster.

Significantly, these public conversations came in many forms – nationalist, statist, and reformist. As the reality of a lasting catastrophe settled in, the USSR's republics had to defend their own interests, thus further adding to the disintegration of the Soviet Union. This involved centrifugal nationalist tendencies that had already been brewing, but it was also a jurisdictional matter concerned with finding the resources to rid the affected regions of the negative effects of the catastrophe.

The statist dimension of the response cannot be overlooked either. Despite evident disgruntlement, the idea persisted that only a great power could respond to such a disaster. The logic was awkward – only a great power could respond to the great disaster of its own creation – yet this notion has not faded. The clean-up was transformed into a massive engineering project, again reminiscent of engineering projects such as the dams the Soviets had built over the years. The only difference was that, instead of taming nature, the Soviets were now taming themselves. The soldiers and engineers involved in Chernobyl almost all had tragic ends, but they were portrayed with the same enthusiasm as were members of work brigades on the BAM railway or construction workers after the earthquake in Tashkent. Even in vastly different times, under new leadership, and with plans to reform, the Soviets fell back on an old formula that they believed had worked in the past.

The reformist movement was not simply anti-statist for the disaffected had nuanced opinions. Overwhelmingly, public opinion suggested something was deeply wrong with the system: the Communist Party had failed miserably but not all had been lost. As the women in the photograph discussed earlier indicate, dissatisfaction with a bureaucratic ministry need not be equated with dissatisfaction with Soviet science. These women did not want Chernobyl's problems solved by foreign intervention. In the Crimean peninsula, the most active and respected voices came from Soviet scientists – people much like others who had been educated in Soviet institutions. In this respect, activists in civil society had strong ties to the state that formed them. They had strong disagreements with the state and seized on the catastrophe to express their opinions in a way that had not been open to them before. This does not necessarily imply that these voices were anti-statist, even though they did not subscribe to the triumphalist Soviet portrayal of the accomplishments of the engineers.

Shortly thereafter, these debates about the future of nuclear power in the western areas of the Soviet Union became intertwined with another disaster – the 1988 Armenian earthquake. Just as Armenians were promising brotherly help to their stricken Ukrainian friends, the latter had to reciprocate and send goods to Armenia. The Armenian nuclear power plant fortunately resisted the earthquake and did not explode, but huge parts of Armenian territory were reduced to rubble. Although the Soviets continued to be preoccupied with the clean-up not just at Chernobyl but also throughout the contaminated areas of Ukraine, Belarus, and the Russian SFSR, it marched into Armenia with the same attitude it always had. This time, however, something had to give.

6

December 1988: Armenia

By the summer of 1988, the Chernobyl disaster was already two years old. After Chernobyl, the Central Committee and related ministries had refused to consider public opinion; to feed the energy needs of a powerful state, it wanted to forge ahead with plans that had been developed in the Brezhnev years. Yet the political and social situations were changing faster than officials in Moscow could grasp. Scientists and activists had had their first public meeting in the Crimean peninsula to mobilize opinion against the government's plan to finish construction of a nuclear power plant there. At the Chernobyl reactor, the sarcophagus had been built, but now Soviet authorities were dealing with public discontent at both republican and regional levels. The apparent success of the sarcophagus was overshadowed by the thousands of people who were living in radioactive environments, had precious few resources with which to purchase healthy food, and were applying political pressure on their increasingly vocal party representatives to petition central authorities for change.

Chernobyl, however, became just one of a series of problems. By 1988, the full weight of nationalist issues had come to the fore, the economy was stumbling, and, in the international arena, the Soviets had ceded ground to their American rivals. After she became a people's deputy of the USSR from the Zhitomir region in the spring of 1989, A.A. Iaroshinskaia observed that there was precious little time to speak about Chernobyl because representatives from around the Soviet Union sought empathy for and responses to specific crises – economic, national, natural, or otherwise. It was not that Gorbachev specifically wanted to hush up Chernobyl but, rather, that Chernobyl was swamped by problems that were the "sad results of seventy years of one-party rule."[1] A long queue was visible behind the microphone where delegates had an opportunity to voice their concerns. Another natural disaster supplied another challenge to an already overburdened state and dissatisfied population.

An earthquake on the southern periphery of the Soviet Union was hardly news, but the timing and the location inserted it into a highly contested social situation. In December 1988, the Armenian earthquake struck in a region where nationalist relations were at the breaking point. The Transcaucasian areas and Baku on the coast of the Caspian Sea were entangled in heated nationalist clashes that were proving too much for the Gorbachev regime to handle.[2] Soviet authorities were confronted with the dual problem of ethnic conflict and natural disaster. Internationally, the earthquake evolved into a news item. In contrast to Chernobyl, for which the Soviets were reluctant to accept international contributions, after the Armenian earthquake mass humanitarian aid was welcomed: this phenomenon has been referred to as the "fall of the humanitarian wall."[3] Finally, as Gorbachev discussed the response with his advisors in Moscow, conservatives mounted challenges to his reform program, leaching energy from the recovery.

Like previous chapters, this chapter emphasizes that natural disasters are not external events that suddenly strike a population but, rather, integral elements of long-standing socio-cultural patterns. Despite all the evident change and confusion, organizational shortcomings, and criticism of the quality of Soviet cement, the reconstruction of cities and the rehabilitation of people's lives moved forward. The heroism of previous rescue operations was absent, but, for years thereafter, the Soviet Union worked to overcome the 1988 Armenian earthquake. This earthquake brought with it issues that once again involved all levels of society. It was not just about housing in Armenia but also about housing refugees in Moscow and organizing fundraisers in Latvia. Different republics were having their relationships redefined as the earthquake forced continued interaction right up until the final demise of the Soviet Union. In this regard, the earthquake can be examined from three interesting perspectives. The first looks at the relief effort as a tool with which the Armenian authorities renegotiated their relationship with Moscow. The second explores how the earthquake affected other republics – not only as a positive force harnessed to independence movements but also as an economic burden in troubled times. The third perspective explores the fate of evacuees who, living in other areas of the Soviet Union, found themselves marginalized.

The initial Soviet response was remarkable because it more closely resembled the response to Tashkent than that to Chernobyl. Authorities believed they could mobilize the resources of a great state, rely on the friendship of peoples, and transform a tragedy into a public relations triumph. Donald Miller and Lorna Miller note the construction aid from Uzbekistan, a republic absent from Chernobyl. Azerbaijan, which had participated in Chernobyl and was almost at war with Armenia, was required to send construction crews. Unlike Chernobyl, where republics had been selectively invited to help, in Armenia, authorities were returning to an older formula. In essence, Soviet authorities continued to disconnect a natural tragedy from its human environment and were thus unable to integrate it into the broader set of experiences that conditioned the lives of the Armenians and Azerbaijanis who lived in the region.

What was new about the Armenian earthquake was the extent of foreign assistance. When looking at the scope of international aid in the city of Spitak, Miller and Miller present the statistics as though the Russian, Uzbek, and Estonian construction crews were part of international aid projects rather than the regular domestic assistance conducted in accordance with Soviet practices.[4] De jure, their assertion is misleading because the Russians, Uzbeks, and Estonians, unlike the Norwegians and the Swiss, participated because of directives from Moscow. De facto, their assertion is much more interesting. The traditional Soviet manner of dealing with disasters was still in effect, but it now dovetailed with foreign methods of assistance. The close proximity to these foreign workers exposed the basic tenets of heroic Soviet recoveries to an international audience. This interconnection between domestic and international assistance requires further exploration.

If the international community brought relief, the inter-ethnic composition of the region exacerbated a complex situation. Heightened national tensions influenced the response to the earthquake and drew it into a national struggle between two republics, Armenia and Azerbaijan, which were seeking more independence from the USSR and from each other. The first public struggles came about ten months before the earthquake, when Armenians living in Karabagh, an Armenian enclave within the republic of Azerbaijan, demonstrated in favour of union with Armenia.[5] Soon after the demonstrations, the Karabagh soviet voted to support the integration of Karabagh into Armenia.[6] Gorbachev wanted to keep the original borders intact, but he had no control over public reaction as thousands of people poured into the streets of Erevan to celebrate the decision of the Karabagh soviet.[7] The demonstrations had their effect in Azerbaijan as well, where crowds in Sumgait took to the streets and subjected Armenians to acts of violence, resulting in over thirty fatalities.[8] Gorbachev could not guarantee the safety of citizens, and, as much as he emphasized the multinational principles of the Soviet Union, he did nothing to temper the growing discord between these two nationalities. In some cases, local authorities abetted or even encouraged the violence.[9] When the Soviet government declared martial law in December 1988, the situation was close to untenable and only worsened with the earthquake. A year after the earthquake, in the midst of the recovery process, the Armenian Supreme Soviet announced that Karabagh had been reunified with Armenia, and soon thereafter the Armenian Soviet Socialist Republic became the Republic of Armenia. This was, of course, a time when the Supreme Soviet of the Soviet Union was undergoing major transformations in Moscow and setting out on a pseudo-democratic path.[10] None of these administrative declarations did anything to reduce tensions between the two nationalities. Nor did they reduce tensions in other areas of the Soviet Union as nationalist movements fed off of each other.[11]

Amidst these nationalist tensions emerged a conservative backlash to Gorbachev's attempts at political reform. Although Brezhnev had yet to secure his monopoly on power at the time of the Tashkent earthquake, no severe internal divisions threatened the unity of the Communist Party. Similarly, at the time of Chernobyl, the Communist Party confronted the tragedy as a unified force. The first cracks, however, were beginning to show months before the Armenian earthquake. In March 1988, *Sovetskaia Rossiia* published a letter nominally written by schoolteacher Nina Andreeva.[12] The letter contained positive words about Stalin and sharply criticized the pluralist and anti-socialist tendencies now manifest in Soviet society. While Andreeva worried about the youths she taught, high-ranking conservatives worried that they were losing social and political control. At the Nineteenth Party Congress in June 1988, conservatives voiced their disgust at the excesses of glasnost.

From Gorbachev's perspective, the Nineteenth Party Congress was a point of no return, a point at which the parameters of Soviet politics were irreversibly changed. New electoral procedures were introduced for party secretaries, the Central Committee apparatus was reorganized, and the platform for fundamental debate was extended.[13] While democratic observers welcomed them, these changes further destabilized the situation in the Soviet Union. Gorbachev had promised a reform platform, but his ability to steer it was challenged by social and regional groups that had little respect for institutional timing: they made their own decisions before Gorbachev had time to react. Gorbachev was so overwhelmed with a host of problems that "no one had any time to think, let alone rethink old assumptions."[14] And it was in the shadow of these altered circumstances that a natural catastrophe struck the heart of Armenia on 7 December 1988.

Unlike the early morning disasters in Ashgabat, Tashkent, and Chernobyl, the Armenian earthquake struck in the middle of the day. Shortly before noon, the earth shook approximately fifty kilometres to the northwest of Leninakan, the second largest city in Armenia.[15] The first shock, which registered 6.9 on the Richter scale, destroyed scores of villages, two major cities, and barely spared an atomic power plant.[16] Thousands of people across western Armenia died immediately or were trapped under heaps of rubble. As the days passed, it became increasingly difficult for rescue crews to find survivors. A chief Soviet spokesperson somewhat callously stated: "With every day the moans are decreasing."[17]

Because of the timing, the earthquake struck when men and women were at work, children at school, and housewives and the elderly at home. A teacher at a school in Leninakan remembered feeling the first "jolt" and then telling students to get out of the building. Four minutes later, a second shock with a 5.8 magnitude destroyed the school and ended the lives of the majority of students.[18] Leninakan, which had a population of approximately 300,000, lost about 75 per cent of its infrastructure.[19] In the immediate aftermath of the shocks help came not from institutions but, as is common in disasters, from the victims themselves.[20] A factory director from Spitak had been driving home at the moment of the earthquake, unsure of what had actually happened. When he entered Spitak and saw the horror, he got a truck and drove to Erevan. He returned with sixty young men who managed to remove ten students from under the rubble. So many individuals were driving from Erevan to Leninakan that there were traffic jams along the route.

One should be reluctant to quantify such emotional trauma. According to approximations, within ten days of the earthquake, twenty-five thousand were confirmed dead (though the actual toll was believed to be considerably higher), forty thousand had been extracted from the rubble, and about half a million were rendered homeless in cities and villages alike.[21] With respect to the nature of the damage, opinions diverge since Soviet reports emphasized the quality of the construction techniques used in their high-rises. Pierre Verluise writes that buildings erected both before and after 1950 were equally capable of protecting inhabitants. Low-lying buildings with proper masonry did as well as did recently built "prefabricated buildings of 9 to 16 stories."[22] These are not uncontested claims, but aerial photographs of Spitak certainly show a mixed survival pattern. In reality, the earthquake was so strong that it easily overwhelmed the most advanced engineering techniques.

While Spitak and Leninakan suffered extensive damage, Erevan (the capital) survived unharmed. Although Erevan was outside the earthquake zone it provides an example of the different tensions that pervaded Armenia at the time. On the night of 7 December, Yuri Rost, a Soviet photographer, flew from Moscow to Erevan. On the flight, he sensed the fear of travellers who had heard about the earthquake but who had few details about the personal fates of its victims. During the flight, the plane passed over the Armenian atomic power station and "people in the window seats looked down apprehensively." Fortunately, "it looked undamaged" – an observation that would turn out to be correct.[23]

In the city of Erevan, Rost saw "no sign of the earthquake."[24] The city had been spared a natural disaster, but it had its own political tensions. Rost was struck by the armoured vehicles on streets that were completely abandoned at night – an unlikely scenario in the aftermath of an earthquake. Despite the apparent calm, Erevan, as Armenia's capital, had to deal immediately with rescue operations in the disaster zone as well as with military operations concerned with nationalist conflicts. At the airport, Rost had been struck by the continuous flow of helicopters returning from Spitak with dead and mutilated bodies.[25] Despite appearances, Erevan was not at rest.

At that moment, the Soviet leader was in New York City preparing to give a speech to the United Nations and to establish the framework for a dialogue with the recently elected Bush administration. Even if he was aware of the Armenians protesting near his quarters, he hardly could have expected that he would shortly be heading to Armenia. His speech at the United Nations came after the earthquake, but he had to end his trip to the United States prematurely and cancel visits to Cuba and Britain.[26] Whereas in New York City he had been met with much fanfare, his reception in Armenia quickly became embroiled in ethnic, regional, and Soviet politics.

When Brezhnev arrived in Tashkent in 1966, he arrived together with Kosygin and gave a resounding speech in the heart of town. Since the Armenian earthquake struck a large geographic area, Gorbachev did not arrive in a central location, where he could follow Soviet practice and promise the reconstruction of whatever had been destroyed; rather, he had to travel between cities and to evaluate each situation on its own. Nikolai Ryzhkov, the head of the Soviet Council of Ministers, had arrived before Mikhail and Raisa Gorbachev had a chance to cross the Atlantic. Upon the arrival of the Soviet leader, Ryzhkov had to convince Gorbachev's entourage to forego his limousine and ride in a red Ikarus bus.[27] Adding to the complexity of the situation, the relief effort was already experiencing problems. A military plane on a relief mission crashed, killing seventy-eight people.[28] Within twenty-four hours of the first crash, a Yugoslav Air Force plane crashed in the congested Erevan airport.[29] Because they had passed over Turkey and Azerbaijan, rumours quickly spread that the planes had been sabotaged (an additional rumour suggested that Russians had conducted an underground atomic explosion to provoke the earthquake).[30]

Rather than give a speech from a podium, Gorbachev mingled freely with crowds to express his sympathies. These meetings were not, however, without tension as the tragedy never succeeded in erasing ongoing ethnic struggles or the knowledge that, earlier that same year, Gorbachev had failed to support the union of Karabagh and Armenia. Along his route, he met protesters who wanted to debate the future of the Karabagh region. In the capital of Armenia, scores of protesters were in the streets and clashed with Soviet troops. In an evening news program, Gorbachev vented his frustrations, asking: "To behave like this at such a time – what sort of morals do these people have?" Gorbachev also accused the Karabagh Committee of linking rescue help with its nationalist program.[31] The nationalist sentiment in Armenia was not the only problem as residents had, in general, lost trust in the Soviet government. The evacuation of children had been standard practice since at least the time of the Ashgabat earthquake, but such evacuation was now being looked upon as a form of abduction. A women's committee was formed to oversee the movement of orphans because there was a fear that the children would be separated from their homeland. Stunned, Gorbachev asked whether they thought the Soviets were going to "deport the Armenians to Siberia."[32] At the same time, the streets in Baku were filling with people. Crowds of youths in Baku proclaimed that the earthquake was Allah's punishment of the Armenian people.[33] No wonder Gorbachev was worried that the country was heading into an abyss.[34]

The immediate Soviet reaction to the earthquake indicated that little or nothing had been done to reform the disaster response system. The Soviet Union still insisted on bringing in work crews from other republics and ran into the problems already evident in 1966, when there was less at stake. With national conflicts erupting throughout the Soviet Union, it seemed foolish to appeal to the friendship of peoples. Yet, as though nothing had changed, the Soviets set up an ad hoc commission to deal with the earthquake and distributed exact construction numbers to various republics and ministries. In the old days, Soviet authorities published healthy percentages that showed how far the plan had exceeded expectations; now, they faced the embarrassing fact that Armenian print media were publishing percentages that did not come close to meeting the 100 per cent mark. Internally, the Soviet commission received disappointing statistics about the number of workers who had even bothered to make the journey. Whereas the plan called for about twenty-four hundred workers from Uzbekistan, only five hundred had appeared in Spitak; in Leninakan, less than 60 per cent of the planned Ukrainian contingent was on site.[35]

The lack of commitment was more than numerical as each republic had its own reasons for shirking its duties. In many cases, the local republics cited the incompetency of Armenians and their inability to establish construction parameters. In the summer of 1989, the leadership in Moscow asked that the republics explain why the reconstruction process was just crawling along. The Ukrainians complained about delays at the republic and union levels. Because no housing had been supplied for their workers in Leninakan, they could not send more people.[36]

Under these circumstances, the friendship of peoples was placed under significant strain. For instance, the Armenians had asked a Ukrainian construction company to increase the size of a building for the pedagogical institute in Kirovakan at the same time as the

Ukrainians were struggling to complete their original commitment. Not only did the Ukrainians have added pressures at home, but they also had to "help" with construction projects in West Siberia and the non-black soil zones of the RSFSR.[37] On site, the Ukrainians had to deal with supply shortages that left them idle for hours and had to wait a "criminally" long time for the Armenians to approve building sites for construction. Because of the delays, workers returned home before construction had been finished, and, after six months, the turnover rate hovered at around 60 per cent.[38] Projects were begun by one crew and finished by another.

When the Armenians complained in the spring of 1990 that the Ukrainians had not delivered enough meat to their meat-processing units, leaving thousands of workers with nothing to do, the Ukrainians responded that many transporters had refused to travel to the dangerous Transcaucasian republics and that, while they would try to improve delivery, nothing could be guaranteed.[39] By the summer of 1990, the Ukrainians were ready to pull out because the situation had become too chaotic. Ukraine had asked Armenia to bring order to its railways and its domestic situation but nothing had been done. Wagons carrying construction materials were being "seized" en route and arrived at their destinations "empty." Workers refused to go to Armenia because the situation there was too dangerous.[40] Ukraine had also been asked to find housing for Soviet citizens who were arriving not only from the earthquake-affected areas in Armenia but also from Azerbaijan, where the ethnic situation had become untenable. The Zaporizhzhia region reported that it had some room in empty and dilapidated homes for evacuees from Azerbaijan but that much of the space had already been taken up by earthquake evacuees.[41] Other regions refused evacuees from the Transcaucasian areas because they had already made space for evacuees from Chernobyl, which was much closer to home.[42] Much as in Tashkent, the state had set decadal quotas of evacuees for each region to house, even though many regions ended up refusing to do so. And, also as in Tashkent, numerous evacuees refused to resettle in rural areas.[43]

The Georgians complained about being shuffled from one construction site to another, and the Belarusians complained about standing around because the supplies could not be delivered as a result of the train blockade in Azerbaijan. The authorities in Tadjikistan claimed that, because they had not been receiving sufficient resources to recover from a deadly earthquake in their own republic, they were

6.1 A photo collage suggesting harmonious aid from Ukraine: "Sturdy buildings grow." Published in *Molod' Ukraini*, 12 December 1989.

experiencing extreme difficulties providing help at home, let alone in Armenia.[44] Of course, the strains were not just emerging along national lines: bureaucrats were also reluctant to extend aid. The Ministry of Agriculture (*Gosagroprom*) in the RSFSR insisted on limiting its aid to rural areas and did not want to get involved in Kirovakan.[45]

Various authorities protested the circumstances most vociferously. The city of Moscow, which typically sent its own contingent in times of need, complained that the Armenians refused to deliver construction materials.[46] More pointedly, questions were raised about Moscow's role as a "staging post" for refugees: Why did thousands of Russians have to work in the earthquake zone when Armenian evacuees had no work? Russia had a big heart and happily shared what it had with those in need, but were these "sacrifices" always necessary?[47] These last comments came in February 1990, when the Armenian Supreme Soviet had already taken steps to augment its legal power vis-à-vis the Kremlin and just before the Baltic state passed laws proclaiming Latvian, Lithuanian, and Estonian as the official languages of Latvia, Lithuania, and Estonia, respectively.[48] Thus Muscovite reluctance contained more than just a tinge of the Russian nationalism that was emerging at this time.[49]

The decision to send Azerbaijani work crews was also questionable. In the summer of 1989, Azerbaijanis not only grumbled that the Armenians were slow to organize construction opportunities for them but also fumed about a worsening situation in which local Soviet and law-enforcement organs were "enflaming" tensions between nationalities (Azerbaijani workers had been attacked and their equipment damaged). Since Armenian authorities could not guarantee the safety of these workers, many of the latter simply returned home.[50] Insisting on having all member republics provide support only aggravated an increasingly fragile ethnic equilibrium. Furthermore, Gorbachev's promise to rebuild Armenia in two years, with republican and ministerial construction crews, made it much easier for critics to highlight the weaknesses of the Soviet state.

Naturally, Armenians did not simply agree with these accusations. In correspondence with Moscow and in local newspapers, they lamented the lack of support they had received. By the summer of 1989, they expressed to the Council of Ministers their dissatisfaction with almost all the republics. According to their records, Turkmenistan had completed 12 per cent of its projects, Latvia 15 per cent, and Georgia 13 per cent.[51] In March 1989, the Armenian youth newspaper reported that the work of the Kazakh work crews had come to a standstill.[52] A month later the newspaper had to allay fears that the construction workers would be living in the buildings they erected. It told readers that the workers were only in Armenia "on business" (*v komandirovke*) and would return home once their work had been completed.[53] Not surprisingly, Armenians were unwilling to speak positively about the assistance received from Azerbaijan. One community refused to accept food aid from Azerbaijani authorities because it feared it might contain poison. Nor did Armenians want financial aid because they figured such aid had once belonged to their "murdered compatriots in Sumgait and other parts of Azerbaijan."[54] The train blockade that prevented construction goods and other materials necessary for the aid program certainly poisoned the atmosphere, but Armenians also complained about Azerbaijani attempts to sabotage their construction work. Azerbaijan had lowered the wages of its workers to such an extent that most of the qualified ones had picked up and left.[55] This explanation differs substantially from the Azerbaijani explanation presented above, but the actual circumstances are not at issue here. What it is important to realize is that the issues between and among these republican building crews inexorably drew two Soviet "friends" into conflict.

And what began poorly did not end any better. In the early winter of 1990, the party secretary from the Gugarsk region wrote an open letter to Gorbachev and Ryzhkov stating that people were losing faith in the rebuilding process. The letter was carefully couched in traditional Soviet language, with references to "indestructible" friendship and emphasizing that the blame for the disastrous circumstances should be placed on bureaucrats and not on the Russian people. But the tone was despairing. No one had expected that the reconstruction decree emanating from the Communist Party in Moscow would be treated as a "recommendation" and not as an order.[56] By the fall of 1990, the Council of Ministers in Armenia informed Ryzhkov in Moscow that, although only 10 per cent of the building projects had been completed, the republics "refused to continue work in Armenia" as long as they had to spend their own capital.[57] Republican levels of government and their official construction crews had a hard time fulfilling Gorbachev's wish to complete the reconstruction within twenty-four months, and most of the republics quickly lost interest in doing so as they tended to their own concerns.

Aid was not limited to rebuilding projects and arrived in other forms. Newspapers around the Soviet Union gave cautious assessments of the recovery. In the days after the earthquake, *Pravda* stepped into action with headlines that often contained words such as "brothers" or "brotherhood." The articles listed the sympathies and aid that was being collected throughout the Soviet Union. Tashkent, Baku, Dushanbe, and Vladivostok contributed medication or foodstuffs.[58] This aid was promised in the form of supplies, money, and local work. *Pravda*'s commentaries did not mention the national conflict in Azerbaijan and differed little from what they had been in 1966.

A group of student volunteers had travelled from Sverdlovsk (now Ekaterinburg) in the Urals with an eye to helping. When they arrived, they were told that construction would get along well enough without them because the worksite needed "specialists and not enthusiasts." Despite this criticism, they reported that they eventually provided effective aid.[59] Armenian student brigades were forming in the spring of 1989, and many wanted to volunteer with the reconstruction; finally, "the word 'volunteer'... could actually be pronounced without any subtext."[60] In yet another form of aid, Armenian children were evacuated to the Albatross pioneer camp in Latvia, where they played games and listened to songs. After Tashkent, children had been sent to pioneer camps where they listened to traditional national songs; now, after Armenia, they were listening to Latvian national songs and learning about Latvian history, and this was politically explosive. When teaching the children about the activities of the Latvian-Armenian Society, the notion of independence could not have been far from teachers' minds.[61] In Riga, artists donated sculptures and paintings for an auction, the proceeds of which were to benefit the children of Armenia.[62] This aid was voluntary and clearly political.

Not all aid was on such a scale. In a way reminiscent of past catastrophes, individuals and organizations wrote letters to newspapers or approached party officials offering various forms of philanthropy. A ninety-six-year-old woman wrote Gorbachev that she had space in her apartment to house orphaned children (at about the same time, *Pravda* was trying to dispel rumours that children being sent outside the boundaries of Armenia would not be allowed to return).[63] A soldier wrote Marshal Iazov asking to be sent to Armenia.[64] Schoolchildren in Grade 10 in Nizhnekamsk wrote Nikolai Ryzhkov in Moscow to tell him they had space for schoolchildren who had lost their homes.[65] The Crimea Philharmonic Orchestra wrote the party secretary in Armenia and offered the proceeds of a charity concert.[66] Soviet authorities portrayed these efforts as exemplary of the unity of the Soviet people.

In the transitional atmosphere of 1988, volunteer and charitable activity has to be qualified: How much of this charitable activity can be considered constituent of civil society? The Crimea Philharmonic Orchestra voluntarily raised money, but it was still a state philharmonic orchestra transferring funds to state officials in Armenia. Individuals freely offered money but had no necessary connection with associational life, and the giving patterns were those typically found within the authoritarian context of Soviet life. The art auction in Riga had weaker ties to the state and was more closely linked to political ambitions. Similarly, the Latvian pioneer camp saw charitable activity intersect with separatist political tendencies. Activity in the pioneer camp was not a subtle form of civil society, such as the one presented in Robert Putnam's *Bowling Alone*, in which superficially innocent associations exert pressure on a wider web of political decisions.[67] If the act of volunteering is constituent of civil society, then all the above activities can be qualified as belonging to the realm of civil society. If civil society requires explicit rather than implicit political activity, then only the Latvian case receives its membership card.

Despite all the volunteer work, the Soviets struggled to rebuild Armenia from within and to find housing for evacuees. This effort compounded an existing problem as Armenians and Azerbaijanis had started to flee the southern regions before the earthquake: thousands of people were already in motion. Azerbaijanis complained that they had been mishandled in their native villages, Armenians complained about their living conditions in Moscow, and Muscovites wanted the evacuees to find housing elsewhere in the RSFSR.

In the village of Saral in the Spitak region, Azerbaijanis submitted a community petition to the Kremlin in which they claimed that they had been forcefully evacuated, both before and after the earthquake, from their native habitat. Furthermore, the villagers resented the absence of aid after the tragedy. They had been denied the aid that everyone was supposed to receive because, as they were told, they had voluntarily swapped homes with a village on the Azerbaijani side and thus had no claims to make.[68] After the earthquake, they were repeatedly told that, because they had left prior to the earthquake, they would not receive compensation for moveable property.[69] According to these villagers, a fraction of the residents had left the village before the earthquake because they received "active" help from party officials. Fewer than ten days before the earthquake, villagers were forced onto buses and driven away, only to be met en route by Armenian bandits who attacked the bus. These villagers no longer had the impression that they were living in a great socialist state; rather, it felt more like a frontier *kishlak* in Afghanistan.

Marc Elie has taken a closer look at the case of Saral and focuses on a number of important themes. First, the very fact that Saral was a village meant that it was marginalized in an official recovery story that had cities in mind.[70] Second, the displacement of people due to the earthquake was not a singular event but part of a long drawn out process in which Azerbaijanis moved out of Armenia and Armenians moved out of Azerbaijan: this evacuation, and behaviour in general, was not simply a function of the natural disaster.[71] Finally, Elie makes the point that the earthquake exposed the vulnerability of minority groups and thus presented an opportunity that could be exploited; officials manipulated the indemnification of these villagers and redirected funds that otherwise could have helped with the reconstruction. These thoughts lead back to those disaster theorists who stress vulnerability at times of disasters.[72] Migrants had difficulties because they had lived as Azerbaijanis on Armenian soil.

The Armenians who were evacuated to the RSFSR and beyond could escape the earthquake, but their new living arrangements were less than satisfactory. In 1990, the Armenian Council of Ministers reported that over three hundred people were sleeping in the corridors of the Armenian offices in Moscow. Many were evacuees fleeing ethnic tensions in Baku, but it quickly became difficult to distinguish between the two types of refugees.

Reports about the evacuees from Azerbaijan did not specifically address the earthquake evacuees, but, in evaluating the evacuee problem, they touched upon inadequacies that were reminiscent of what had happened in Tashkent. The central authorities assigned specific numbers (in this case, multiples of five) to Soviet ministries, who were then supposed to find housing for the evacuees they had been assigned.[73] In their turn, the ministries discovered that the evacuees preferred to be in Moscow or the Moscow region and refused to go elsewhere.[74] They were insulted by the notion that city dwellers should be resettled in rural areas.[75] The Kremlin had expressed its willingness to resettle these earthquake victims but, as was the case in Tashkent, had already made it clear that it did not want the evacuees in the Soviet or former Imperial capital.[76] A high concentration of evacuees in Moscow would have political consequences. In January 1990, evacuees in Moscow were becoming impatient and organized unsanctioned meetings. Officials believed this could have been avoided if the evacuees had been allocated to distant cities.[77] Ministries who had been assigned evacuees were also responsible for finding them employment, certainly an unenviable task in the perestroika period. Yet the "overwhelming majority" of evacuees turned down the jobs that were offered to them.[78] This pattern echoes the situation during the Tashkent earthquake, when evacuees selectively accepted or rejected the help that was offered to them.

The reluctance of member republics to aid in reconstruction or to house evacuees was to a degree welcome in Armenia because the isolation of Armenians served its agenda of gaining greater independence. Armenian authorities were not slow to exploit this opportunity and were soon submitting reports to Moscow arguing that the earthquake had had such a devastating economic effect on the region that the structure of the economy would have to be entirely rethought. The answers lay not within the Soviet Union but beyond its borders, where an Armenian diaspora had better resources to finance the recovery and put Armenia's economy on a new footing. Importantly, Armenians were not just asking the diaspora for donations; rather, they wanted it to restructure how money flowed in and out of the country. In a carefully worded report to Ryzhkov in Moscow, the Armenian academician A.G. Aganbegian and the Armenian people's deputy Galina Vasil'evna Starovoitova (born in Cheliabinsk in the RSFSR) argued that, after the Soviet state had provided such huge amounts of financial aid to Armenia, Armenians could hardly expect more state funds at the expense of other republics.[79] Since Armenia had to find its own solutions, it required new investment mechanisms. Rather than giving "straight aid to the suffering regions," Aganbegian and Starovoitova wanted the Armenian diaspora to lease land and to establish vacation locales and other businesses. Ideally, Armenia would be transformed into a "zone of free enterprise." The report also envisions transforming the airport in Erevan into an international airport, with flights from all over the world (not just Los Angeles, as was already the case).[80] The earthquake was surely no small inspiration since the "entire world" had arrived at the airport in the form of aid workers.[81] This system would work most effectively if Armenia's Ministry of Foreign Affairs had its authority increased. If it had its own representation abroad and had the authority to issue visas, it could facilitate foreign investment.[82] This increased investment would require the complete modernization of Armenia's transportation infrastructure.[83] Armenians, much like Ukrainians after Chernobyl, wanted to shift their entire economy. The earthquake had ruined a significant portion of the industrial sector, but it made little sense to rebuild heavy industry; rather, Aganbegian and Starovoitova wanted to focus on light industry (the argument was not purely economic for, since Chernobyl, a greater awareness of ecological factors had been developing).[84] These original demands were put forth in 1989, and Armenia continued to press the issue. In 1990, the Central Committee in Erevan listed obstacles to these plans: the ruble was not a convertible currency, foreign investment required too much coordination of bureaucratic organs, and foreign investors had no guarantees.[85]

These requests leveraged the earthquake to pull Erevan away from Moscow, yet there was a degree of overlap with Muscovite interests. As a result of perestroika and the upheavals throughout the empire, Moscow was considering new economic directions for the entire Soviet Union. Plans were under way to enable the republics to be more self-administrating and self-financing. Yet reforming, or what really amounted to dismantling, an entire economic system was not unproblematic. Officials worried that if Armenia received special tariffs for the import of foreign goods, then the Soviet Union would cease to be a federation and a unified economic zone.[86] The Ministry of Foreign Economic Relations worried that, without internal tariffs between the republics, it made no sense for Armenia to have special tariffs of its own.[87] In addition to these reservations, the head of the newly created Commission of Extraordinary Situations did not believe that Armenia could emerge from the crisis on its own. This view presupposed the increasingly anachronistic notion that help would come from within and not from without.[88] The Soviet ministries' reservations, if not outright opposition to the Armenian recovery plans, were expected with the influx of international assistance that started to pour in almost immediately after the tragedy.

The first announcement in *Pravda* celebrated the willingness of Cubans to send aid workers from the "island of freedom," the same island that later opened its arms to the children of Chernobyl.[89] Yet the Cuban effort was quickly overshadowed by the relief plans coming from Western countries. Even *Pravda* reported the successful fundraising efforts of the British.[90] On the one hand, officially the aid was presented as a fundamental new direction in international relations;[91] on the other hand, publicists used the aid as a foil to expose the poor Soviet relief efforts.[92]

International relief efforts were essential but not unproblematic. Norway sent housing to provide shelter for Norwegian workers who were constructing a hospital in Spitak, but it discovered that the housing had been reassigned to Leninakan.[93] In addition to financial help, the Milanese Merchants Union had sent equipment to help bake bread and provide food. The Italian Embassy had to intervene in December 1989, when it was discovered that, although the ovens had been delivered, they were lying unused and exposed to adverse climatic conditions. The Italian Embassy asked the Soviet authorities to contact Armenian authorities, not understanding how little influence the Muscovites could exert.[94]

British aid demonstrated the close links between humanitarian action and political policy. In 1990, Margaret Thatcher visited the Soviet Union and planned a stop at Lord Byron School in Leninakan, a school that had been built as a gift from the British. Thatcher upset the desired image of a Soviet leader rushing to the scene of a disaster to solve problems in front of adoring crowds. When she arrived throngs of peoples welcomed her but took advantage of her visit to display banners that, among other things, protested the slow Soviet response.[95] She also upset traditional naming practices. Leninakan, which would soon be renamed Gyumri, had already been renamed after the first Soviet leader. After the British prime minister's visit, a street in this city was redesignated to bear her name.

Beyond providing resources, international aid revitalized an important Soviet public association – the Soviet Red Cross and Red Crescent. Ironically, the Soviet insistence upon maintaining public associations that were nevertheless dominated by state institutions in Moscow ensured that the Soviet Red Cross had a functional organizational structure and that, once the opportunity availed itself, it could quickly be integrated into the activities of the International Red Cross. The Soviet Red Cross played a role at Chernobyl, but it truly revived its activities in Armenia. Thereafter, it became heavily involved in the aftermath of Chernobyl, with the train accident in Bashkiriia, and with an earthquake in Tadjikistan in January 1989. For the first time since the 1920s, the Soviet Red Cross cooperated with its international counterparts and subjected itself to international scrutiny.

Members of the International Red Cross arrived in Armenia to assist and evaluate the effectiveness of the response to the earthquake.[96] National branches of the Red Cross from Europe rescued children from the rubble and found them safe places to live in Italy and Hungary.[97] While foreign branches offered assistance, reviews of the work of the Soviet Red Cross were submitted to International Red Cross headquarters in Geneva. Officials of the International Red Cross were concerned that mountains of unnecessary goods, especially unclean clothing, had been sent to the Soviet Union. They voiced concern about the arrival of medicine that was past its safe date of use.[98] Goods arriving in Moscow were not marked, so it took precious time to identify the material designated for Armenia.[99] The earthquake accelerated the reintegration of the Soviet Red Cross's activities into the international community.

The above visit stimulated a similar visit four years after Chernobyl, when a delegation from the International Red Cross toured the affected areas. It recognized that the Soviet Red Cross had strengthened its image as a result of what had happened in Armenia. Because numerous Soviet newspapers carried stories about the Red Cross and its humanitarian activities, these were known to a widespread Soviet audience.[100] Residents around Chernobyl thus mistrusted the Red Cross less than they did the Soviet state. This international delegation pushed for the Soviet Red Cross to publish its activities in bulletins, and it encouraged the Soviets to raise money through charity concerts and lotteries.[101]

The catastrophes played a critical role in revitalizing the Soviet Red Cross as a non-governmental organization, which, albeit nominally apolitical, influenced people's thinking about the Soviet government.[102] The Soviet Red Cross was not just interested in receiving international aid; it also envisaged providing foreign assistance. It wanted its volunteers to receive extra compensation and foreign currency to cover costs abroad.[103] Despite all the problems on the home front, the Soviet Union provided aid to Iran when a massive earthquake struck the northern part of that country in June 1990.[104] Soviet authorities recognized deficiencies in the aid it could provide, including getting permission for aid workers to travel internationally.[105] When the Commission for Extraordinary Situations drafted plans to systematize international response efforts, the Soviet Red Cross responded by suggesting that its influence be expanded. It wanted the effective right to independently decide to help internationally and it wanted the Commission for Extraordinary Situations to recognize that not just ministries and bureaucratic departments but also "public and other organizations" were important players in relief efforts.[106] The national branches of the Red Cross had historically worked closely together with their respective states, so the Soviet Red Cross was breaking new ground in its efforts to distinguish itself from the state.[107] The rebirth of the Red Cross as an independent organization signalled a new era in Soviet rescue operations.

The social and political circumstances surrounding the Armenian earthquake were unique for many reasons. For the first time, the Soviet Union had to deal with two massive disasters simultaneously. The Chernobyl reactor had exploded two years earlier, but the problems stemming from it were no less urgent as radioactive levels throughout the area were a major concern. Economically weakened and with rising political tensions in Moscow, the state could not hope to deal with the Armenian recovery in the same manner as had the Brezhnev administration. Unfortunately, despite all the lessons that could have been learned, Gorbachev and his advisors pushed forward in a rather non-reformist spirit. They pulled a dusty Soviet playbook from the drawer and sought to mobilize the spirit of Soviet citizenry with old ideas – the friendship of peoples, building quotas, and triumphal news stories about heroic construction crews. Perhaps the quick rebuilding of the sarcophagus had created the illusion that Soviet engineers could still successfully storm any fortress. However, the damage from the Armenian earthquake was spread over a large area, and no single rebuilding project presented an appropriate media opportunity to highlight the achievements of the Soviet state. Instead, Gorbachev was forced to fight a rearguard action as Armenia sought its own solutions and harnessed the catastrophe to promote its national identity. While Gorbachev decided to play a more public role in Armenia than he did at Chernobyl, his increased public presence just made his weaknesses clear for all to see.

Instead of reinforcing the vaunted Soviet slogan, the earthquake undermined the friendship of peoples, especially among Armenia's neighbouring republics. At Ashgabat, the friendship of peoples had a regional meaning, being strongest among the Central Asian republics. In Armenia, the unravelling of this friendship may be seen most clearly in two Transcaucasian republics: Armenia and Azerbaijan. The earthquake did not cause disagreements between Armenians and Azerbaijanis as tensions had flared about a year before it occurred; rather, it brought to the fore the impossibility of the situation and the complete absence of domestic solutions. The earthquake accelerated disillusionment on the southern periphery of the USSR.

If the ethnic tensions at the end of the Soviet era are well known to all, the international dimension of the rescue operation is not. Despite its adherence to stale formulae, the Soviet government did not block international aid. Of course, this enabled Armenians to reach out to their compatriots around the world in the hope of achieving both recovery and political independence. In addition, Soviet citizens in Armenia received their first mass exposure to the West. These people had long become accustomed to Western wares and Western-style Soviet cinema, but they were rarely directly exposed to the West unless they travelled there. After the earthquake, Armenia became a mobile United Nations site and a little multi-ethnic enclave. International assistance was not always effective as goods were lost in transit or forgotten in warehouses, but it introduced a social dimension that was lacking in previous disaster situations. With the creation of expansive international relations and plans for independent overseas representation, the Armenian earthquake further accelerated centrifugal trends that Gorbachev could not control.

Since the rescue operations after the Armenian earthquake had an element of political and diplomatic pluralism absent in past reconstruction efforts, it is tempting to characterize the response as symbolic of perestroika and glasnost: new economic approaches and an international openness were certainly evident after the earthquake. Yet to brand the response with such general terms, the terms most closely associated with Gorbachev's tenure as general secretary, overlooks the subtle and not-so-subtle distinctions that changed the Soviet Union year by year and month by month (rather than from one administration to the next). Although Chernobyl exploded in the perestroika era, the situation in 1986 in the Soviet Union was distinct from what it was when the earth trembled in Armenia. Instead of referring to perestroika, we might choose to speak about early, middle, and late perestroika. But even these designators overlook regional specifics – Ukraine was dealing with different problems than Armenia – which may have been of secondary concern in Moscow but nevertheless determined the outcome of events in the regions themselves. Perestroika affected events in Armenia, but this umbrella term should not distract the analyst from radical regional divergences and the temporal differences that made 1986 in Ukraine seem like decades before 1988 in Armenia. Time was not linear under Gorbachev.

Conclusion

Today, disasters continue to invigorate social and cultural debate. On 7 July 2012, a massive flood swept into the town of Krymsk in the southern part of the Russian Federation. The rising water levels devastated whole sections of the town, and more than one hundred people were reported to have lost their lives. With a rising death toll and a faltering rescue effort, the media reported growing discontent with the state's management of the crisis. Into the gap stepped volunteers who were morally concerned about the fate of the victims and eager to publicize the weaknesses of the Russian state. The Russian opposition newspaper *Novaia gazeta* reported that communication had been lost between people and the authorities (*narod i vlast'*).[1] Internationally, a *New York Times* journalist compared the delayed reporting of Chernobyl in the news to the immediate spread of information after the flooding in Krymsk.[2] In an even stronger assessment, the volunteer effort was portrayed as "a blueprint for a new form of civil society." The volunteer work being performed could contribute to the "idea that citizens can organize, be responsible for one another, and ultimately have an effect on how Russia governs itself."[3] The *Neue Zürcher Zeitung* published an article about the Kremlin's fear of the new Russian *Bürger* (*Citizen*): "The Kremlin demands subjects, but these subjects have long since become citizens."[4]

The Krymsk disaster and the commentary it provoked vividly illustrate not only how much has changed over the years but also how much has remained the same. The continued inability of the Russian government to deal adequately with the aftermath of disasters is a common motif. But another equally recurrent motif is the desire to juxtapose the weaknesses of a modern bureaucratic state with the actions of an organized society of volunteers who fill gaps in the bureaucratic woodwork and, in return, expect a greater say in the political life of the country. In 2012, the emphasis on these energetic volunteers intimates that Russian society has slowly wakened from a long slumber. For some historians, this slumber has lasted a millennium; for others, it was induced with a collective sleeping pill around 1917. The author of the *New York Times* article gives the distinct impression that such volunteer activity is foreign to the spirit of the Soviet years. Yet these are all versions of the state-versus-society trope, which continues to dominate analyses of life in the Russian Federation.

A study of the Soviet past, however, presents a more diverse picture than that presented in the above newspapers. No single, simple narrative can neatly package the experience of disasters in the Soviet Union. Where one expects parallels, one finds disparities, and where one anticipates divergences, one sees peculiar similarities. Thus, before assessing the disaster performance of the Soviet and Russian states, we must look again at original ideas about disasters. If we remember, Kenneth Hewitt argues that disasters must not be seen as isolated events but, rather, as extensions of the specific societies within which they occur. He criticizes scientists for separating natural phenomena from social phenomena. Although he did not focus on the Soviet experience, his thoughts are certainly valid in this context.

Theories of disaster may be matched with empirical issues. The role of the media, as important in Chicago as in Chernobyl, was critical throughout the twentieth century. The presentation of news in an authoritarian state is a fundamental aspect of everyday life, but it changes constantly – and not just according to greater or lesser degrees of censorship. Evidently, each regime had its own media strategy, depending upon the pressing issues of the day. In a strange way, the media, combined with a personal system of morality, led hundreds of thousands of people to volunteer. Despite the fact that citizens continuously volunteer their time to deal with the aftermaths of floods, earthquakes, and so on, writers have ignored the phenomenon of volunteering in the Soviet Union. Volunteering was not a straightforward altruistic affair; rather, it was representative of a complex set of values, ranging from individual expression to statist coercion. At each disaster, responders' attitudes were affected by specific political and social concerns. For its part, the bureaucratic response to earthquakes is incredibly complex, continually revealing changing attitudes across vast periods of time.

Soviet censorship appears in a more nuanced light when studied through the lens of disasters. Publication laws placed restrictions on the coverage of natural disasters, but this did not mean they went unreported or that they were always reported in the same way, There was never any blanket policy to determine what did or did not appear in the press. The Crimean earthquake was reported immediately, and, although scientists dominated the discussion, details of the tragedy were abundant in newspapers. The reporting was much less centralized than it was for other disasters as the RSFSR led the reconstruction efforts; thus, republican news organs in the RSFSR emerged as the dominant mouthpieces. The Crimean earthquake occurred shortly before Stalin's totalitarian turn, but, even in the late Stalinist years, reporting on the quakes did not follow a single pattern. In 1948, the Stalinist regime reported the deadly Ashgabat earthquake, which killed tens of thousands of people, much more quickly than the Gorbachev regime published news on Chernobyl. All-union reporting on the Ashgabat catastrophe quickly subsided, but local news organs did not hesitate to publish both laudatory and critical stories about the reconstruction. Under Brezhnev, the state strongly encouraged news and specialized journals to issue articles about the Tashkent earthquake, and the disaster became the centre of a media circus. Although international reporters were suspiciously absent, the earthquake enjoyed coverage in a range of media outlets – radio, film, newspapers, scholarly and scientific works, popular stories (such as Peskov's *Tashkent: Catastrophe and Courage*), and Soviet foreign-language publications abroad.

The state obviously wanted to frame disasters according to its own needs, with the result that political circumstances determined their presentation. In the 1920s, the Crimean earthquake immediately became front-page news, establishing the importance of the Crimean peninsula as a sanatorium for all subjects of the Soviet Union; thus, a political need necessitated spreading the word about the disaster. Moreover, scientists engaged in public discussions, using the authority of their scientific voices to explain the phenomenon and to argue that officialdom had the situation under control. The nature of science at hand – seismology in the 1920s – made it easier for these scientists to express themselves: they were not considered the pride of a communist state, as were nuclear physicists in the 1980s. Thus, unlike the Chernobyl situation, the Crimean situation did not require immediate censorship. Although Gorbachev later favoured less media control, the political circumstances in the spring of 1986 made censorship almost inevitable. Chernobyl struck at the heart of Soviet scientific pride and threatened to add a full-scale political crisis to the economic crisis Gorbachev was already facing. Moreover, Chernobyl had an international dimension that was absent in other major catastrophes.

Scientists, hardly the standard-bearers of political debates, played critical roles in the media. In 1928, the authors published in *Zemletriasenie v Krymu* were almost exclusively scientists. During the Crimean disaster, they not only offered valid messages but also misled: erudite claims about the peninsula slipping into the sea could not be retracted. In Ashgabat, science appeared to play little or no part in the public eye, whereas in Tashkent attention fell upon seismologists. Seismologists were in an enviable position because they enjoyed renown without responsibility; few people expected them to predict the next great shake. After Chernobyl, scientists were again in the news. The explosion seemed to stir the foundations of Soviet science, but scientists did not suffer as they expressed outrage in commissions and in regional newspapers. They successfully limited the construction of further nuclear power plants while adamantly defending the reputation of Soviet science against its ruin at the hands of an inept bureaucracy. As the photograph of the women outside the Crimean nuclear power plant testifies, even activists continued to trust Soviet scientists.

Despite the variety of these voices, common factors conditioned the reporting: a death toll counted more than destruction, urban areas counted more than rural ones, and the historical relationship between disasters was continually ignored. This had awkward consequences over the years. Soviet newspapers reported deaths in Iran but not those in Ashgabat, just across the border, even though they were caused by the same earthquake. After a mining explosion in Ukraine days after the earthquake in Tashkent, the regional newspaper mentioned human losses but gave no further details. In many ways, the death toll did not intimidate authorities, but the prospect of civil disobedience at the inevitable funerals did.

The location of the tragedy also played its part in the reporting. Both Tashkent and Ashgabat were located on the far periphery of the former Russian Empire and the Soviet Union, so, in a sense, they could be forgotten. Yet Tashkent had been the site of a major international diplomatic effort and was the fourth largest urban agglomeration in the Soviet Union. It received attention in a way that Ashgabat did not. Outside urban centres, rural disasters were conveniently neglected. This may have reflected an age-old Bolshevik prejudice against peasants, but it was also a political convenience. Little political currency was to be gained from highlighting rescue efforts in remote areas that had been flooded; Soviet authorities were less concerned with this form of natural disaster. A flood in an ethnic Russian area never became a news item in the same way as did an earthquake in Central Asia. It is not by chance that a *derevenshchik* (ruralist) like Valentin Rasputin, who wanted to highlight Russian peasant culture, wrote about floods and fires rather than earthquakes. One can surmise that the *derevenshchiki* preferred ethnic Russian natural disasters to the earthquakes that ripped through Central Asia. Nor is it insignificant that a Jewish author, Lazar Karelin, chose to write a fictional piece about Ashgabat's tragedy.

In addition, connections were rarely made between disasters (or even smaller accidents) as it was Soviet strategy to isolate these incidents in the minds of Soviet citizens, thus furthering the state's control of memory. Attempts to steer memory were not limited to revolutionary history or the class struggle as disasters were presented as individual occurrences, even if well-worn historical themes such as the friendship of peoples kept reappearing. Occasionally, the question of compensation required mention of another tragedy. For example, a letter published in a Crimean newspaper in 1966 sympathized with Tashkentites, the Crimean peninsula having experienced a similar upheaval in 1927. The linking of disasters was, however, the exception rather than the rule. Although much of the information about the Crimean and Ashgabat earthquakes was readily available in published sources, state officials refrained from linking response strategies to Tashkent. The radioactive aspect of Chernobyl made it a special case, but even after the Armenian earthquake little effort was made to draw lessons from the past. Seismologists continued to monitor the crust of the earth and engineers sought to improve building techniques, but this activity did not situate the response within broader historical and social issues. To a degree, this behaviour was not unusual. This was precisely the approach Hewitt criticized in Western analyses, which reduced natural disasters to their scientific components.

These written sources only tell part of the story. In the theatres, film directors offered consistent reminders of disasters, even if the moral of the story continued to change. In 1926, only a year before the Crimean earthquake, Amo Bek-nazaryan filmed *Namus* and provided graphic images of earthquake destruction. In 1958, *Poema o more* took advantage of the cultural thaw and enabled viewers to question the flooding of villages as a byproduct of hydroelectric energy production. Whereas these films had a provocative edge, others emphasized heroism. Malik Kaiumov's *Tashkent, Earthquake* reveals the destruction wrought by the Tashkent earthquake but focuses on individuals who successfully resuscitated the city. In the dramatic fictional film *Ekipazh* from the late 1970s, the directors combine an earthquake with an air catastrophe to highlight not only modern perils but also the ability of Soviet pilots to overcome extreme danger. The message shifts, but the movie theatre reminded visitors that disaster was never that far away.

Clearly, the Soviets made much use of modern media after the Tashkent earthquake, but little has been said about the personal use of media. As the Soviet Union placed more emphasis on consumerism in the 1960s, consumer toys became available to Soviet citizens. The state had its official photographers, but residents could save their kopeks and purchase cameras. Unfortunately, family albums and photographs from hobby photographers have not received just treatment. Without individual interviews and access to family memory, an important component of disaster analysis remains unexamined. Visual analysis, so critical in our contemporary world, will not only further the researcher's understanding of the tragedies but it will also indicate how residents kept alive memories of these difficult days when the public press had long stopped reporting on it.

Beyond the published words, photographs, and films that framed the experience of catastrophe for those outside the danger zone, disasters were characterized by the history of massive volunteer efforts. The history of almost all disasters, from the late tsarist period to the present, is about volunteer activity. In all the cases studied here, volunteers responded en masse. Whether volunteer activity manifested itself in the form of financial donations after the Crimean earthquake, as citizen militias in the immediate wake of the Ashgabat earthquake, or in the shape of Leningradites volunteering to travel to Tashkent, Soviet citizens did not hesitate to mobilize. The social nature and political context of their actions differed depending upon the circumstances, but there was no lack of energy emanating from the populace. Soviet citizens wrote to newspapers expressing their desire to provide assistance, and others travelled great distances to become directly involved. Nikolai Savenko abandoned his family in St Petersburg to help in Tashkent. In the case of Vasilii Karpenko, fact followed fiction as his reading of *Tashkent: City of Bread* influenced his decision to travel to Uzbekistan. Of course, these were not the only two cases – scores of other volunteers had personal decisions to make as well. Unfortunately, volunteering in the Soviet Union has been overlooked or underestimated because it has been tied to the coercive practices of the authoritarian state.

The challenge is to recognize both the coercive element emanating from statist authorities and the personal motives for volunteering. Soviet media organs attached a specific meaning, with coercive undertones, to the term "volunteer." When *Turkmenskaia iskra* published articles about a *subbotnik* or a *voskresnik* (respectively translated as "a Saturday" and "a Sunday," days when Soviet citizens were called upon to volunteer in their communities), volunteers appeared because these activities were a component of the party program. In 1966, the state issued quotas indicating the living space each republic was to build and the number of refugees each republic "volunteered" to house. In 1986, workers presented as volunteers were conscripted to work in the thirty-kilometre zone. Beyond these rigid numbers and forced mobilizations, the state fully understood that it had to tempt those who were going to volunteer. Special pay rates were used to lure volunteers to Tashkent and Chernobyl. At Chernobyl, Valerii Legasov admitted the state employed this tactic, seeing it as one component in the larger phenomenon of volunteering.

Similarly, the sheer numbers of volunteers quantify but do not qualify the nature of the phenomenon. Sociologists suggest that, right after a disaster, volunteering is often a function of altruism – the assistance transcends specific ideological requirements and draws on spontaneous moral principles common around the globe. Even if postmodernism tries to subvert such "objective" principles of morality as altruism, it is not a stretch to suggest that whatever personal reasons a subject might have, she or he is not clearing rubble or providing medical assistance for ideological reasons. The relative absence of ideology in the Komsomol minutes of 1966 is a good indication that ideology was not a priority in Tashkent.

Volunteer work in the long term is, however, seldom based on pure altruism – the 1966 minutes of the Komsomol tell us this much as well. This being so, how can we distinguish between an individual who volunteered for personal benefit and the one who did so for public benefit as only the latter fits theoretical notions of civil society? Where does altruism end and individual benefit begin? Of course, a final answer might be difficult to come by since each individual, as Nietzsche suggests in *Beyond Good and Evil* (*Jenseits von Gut und Böse*), is the battleground of competing value systems. This limitation notwithstanding, it is certainly instructive to reiterate the diversity of volunteer experience in these tragic circumstances and how individuals superimposed personal desires on external displays of altruism.

After the initial shock of each tragedy, volunteers had a moment to consider how and why they wished to involve themselves. In the Crimean peninsula, because of transportation issues, physical volunteering from around the Soviet Union was much less common than it was in other areas. Furthermore, the state did not create incentives for volunteers; instead, citizens made financial contributions or entertainers organized benefit events to raise funds. In the Crimean peninsula and Ashgabat, residents, not the state, were instrumental in rebuilding neighbourhoods. Volunteering in these instances was a function of natural rather than statist necessity.

In these disaster scenarios, volunteering emerged as an individual rather than as a collective phenomenon. Veritable volunteer organizations such as VOOPIK operated in the Soviet Union, but during disasters volunteering was by and large performed on an individual basis. As an association, the Soviet Red Cross existed throughout the twentieth century, but it rarely played a dominant role. Moreover, there is scant evidence that volunteering built a lasting sense of community (as one might expect with a volunteer fire department in the United States or with a sporting association in Imperial Germany). The Tashkent experience in 1966 spoke to the individualism involved in volunteering: Vasilii Karpenko followed his own literary imagination. Whereas one worker chose to travel to Tashkent because his family had lived there during the Second World War, a long-standing Komsomol member selected a building project in Tashkent over one in Kazakhstan. In Armenia, Soviet citizens volunteered for work brigades and accepted Armenian children into their regions. But the geopolitical realities of the perestroika era put limits on volunteering: most citizens were too preoccupied with their own problems to focus on Armenia. Volunteer truck drivers wavered when faced with military dangers in the region; sending money and supplies became the preferred form of volunteer activity. The associational aspect of volunteering was, not surprisingly, restricted to international organizations.

Individuals also received rewards for volunteering. Monetary incentives were distributed to individuals in Tashkent and in Chernobyl, but volunteering had other attractions as well. Travel to and from Tashkent was subsidized, and, when in Tashkent, youths could do as they pleased as long as they did not confront the regime. Chernobyl was radically different in this respect because no one wanted to linger in a radioactive zone. Here the financial component played a greater role, with remuneration being inversely proportional to the level of expected radioactive exposure. These examples are not meant to undermine the force of altruism but, rather, to add a layer of complexity to the endless Soviet references to volunteers.

With regard to the Cold War, it is worth noting that the Soviet Red Cross was the biggest loser. During the Crimean earthquake, the organization was involved at many levels, but thereafter its usefulness subsided. The Turkmenistan branch of the Red Cross was active during the Ashgabat earthquake but spent most of its time conducting educational exercises; throughout the Soviet Union the Red Cross had lost much of its independence and, especially after the Second World War, ceased to contribute medical assistance at critical moments. Only after the Armenian earthquake did the organization experience a revival, reassert itself, and redefine its mission. In 1988, it certainly helped that the organization had retained a bureaucratic structure throughout the Soviet years as this enabled it to easily mobilize when the time came. Not surprisingly, independent associational activity only emerged in the context of perestroika, and even then it was weak. After Chernobyl, independent organizations struggled to have their statutes recognized.

The relationship between volunteer activity and civil society requires attention, even if the latter may be losing its intellectual energy as an analytical concept. Volunteer activity is frequently equated with civil society because of the connection between active/engaged citizens and democracy. A popular Tocquevillian notion underlies this thought – the volunteer might not even be aware that he or she is receiving a political education, but the very act of volunteering is a component of political life and implicitly or explicitly exerts pressure on state-level institutions. In the Soviet Union and Russia, volunteer activity was widespread, yet a link between this volunteer activity and political activism appears muted indeed. Ironically, in the communist state, volunteering was an individual rather than an associational phenomenon. Even if this last assertion distances Soviet volunteering from its Tocquevillian cousin, it does not diminish the sociological importance of volunteering throughout the Soviet and post-Soviet period.

This much can be said about volunteer activity, but what conclusions can be drawn about the Soviet and Russian governments that handled the rescue operations? At first glance, this question has a straightforward answer: the totalitarian state took direct control of the disaster response but performed dismally. Of course, this answer is unsatisfactory because it ignores important nuances concerning the attitude and performance of each separate administrative level of the Soviet state. Therefore, even if we accept that the Soviet response was underwhelming, we must still juxtapose the performance of individual administrations. In short, Brezhnev orchestrated the most efficient centralized response effort, whereas Gorbachev orchestrated the least efficient, overseeing two utterly chaotic disasters. The least centralized efforts came in the 1920s and 1940s in the NEP and Stalinist years. Regardless of the time period, however, the disasters exposed weaknesses as nature overwhelmed the pretense of organized Soviet rule.

In a rare move in post-revolutionary history, the authorities responsible for the rehabilitation of the Crimean peninsula made it perfectly clear that the state had only limited capacities to respond. When discussing the issue with peasants, the state made every effort to explain that the victims could only expect moderate support. The RSFSR and not the USSR was responsible for guaranteeing the reconstruction of its southern coast. Similarly, the Ukrainian SFSR created its own committee to respond to the crisis. With limited resources at the regional level and little funding emanating from the Kremlin, the RSFSR had no choice but to be careful about the allocation of resources and to enunciate the limits of its own responsibility. The restraint shown by the RSFSR runs counter to the authoritarian tendencies Sorokin envisaged when democratic regimes responded to crises. After the rejection of "War Communism" in the early 1920s, and at the tail end of the NEP era (when the Soviet Union flirted with micro-capitalist policies), the limited involvement of the state is explicable: Stalin had yet to transform the state into an omnipresent force.

Yet the response in the Crimean peninsula shared certain similarities to the response in the aftermath of the Ashgabat earthquake. Clearly, the state had to create the illusion that Moscow was responsible for the recovery of Ashgabat: it adopted a restrained approach to reconstruction without advertising the limits of its support. In the emerging Cold War, the state could not afford to reveal the limitations of its power. Stalin was willing to issue building decrees and the like, but he was hesitant to commit extensive resources or money that was being redirected to bomb projects. Despite the image of a highly centralized Stalinist state, the recovery effort in Ashgabat was closer to the Crimean recovery effort than it was to the finely tuned orchestration of the Tashkent recovery.

Eighteen years after Ashgabat and twenty-one years after the end of the Second World War, the Soviet Union had changed economically and politically. In essence, the reconstruction of Tashkent represented a radical break from the past and a high point in the mobilization of resources to limit the effects of natural caprice. The city's diplomatic importance and the need of the new leadership to assert itself publicly have already been mentioned, but this certainly was not the sole motive for such a gargantuan response. While Chernobyl was more dramatic because of its relationship to the atomic energy industry, the recovery effort in Tashkent was much more all-encompassing. In the Uzbek capital, architects, construction workers, Komsomol members, scientists, and party officials became involved in a transformative project that lasted for years. Moscow had the authority to push the reconstruction forward, though much of the planning emerged from the peculiarities of regional and public organizations.

In fact, the response reflected general advances in the Soviet Union as much as it did the outlook of the leadership. For example, Brezhnev and Kosygin's arrival in Tashkent on the day after the earthquake was not just a function of their own decisions but also of a Soviet society accustoming itself to air travel. The mobility of the leadership represented the increased physical mobility of Soviet citizens. In this respect, the arrival of Brezhnev and Kosygin was little different from the arrival of thousands of workers. Similarly, the production of the film *Tashkent, Earthquake*, a melodramatic documentary, reflected shifting priorities in 1960s Soviet filmmaking rather than something specific about natural disasters or the scientific qualities of earthquakes. The film memorializes the earthquake through the use of the aesthetic sensitivities of the 1960s. The arrival of the Komsomol and its worker brigades belonged less to crisis response than to the regular shipping of youth around the Soviet Union to help with various building and reconstruction projects. Tashkent was much more "business as usual" than were either the Crimean peninsula or Ashgabat. This explains why little effort was made to create a standing bureaucratic ministry to deal with such emergencies. I.T. Novikov led a committee to coordinate the various organs summoned to Tashkent, but this committee was temporary. The response to the earthquake was presented as exceptional, but it simply mobilized existing structures (albeit in a very large way). This attitude towards natural disasters only changed after the Armenian earthquake.

In 1966, the centralized state had a firm hand in guiding the disaster response, but all sorts of cracks permitted unexpected behaviour. The state, even during a major event involving media (such as the reconstruction of Tashkent) did not have absolute control. The regional Komsomol committees continually reported inadequacies on construction sites and distractions everywhere else. The case of architecture in Tashkent further illustrates this point. It would be foolish to argue that the centralized bureaucracy had no role in the reconstruction of Tashkent – state-sponsored bulldozers razed the centre of town to rebuild the city according to a general plan designed in Moscow. Yet the ultimate vision for the city was much more diverse than anything contained within a single plan. The military was responsible for the construction of one suburb, the union republics mixed their designs in Chilanzar, and local architects debated the relationship between old and new, between Uzbek and Soviet, and between Soviet and Western. When Uzbek architects complained about the haphazard layout of new buildings, they were only pointing out how individual republics often had their own way of doing things.

This should not, however, be seen as a weakness of the Soviet state since absolute control may not have been the goal in the first place. In his analysis of the Imperial Russian government, George Yaney assesses the degree to which the tsarist autocracy was transforming its bureaucracy into a more efficient apparatus based on merit and education rather than on rank. While he argues that the Imperial government was systematizing its bureaucracy, he maintains that a degree of desystematization was to its benefit. The ambiguous zones that lacked systematization gave the state more room for manoeuvring while giving outlying officials a greater sense of freedom (even though the state was prepared to intervene when necessary). Similarly, the disorganization at the republican level was not necessarily always of concern to Soviet officials.

At the outset, the response at Chernobyl appeared to repeat the highly centralized response at Tashkent. Although Gorbachev had already started to consider reducing the state's role in everyday life, at Chernobyl the state took complete control. From the firefighters who rushed to the scene in the early morning of 26 April to the evacuation of Pripyat to the conscription of liquidators and to the construction of the sarcophagus, the state orchestrated the rescue (no matter how ill-fated the outcome). Yet this approach only lasted for a very short period and, where it did persist, it was only at the power plant itself.

Across the western part of the Soviet Union, Chernobyl had set new processes in motion. The extreme situation required an extremely centralized solution, but member republics, such as Ukraine and Belarus, quickly developed their own approaches to ridding territory of radioactive elements and providing succor to victims – these independent voices ultimately played a part in the slow disintegration of the Soviet Union. Volunteers arrived from other republics to help with the construction of Slavutich, but their involvement was much more limited than it was at Tashkent. Chernobyl was instrumental in mobilizing citizen groups, but their immediate concerns were not always their home city. The protesters in the Crimean peninsula were more focused on their own region than they were in offering assistance to the northern parts of Ukraine, and they were almost indifferent to the consequences in Belarus. Each region and each interest group expressed its own demands.

In Armenia, the situation had changed once again and not simply because a radioactive explosion is different from an earthquake. Gorbachev had learned a lesson that Brezhnev could have easily taught him: a leader should appear at the site of a disaster. Absent in Chernobyl and even Kyiv, Gorbachev appeared, with some prodding, in Armenia. However, his public appearance made him the focus of blame. Gorbachev started the rescue efforts with a traditional Soviet template, which was swept aside by current events. Even international relief was not a magic bullet, having problems of its own, but it signalled a radical shift in policy. The earthquake exposed Armenia to such a vast array of novel worldviews that the Armenian declaration of independence in August 1990 was no surprise.

Rarely were disasters limited to the event itself. When the bus went over the bridge in Kyiv in 1966, it was not an isolated incident but a reflection of Soviet financial reward practices. After the Soviets had rebuilt Ashgabat to their satisfaction, life did not return to normal. Many residents spent decades in temporary housing and thus had to cope not only with the loss of loved ones but also with having to reposition themselves within the grid of a new city. In Tashkent, residents were relocated from the centre of town, from private dwelling to public building, and some even relocated to live closer to relatives on the western edge of the Soviet Union. They brought their memories to communities far from where the disaster had struck. These disasters lingered in the minds of residents even if Soviet officials had their own agenda.

These disasters rarely involved diplomatic sparring or caused the international tensions characteristic of the Cold War, but they do suggest that the Iron Curtain was not as impenetrable as ideologists on both sides wanted to believe. To be sure, the response in Ashgabat was shrouded in secrecy, and the Soviet builders, hardly troubled by issues of design, did not look to Western architects for inspiration. By 1966, disaster clearly and succinctly exposed the Soviet Union's admiration for the West. Residents may not have known the names of Le Corbusier and Moshe Safdie, but they were soon walking down streets that showed more than just a touch of Western architectural design. The Soviets were not ready to accept foreign assistance and become members of a global community of first responders, but Western elements were visible throughout Tashkent. It might be exaggerating to write of a sexual revolution in the Soviet 1960s, but the mores of the Komsomol in Tashkent paralleled trends in Western Europe and the United States. Even in film, the Iron Curtain was opening. The Soviet disaster film *Ekipazh* had been directed in the spirit of *Earthquake*, starring Charlton Heston, and *The Towering Inferno*, starring Steve McQueen. If we are reluctant to admit that the Soviet Union copied the West, we can at least conclude that attitudes and behaviour during disasters had strong parallels with those in the West. Much of this is not new as Soviet efforts at consumerism have been well-documented, but these thoughts insert attitudes towards disasters deep into the rhythm of daily life.

In the Soviet era, disasters were linked not only to Marxist-Leninist values but also to the core values of a multi-ethnic state; disasters were a testing ground for gauging the strength of multi-ethnic friendship. The Soviets wrote extensively about the friendship of peoples, but to what degree did this friendship manifest itself in difficult situations? In the NEP years, the Bolshevik Party emphasized cultural diversity and promoted national languages and local traditions, but the rescue operation in the Crimean peninsula paid little attention to ethnic volunteer efforts. Officials hoped to receive assistance from throughout the Soviet Union but did not place high expectations on their appeals. In Ashgabat, assistance came from far and wide but in a particular form. The Russian Federation played a minimal role, even though medical and technical expertise was flown in from Moscow and St Petersburg, implicitly recognizing the role of Russians as the older brother in the friendship of peoples. The responsibility for the mass migration of workers to Ashgabat and the emigration of children to safe havens was not executed equitably across the Soviet Union. The Central Asian republics assisted each other while the northern and western republics remained at a distance, even if they made small gestures through the provision of supplies. The Stalinist government either did not understand the political potential of a natural disaster or saw no need to dramatize the involvement of member republics such a short time after the deportation of Chechens and Crimean Tatars to Central Asia.

In 1966, the slogan "friendship of peoples" had become entrenched in Soviet life, both socially and politically, so the Brezhnevite state quickly incorporated it into its disaster relief efforts. Before the earthquake struck Tashkent, *Pravda Vostoka* was celebrating the decade of Belarusian culture and *Literaturnaia gazeta* had just made a tourist's stop in Alma Ata, where it lauded the work of Russian colonizers. However, as a financial commitment, celebrating Belarusian culture differed fundamentally from shipping in thousands of workers to construct buildings that could have been erected with local labour. Costs were unexpectedly amplified due to attrition rates when workers came and went. The friendship of peoples caused major cost overruns.

Tying the disaster response to the idea of friendship of peoples had other consequences as well. If Ashgabatites sent their children to other Central Asian republics, Tashkentites sent their children to Moscow and the Black Sea. With increased mobility in the Soviet Union, it was possible to send people far and wide. The process was haphazard and rife with problems, but many Tashkentites did settle in western areas of the Soviet Union. The process was most attractive to migrants who could return to relatives in Ukraine, thus transforming an evacuation into a homecoming.

Two decades later, the friendship of peoples played a diminished role at Chernobyl. As central party officials were slowly coming to terms with a burgeoning economic crisis, they must have been aware that an appeal to the friendship of peoples was too costly a step. In traditional fashion, the Soviets prided themselves on the "volunteers" who arrived from all corners of the union, but responsibility lay primarily with the three core Slavic republics – Belarus, Russia, and Ukraine. Working crews from Armenia and other republics contributed to the construction of Slavutich, but this aid was limited and never became a central propaganda crutch.

The explosion at Chernobyl was the last instance when the slogan "friendship of peoples," even in reduced form, could be employed to positive effect. After the Armenian earthquake, the state stubbornly promoted the friendship of peoples, but the political weight of a reborn nationalism quickly overwhelmed party slogans. The ineffectiveness of the slogan went hand in hand with the Communist Party's diminishing strength. With assistance pouring in from international sources, the friendship of peoples only made sense at an international level.

In the Soviet and Russian tradition, it should come as no surprise that the state – in its central and regional form – played a major role after natural tragedies. But the Soviets never did have complete control over the land in which they lived. Disasters imposed themselves on Soviet institutions and on the natural landscapes. A scholar of language can point out that, for almost seventy years, the Soviet state controlled the discourse of disasters as it manoeuvred between the *avariia* and *stikhiinoe bedstvie* of its own choosing. These linguistic gymnastics were certainly expressive of state desire; however, as John Searle so eloquently argues, desires are not always fulfilled in the real world.[5] When disaster struck, as it often did, the state scrambled to deal with it. Each Soviet leadership had its own approach, but no matter the effort at polishing the circumstances, the state remained a small player when compared to the natural forces it confronted.

Unfortunately, gaps persist in our understanding of disasters, and it is still difficult to separate the effects disasters have had on social strata. The multi-ethnic response has been commented upon, and the efforts to evacuate children add another dimension to disaster response, but this does not exhaust the possibilities. Eric Klinenberg explores the fate of senior citizens who lived alone in Chicago, but no similar evidence is readily available for the Soviet Union. Precious few clues indicate how vulnerable groups fared in disaster situations; the sources are silent on their fate. Limitations emerge, in part, because the current authoritarian regimes in Uzbekistan and Turkmenistan have created a restrictive climate for expression. Survivors of the earthquakes in Ashgabat and Tashkent still live in these cities, but their stories have only been told in short snippets. Oral histories have long since been a key component of the historian's trade. This is most evident regarding the religious aspects of the earthquakes. Religious artefacts and religious art belong to the story of natural disasters, and appeals to the Koran arose after the Tashkent earthquake in 1966. Despite the Soviet Union's restrictions on artistic production, one can expect that, in one form or another, there exists religious art that depicts these tragedies. The concrete evidence, however, remains to be discovered. After the Haiti earthquake in 2010, an upsurge of religious art filled the material void in which residents found themselves.[6] Unfortunately, so far the evidence regarding the Soviet Union is limited. The next step for researchers is to document these personal stories before they fade from memory.

These limitations notwithstanding, we can posit an arc by which to evaluate the state's aptitude for understanding disasters as more than just geological phenomena. The Brezhnev government stands at the peak of this arc. It is no accident that the documentation of the Tashkent earthquake far exceeds that of other disasters: it became a cause célèbre for communists. The RSFSR of the 1920s finds itself on the curves of the arc. It understood the political and social importance of the disasters, yet was less than successful in mobilizing support to convert natural disasters into political capital. Stalin and Gorbachev find themselves at the bottom ends of the arc. Ashgabat was comparatively neglected, whereas the reaction to the Chernobyl explosion and the Armenian earthquake spiralled out of control. In no case, however, should the extent of state control be exaggerated for, even in 1966, numerous elements of the response slipped out of the hands of the leadership in the Kremlin.

Disasters easily upset the rhythms of human beings, animals, and plant life. Disasters in the Soviet Union were, of course, not unique. In Peru, Japan, and the United States, humans had their life patterns disrupted by water rising, earth shaking, and wind swirling. In the southern areas of the Soviet Union and in Los Angeles, lore has it that animals were able to sense tremours well in advance of humans, thus sharing their sense of peril. Just as Western governments struggled to cope with these disasters, so did the Soviet Union.

This history must now take its leave from the state and say a few words about the residents who are still dealing with natural and human-made disasters. As the environment continues to change, neither the Russian Federation nor the other Soviet successor states have long-term answers to disasters. Thus, citizens will continue to develop creative ways to deal with these upheavals as they occur. As media technologies expand, they will have more venues for expressing themselves and will give researchers better access to the structural and, equally important, emotional swings that go hand in hand with catastrophes. Even as scientists gather more data about our unpredictable planet, we cannot truly come to terms with disasters unless we integrate the behaviour of individuals with the behaviour of their communities. It is my hope that this study has taken a step in that direction.

Notes

INTRODUCTION

1 *Toshkent 1966 iil silsilasi*, n.p.

2 Ibid.

3 James Oberg has written a catalogue of disasters, but his book does not place these disasters within a broader socio-cultural setting. See Oberg, *Uncovering Soviet Disasters*.

4 Stronski, *Tashkent*, 256.

5 In German and French, see Beck, *Risikogesellschaft*; Waldherr, *Erdbeben*; Schmidt, "*Wolken krachen*"; Quenet, *Les tremblements de terre aux XVIIe et XVIIIe siècles*; Acot, *Catastrophes climatiques*; Beck, *Weltrisikogesellschaft*; Briese and Günther, "Katastrophe"; Walter, *Katastrophen*; Utz, *Kultivierung der Katastrophe*. An exception is Marc Elie's work on the Armenian earthquake. See Elie, "Au centre d'un double malheur"; and Miller and Miller, *Armenia*, 14.

6 Medvedev, *Nuclear Disaster in the Urals*.

7 Mickiewicz, *Split Signals*, 29.

8 Mickiewicz emphatically differentiates Gorbachev from his predecessors. See Mickiewicz, *Split Signals*, 136–7.

9 On social and cultural diversity, see Lahusen and Kuperman, *Late Soviet Culture*; Stites and von Geldern, *Mass Culture in Soviet Russia*; Clark, *Soviet Novel*. On life in a Soviet provincial town, see Kotkin, *Magnetic Mountain*.

10 Kadyrov, *Ashkhabadskaia katastrofa*, 132.

11 Medvedev, *Nuclear Disaster in the Urals*, 19–23.

12 Karelin, "Zemletriasenie."

13 Leonid Gaidai, *Kavkazskaia plennitsa*; Vladimir Motyl', *Beloe solntse pustyni* (Mosfil'm, 1970); Eldar Riazanov, *Ironiia sud'by, ili s legkim parom!* (Mosfil'm, 1975); Eldar Riazanov, *Vokzal dlia dvoikh* (Mosfil'm, 1982).

14 Anthony J. Lukas, "Old Uzbek City Is Enjoying a New Day in the Sun," *New York Times*, 1 October 1966.
15 For a discussion on the secretive response to the Tangshan earthquake in China in 1976, see Chen, "Resist the Earthquake and Rescue Ourselves."
16 Kaiumov, *Tashkent, zemletriasenie* (Kinostudiia dokumental'nykh fil'mov Uzbekistana, 1968). This film is located at *Rossiiskii gosudarstvennyi arkhiv kinofotodokumentov* (RGAKFD), 20776.
17 Bacon and Sandle, *Brezhnev Reconsidered*.
18 Marples, *Chernobyl and Nuclear Power*, 115–80.
19 Baranovs'ka, *Sotsial'ni ta ekonomichni naslidki Chornobil's'koi katastrofy*; *Kniga pamiati k 25-i godovshchine avarii na Chernobylskoi atomnoi elektrostantsii*.
20 Ryzhkov, *Prem'er*, 164–84.
21 Suny, *Revenge of the Past*, 133, 141.
22 L. Moiseeva, "Eto 26-e aprelia," *Tribuna energetika*, 10 April 1988.
23 Conquest, *Harvest of Sorrow*.
24 Qualls, *From Ruins to Reconstruction*.
25 Malia, *Soviet Tragedy*.

CHAPTER ONE

1 Voltaire, "Lisbon Earthquake."
2 Sorokin, *Man and Society in Calamity*, 125. Sorokin's subheading is "Specific Increase of Totalitarianism in Response to Sundry Calamities."
3 Ranft and Selzer, "Städte aus Trümmern," 24.
4 Officer, *When the Planet Rages*.
5 Hewitt, "Idea of Calamity in a Technocratic Age," 25.
6 Nietzsche, "Ecce Homo," 1145.
7 Utz, *Kultivierung der Katastrophe*, 115–48.
8 Dostoevsky, *Crime and Punishment*, 430.
9 Sunstein, *Laws of Fear*, 43 (emphasis in original).
10 Beck, *Risikogesellschaft*; Beck, *Risk Society*.
11 Beck, *Risk Society*, 23.
12 Ibid., 43.
13 Oliver-Smith, "Theorizing Disasters," 32.
14 Elie, "Au centre d'un double malheur."
15 Oliver-Smith, *Defying Displacement*, 146.
16 Klinenberg, *Heat Wave*.
17 Gaillard and Le Masson, "Traditional Societies' Response to Volcanic Hazards in the Philippines." See also Oliver-Smith, *Martyred City*.

18 Schubert, "Great Fire of Hamburg," 221.

19 Ibid., 227.

20 Beissinger, *Nationalist Mobilization and the Collapse of the Soviet State*, 14–15.

21 Briese and Günther, "Katastrophe," 157.

22 Quoted in Klinenberg, *Heat Wave*, 16 (emphasis added). See also Steinberg, *Acts of God*.

23 Klinenberg, *Heat Wave*, 22.

24 Ibid., 23.

25 Allen Barton began his classic study of communities in disaster with a tornado in Arkansas in 1952. See Barton, *Communities in Disaster*, 3–10.

26 Zoshchenko, "Earthquake."

27 In the Kazakh film *Angel with a Skullcap* (*Angel v tiubeteike*), the main character drops exercise weights on the floor, waking the neighbour below him. The neighbour awakens, sees the chandelier shake, and cries "Earthquake." See Shaken Aimanov, *Angel v tiubeteike* (Kazakhfil'm, 1968).

28 Elias, *Time*, 39.

29 Corbin, *Village Bells*.

30 Herbert, *Victorian Relativity*, 172–3.

31 Hanson, *Time and Revolution*. Hanson differentiates between rational time and charismatic time. In charismatic time, the leadership stands above normal considerations of time and is in a position to reorder events.

32 For a complex explanation of aspect and the distinction between the perfect and the imperfect, see Comrie, *Aspect*. By the same author, see *Tense*. The intricacies of twentieth-century Russian are presented in Comrie et al., *Russian Language in the Twentieth Century*.

33 On the role of language in Soviet history, see Halfin and Hellbeck, "Rethinking the Stalinist Subject." See the introduction in Hellbeck, *Revolution on My Mind*.

34 Wittgenstein, *Philosophical Investigations*.

35 In English, we differentiate between a disaster and an emergency. Dennis E. Wenger writes: "As opposed to a disaster, a community emergency does not represent a crisis state. In this instance an event may occur which places demands upon the traditional structure; however, the institutionalized, crisis management components of the system are able adequately to meet these demands by established mechanisms." For example, a fire department attends to a burning home but other measures are required to deal with forest fires. See Wenger, "Community Response to Disaster," 27. Allen H. Barton defines a disaster as "part of the larger category of *collective stress situations*. A collective stress situation occurs when *many members of a social*

system fail to receive expected conditions of life from the system." See Barton, *Communities in Disaster*, 38 (emphasis in original).

36 In English and French, the word "catastrophe" had theatrical and poetic connotations until at least the seventeenth century. See Michael O'dea, "Le mot 'catastrophe,'" 36–7. For an extensive history of the word in a German environment, see Briese and Günther, "Katastrophe."

37 See the corresponding entry in Dal', *Tolkovyi slovar' zhivogo velikorusskogo iazyka*.

38 Ellen Mickiewicz writes that a 1985 earthquake in Tadzhikistan was referred to as an *avariia*. This is highly unlikely and, if true, a very rare exception. See Mickiewicz, *Split Signals*, 137. In what might be a unique case, a film reviewer in 1980 employed the words *avariia*, *stikhiia*, and *katastrofa* in the same sentence. This close juxtaposition of all three terms is exceptionally rare and perhaps was only permitted in the context of fictional films. See Maslovskii, "Khronika podviga," 5.

39 *Avariia* is related to the German *Havarie* and apparently has its origins in Arabic.

40 It has also been referred to as an accident, which has bothered some researchers. See Lemarchand, *La vie contaminée*, 170.

41 Men'shikov, *Sovetskaia ekonomika*; Dmitrii Oreshkin, *Aral'skaia katastrofa.*

42 For an analysis of attempts to control the discourse of the Chicago heat wave in 1995, see Klinenberg, *Heat Wave*, 23.

43 Stone, *Policy Paradox*, 219.

44 Quoted in Stone, *Policy Paradox*, 218.

45 On the transition from brotherhood to friendship, see Martin, *Affirmative Action Empire*, 432–60.

46 See, for example, Suny, *Revenge of the Past*; Hosking, *Beyond Socialist Realism*, 50–83; Simon, *Nationalism and Policy*; Pipes, *Formation of the Soviet Union*.

47 See Rabusseau, *Les neiges labiles*; Utz, *Kultivierung der Katastrophe*, 115–47. Avalanches were not absent in Soviet literature and film. The film *Dead Mountaineer's Hotel*, based on the novel by Boris Strugatsky, has an avalanche as the backdrop to the drama. See Grigorii Kromanov, *Dead Mountaineer's Hotel* (1979).

48 Ziiaev, *Tsentr Tashkenta*, 17.

49 Turnerelli, *L'incendie de Kazan 1842*.

50 Rüthers, *Moskau bauen von Lenin bis Chruscev*, 212.

51 This theme is addressed in Meuser et al., *Zwischen Stalin und Glasnost*.

52 On Dnepropetrovsk, see Rassweiler, *Generation of Power*, 142. On the BAM railway, see Christopher J. Ward, *Brezhnev's Folly: The Building of BAM and*

Late Soviet Socialism (Pittsburgh, PA: University of Pittsburgh Press, 2009).

53 Stronski, *Tashkent*, 255.

54 Gilbert, "Reply to Hewitt," 98.

55 Solnit, *Paradise Built in Hell.*

56 For a philosophical explanation of the Lockean strain, see Taylor, "Liberal Politics and the Public Sphere." For a discussion on the Habermasian strain, see Calhoun, *Habermas and the Public Sphere*.

57 The Orthodox Church, for example, collected massive amounts of goods by having people drop them off. "Tserkov' ob"iavila sbor veshchei dlia postradavshikh," *Izvestiia Mordovii*, 8 April 2010.

58 This is one of Robert Putnam's primary concerns with the recent transformation of volunteer work in the United States. See Putnam, *Bowling Alone*.

59 Lindenmeyr, *Poverty Is Not a Vice*; Valkenier, *Russian Realist Art*; Raeff, *Understanding Imperial Russia*; Koenker and Rosenberg, *Party, State, and Society*; Kollman, *By Honor Bound*; White, *Russia Goes Dry*; Shearer, *Industry, State, and Society*; Ashwin, *Gender, State, and Society*; Gorshkov, *Russia's Factory Children*.

60 Robbins Jr, *Famine in Russia*.

61 See, among others, Lindenmeyr, *Poverty Is Not a Vice*; Bradley, "Volunteer Associations."

62 Mersiianovaia and Iakobson, *Potentsial i puti razvitiia filantropii v Rossii*, 224–5.

63 Peris, *Storming the Heavens*, 63.

64 Ibid., 63, 67.

65 Gestwa, *Die Stalinschen Grossbauten des Kommunismus*, 452–3. See also Vail' and Genis, *60-e—mir sovetskogo cheloveka*.

66 Weiner, *Little Corner of Freedom*.

67 Ibid., 406–28.

68 John Dunlop recognizes the problems they caused for the regime but hesitates to link them with the values of civil society. See Dunlop, *Faces of Contemporary Russian Nationalism*, 63–92.

69 Putnam, *Bowling Alone*.

70 On the rebuilding of a socialist Polish city, see Goldman, "Warsaw."

71 Alexander Dovzhenko and Iuliia Solntseva, *Poema o more* (Mosfil'm, 1958). Dovzhenko died in 1956 and his wife completed the project.

72 Rasputin, *Farewell to Matyora*. This story was made into a film. See Elem Klimov, *Proshchanie* (1981).

CHAPTER TWO

1 Cohen, *Bukharin and the Bolshevik Revolution*, 177.
2 Gladkov, *Cement*, 209–10.
3 On architecture, see Hudson, *Blueprints and Blood*.
4 For an interesting analysis of Trotsky's attitude towards Stalin, see Isaac Deutscher's review of Trotsky's *Stalin*, in Deutscher, "Trotsky on Stalin," 78–90.
5 "Razrusheniia v raione Alupki," *Pravda*, 15 September 1927.
6 "Ofitsial'noe soobshchenie," *Krasnyi Krym*, 24 September 1927. The rumour was also mockingly reported in the *New York Times*. See "Quakes in Crimea Drive Nepmen Away," *New York Times*, 25 September 1927.
7 Markevich, "Letopis' zemletriasenii v Krymu," 69–70.
8 The basic parameters of the scale are reprinted in Rost, *Armenian Tragedy*, 193. It is also readily available on the internet. It has been modified since the Crimean earthquake, but the essential idea remains. First, the scale rates an earthquake according to its effect on human structures. Second, the lower levels describe impact on human beings, whereas the higher levels describe the impact on buildings. See also Ulomov, *Vnimanie!*, 56–60. Ulomov presents the Medvedev-Sponheuer-Karnik scale (also known as MSK-64) developed in 1964 and designed in the spirit of previous intensity scales that take into consideration the impact on human communities and buildings.
9 Dvoichenko, "Chernomorskie zemletriaseniia 1927 goda v Krymu," 77.
10 Shimanovskii, "Soobshchenie o Krymskom zemletriasenii 12 sentiabria 1927 goda," 43–5.
11 Dvoichenko, "Chernomorskie zemletriaseniia 1927 goda v Krymu," 84–5.
12 Ibid., 93.
13 Ibid., 94.
14 Allworth, *Tatars of Crimea*, 4, 33.
15 GA RF, f. A-482, op. 1, d. 617, l. 213–20.
16 Amo Bek-nazaryan, *Namus* (1926). The film was based on a late nineteenth-century novel by Aleksandr Shirvanzade. The novel is set in Shemakha in Azerbaidjan. In 1859, a massive earthquake struck the regional centre, and the town never really recovered as nearby Baku rode the oil boom. Thus Shemakha offers a striking example of a city that did not rise from the proverbial ashes. See Shirvanzade, "Namus," 123–37.
17 Petrov and Il'f, *Dvenadtsat' stul'ev*, 330–1. The story was written shortly after the earthquake. The panic is also evident in the film version from 1971, a

time when the Brezhnev government did not like to associate panic with disasters. See Leonid Gaidai, *Dvenadtsat' stul'ev* (1971).

18 "Plody paniki," *Krasnyi Krym*, 14 September 1927.

19 "Pravitel'stvennoe soobshchenie," *Krasnyi Krym*, 13 September 1927.

20 "Na pomoshch' vsesoiuznoi zdravnitse," *Krasnyi Krym*, 24 September 1927.

21 On the NEP economy, see Nove, *Economic History of the USSR*, 115, 117.

22 GA RF, f. A-259, op. 11[b], d. 2407, l. 45–6.

23 GA RF, f. A-259, op. 12[a], d. 305, l. 89.

24 GA RF, f. A-259, op. 12[a], d. 305, l. 84–5.

25 GA RF, f. A-259, op. 32, d. 23, l. 228.

26 GA RF, f. A-259, op. 32, d. 23, l. 243–4.

27 GA RF, f. A-259, op. 12 [a], d. 305, l. 92.

28 GA RF, f. A-259, op. 11 [b], d. 2407, l. 138. Insurance debates were not hidden from the public. Officials wanted to find ways to make voluntary insurance mandatory, so there was funds to cover all sorts of natural disasters. See Semeshko, "Strakhovanie ot stikhiinykh bedstvii," 14.

29 GA RF, f. A-259, op. 12[a], d. 305, l. 86.

30 GA RF, f. A-259, op. 12[a], d. 305, l. 78.

31 GA RF, f. A-259, op. 12[a], d. 305, l. 77.

32 GA RF, f. A-259, op. 11[b], d. 2407, l. 176; GARF, f. A-259, op. 12[a], d. 305, l. 79.

33 GA RF, f. A-259, op. 11[b], d. 2407, l. 36.

34 GA RF, f. A-259, op. 12[a], d. 305, l. 81; GARF, f. A-259, op. 11[b], d. 2407, l. 187.

35 GA RF, f. A-259, op. 11[b], d. 2407, l. 67.

36 GA RF, f. A-482, op. 1, d. 617, l. 52. On Stalin's advocacy of the phrase "friendship of peoples" in the 1930s, see Martin, *The Affirmative Action Empire*, 440. Martin refers to the phrase as a metaphor but does not explain what it is a metaphor for (probably because it is not a metaphor).

37 "Dagestan otpravil v Krym 3 vagona stekla," *Krasnyi Krym*, 20 October 1927. "Pomoshch' Belorussii," *Krasnyi Krym*, 21 October 1927. See also TsDAVO, f. 452, op. 1, d. 1, l. 71.

38 GA RF, f. A-482, op. 1, d. 617, l. 64.

39 GA RF, f. A-482, op. 1, d. 617, l. 150.

40 Grinberg, *Moskovskii teatr operetty*, 203.

41 GA RF, f. A-259, op. 11[b], d. 4017, l. 3.

42 GA RF, f. A-482, op. 1, d. 617, l. 291–2.

43 GA RF, f. A-482, op. 1, d. 617, l. 338.

44 GA RF, f. A-482, op. 1, d. 617, l. 52, 125.

45 TsDAVO, f. 452, op. 1, d. 1, l. 51.

46 TsDAVO, f. 452, op. 1, d. 1, l. 88.

47 GA RF, f. A-259, op. 32, d. 23, l. 218–19.
48 Korshunov, *Mogut li evrei rabotat na zemle*, 23–5. See also Dekel-Chen, *Farming the Red Land*; Levin, *O pereselenii evreiskoi bednoty v Krym i Birobidzhan*.
49 Dekel-Chen, *Farming the Red Land*, 102. Polian, *Against Their Will*, 66.
50 At a broad level, the First All-Russian Congress of Resettlement Officials had met in March of 1927 to discuss solutions to the imbalanced population distribution in the Soviet Union. See Polian, *Against Their Will*, 65–6.
51 GA RF, f. A-259, op. 32, d. 23, l. 229.
52 GA RF, f. A-259, op. 32, d. 23, l. 242.
53 Stites, "Bolshevik Ritual Building in the 1920s," 302.
54 Saidbaev, *Islam i obshchestvo*, 189.
55 GA RF, f. A-259, op. 32, d. 23, l. 219.
56 GA RF, f. A-259, op. 32, d. 23, l. 229.
57 GA RF, f. A-259, op. 11[b], d. 2407, l. 177. See "Vozmozhna li novaia katastrofa v Krymu," *Pravda*, 20 September 1927.
58 GA RF, f. A-259, op. 32, d. 23, l. 234.
59 GA RF, f. A-259, op. 32, d. 23, l. 250.
60 GA RF, f. A-259, op. 32, d. 23, l. 157.
61 Markevich, "Letopis' zemletriasenii v Krymu," 64. Herodotus wrote about earthquakes in other contexts as well. He reported on Greek soldiers who, after an earthquake, gave offerings to the gods before the battle of Salamis. The soldiers hoped thereby to get the gods on their side before entering battle. See Waldherr, *Erdbeben*, 112.
62 GA RF f. R-9501, op. 1, d. 38, l. 81.
63 Semeshko, "Krasnyi Krest vo vremia zemletriaseniia v Krymu," 3.
64 "Chto pokazalo pravitel'stvennoe obsledovanie iuzhnogo berega," *Krasnyi Krym*, 10 December 1927.
65 Semeshko, "Krasnyi Krest vo vremia zemletriaseniia v Krymu," 3.
66 GA RF, f. R-5446, op. 22, d. 2782, l. 6.
67 On the initial atomic tests in the Soviet Union, see Holloway, *Stalin and the Bomb*, 213–23.
68 Kadyrov, *Ashkhabadskaia katastrofa*, 11.
69 Cattell, "Soviet Cities and Consumer Welfare Planning," 258–9. Major cities such as Moscow and Kyiv already had general plans, but they were the exception. On Kyiv, see Ignatkin, "Stroitel'stvo i arkhitektura sovremennogo Kieva," 2:641–2.
70 Kadyrov, *Ashkhabadskaia katastrofa*, 20–4.
71 See the photographs inserted in Kadyrov, *Ashkhabadskaia katastrofa*.
72 Nalivkin, *Vospominaniia ob Ashkhabadskom zemletriasenii 1948 goda*, 9–10.
73 Ibid., 14.

74 "O zemletriasenii v raione g. Ashkhabada," *Pravda*, 7 October 1948.

75 "V pravitel'stvennoi komissii Soveta Ministrov SSSR po likvidatsii posledstvii zemletriaseniia v raione goroda Ashkhabada," *Pravda*, 9 October 1948; "O merakh pomoshchi naseleniiu, postradavshemu ot zemletriaseniia v g. Ashkhabade," *Pravda*, 9 October 1948.

76 "Zemletriasenie v Irane," *Pravda*, 8 October 1948.

77 "Pervoocherednye meropriiatiia pravitel'stva Turkmenskoi SSR po likvidatsii posledstvii zemletriaseniia," *Pravda*, 11 October 1948.

78 More recent efforts have been made to determine a realistic death toll. See Kadyrov, *Ashkhabadskaia katastrofa*.

79 "200 Killed by Quake in Famed Iranian City," *New York Times*, 7 October 1948.

80 Klychmuradov, *Ashkhabadskoe zemletriasenie i pomoshch' narodov SSSR*, 4.

81 GA RF, f. R-5451, op. 43, d. 705, l. 360.

82 GA RF, f. R-5451, op. 43, d. 705, l. 359.

83 Nalivkin, *Vospominaniia ob Ashkhabadskom zemletriasenii 1948 goda*, 11.

84 GA RF, f. R-5446, op. 50a, d. 586, l. 15.

85 Nalivkin, *Vospominaniia ob Ashkhabadskom zemletriasenii 1948 goda*, 15.

86 Ibid., 13.

87 Klychmuradov, *Ashkhabadskoe zemletriasenie*, 57–61.

88 *Turkmenskaia iskra* published a photograph of lumber arriving from afar. See *Turkmenskaia iskra*, 24 November 1948.

89 Klychmuradov, *Edinstvo armii i naroda*, 20.

90 V. Tunin, "Odna sem'ia," *Turkmenskaia iskra*, 20 October 1948.

91 "Spasibo starshemu bratu," *Turkmenskaia iskra*, 15 February 1950.

92 "Stalinskaia druzhba narodov," *Turkmenskaia iskra*, 22 October 1948.

93 GA RF, f. R-1235, op. 122, d. 368, l. 21–2.

94 GA RF, f. R-5446, op. 57a, d. 65, l. 8.

95 "Stroiteli Uzbekistana pomogaiut vosstanavlivat' Ashkhabad," *Turkmenskaia iskra*, 8 June 1949.

96 See "Pervoocherednye meropriiatiia pravitel'stva Turkmenskoi SSR po likvidatsii posledstvii zemletriaseniia."

97 "Sdelaem Ashkhabad eshche krashe, chem prezhde," *Turkmenskaia iskra*, 9 March 1949; Iv. Ruchkin, "Tak li gorodskoi sovet dolzhen rukovodit' vosstanovleniem Ashkhabada?," *Turkmenskaia iskra*, 19 March 1949.

98 Ruchkin, "Tak li gorodskoi sovet dolzhen rukovodit' vosstanovleniem Ashkhabada?"

99 "Sobranie partiinogo aktiva g. Ashkhabada," *Turkmenskaia iskra*, 13 August 1949.

100 "Govoriat peredoviki stroek Ashkhabada," *Turkmenskaia iskra*, 14 October 1949.

101 V. Velikzhanin, "Ashkhabadproekt 'proektiruet,'" *Turkmenskaia iskra,* 7 May 1950.
102 V. Dronov, "O kontrole za stroitel'stvom v Ashkhabade," *Turkmenskaia iskra*, 17 November 1950.
103 GA RF, f. R-5446, op. 51, d. 3100, l. 165, 167. Five years before the earthquake, the seismological co-efficient had been reduced to economize on building costs. See "V seismoopasnoi zone," *Vechernii Ashkhabad*, 8 August 1989.
104 See Aman, *Architecture and Ideology*, 56.
105 See, for example, Klychmuradov, *Ashkhabadskoe zemletriasenie*.
106 Ruchkin, "Tak li gorodskoi sovet dolzhen rukovodit' vosstanovleniem Ashkhabada?"
107 L. Gaidai, "Strogo sobliudat' tipovye proekty," *Turkmenskaia iskra*, 26 March 1950.
108 M. Shermenev, "Strakhovoe vozmeshchenie postradavshim ot zemletriaseniia," *Turkmenskaia iskra*, 28 November 1948.
109 Kadyrov, *Ashkhabadskaia katastrofa*, 16.
110 A. Rakhmanov, "Khoshar zatiagivaetsia," *Turkmenskaia iskra*, 28 November 1948.
111 Kadyrov, *Ashkhabadskaia katastrofa*, 26.
112 N. Strunkina, "Pensionerka: 40 let v barakakh," *Vechernii Ashkhabad*, 13 September 1989.
113 "Vosstanovlenie Ashkhabada – krovnoe delo Komsomola," *Turkmenskaia iskra*, 29 April 1949.
114 GA RF, f. R-9501, op. 2, d. 1100, l. 57.
115 Ibid., l. 55.
116 Ibid., l. 60.
117 Ibid., l. 78–82.
118 GA RF, f. R-9501, op. 2, d. 1218.
119 "Ashkhabad," *Turkmenskaia iskra*, 7 November 1948.
120 GA RF, f. R-9501, op. 2, d. 1218, l. 130, 192.
121 The evacuation of children is a controversial topic in England. For an optimistic evaluation of the English evacuation of children, see Julie Summers, *When the Children Came Home: Stories of Wartime Evacuees* (London: Simon and Schuster, 2011). For a more tragic and comic perspective, see the BBC podcast of Katie Hims's *The Wrong Label* at http://www.bbc.co.uk/radio/player/b010t6h0. The story of Spanish children evacuated to the Soviet Union during the Spanish Civil War is told in Jaime Camino, *Los Niños de Rusia* (2001).
122 "Children in War-Time: Has Evacuation Failed?," *Times of London*, 30 January 1940.

123 Sh. Kadyrov, "Taina 48-go goda," *Vechernii Ashkhabad*, 27 July 1989; Sh. Kadyrov, "Nuzhna pravda," *Vechernii Ashkhabad*, 1 February 1989.

124 Kakamurat Ballyev, "Vechnaia vesna rastsvetaet v dushe naroda," *Neitral'nyi Turkmenistan*, 5 October 1998.

125 Bial'kin, *Tragediia i podvig Ashkhabada*. The documents published in this book come almost exclusively from official Soviet sources.

126 Rousso, *La dernière catastrophe*.

127 Melikov, *Khronika istorii Ashkhabada*, 120.

CHAPTER THREE

1 Jean Wetz, "La rencontre indo-pakistanaise de Tachkent: M. Kossyguine a réuni mardi matin M. Shastri et le maréchal Ayoub Khan avant l'ouverture de la séance plenière," *Le Monde*, 5 January 1966.

2 J. Anthony Lukas, "Ayub and Shastri Arrive in Soviet: Meet Today at Tashkent on 18-Year Kashmir Dispute," *New York Times*, 4 January 1966.

3 J. Anthony Lukas, "Old Uzbek City Is Enjoying a New Day in the Sun," *New York Times*, 9 January 1966.

4 Jean Wetz, "Le conflit indo-pakistanais: Le succès de la conférence de Tachkent dépend des 'suggestions' que les Russes pourraient faire sur le Cachemire," *Le Monde*, 6 January 1966. The same correspondent also noted the model trains in the new toy stores but suggested that they, like the diplomatic talks, were easy to derail. See Jean Wetz, "À la conférence indo-pakistanaise de Tachkent: M. Kossyguine confère longuement avec les deux protagonistes toujours en désaccord sur l'ordre du jour des travaux," *Le Monde*, 8 January 1966.

5 Orekhov, *Velikii khashar*, 12.

6 Ziiaev, *Tsentr Tashkenta*, 17.

7 *Toshkent 1966 iil silsilas*.

8 Ibid. See also Ulomov's scientific analysis of the Tashkent earthquake in Ulomov, *Vnimanie!*

9 Peskov, "Tashkent," 42.

10 Ibid.

11 Aldylov et al., *Gorod, rozhdennyi dvazhdy*, 23.

12 *Toshkent 1966 iil silsilasi*.

13 "L.I. Brezhnev i A.N. Kosygin v Tashkente," *Pravda*, 27 April 1966.

14 Brezhnev was "first secretary" until the Party Congress, which reintroduced the title "general secretary." The title was most often associated with Joseph Stalin.

15 The speech is printed in Arkhangel'skii, *Tashkent*.

16 Vladimir Amlinskii, "Zemletriasenie i liudi," *Literaturnaia gazeta*, 17 May 1966.
17 Orekhov, *Velikii khashar*, 8.
18 GA RF, f. A-259, op. 45, d. 4912, l.69.
19 Chen, ""Resist the Earthquake and Rescue Ourselves."
20 On the laws, see RGANI, f. 5, op. 33, d. 235, l. 141.
21 N. Matchanov, "Tashkentskii khashar," *Novyi mir* 8 (August 1972): 205–16.
22 "L.I. Brezhnev i A.N. Kosygin v Tashkente," *Pravda*, 27 April 1966; "Zemletriasenie v Tashkente," *Pravda*, 27 April 1966.
23 Walter, *Katastrophen*, 136–8.
24 "Ikh imena nazyvaet narod," *Pravda Vostoka*, 27 April 1966; "L.I. Brezhnev i A.N. Kosygin v Tashkente," *Pravda Vostoka*, 27 April 1966; "Do novykh vstrech, Belarus'," *Pravda Vostoka*, 27 April 1966.
25 I. Liaskalo, "I vse zhe chelovek sil'nee," *Pravda Vostoka*, 29 June 1966.
26 V. Krinitskii and M. Arnautov, "Dni, polnye muzhestva," *Pravda Vostoka*, 8 July 1966.
27 GA RF, f. R-5446, op. 100, d. 265, l. 1.
28 M. Tiupaev, "My videli vashu stolitsu," *Pravda Vostoka*, 4 May 1966.
29 P. Il'khamov, "Luchi druzhby – s 'golubogo ekrana,'" *Pravda Vostoka*, 4 May 1966.
30 Nikolai Gribachev, "Tashkent v mae," *Pravda Vostoka*, 17 May 1966.
31 Kh. Iakh'iaev, "Za obraztsovyi obshchestvennyi poriadok," *Pravda Vostoka*, 14 May 1966.
32 M. Rubanov, "I zorche, i strozhe," *Pravda Vostoka*, 31 May 1966.
33 "Spekulianta – po rukam! Reid po rynkam Tashkenta," *Pravda Vostoka*, 12 July 1966.
34 Shlapentokh, *Public and Private Life*, 212.
35 GA RF, f. R-5451, op. 58, d. 4172, l. 87.
36 GA RF, f. R-5446, op. 100, d. 1271, l. 126.
37 "Gosstrakhovskii veksel'. Nashi interv'iu," *Pravda Vostoka*, 8 June 1966.
38 "Gosstrakhovskii veksel," *Pravda Vostoka*, 18 June 1966.
39 "Druzheskaia pomoshch' Tashkentu," *Stroitel'naia gazeta*, 20 May 1966; "Tashkentu – kliuchi ot bratskogo milliona," *Stroitel'naia gazeta*, 22 May 1966; "Geroicheskie budni stroitelei Tashkenta," *Stroitel'naia gazeta*, 1 June 1966; An. Vetrov and V. Zotov, "Front i tyl," *Stroitel'naia gazeta*, 13 July 1966.
40 V. Faians, "Tashkent – eto ekzamen," *Stroitel'naia gazeta*, 6 June 1966.
41 K. Kriukov, "Sokhranit' arkhitekturnye pamiatniki Tashkenta," *Stroitel'naia gazeta*, 22 February 1967.
42 See L. Volgin, "Vstrecha v Tashkente," *Literaturnaia gazeta*, 6 January 1966;

A. Iakubov, "Vo imia druzhby bratskikh kul'tur," *Literaturnaia gazeta*, 20 January 1966.

43 A. Alimzhanov, "Alma-Ata: Otsiuda step' nachinaetsia," *Literaturnaia gazeta*, 13 January 1966. See also Valentin Shatskov, "Vladivostok: Na 'kraiu zemli'," *Literaturnaia gazeta*, 22 January 1966.

44 Vladimir Amlinskii, "Zemletriasenie i liudi," *Literaturnaia gazeta*, 19 May 1966.

45 Takuma, "Human Behavior in the Event of Earthquakes," 162.

46 Stites, *Russian Popular Culture*, 168.

47 "Bratskaia pomoshch' Tashkentu," *Literaturnaia gazeta*, 25 June 1966; A. Khmelik, "Deti Tashkenta," *Literaturnaia gazeta*, 30 June 1966.

48 Malik Kaiumov, *Tashkent, zemletriasenie* (Kinostudiia dokumental'nykh fil'mov Uzbekistana, 1968).

49 Peskov, "Tashkent." This was also published in *Pravda Vostoka*. See V. Peskov, "Drama i podvig Tashkenta," *Pravda Vostoka*, 19 May 1966.

50 RGAE, f. 339, op. 3, d. 2470, l. 31.

51 TsDAGO, f. 1, op. 24, d. 6172, l. 1.

52 "V Tashkente vse spokoino," *Komsomolets Donbassa*, 29 April 1966; "Rekordsmeny podzemnykh gorizontov," *Komsomolets Donbassa*, 1 May 1966.

53 "Robitnikam i robitnitsiam, inzhenerno-tekhnichnim pratsivnikam i sluzhbovtsiam shakhti imeni Rumiantseva Donets'koi oblasti," *Radians'ka Donechchyna*, 30 April 1966.

54 Official documents suggested that thirteen people died as a result of the earthquake. See GA RF, f. R-5446, op. 100, d. 267, l. 1. Eric Klinenberg noted that the Chicago heat wave in 1995 had a higher death toll than did the San Francisco earthquake in 1989, though it generated comparatively little media interest. He explains the difference, in part, as being due to the fact that victims in heat waves tend to be members of marginalized groups. See Klinenberg, *Heat Wave*, 17.

55 After a tram accident in L'viv in 1972, officials reported that no provocative incidents occurred at the funeral. See TsDAGO, f. 1, op. 25, d. 718, l. 86.

56 TsDAGO, f. 1, op. 24, d. 4554, l. 40–1.

57 Ibid., l. 42–3.

58 RGANI, f. 5, op. 33, d. 235, l. 141. On the restrictions, see also Mickiewicz, *Media and the Russian Public*, 54.

59 RGANI, f. 5, op. 33, d. 235, l. 138.

60 Ibid., l. 139. See V. Gol'tsov, "Podvig v nebe: Rasskaz o muzhestve i masterstve ekipazha samoleta Viktora Mostovogo," *Pravda*, 15 October 1963. See Eldar Riazanov, *Neveroiatnye prikliucheniia ital'iantsev v Rossii* (1974). The

1979 film is Aleksandr Mitta's *Ekipazh* (1979). *Ekipazh* was not the first disaster film. In 1962, Grigorii Nikulin directed a film about a transatlantic flight that was the subject of a terrorist attack. The subject matter was a Western, not a Soviet, plane. See Grigorii Nikulin, *713-i prosit posadku* (1962). *Alarming Sunday* is of the same genre as *Ekipazh* and features courageous Soviet firefighters extinguishing a port fire; in this case, however, the ship is foreign owned. See Rudol'f Fruntov, *Trevozhnoe voskresen'e* (1983).

61 RGANI, f. 5, op. 33, d. 235, l. 140. This incident was dramatized twenty-five years later in Oles Honchar's *The Black Ravine*, 25 March 2012. Available at http://www.utoronto.ca/elul/English/Bilenko/Honchar-Black-Ravine.pdf.

62 RGANI, f. 5, op. 33, d. 235, l. 141. This issue resurfaced with Chernobyl, when V. Shcherbytskii, first party secretary of the Communist Party of Ukraine, made a similar point in 1986. See TsDAGO, f. 1, op. 25, d. 2995, l. 71.

63 Quoted in Roth-Ey, *Moscow Prime Time*, 159.

64 Vasilii Shukshin, *Zhivet takoi paren'* (Tsentral'naia kinostudiia imeni M. Gor'kogo, 1964). In this story, the main character is played by a young Leonid Kuravlev. *V kvadrate 45*, from the early 1950s, also had a rescue theme. See Iurii Vyshinskii, *V kvadrate 45* (1955).

65 Shortly thereafter Goriunov was reassigned as Soviet ambassador to Kenya.

66 Liaskalo, "I vse zhe chelovek sil'nee."

67 GA RF, f. R-5446, op. 100, d. 265, l. 1.

68 Ibid., l. 125.

69 GA RF, f. A-259, op. 45, d. 5343, l. 87–8.

70 Ibid., l. 89, 91.

71 Piers Blaikie et al., *At Risk*, 126.

72 "V atmosfere teploty i vzaimoponimaniia: Ot'ezd prezidenta Frantsii v Novosibirsk," *Pravda*, 24 June 1966.

73 Steinberg, *Acts of God*, 29–30. With respect to the media in general, David Alexander suggests that "television is virtually capable of turning public response on or off like a tap." See Alexander, *Confronting Catastrophe*, 139–40.

74 Quoted in Steinberg, *Acts of God*, 26.

75 "Violent séisme à Tachkent. MM. Brejnev et Kossyguine sont allés sur place," *Le Monde*, 27 April 1966.

76 "La terre a tremblé de nouveau à Tachkent," *Le Monde*, 28 April 1966.

77 Kaiumov, *Tashkent, zemletriasenie*.

78 GA RF, f. A-596, op. 1, d.2035, l. 107.

79 Ibid., l. 109.

80 Ibid., l. 120.

81 Peskov, *Puteshestvie c molodym mesiatsem*, 267–81.

82 The story did not reappear in the modified English-language version of this collection of stories. The English translation is in fact a translation of a Russian modification, *Otechestvo* (1972), of the original collection. See Peskov, *This Is My Native Land*.
83 Kornilov, *Tashkentskii dnevnik*. See also U. Abdurazzakov and Pulatov. G, *Gorod, pobedivshii stikhiiu* (Tashkent: Izd-vo Uzbekistan, 1974).
84 Aldylov et al., *Gorod, rozhdennyi dvazhdy*, 23.
85 Chikov and Zhuravlev, *Mesto podviga*.
86 Orekhov, *Velikii khashar*; Matchanov, "Tashkentskii khashar."
87 The Oxford Uzbek-English dictionary defines *khashar* as follows: "Mutual help given in agricultural works by peasants." See *Uzbek-English Dictionary*, 174.
88 Matchanov, "Tashkentskii khashar," 214.
89 Orekhov, *Velikii khashar*, 21.
90 Matchanov, "Tashkentskii khashar," 211.
91 Ibid., 212.
92 This separation is critical in Habermas, *Structural Transformation of the Public Sphere*.
93 "Vchera v Tashkente v torzhestvennoi obstanovke otkryt monumental'no-skulpturnyi kompleks," *Pravda Vostoka*, 21 May 1976.
94 On the shifting nature of clan politics in Central Asia, see Collins, *Clan Politics and Regime Transition*.
95 E. Ishmukhamedov, *Proshchai, zelen' leta* (Uzbekfilm, 1985).
96 Sardor Iskhakov, *Stolitsa druzhby i tepla* (RDK-Film, 2011).
97 Aldylov et al., *Gorod, rozhdennyi dvazhdy*, 23. The time reference appears a little into the story in Orekhov, *Velikii khashar*, 7.
98 On the importance of time in a social context, see Elias, *Time*.
99 TsDAGO, f. 1, op. 24, d. 6347, l. 31, 33, 39.

CHAPTER FOUR

1 Hudson, *Blueprints and Blood*.
2 Kotkin, *Magnetic Mountain*.
3 Quoted in B.M. Frolic, "New Moscow City Plan," 276.
4 Bouvard, *Le métro de Moscou*, 16.
5 Crews, "Civilization in the City." On the 1920s in the USSR, see Hudson, *Blueprints and Blood*.
6 The Western links are mentioned in Plesnevich, "Krizisy sovetskoi arkhitektury," 6–7.
7 The All-Russian Society for the Preservation of Historical and Cultural

Monuments went to great efforts to preserve architectural treasures. See Dunlop, *Faces of Contemporary Russian Nationalism*, 66–85.

8 Orekhov, *Velikii khashar*, 12.

9 Gladkov, *Cement*, 65.

10 On the role of concrete in design, see Banham, "New Brutalism." See also Legault, "Idea of Brutalism in Canadian Architecture."

11 General plans for the city had been made in 1938, 1954, 1964, and then 1967.

12 A. Mukhamedshin, "Tashkent zavtra," *Stroitel'stvo i arkhitektura Srednei Azii* 1, 10 (1964): 9–10.

13 Merport, *Novoe stroitel'stvo v Tashkente*, 1–6.

14 RGAE, f. 4372, op. 66, d. 2822, l. 46.

15 Burshtein, "Kakova seismichnost' Tashkenta?," 36.

16 Ibid., 37.

17 GA RF, f. R-5446, op. 100, d. 264, l. 4.

18 Ibid., l. 11.

19 This is commented upon in Stronski, *Tashkent*.

20 S. Blagov, "Kliuchi ot gorodskikh vorot," *Pravda Vostoka*, 22 May 1966. This phenomenon was not unique to the Soviet Union. After the destruction of Dresden during the Second World War, structures that had withstood the bombing were removed to make way for the new socialist city. See Meinhardt, "Der Mythos vom 'Alten Dresden' als Bauplan," 181.

21 Lewin, *Gorbachev Phenomenon*, 31. This attitude was not unique to the Soviet Union. After the San Francisco earthquake in 1906, David Hudson Burnham, who had formally submitted a new urban plan to city hall a day before the earthquake, rushed back from Paris to have his plan for a radically new San Francisco "implemented immediately." Ultimately, officials decided to maintain the original grid plan of the city. Starr, *California*, 176.

22 Iu. Mukimov, "Tashkent. Takim on budet," *Pravda Vostoka*, 15 August 1967.

23 Chebotareva, "V zashchitu plotnoi maloetazhnoi zastroiki," 18.

24 Kosinskii, "Bukhara," 19.

25 Kriukov and Notkin, "Rekonstruktsiia drevnikh gorodov i problemy sokhraneniia pamiatnikov arkhitektury Uzbekistana," 28–9.

26 Shvidkovskii, "Puti rekonstruktsii drevnikh gorodov," 18.

27 "Neizgladimoe vpechatlenie proizvelo na diplomatov," *Pravda Vostoka*, 19 May 1967. Photograph by I. Dushkin.

28 *Pravda Vostoka*, 23 June 1967.

29 Shvidkovskii, "Puti rekonstruktsii drevnikh gorodov," 18–21.

30 Ibid., 21.

31 Man'kovskaia, "O rabote sektsii istorii arkhitektury," 21.
32 Dunlop, *Faces of Contemporary Russian Nationalism*, 66.
33 GA RF, f. A-639, op. 1, d. 6, l. 88–90.
34 GA RF, f. A-639, op. 1., d. 77, l. 98.
35 Al'bert Mkrtchian and Edgar Khozhikian, *Opekun* (1970).
36 GA RF, f. A-639, op. 1, d. 41, l. 25.
37 GA RF, f. A-639, op. 1, d. 265, l. 79. These comments were intended for *Nauka i zhizn'* but do not appear to have been published.
38 GA RF, f. A-639, op. 1, d. 265, l. 70.
39 GA RF, f. A-639, op. 1, d. 6, l. 146. The hotel was removed in 2006.
40 V.N. Manakova, "Arkhitektura kafe 'Golubye kupola' i chaikhany na bul'vare imeni V.I. Lenina," *Stroitel'stvo i arkhitektura Uzbekistana* 7 (1971): 33–4.
41 Quoted in Legault, "Idea of Brutalism in Canadian Architecture," 321.
42 Fitzpatrick, "Popular Sedition in the Post-Stalin Soviet Union," 3. This theme has been explored in detail in Bellat, *Amériques-URSS*. On Tashkent, specifically, see pp. 216–20.
43 Meuser et al., *Zwischen Stalin und Glasnost*, 43.
44 Camus, "Fabrication industrielle de huit logements par jour dans la région parisienne." The materials were also used in other areas of Eastern Europe. See Zarecor, "Rainbow Edges."
45 RGAE, f. 339, op. 3, d. 2470, l. 102–3.
46 Ibid., l. 95.
47 Savitsky, "New Trends in Architecture." This theme finds extensive poetic and comedic expression in the film *Irony of Fate* (1975).
48 Korobovtsev, "Tashkent," 10 (1971): 19.
49 Ibid., 20.
50 Ibid., 21. Korobovtsev took this quote from an interview in an article in *Literaturnaia gazeta*.
51 Korobovtsev, "Tashkent," 12 (1971): 26. A Muscovite parallel with Moshe Safdie is also mentioned in Bellat, *Amériques-URSS*, 222.
52 Ikonnikov, *Soviet Architecture of Today*, plate 36.
53 Korobovtsev, "Tashkent," 12 (1971): 28.
54 Ibid., 10 (1971): 21.
55 Korobovtsev, "Tashkent," 10 (1971): 19.
56 "Zdes' b'etsia serdtse Tashkenta," *Pravda Vostoka*, 11 June 1967.
57 On the size and function of the makhalla, see Moiseeva, "Narodnye traditsii i sovremennoe gradostroitel'stvo," 79.
58 Korobovotsev quotes Le Corbusier to support the construction of taller buildings. See Korobovtsev, "Tashkent," 10 (1971): 22–3.

59 Hudson, *Blueprints and Blood*, 139.
60 Meuser et al., *Zwischen Stalin und Glasnost*, 30.
61 The Western influences are discussed in Meuser et al., *Zwischen Stalin und Glasnost*, 27.
62 Mackenzie, "Tashkent," 215.
63 Irbutaev, "V makhalle Iangi-Khaiat," 7.
64 Ibid., 8. On the continued presence of religious officials in the makhalla, see Ro'i, *Islam in the Soviet Union*, 333–4, 342.
65 Irbutaev, "V makhalle Iangi-Khaiat," 9.
66 Ibid., 10. On general Brezhnev tactics to encourage atheism through persuasion and the encouragement of atheism, see Bociurkiw, "Religion in the USSR after Khrushchev." At the same time, there was an increase in religious activism.
67 Khamidov, "O makhalle i ee vliianii," 53.
68 Chebotareva, "Opyt proektirovaniia eksperimental'nykh mikroraionov-makhallia v Tashkente," 11.
69 Moiseeva, "Narodnye traditsii i sovremennoe gradostroitel'stvo," 79.
70 Ibid., 80.
71 Celik, *Urban Forms and Colonial Confrontations*, 38–43.
72 Askarov, "Dom i dukh starogo Tashkenta kontsa XX veka," 5.
73 Plesnevich, "Prostranstvennoe myshlenie," 14.
74 Plesnevich, "Krizisy sovetskoi arkhitektury," 6.
75 A. Aulov, "Tashkent mnogoetazhnyi," *Pravda Vostoka*, 7 July 1967.
76 Korobovtsev, "Zhilishche v tsentre Tashkenta," 4.
77 Travianko, "Kachestvenno proektirovat' i zastraivat' novye mikroraiony Tashkenta."
78 GA RF, f. A-259, op. 45, d. 4912, l. 3.
79 GA RF, f. A-259, op. 45, d. 5342, l. 25.
80 GA RF, f. A-259, op. 45, d. 4912, l. 4.
81 Ibid., l. 23. On central intervention in regional economics and its negative consequences, see Rutland, *Politics of Economic Stagnation*, 49–72.
82 RGAE, f. 339, op. 3, d. 2687, l. 67.
83 GA RF, f. R-5446, op. 100, d. 266, l. 117.
84 TsDAVO, f. 4906, op. 4, d. 2315, l. 57, 54, 56. The RSFSR also complained about the costs associated with seismological construction. See RGAE, f. 339, op. 3, d. 2687, l. 58.
85 RGAE, f. 339, op. 3, d. 2687, l. 47.
86 TsDAVO, f. 4906, op. 4, d. 2315, l.52.
87 TsDAVO, f. 4906, op. 4, d. 2324, l. 18–19.
88 GA RF, f. R-5446, op. 100, d. 265, l. 53, 41–9.

89 GA RF, f. R-5446, op. 100, d. 265, l. 127, 132.

90 Ibid., l. 99.

91 On disruptive supply and production in the 1930s, see Filtzer, *Soviet Workers and Stalinist Industrialization*, chap. 7.

92 RGAE, f. 339, op. 3, d. 2470, l. 201.

93 RGAE, f. 339, op. 3, d. 2687, l. 24–8.

94 Ibid., l. 120.

95 The BAM railway project also had a very high attrition rate, which added to migration costs and reduced the familiarity individual workers had with the projects. See Mote, "BAM after the Fanfare," 53.

96 RGAE, f. 339, op. 3, d. 2470, l. 200.

97 RGAE, f. 339, op. 3, d. 2687, l. 121.

98 Taubman, *Governing Soviet Cities*, vii. Taubman quotes the mayor of Chervonograd about the building trusts in his town: "All they care about is chalking up square meters. They don't even care if no grass grows around the houses."

99 GA RF, f. R-5446, op. 100, d. 265, l. 152–3.

100 RGAE, f. 339, op. 3, d. 2687, l. 40–2.

101 Ibid., l. 157.

102 Davidow, *Soviet Union through the Eyes of an American*, 68–9 (emphasis in original).

103 Chikov and Zhuravlev, *Mesto podviga*, 24, 65.

104 Aldylov et al., *Gorod*, 45.

105 Grid patterns go back to the rational planning of the eighteenth-century Enlightenment city. Odessa was a prime example in the Russian context. See Skinner, "Trends in Planning Practices," 141.

106 GA RF, f. R-5446, op. 101, d. 351, l. 5.

107 RGAE, f. 339, op. 3, d. 2470, l. 228.

108 RGAE, f. 4372, op. 66, d. 2822, l. 22.

109 Ibid., l. 15.

110 Ibid., l. 16.

111 TsDAGO, f. 1, op. 25, d. 1570, l. 15, 17.

112 K. Kriukov, "Sokhranit' arkhitekturnye pamiatniki Tashkenta," *Stroitel'naia gazeta*, 22 February 1967.

113 Solzhenitsyn envisioned Brezhnev's bulldozer "scraping Russia from the face of the earth." See Solzhenitsyn, *Mortal Danger*, 28.

114 Ikramov, "Giulistan," 36. The bulldozer also played a critical role in *Poem about the Sea*, in which it destroys the homes of villagers. See Alexander Dovzhenko and Iuliia Solntseva, *Poema o More* (Mosfil'm, 1958).

115 B. L'vov, "V chem ne vinovata stikhiia," *Stroitel'naia gazeta*, 9 September 1966.

116 GA RF, R-5451, op. 58, d. 3215, l. 71.
117 Ibid., l. 47.
118 GA RF, f. R-5461, op. 58, d. 346, l. 59. Delays with the palace of culture were not unique to Uzbekistan. In the early 1950s, a similar scandal erupted in Turkmenistan. See "Turkmenistan," 81.
119 GA RF, f. R-5451, op. 58, d. 3215, l. 68.
120 Ibid., l. 29, 31.
121 TsDAGO, f. 1, op. 24, d. 6348, l. 46. The bus driver denied money was a motivation, but he did receive three rubles.
122 TsDAGO, f. 1, op. 24, d. 6347. This accident was reported in *Vechirniy Kyiv* in a small box on the third page. The box reported that an accident with casualties had occurred and that a commission had been established to look into the incident. See *Vechirniy Kyiv*, 26 April 1967.
123 TsDAGO, f. 1, op. 24, d. 6347, l. 12.
124 Ibid., l. 10.
125 TsDAGO, f. 1, op. 25, d. 1269, l. 157–8.
126 Ibid., l. 159.
127 Sardor Iskhakov, *Stolitsa druzhby i tepla* (RDK-Film, 2011).
128 Ibid.
129 Ibid. A film version of this novel appeared in 1968 under the same title. See Abbasov Shukhrat, *Tashkent – gorod khlebnyi* (1968).
130 GA RF, f. A-259, op. 45, d. 6060, l. 8.
131 Ward, *Brezhnev's Folly*, 48, 90. The volunteering in the case of BAM was not such a point of emphasis as it was in Tashkent. On compensation, see also Rassweiler, *Generation of Power*, 100–2.
132 On the cost overruns this caused, see TsDAVO, f. 4906, op. 4, d. 2324, l.54.
133 TsDAGO, f. 1, op. 32, d. 2482, l. 7.
134 "V stroitel'stve novogo Tashkenta aktivnoe uchastie prinimaiut studenty uchebnykh zavedenii stolitsy respubliki," *Komsomolets Uzbekistana*, 21 May 1966.
135 *Komsomolets Uzbekistana*, 31 May 1966.
136 On the Komsomol at Dneprostroi, see Rassweiler, *Generation of Power*, 170–2.
137 TsDAGO, f. 7, op. 20, d. 132a, l. 1–3.
138 TsDAGO, f. 7, op. 20, d. 358a, l. 9.
139 TsDAGO, f. 7, op. 20, d. 355, l. 3, 29–30.
140 TsDAGO, f. 7, op. 20, d. 249, l. 39.
141 TsDAGO, f. 7, op. 20, d. 355, l. 31.
142 TsDAGO, f. 7, op. 20, d. 355, l. 33.
143 TsDAGO, f. 7, op, 20, d. 356, l. 6–7.

144 TsDAGO, f. 7, op. 20, d. 249, l. 10, 94–5.

145 Ibid., l. 9. On the availability of alcohol, the negative effects of its consumption, and the increasing consumption levels from the 1960s onwards, see Treml, *Alcohol in the USSR*. See also S. Strumilin and M. Sonin, "Alkogol'nye poteri i bor'ba s nimi," *Ekonomika i organizatsiia promyshlennogo proizvodstva* 4 (1974): 30–44.

146 TsDAGO, f. 7, op. 20, d. 914, l. 31.

147 Ibid., l. 6.

148 On the lack of experience in the immediate postwar period, see Fürst, *Stalin's Last Generation*, 52.

149 TsDAGO, f. 7, op. 20, d. 914, l. 116.

150 Shlapentokh, *Public and Private Life*, 109.

151 Ibid., 110.

152 TsDAGO, f. 7, op. 20, d. 249, l. 35.

153 TsDAGO, f. 7, op. 20, d. 356, l. 17.

154 TsDAGO, f. 7, op. 20, d. 249, l. 49, 73.

155 Ibid., l. 58.

156 TsDAGO, f. 7, op. 20, d. 3838, l. 72, 79.

157 TsDAGO, f. 7, op. 20, d. 249, l. 44.

158 TsDAGO, f. 7, op. 20, d. 356, l. 18.

159 TsDAGO, f. 7, op. 20, d. 249, l. 21.

160 TsDAGO, f. 7, op. 20, d. 137, l. 32. Attendance figures for the next Sunday were unavailable.

161 TsDAGO, f. 7, op. 20, d. 137, l. 36.

162 TsDAGO, f. 7, op. 20, d. 136, l. 21.

163 Ibid., l. 34.

164 Comrie et al., *Russian Language in the Twentieth Century*, 210.

165 TsDAGO, f. 7, op. 20, d. 356, l. 82.

166 Ibid., l. 14.

167 Malik Kaiumov, *Tashkent, zemletriasenie* (Kinostudiia dokumental'nykh fil'mov Uzbekistana, 1968).

168 Kozlov, "Meaning of Sedition," 25–7.

169 Quoted in Kozlov, "Meaning of Sedition," 28, 48, 50.

170 Kozlov, "Meaning of Sedition," 27.

171 RGANI, f. 5, op. 59, d. 3, l. 7.

172 Fitzpatrick, "Popular Sedition in the Post-Stalin Soviet Union," 11.

173 RGAE, f. 339, op. 3, d. 2470, l. 194.

174 RGAE, f. 339, op. 3, d. 2470, l. 119–20.

175 "Priglashaem k Chernomu moriu," *Pravda Vostoka*, 27 May 1966.

176 TsDAVO, f. 2, op. 13, d. 1715, l. 62.

177 GA RF, f. R-5446, op. 100, d. 267, l. 82.
178 TsDAVO, f. 2, op. 13, d. 1715, l. 195.
179 TsDAVO, f. 2, op. 13, d. 1715, l. 134.
180 TsDAGO, f. 1, op. 31, d. 3046, l. 98.
181 TsDAVO, f. 2, op. 13, d. 1715, l. 58.
182 TsDAVO, f. 2, op. 13, d. 2608, l. 11.
183 TsDAVO, f. 2, op. 13, d. 1715, l. 170.
184 TsDAGO, f. 1, op. 31, d. 3046, l. 28.
185 TsDAVO, f. 2, op. 13, d. 1715, l. 53.
186 TsDAVO, f. 2, op. 13, d. 2608, l. 13, 69.
187 Manley, *To the Tashkent Station*, 249–50.
188 "Tashkentskie rebiata v Podmoskov'e," *Komsomolets Uzbekistana*, 12 June 1966.
189 "Bratskaia pomoshch' Tashkentu," *Literaturnaia gazeta*, 25 June 1966.
190 "Gruziia: 'Tashkent' v 'Rustaveli,'" *Komsomolets Uzbekistana*, 14 August 1966.
191 A. Khmelik, "Deti Tashkenta," *Literaturnaia gazeta*, 30 June 1966.
192 GA RF, f. R-5446, op. 100, d. 214, l. 6.
193 GA RF, f. R-6991, op. 6, d. 51, l. 49.
194 Sh. Tashpulatov, "Zemletriasenie i religiia," *Pravda Vostoka*, 25 October 1966.
195 R. Izattulaev, "Kak ia voiuiu s religiei – zametki ateista," *Pravda Vostoka*, 8 December 1966.
196 R. Babadzhanova, "Ateisty v nastuplenie," *Pravda Vostoka*, 13 January 1967.
197 Saidbaev, *Islam i obshchestvo*, 189.
198 RGANI, f. 5, op. 60, d. 24, l. 76.
199 On the persistence of festivals after Khrushchev's anti-religion campaigns, see Ro'i, *Islam in the Soviet Union*, 489–508, esp. 508.
200 G. Kolobov, "Pervymi k finishu," *Pravda Vostoka*, 22 July 1967.
201 See MAKSAN 10 (1991): 7–8.
202 TsDAGO, f. 1, op. 25, d. 1269, l. 79, 87.
203 GA RF, f. R-5446, op. 140, d. 291, l. 27; GA RF, f. R-5446, op. 144, d. 309, l. 1.
204 L. Moiseeva, "Eto 26-e aprelia," *Tribuna energetika*, 4 October 1988.

INTERLUDE

1 Film history is, of course, a vibrant field, but it, like art history, is specifically visual. On history and film, see Rosenstone, "Introduction."
2 On television, see Stites, *Russian Popular Culture*, 168–70.
3 Gillespie, *Russian Cinema*.
4 Youngblood, *Russian War Films*.

5 Amo Bek-nazaryan, *Namus* (1926). The earthquake is mentioned, but its significance as a natural disaster is not discussed, in Youngblood, *Movies for the Masses*, 87–8.
6 Despite extensive attention to Dovzhenko, this film went unmentioned in Peter Kenez's history of Soviet film. See Kenez, *Cinema and Soviet Society*. It is of course possible that the film was difficult to come by, whereas now it is easily available on the internet.
7 Karelin, "Zemletriasenie."
8 A. Speshnev, *Khronika nochi* (Belarus'fil'm, 1972); A. Kosarev, *Kogda drozhit zemlia* (Mosfil'm, 1975).
9 Aleksandr Mitta, *Ekipazh* (Mosfil'm, 1979).
10 Denise Youngblood writes: "film as a medium is poorly suited to the transmission of factual information if it is to remain true to its own aesthetic imperatives." See Youngblood, "Repentance," 140.
11 Dmitrii Svetozarov, *Proryv* (Lenfil'm, 1986).
12 Razlogov, "Mezhdu zrelishchem i povestvovaniem," 65.
13 Youngblood, *Russian War Films*.
14 It is briefly fictionally portrayed at the very end of Leonid Gaidai, *Dvenadtsat' stul'ev* (1971). This was taken from the original story. See Petrov and Il'f, *Dvenadtsat' stul'ev*, 330–1.
15 RGAKFD (*Rossiiskii gosudarstvennyi arkhiv kinofotodokumentov*) no. 18100, *Zemletriasenie v Ialte* (1927).
16 RGAKFD no. 8449, *Zemletriasenie v Ashkhabade* (1948), reel 2.
17 RGAKFD no. 19485, *Skop'e – gorod tragedii i bratstva* (1964).
18 RGAKFD no. 8449, *Zemletriasenie v Ashkhabade* (1948), reel 2.
19 Ibid., reel 5.
20 Ibid.
21 Ibid., reel 2.
22 Nalivkin, *Vospominaniia ob Ashkhabadskom zemletriasenii 1948 goda*, 11.
23 RGAKFD no. 8449, *Zemletriasenie v Ashkhabade* (1948), reel 5.
24 Iv. Ruchkin, "Tak li gorodskoi sovet dolzhen rukovodit' vosstanovleniem Ashkhabada?" *Turkmenskaia iskra*, 19 March 1949.
25 RGAKFD no. 7039, *Novosti dnia No. 31* (1951).
26 RGAKFD no. 21039, *Po Sovetskomu Soiuzu No. 5* (1964).
27 RGAKFD no. 30796, *Poka grom ne grianet…* (1989), dir. S. Kheifets.
28 RGAKFD no. 29979, *Zemletriasenie* (1989), dir. V. Troshkin, reel 6; RGAKFD no. 30796, *Poka grom ne grianet…* (1989), dir. S. Kheifets.
29 RGAKFD no. 18909, *Navodnenie v Primorskom krae* (1950).
30 Medvedev, *Nuclear Disaster in the Urals*.

31 Mikhail Romm, *9 dnei odnogo goda* (1962); Grigorii Nikulin, *713-i prosit posadku* (1962).

32 "Podvig na Zeravshane," Sovetskii ekron 14 (July 1964): 3. It is unclear what happened to *Seven Beauties*.

33 Malik Kaiumov, *Tashkent, zemletriasenie* (Kinostudiia dokumental'nykh fil'mov Uzbekistana, 1968).

34 "Vsesoiuznyi khashar," 10–11; V. Peskov, "Tashkent 700 dnei spustia," 4–5. This last article was reprinted from *Komsomol'skaia pravda*, where it was published exactly two years after the earthquake.

35 RGAKFD no. 20776, *Tashkent, zemletriasenie* (1968), reel 2.

36 George Seaton and Henry Hathaway, *Airport* (1970); Mark Robson, *Earthquake* (1974); John Guillermin, *The Towering Inferno* (1974). This is not to say that these American directors had seen *Tashkent, Zemletriasenie*.

37 Sobolev, "Meniaiushchiisia i neizmennyi," 16–17.

38 Eldar Riazanov, *Neveroiatnye prikliucheniia ital'iantsev v Rossii* (1974).

39 RGANI, f. 5, op. 33, d. 235, l. 139.

40 An exception to this is the film *Piat' minut do katatstrofy*, but the main characters in this film were foreigners, thus the Soviets would not be associated with the catastrophe. Moreover, the film is closer to the sci-fi genre. See P. Popogrebskii, *Piat' minut do katastrofy* (Kievskaia studio imeni A.P. Dovzhenko, 1978). For a review of this film, see Kichin, "Eksperiment," 4–5.

41 A. Nugmanov, *Medeo. Dni i nochi muzhestva.* (Kazakhfil'm, 1973).

42 Kosarev, *Kogda drozhit zemlia*. The rocky outcrop was not a complete novelty. In the 1930s, the Swiss village of Linthal dealt with a rocky outcrop that threatened its existence. The social, economic, and political dimensions of a potential but not actual catastrophe are explored in Zopfi, *Kilchenstock*. Years after all the village discussions, and at a time when the villagers felt safe again, an outcrop did collapse and caused substantial damage. The story offers a rural perspective to contrast with the industrial designs of the Soviets.

43 Mamaladze, "Probnyi kamen' temy."

44 Quoted in Mamaladze, "Probnyi kamen' temy," 73.

45 Plakhov, "V razrezhennom prostranstve."

46 Vladimir Bortko, *Komissiia po rassledovaniiu* (Lenfil'm, 1978).

47 Marples, *Chernobyl and Nuclear Power*, 100–1.

48 Aleksandr Mitta, *Ekipazh* (Mosfil'm, 1979).

49 Maslovskii, "Khronika podviga," 5; Vasil'eva, "Eto vysokoe trudnoe nebo." The exception is *Literaturnaia gazeta*.

50 Andrei Maliukov, *34-i skoryi* (Mosfil'm, 1981); Rudol'f Fruntov, *Trevozhnoe voskresen'e* (1983).

51 Later disaster films are reviewed in Berman, "Davaite igrat' na svoem pole."

52 Plakhov, "Vse ruzh'ia streliaiut," 74–5.

53 Vasil'eva, "Eto vysokoe trudnoe nebo," 14–15. In an interview given in 2008, the director Mitta said he had filmed the star, Sasha Iakovleva, showing her "beautiful body," but the scene was not included in the film. See Valerii Kichin, "Kogda b vy znali, iz kakogo siura," *Rossiiskaia gazeta*, 28 March 2008.

54 RGAKFD no. 22020, *Ashkhabad* (1949), reel 1.

55 Berman, "Davaite igrat' na svoem pole," 55.

56 The Sao Paolo fire received a visual quote in Grigorii Kromanov, *Dead Mountaineer's Hotel* (1979).

57 "A Soviet Film Maker at Chernobyl in '86 is Dead of Radiation," *New York Times*, 30 May 1987.

58 RGAKFD no. 31506, *Sovetskii voin No. 4* (1989); RGAKFD no. 30521, *Voz'mu tvoiu bol'* (1989), reel 1; RGAKFD no. 30796, *Poka grom ne grianet…* (1989), reel 1.

59 RGAKFD no. 31598, *Zheleznodorozhnaia katastrofa v Bashkirii* (1989), reel 1.

60 RGAKFD no. 31370, *Sled* (1990), reels 1 and 2.

61 Berman, "Davaite igrat' na svoem pole."

CHAPTER FIVE

1 TsDAGO, f. 1, op. 25, d. 2870, l. 3. On earlier slip-ups in radio, see Lovell, *Russia in the Microphone Age*, 39.

2 TsDAGO, f. 1, op. 25, d. 2870, l. 15.

3 Ibid., l. 8.

4 Marples, *Chernobyl and Nuclear Power*, 170.

5 Ryzhkov, *Prem'er*, 164.

6 RGANI, f. 89, op. 53, d. 88, l. 1; Marples, *Chernobyl and Nuclear Power*, 141.

7 Ryzhkov, *Prem'er*, 216.

8 Ibid., 207.

9 See Zubok, *Failed Empire*, 288–9 for a brief talk about Chernobyl that portrays it as a military event.

10 For an analysis that isolates Chernobyl within the context of the Soviet Union, see Lemarchand, *La vie contaminée*.

11 One early Russian documentary account puts the two catastrophes side by side. See Tarakanov, *Dve tragedii XX veka*.

12 Marples, *Chernobyl and Nuclear Power*; Marples, *Social Impact of the Chernobyl Disaster*.

13 Marples, *Social Impact of the Chernobyl Disaster*, 113.

14 Legasov, *Lessons of Chernobyl*.

15 On the editing, see Marples, *Social Impact of the Chernobyl Disaster*, 131. "A Soviet Film Maker at Chernobyl in '86 Is Dead of Radiation," *New York Times*, 30 May 1987.

16 Iaroshinskaia, *Chernobyl'*, 73.

17 Tarasevich, "Mi stvorili novii metod dezaktivatsii vod, odiagu i tekhniki"; Novikov, "'Chornobyl'tsi' akademii z chestiu vikonali svoiu misiiu."

18 Baranovs'ka, "Chornobyl' v novitnii istorii Ukraiiny," 163. The medical component of the tragedy has also been written about extensively as the health of children affected by radiation very quickly became a global concern. See Gale and Hauser, *Final Warning*.

19 *Chornobyl'*; *Kniga pam'iati likvidatorov posledstvii avarii na Chernobyl'skoi* AES; *Kniga pamiati k 25-i godovshchine avarii na Chernobylskoi atomnoi elektrostantsii*; *Pamiat' o Chernobyle*.

20 For an institutional prehistory, see Schmid, *Producing Power*.

21 Ibid., 90–1.

22 Marples, *Chernobyl and Nuclear Power*, 81.

23 Ibid., 101.

24 Ibid., 104.

25 A similar point is made in Schmid, *Producing Power*, 138.

26 "Dokument No. 9: Povidomlennia UKDB URSR po m. Kyivu ta Kyivs'kii oblasti do drugogo golovnogo upravlinnia KDB SRSR ta 2-go upravlinnia KDB URSR pro avariinu zupynku 9 veresnia 1982 r. energobloka No. 1 Chornobyl's'koi AES," 10 September 1982, http://www.sbu.gov.ua/sbu/doccatalog/document?id=41859.

27 "Dokument No. 10: Povidomlennia UKDB URSR po m. Kyivu ta Kyivs'kii oblasti do KDB SRSR ta KDB URSR pro resul'tati rozsliduvannia prychyn avariinoi sytuatsii, shcho sklalasia na Chornobyl's'kii AES 9 veresnia 1982 r," 13 September 1982, http://www.sbu.gov.ua/sbu/doccatalog/document?id=41860.

28 "Dokument No. 11: Informatsiine povidomlennia KDB URSR do TsK KPU pro avariinu zupynku 9 veresnia 1982 r. energobloka No. 1 Chornobyl's'koi AES," 14 September 1982, http://www.sbu.gov.ua/sbu/doccatalog/document?id=41865.

29 "Dokument No. 13: Dopovidna zapyska nachal'nika UKDB URSR po m. Kyivu ta Kyivs'kii oblasti golovi KDB URSR pro radiatsiinu obstanovku, shcho sklalasia u raioni roztashuvannia Chornobyl's'koi AES vnaslidok avarii 9 veresnia 1982 r," 30 October 1982, http://www.sbu.gov.ua/sbu/doccatalog/document?id=41889.

30 "Dokument No. 14: Dopovidna zapyska golovy KDB URSR pershomu sekretariu TsK KPU pro radiatsiinu obstanovku, shcho sklalasia v raioni roztashu-

vannia Chornobyl's'koi AES vnaslidok avarii 9 veresnia 1982 r," 5 November 1982, http://www.sbu.gov.ua/sbu/doccatalog/document?id=41890.

31 Nove, *Glasnost' in Action*, 159–60.

32 For detailed analyses of the explosion, see Marples, *Chernobyl and Nuclear Power*; and Zhores, *Legacy of Chernobyl*.

33 Ibid., 17–18.

34 RGANI, f. 89, op. 53, d. 88, l. 1.

35 On the firefighters, see Marples, *Chernobyl and Nuclear Power*, 129.

36 Marples, *Chernobyl and Nuclear Power*, 164.

37 Hériard-Dubreuil and Ollagnon, "De la gestion de l'accident à la réhabilitation des conditions de vie," 59–60.

38 Marples, *Social Impact of the Chernobyl Disaster*, 152.

39 Wenger, "Community Response to Disaster," 35.

40 On memory in a totalitarian context, see Hosking, "Memory in a Totalitarian Society."

41 Pokhodnia, "Vse otsenili geroicheskuiu rabotu nashikh uchenykh."

42 Ibid., 434. A.A. Vovk wrote that the UAS played the lead role in all important scientific matters. See Vovk, "Nauchnaia mysl' operezhala tekhnicheskie vozmozhnosti," 384.

43 Pokhodnia, "Vse otsenili geroicheskuiu rabotu nashikh uchenykh," 438.

44 The Soviets eventually decided not to build the fifth and sixth blocks of the power plant, but they did everything possible to get the existing reactors back on the grid. On 1 October 1986, the first block went back on the grid, and on 5 November the second block started to produce power. The third block was delayed, but it, too, was back on the grid soon enough. The Ukrainian government finally shut the plant down for good on 15 December 2000.

45 Pokhodnia, "Vse otsenili geroicheskuiu rabotu nashikh uchenykh," 434.

46 Kukhar, "Ia niz'ko im vkloniaiusia," 406.

47 Novikov, "'Chornobyl'tsi' akademii z chestiu vikonali svoiu misiiu," 432.

48 Beliaev, *Chernobyl'*, 150.

49 Ibid., 67.

50 See, for example, *Pamiat' o Chernobyle*; *Kniga pamiati k 25-i godovshchine avarii na Chernobylskoi atomnoi elektrostantsii*.

51 *Kniga pamiati k 25-i godovshchine avarii na Chernobylskoi atomnoi elektrostantsii*, 35.

52 Ibid., 39, 35.

53 Ibid., 42–3.

54 Ibid., 39, 41.

55 Vender, *Chernobyl'*.

56 Examples of Odessa and other Ukrainian areas asking for power in the 1960s appear in TsDAGO, f. 1, op. 25, d. 1269; f. 1, op. 24, d. 6030.

57 Gustafson, *Crisis amid Plenty*, 42.

58 Marples, *Social Impact of the Chernobyl Disaster*, 94.

59 Jane Dawson argues that the movements in the Crimean peninsula were nationalist in character. See Dawson, *Eco-Nationalism*, 143–61.

60 Marples, *Social Impact of the Chernobyl Disaster*, 108–9.

61 "Krym – v Krasnuiu knigu?," *Krymskii komsomolets*, 14 May 1988.

62 TsDAGO, f. 1, op. 32, d. 2474, l. 46.

63 TsDAGO, f. 1, op. 32, d. 2583, l. 54.

64 Ibid., l. 57.

65 Marples, *Chernobyl and Nuclear Power*, 90–1.

66 TsDAGO, f. 1, op. 32, d. 2583, l. 58.

67 Ibid., l. 74.

68 Ibid., l. 77.

69 Schmid, *Producing Power*, 139. Scientific opposition was certainly not a new phenomenon since it had been around since the 1920s. See Graham, *What Have We Learned*, 105.

70 Schmid, *Producing Power*, 146.

71 Zubok, *Zhivago's Children*, 340–1.

72 Iu. Anisimov, "My reshitel'no protiv!," *Krymskii komsomolets*, 13 August 1988.

73 Iu. Zamiatin, "Krym i AES nesovmestimy," *Krymskii komsomolets*, 9 September 1989.

74 Nikolai Nozdrachev, "Minery iz Minatomenergo," *Krymskii komsomolets*, 22 July 1989.

75 Sergei Shuvainikov, "Krymskaia AES: Epitsentr problem," *Krymskii komsomolets*, 21 January 1989.

76 Sergei Shuvainikov, "Krymskaia AES na vesakh seismologov," *Krymskii komsomolets*, 26 November 1988.

77 L.S. Borisenko, "Predskazuemo li zemletriasenie?," *Krymskii komsomolets*, 25 March 1989.

78 Iurii Kanin, "Sud'ba Armianskoi AES'," *Krymskii komsomolets*, 7 January 1989.

79 "Bratskaia pomoshch'," *Krymskii komsomolets*, 17 December 1988. See, for example, "Bratskaia pomoshch' Tashkentu," *Literaturnaia gazeta*, 25 June 1966.

80 Wilson, *Ukrainian Nationalism in the 1990s*, 64–8.

81 Kuzio, *Ukraine*, 73–4.

82 Ibid., 79. See also Anatolii Kozub, "Nestoronnim vkhid … zaboroneno?" *Molod' Ukraiiny*, 2 November 1989; Marples, "Greening of Ukraine."

83 Kuzio, *Ukraine*, 98–9.

84 See, for example, Shuvainikov, "Krymskaia AES."
85 Habermas, *Structural Transformation of the Public Sphere*.
86 On Ukrainian historians who linked both tragedies as examples of Ukrainian persecution under Soviet rule, see Marples, *Heroes and Villains*, 4, 20.
87 TsDAGO, f. 1, op. 25, d. 3166, l. 97.
88 TsDAVO, f. 2, op. 15, d. 678.
89 TsDAGO, f. 1, op. 25, d. 3346, l. 22.
90 In 1990, the Central Committee received from local communists a petition to close the plant because of the karst. See TsDAGO, f. 1, op. 32, d. 2816, l. 136.
91 TsDAGO, f. 1, op. 25, d. 3346, l. 24–7.
92 TsDAGO, f. 1, op. 32, d. 2671, l. 1.
93 Earlier doubts about the construction process had already been expressed. See TsDAGO, f. 1, op. 32, d. 2291, l. 47; and Marples, *Chernobyl and Nuclear Power*, 85.
94 TsDAGO, f. 1, op. 32, d. 2671, l. 51.
95 Ibid., l. 53. The idea here was to find another source of energy (water, coal) for creating the electrical energy yet still maintain a power plant on the site.
96 Felicity Barringer, "From Children of Chernobyl, Stories of Flight and of Fears," *New York Times*, 5 June 1986.
97 TsDAGO, f. 1, op. 32, d. 2338, l. 2.
98 Ibid., l. 7–8.
99 GA RF, f. R-5446, op. 162, d. 2009, l. 95, 124.
100 TsDAGO, f. 1, op. 32, d. 2927, l. 82.
101 TsDAGO, f. 1, op. 32, d. 2942, l. 39.
102 Iurii Radchenko, "Politika miloserdiia," *Molod' Ukraiiny*, 10 March 1990.
103 TsDAGO, f. 1, op. 32, d. 2927, l. 83. On Castro, see Liudmila Shevchuk, "Teplo, turbota i banany," *Molod' Ukraiiny*, 28 April 1990.
104 TsDAGO, f. 1, op. 32, d. 2927, l. 82–3.
105 Quoted in Marples, *Chernobyl and Nuclear Power*, 169.
106 TsDAGO, f. 1, op. 25, d. 3165, l. 15.
107 Ibid., l. 17.
108 V. Shcherbonos, "Osniakivs'ka tragediia: Bil', muzhnist', pam'iat," *Komsomol's'kyi gart*, 25 March 1989.
109 Iurii Radchenko, ""Samotne derevo ne prizhivaet'sia"," *Molod' Ukraiiny*, 26 October 1989.
110 TsDAGO, f. 7, op. 20, d. 3837, l. 2.
111 Ibid., l. 2, 9.
112 Ibid., l. 3.

113 "My povynni buty mudry serdtsem ... Leninakan: P'iat' misiatsiv pislia tragedii." *Molod' Ukraiiny*, 23 May 1989.

114 For insights into Slavutich today, see Daniel Wechlin, "30 Jahre nach Tschernobyl: Die sterbende Stadt der Liquidatoren," *Neue Zürcher Zeitung*, http://www.nzz.ch/international/europa/die-sterbende-stadt-der-liquidatoren-ld.15314.

115 Gorits'kii, *Chornobyl'*, 230, 236.

116 RGANI, f. 89, op. 53, d. 19, l. 3.

117 "Nasha obshchaia beda," *Pravda Vostoka*, 28 May 1986.

118 TsDAGO, f. 1, op. 32, d. 2672, l. 3.

119 Gorits'kii, *Chornobyl'*, 252.

120 Ibid., 247.

121 Ibid., 253.

122 See minute 20 of Sardor Iskhakov, *Stolitsa druzhby i tepla* (RDK-Film, 2011).

123 See the photos at the end of Gorits'kii, *Chornobyl'*; V. Svinchuk, "Takim on budet," *Tribuna energetika* (Zelenyi Mys), 10 March 1987.

124 On the massive problems, see Marples, *Social Impact of the Chernobyl Disaster*, 225–38.

125 V. Torchishnik, "Ekzamenuet Slavutich," *Tribuna energetika* (Zelenyi Mys), 26 May 1987.

126 I. Mizhen', "Nakanune novoseliia," *Tribuna energetika*, 15 September 1987; "Dai nazvanie ulitse," *Tribuna energetika*, 17 November 1987.

127 I. Nedil'ko, "Solov'inyi beton Slavuticha," *Tribuna energetika*, 9 June 1987. See the last page of *Tribuna energetika*, 14 July 1987, for the poems.

128 S. Komissarov, "Budni goroda molodykh," *Tribuna energetika*, 13 September 1988.

129 On the positive significance of Slavutich fifteen years later, see Matthew Brzezinski, "The Silver Lining in Chernobyl's Cloud," *New York Times*, 3 September 2000, Sunday Magazine, 40.

130 Gorits'kii, *Chornobyl'*, 193.

131 TsDAGO, f. 1, op. 32, d. 2815, l. 137.

132 TsDAGO, f. 1, op. 25, d. 3089, l. 34.

133 TsDAGO, f. 1, op. 25, d. 3346, l. 4.

134 TsDAGO, f. 1, op. 32, d. 2612, l. 26.

135 TsDAGO, f. 1, op. 32, d. 2338, l. 13. The same document can be found in RGANI, f. 89, op. 53, d. 34, l. 12

136 TsDAVO, f. 2, op. 15, d. 2026, l. 209.

137 TsDAGO, f. 1, op. 32, d. 2943, l. 99–100.

138 Ibid., l. 35.

139 Marples, *Social Impact of the Chernobyl Disaster*, 184.

140 S. Liubchenko, "Sboev v rabote ne budet," *Tribuna energetika*, 20 January 1987.
141 Bogdanovich and Karapetian, *Chernobyl'*, 73.
142 TsDAGO, f. 1, op. 32, d. 2848, l. 156.
143 TsDAGO, f. 1, op. 32, d. 2870, l. 16.
144 TsDAGO, f. 1, op. 32, d. 2848, l. 156.
145 Legasov, *Lessons of Chernobyl*, 12.
146 TsDAGO, f. 1, op. 32, d. 2482, l. 7.
147 Bagdanovich and Karapetian, *Chernobyl'*, 122.
148 TsDAGO, f. 1, op. 32, d. 2816, l. 76.
149 Ibid., l. 90.
150 GA RF, f. R-5446, op. 163, d. 1311, l. 110–11.
151 On the Stakhanovite perks, see Siegelbaum, *Stakhanovism and the Politics of Productivity*, 187–8.
152 TsDAGO, f. 1, op. 32, d. 2612, l. 8–9.
153 TsDAGO, f. 1, op. 32, d. 2671, l. 17.
154 Ibid., l. 20.
155 GA RF, f. R-5446, op. 163, d. 1312, l. 88.
156 Ibid., l. 88.
157 GA RF, f. R-5446, op. 163, d. 1311, l. 8.
158 GA RF, f. R-9654, op. 7, d. 815, l. 153.
159 Bagdanovich and Karapetian, *Chernobyl'*, 50.
160 Ibid., 106–8. Twelve thousand has to be considered a loose number.
161 Putnam, *Bowling Alone*.
162 TsDAGO, f. 1, op. 32, d. 2612, l. 63.
163 Ibid., l. 71.
164 TsDAGO, f. 1, op. 32, d. 2815, l. 39.
165 Ibid., l. 30.
166 Ibid., l. 31.
167 RGAE, f. 4372, op. 67, d. 9744, l. 103.
168 Ibid., l. 271, 273.
169 Ibid., l. 208.
170 Ibid., l. 91.
171 RGAE, f. 4372, op. 67, d. 9739, l. 343.
172 RGAE, f. 4372, op. 67, d. 9744, l. 107.
173 GA RF, f. R-9654, op. 7, d. 815, l. 298.
174 On the sensitivity to the words, see GA RF, f. R-9654, op. 7, d. 815, l. 58, 157.
175 GA RF, f. R-5446, op. 163, d. 1311, l. 18–19.
176 GA RF, f. R-9654, op. 7, d. 815, l. 60.
177 Ibid., l. 35.

178 Ibid., l. 160.
179 Ibid., l. 143–4.
180 RGAE, f. 4372, op. 67, d. 9744, l. 279. More recently, a proposal was made to transform some abandoned villages in the thirty-kilometre zones into UNESCO heritage sites. See Lemarchand, "Le futur pour mémoire," 143.
181 Gur'ianova and Vasil'ev, *Mertvaia zona*, 106. These towns were abandoned after the collapse of the Soviet Union.
182 TsDAGO, f. 1, op. 32, d. 2810, l. 5–9.
183 Ibid., l. 16.
184 Then the full name was *Gosudarstvennaia komissiia Soveta Ministrov po chrezvychainym situatsiiam*. Today in the Russian Federation it exists as the Ministry of Extraordinary Situations, or MChS (МЧС).
185 GA RF, f. R-5446, op. 163, d. 1292, l. 95, 97.
186 Ibid., l. 141.
187 Ibid., l. 131.
188 Altunin, *Grazhdanskaia oborona*, 18.
189 Altunin, *Formirovaniia grazhdanskoi oborony v bor'be so stikhiinymi bedstviiami*.
190 See *Chernobyl Union of Ukraine*, 10 May 2012.
191 Koselleck, *Begriffsgeschichten*.
192 Dupuy, "Tchernobyl," 21.
193 Virilio and Alexievitch, "Être témoins de cet accident du temps," 161.
194 Lemarchand, "Le futur pour mémoire," 147.

CHAPTER SIX

1 Iaroshinskaia, *Chernobyl'*, 71.
2 For a general overview, see Suny, *Revenge of the Past*, 132–8. For an analysis sympathetic to the Azeri side, see Zeynalov, *Le conflit du Haut-Karabakh*.
3 Quoted in Miller and Miller, *Armenia*, 14.
4 Miller and Miller, *Armenia*, 18. For a French perspective that emphasizes international aid, see P. Verluise, *Armenia in Crisis: The 1988 Earthquake*, trans. L Chorbajian (Detroit, MI: Wayne State University Press, 1995).
5 Suny, *Revenge of the Past*, 133.
6 Zeynalov notes that Azeri members were already absent from the vote. See Zeynalov, *Le conflit du Haut-Karabakh*, 198–203.
7 Libaridian, *Modern Armenia*, 206.
8 Ibid. For a slightly different view, see Zeynalov, *Le conflit du Haut-Karabakh*, 201. On Armenian acts of violences against Azerbaijanis, see also Beissinger, *Nationalist Mobilization*, 298. Beissinger notes the ambiguity of accounts.

9 Beissinger, *Nationalist Mobilization*, 299.
10 Payaslian, *Political Economy of Human Rights*, 92. On the Supreme Soviet and its shaky relationship to a democratic institution, see Remington, "Parliamentary Government in the USSR."
11 Beissinger, *Nationalist Mobilization*, 83–4.
12 Nina Andreeva, "Ne mogu postupat'sia printsipami," *Sovetskaia Rossiia*, 13 March 1988.
13 Beissinger, *Nationalist Mobilization*, 82.
14 The quote is from a conversation between Jerry Hough and Gennady Gerasimov, Gorbachev's press spokesperson, in November 1995. See Hough, *Democratization and Revolution*, 206. This is referenced in Beissinger, *Nationalist Mobilization*, 92.
15 Felicity Barringer, "Thousands Feared Dead in Soviet Caucasus Quake," *New York Times*, 8 December 1988.
16 Miller and Miller, *Armenia*, 13.
17 Bill Keller, "Soviet Press Calls the Rescue Effort Bungled and Inept," *New York Times*, 13 December 1988.
18 Verluise, *Armenia in Crisis*, 18.
19 Ibid., 28.
20 Ibid., 19.
21 Alderson, *Armenia*.
22 Verluise, *Armenia in Crisis*, 27.
23 Rost, *Armenian Tragedy*, 96.
24 Ibid., 97.
25 Ibid., 101.
26 Nikolai Ryzhkov suggests that Gorbachev was not in a rush to get into the danger zone. See Ryzhkov, *Prem'er*, 216.
27 Ryzhkov, *Prem'er*, 217.
28 Bill Keller, "Amid the Rubble, Armenians Express Rage at Gorbachev," *New York Times*, 12 December 1988.
29 Keller, "Soviet Press Calls the Rescue Effort Bungled and Inept."
30 Bernard Guetta, "Spitak, ville-tombeau," *Le Monde*, 16 December 1988.
31 Quoted in Keller, "Amid the Rubble"; Benthall, *Disasters*, 113.
32 Keller, "Amid the Rubble."
33 "Manifestations à Bakou: 'Le châtiment d'Allah'," *Le Monde*, 11 December 1988.
34 Keller, "Amid the Rubble."
35 GA RF, f. R-5446, op. 150, d. 278, l. 67.
36 GA RF, f. R-5446, op. 150, d. 282, l. 13.
37 TsDAVO, f. 2, op. 15, d. 1569, l. 8.

38 V. Andronaki, "Voskresenie," *Krymskii komsomolets*, 19 August 1989.

39 TsDAGO, f. 1, op. 32, d. 2833, l. 34, 38.

40 TsDAGO, f. 1, op. 32, d. 2814, l. 37–8.

41 TsDAVO, f. 2, op. 15, d. 1926, l. 17.

42 Ibid., l. 23.

43 Ibid., l. 30.

44 GA RF, f. R-5446, op. 150, d. 282, l. 47–8. The earthquake was on 23 January 1989. It was immediately reported in *Pravda*, which subsequently published news on the relief efforts. See O. Latifi, "V Gissare posle stikhii," *Pravda*, 25 January 1989.

45 GA RF, f. R-5446, op. 150, d. 277, l. 186.

46 GA RF, f. R-5446, op. 150, d. 282, l. 62.

47 O. Sidarov and Iu. Zapadalov, "Podumaem o miloserdii vmeste," *Moskovskaia pravda* (Moscow), 13 Feburary 1990.

48 Simon Payaslian, *The History of Armenia* (New York: Palgrave Macmillan, 2007), 196.

49 Beissinger, *Nationalist Mobilization*, 392–4.

50 GA RF, f. R-5446, op. 150, d. 282, l. 142.

51 GA RF, f. R-5446, op. 150, d. 281, l. 56.

52 "Vopros rebrom: budem nadeiat'sia?," *Komsomolets Armenii*, 18 March 1989.

53 "Doma prednaznacheny dlia mestnykh zhitelei," *Komsomolets Armenii*, 15 April 1989.

54 GA RF, f. R-5446, op. 150, d. 280, l. 6.

55 GA RF, f. R-5446, op. 162, d. 262, l. 79–80. The only workers who remained were Armenian in origin and were from Baku: they could not return home because of the ethnic violence. They had not received their proper pay.

56 GA RF, f. R-5446, op. 162, d. 262, l. 5–6.

57 GA RF, f. R-5446, op. 162, d. 263, l. 34.

58 "Ne ostavim brat'ev v bede," *Pravda*, 9 December 1988.

59 "Nash skromnyi vklad," *Komsomolets Armenii*, 1 January 1989.

60 "My poedem stroit'!," *Komsomolets Armenii*, 24 April 1989.

61 "Na novom meste," *Komsomolets Armenii*, 28 March 1989.

62 "V fond 'Deti Armenii," *Komsomolets Armenii*, 13 April 1989.

63 See Miroslav Buzhkevich, "Vyzov razumu i chesti," *Pravda*, 16 December 1988.

64 Virabian et al., *Spitakskoe zemletriasenie*, 78, 76.

65 Ibid., 62.

66 Ibid., 59.

67 Putnam, *Bowling Alone*.

68 GA RF, f. R-5446, op. 150, d. 2093, l. 6.

69 Ibid., l. 7–12.

70 Elie, "Au centre d'un double malheur," 48.
71 Ibid., 73.
72 Ibid., 70–1.
73 GA RF, f. R-5446, op. 150, d. 272, l. 9.
74 Ibid., l. 22.
75 Ibid., l. 93.
76 Ibid., l. 2.
77 GA RF, f. R-5446, op. 162, d. 180, l. 49.
78 Ibid., l. 56.
79 Starovoitova was actively involved in ethnic disputes for years. See Starovoitova, *Etnicheskaia gruppa v sovremennom sovetskom gorode*; Starovoitova, *Sovereignty after Empire*.
80 GA RF, f. R-5446, op. 162, d. 262, l. 172–3.
81 Bernard Guetta, "'Le monde entier' sur l'aéroport d'Erevan," *Le Monde*, 16 December 1988.
82 GA RF, f. R-5446, op. 162, d. 262, l. 174.
83 Ibid., l. 175.
84 Ibid., l. 171.
85 GA RF, f. R-5446, op. 162, d. 1714, l. 3.
86 Ibid., l. 18.
87 Ibid., l. 21.
88 GA RF, f. R-5446, op. 162, d. 262, l. 192.
89 G. Zafesov and A. Moiseev, "Bratskaia solidarnost' ostrova Svobody," *Pravda*, 11 December 1988.
90 T. Kolesnichenko, "Po marshrutu London – Erevan," *Pravda*, 11 December 1988.
91 V. Nikiforov, "Za dobrotu mysli i chuvstv: Protsess gumanizatsii mezhdunarodnykh otnoshenii nabiraet silu," *Izvestiia*, 1 May 1989.
92 Andrei Pral'nikov, "Proverka gorem: Tragediia Armenii – god spustia," *Moskovskie novosti*, 10 December 1989.
93 GA RF, f. R-5446, op. 150, d. 277, l. 45.
94 GA RF, f. R-5446, op. 150, d. 279, l. 40. A similar situation emerged with respect to aid from Finland. See Verabian et al., *Spitakskoe zemletriasenie*, 495–6.
95 Mary Dejevsky, "Tour Cut Short as Thatcher Is Mobbed in Earthquake City," *Times of London*, 11 June 1990.
96 GA RF, f. R-9501, op. 14, d. 974, l. 33–4.
97 Ibid., l. 36.
98 Ibid., l. 55, 66. This was a general problem. See Emmanuelli, *Les prédateurs de l'action humanitaire*, 191.
99 GA RF, f. R-9501, op. 14, d. 974, l. 56.

100 GA RF, f. R-9501, op. 14, d. 1049, l. 22. For newspaper reporting on the Soviet Red Cross, see GA RF, f. R-9501, op. 14, d. 1062.

101 GA RF, f. R-9501, op. 14, d. 1049, l. 25, 78.

102 Traditionally, the Red Cross is affiliated with but separate from state systems, thus its position as an NGO is rather awkward. See Benthall, *Disasters, Relief, and the Media*, 147. According to Benthall, the Red Cross "cannot be compared precisely with other NGOs, and in a sense is not an NGO at all since its authority derives from decisions made by governments."

103 GA RF, f. R-5446, op. 162, d. 2017, l. 2–3.

104 Although Iran did accept foreign aid, it did not do so without discussion. See "Iran : 'Une épreuve envoyée par Dieu' tandis que le bilan du séisme s'alourdit, les autorités de Téhéran sont divisées sur l'aide étrangère," *Le Monde*, 25 June 1990.

105 GA RF, f. R-5446, op. 162, d. 2017, l. 13.

106 Ibid., l. 38–9.

107 Forsythe, *Humanitarians*, 191–2.

CONCLUSION

1 Andrei Kolesnikov, "Vodnyi Chernobyl," *Novaia gazeta*, 20 July 2012.

2 Ellen Barry, "Russia, Shifting from Soviet Ways, Hesitantly Welcomes Volunteers in Flood Zone," *New York Times*, 15 July 2012.

3 Sasha Senderovich, "Russia's Summer of Idealism," *New York Times*, 18 July 2012.

4 Volker Pabst, "Die Furcht des Kremls vor den Bürgern," *Neue Zürcher Zeitung*, 4 August 2012. The quoted sentence is remarkably similar to claims made about Russians in the Imperial era. See Bradley, "Subjects into Citizens."

5 Searle, *Rationality in Action*.

6 Cosentino, *In Extremis*.

Bibliography

ARCHIVES AND NEWSPAPERS CITED

Archives

GA RF	Gosudarstvennyi arkhiv Rossiiskoi Federatsii [State Archive of the Russian Federation]
RGANI	Rossiiskii gosudarstvennyi arkhiv noveishchei istorii [Russian State Archive of Contemporary History]
RGAE	Rossiiskii gosudarstvennyi arkhiv ekonomiki [Russian State Archive of the Economy]
RGAKFD	Rossiiskii gosudarstvennyi arkhiv kinofotodokumentov [Russian State Film and Photo Archive]
TsDAGO	Tsentral'nyi derzhavnyi arkhiv gromads'kikh ob'iednan' Ukraiiny [Central State Archive of Public Organizations of Ukraine]
TsDAVO	Tsentral'nyi derzhavnyi arkhiv vishchikh organiv vlady ta upravlinnia Ukraiiny [Central State Archive of Supreme Bodies of Power and Government of Ukraine]

Newspapers

Ekonomika i zhizn'
International Herald Tribune
Izvestiia (Moscow)
Izvestiia Mordovii (Saransk)
Komsomolets Armenii (Erevan)
Komsomolets Donbassa (Donetsk)

Komsomolets Uzbekistana (Tashkent)
Komsomol'skaia pravda (Moscow)
Komsomol's'kyi gart (Chernihiv)
Krasnyi Krym (Simferopol)
Krymskii komsomolets (Simferopol)
Le Monde (Paris)
Literaturnaia gazeta (Moscow)
Molod' Ukraiiny (Kyiv)
Moskovskaia Pravda (Moscow)
Nauka i religiia (Moscow)
Neue Zürcher Zeitung (Zürich)
New York Times
Novyi mir (Moscow)
Pravda (Moscow)
Pravda Vostoka (Tashkent)
Radians'ka Donechchyna (Donetsk)
Rossiiskaia gazeta (Moscow)
Soviet Life
Stroitel'naia gazeta (Moscow)
Stroitel'stvo i arkhitektura Srednei Azii (Tashkent)
Stroitel'stvo i arkhitektura Uzbekistana (Tashkent)
Times of London
Tribuna energetika (Zelenyi Mys + Pripyat)
Turkmenskaia iskra (Ashgabat)
Vechernii Ashkhabad (Ashgabat)
Vechirniy Kyiv (Kyiv)

BOOKS AND ARTICLES

"1,400 Feared Dead in New Soviet Quake; Tadzhikistan." *Times of London*, 24 February 1989.

Abdurazzakov, U., and G. Pulatov. *Gorod, pobedivshii stikhiiu*. Tashkent: Izdvo Uzbekistan, 1974.

Abdusamatov, Kh. Sh., and S.r. Adylov. *Tashkent v period razvitogo sotsializma*. Tashkent: Fan, 1983.

Abrosimov, P.V., and N.V. Baranov. *Stroitel'stvo i rekonstruktsiia gorodov*. Moscow: Gos. Izd. lit. po stroit. i archit., 1958.

Acot, Pascal. *Catastrophes climatiques, désastres sociaux*. Paris: Presses universitaires de France, 2006.

Alderson, Andrew, ed. *Armenia: The Agony, the Hope*. London: Express Newspapers, 1989.

Aldylov, S., P. Maksumov, and F. Tursunov. *Gorod, rozhdennyi dvazhdy*. Moscow: Znanie, 1970.

Alexander, David. *Confronting Catastrophe: New Perspectives on Natural Disasters*. Oxford: Oxford University Press, 2000.

Allworth, Edward. *The Modern Uzbeks: From the Fourteenth Century to the Present – A Cultural History*. Stanford, CA: Stanford University Press, 1990.

– *The Tatars of Crimea: Return to the Homeland*. Durham, NC: Duke University Press, 1998.

Altunin, A. *Formirovaniia grazhdanskoi oborony v bor'be so stikhiinymi bedstviiami*. Moscow: Stroiizdat, 1978.

– ed., *Grazhdanskaia oborona*. Moscow: Voennoe izdatel'stvo, 1985.

Aman, Anders. *Architecture and Ideology in Eastern Europe during the Stalin Era: An Aspect of Cold War History*. Cambridge, MA: MIT Press, 1992.

Arkhangel'skii, V.A., ed. *Tashkent - gorod bratstva*. Tashkent: Izd-vo TsK KP Uzbekistana, 1969.

Ashwin, Sarah. *Gender, State, and Society in Soviet and Post-Soviet Russia*. London: Routledge, 2000.

Askarov, Sh. "Dom i dukh starogo Tashkenta kontsa XX veka." *Arkhitektura i stroitel'stvo Uzbekistana* 1 (1991): 4–8.

Autier, P., M.C. Ferir, A. Hairapetien, A. Alexanian, V. Agoudjian, G. Schmets, G. Dallemagne, M.N. Leva, and J. Pinel. "Drug Supply in the Aftermath of the 1988 Armenian Earthquake." *Lancet* 335, no. 8702 (1990): 1388–90.

Babaev, Agadzhan. *Nash Ashkhabad*. Ashkhabad: Turkmenistan, 1970.

Bacon, Edwin, and Mark Sandle, eds. *Brezhnev Reconsidered*. New York: Palgrave, 2002.

Banham, Reyner. "The New Brutalism." In *As Found: The Discovery of the Ordinary*, ed. Claude Lichtenstein and Thomas Schregenberger, 128–35. Baden, CH: Lars Müller Publishers, 2001 [1955].

Baranov, N.V. *Osnovy sovetskogo gradostroitel'stva*. Moscow: Stroiizdat, 1966.

– *Istoricheskie goroda SSSR: Novoe i staroe*. Moscow: Stroiizdat, 1987.

Baranovs'ka, N.P. "Chornobil' v novitnii istorii Ukraiiny: Vlada i suspil'stvo." PhD diss., Ukrainian Academy of Sciences, 2006.

– *Sotsial'ni ta ekonomichni naslidki Chornobil's'koi katastrofy*. Kyiv: Ukrainian Academy of Sciences, 2001.

Barkhin, Mikhail Grigor'evich. *Gorod: 1945–1970: Praktika, proekty, teoriia*. Moscow: Stroiizdat, 1974.

Barton, Allen. *Communities in Disaster: A Sociological Analysis of Collective Stress Situations*. Garden City, NY: Doubleday, 1969.

Bater, James H. *The Soviet City: Ideal and Reality*. London: E. Arnold, 1980.

– *St. Petersburg: Industrialization and Change*. Montreal and Kingston: McGill-Queen's University Press, 1976.

Beck, Ulrich. *Risikogesellschaft: Auf dem Weg in eine andere Moderne*. Frankfurt am Main: Suhrkamp, 1986.

– *Risk Society: Towards a New Modernity*. Newbury Park, CA: Sage, 1992.

– *Weltrisikogesellschaft*. Frankfurt am Main: Suhrkamp, 2007.

"Beda Armenii - gore obshchee: Prebyvanie M.S. Gorbacheva v Armianskoi SSR." *Pravda*, 11 December 1988.

Beissinger, Mark R. *Nationalist Mobilization and the Collapse of the Soviet State*. Cambridge: Cambridge University Press, 2002.

Beliaev, I.A. *Chernobyl': Vakhta smerti*. Moscow: IzdAT, 2006.

Bellat, Fabien. *Amériques-URSS: Architectures du défi*. Paris: Chaudun, 2014.

Benthall, J. *Disasters, Relief, and the Media*. New York: St Martin's Press, 1993.

Berlioz, Jacques. *Catastrophes naturelles et calamités au Moyen Âge*. Sismel: Edizioni del Galluzzo, 1998.

Berman, Boris. "Davaite igrat' na svoem pole." *Iskusstvo kino* 10 (1987): 51–60.

Bevir, Mark, and Hans Erich Boedeker, eds. *Begriffsgeschichte, Diskursgeschichte, Metapherngeschichte*. Göttingen: Wallstein, 2002.

Bial'kin, Anatolii. *Tragediia i podvig Ashkhabada: Dokumenty, materialy i vospominaniia ochevidtsev zemletriaseniia*. Moscow: Zarnitsy, 2005.

Bikmukhametov, Robert. *Doroga ostaetsia*. Moscow: Sovetskii pisatel', 1969.

Blaikie, Piers, Terry Cannon, Ian Davis, and Ben Wisner. *At Risk: Natural Hazards, People's Vulnerability, and Disasters*. London: Routledge, 1994.

Blumenberg, Hans. *Schiffbruch mit Zuschauer*. Frankfurt am Main: Suhrkamp, 1997.

Bocharov, Iu. P., and Orest K. Kudriatsev. *Planirovochnaia struktura sovremennogo goroda*. Moscow: Stroiizdat, 1972.

Bociurkiw, Bohdan. "Religion in the USSR after Khrushchev." In *The Soviet Union under Brezhnev and Kosygin: The Transition Years*, ed. John W. Strong, 135–55. New York: Van Nostrand Reinhold, 1971.

Bodenschatz, Harald, Christiane Post, and Uwe Altrock. *Städtebau im Schatten Stalins: Die internationale Suche nach der sozialistischen Stadt in der Sowjetunion 1929–1935*. Berlin: Braun, 2003.

Bogdanovich, A., and T. Karapetian. *Chernobyl': Trevozhnaia komandirovka. Staryi Oskol. Dokumental'no-publitsisticheskii sbornik*. Staryi Oskol: Tsentr obshchestvennykh sviazei i reklamy OAO "OEMK," 2006.

"Bol' i zabota armianskogo naroda - bol' i zabota vsei strany." *Pravda*, 13 December 1988.

Bouvard, Josette. *Le métro de Moscou: La construction d'un mythe soviétique*. Paris: Ed. du Sextant, 2005.

Bovin, Aleksandr. *XX vek kak zhizn': Vospominaniia*. Moscow: Zakharov, 2003.

Bradley, Joseph. "Russia's Parliament of Public Opinion: Association, Assembly and the Autocracy, 1906–1914." In *Reform in Modern Russian History: Progress or Cycle?*, ed. Theodore Taranovski, 212–36. Cambridge: Cambridge University Press, 1995.

– "Subjects into Citizens: Societies, Civil Society, and Autocracy in Tsarist Russia," *American Historical Review* 107 (October 2002): 1094–123.

– "Volunteer Associations, Civic Culture and Obshchestvennost' in Russia." In *Between Tsar and People: Educated Society and the Quest for Public Identity in Late Imperial Russia*, ed. Edith Clowes, Sam Kassow, and James L. West, 131–48. Princeton, NJ: Princeton University Press, 1991.

Briese, Olaf, and Timo Günther. "Katastrophe: Terminologische Vergangenheit, Gegenwart und Zukunft." *Archiv für Begriffsgeschichte* 51 (2009): 155–95.

Brumfield, William Craft. *A History of Russian Architecture*. Cambridge: Cambridge University Press, 1993.

– *The Origins of Modernism in Russian Architecture*. Berkeley: University of California Press, 1991.

Bukhanov, M.S. *Kogda brat v bede*. Tashkent: Uzbekistan, 1969.

Bulatov, Mitkhat. *Osobennosti i printsipy progressivnogo resheniia planirovki i zastroiki g. Tashkenta*. Moscow: n.p., 1960.

Burshtein, I.N. "Kakova seismichnost' Tashkenta?" *Stroitel'stvo i arkhitektura Srednei Azii* 5 (1964): 36–7.

Burton, Ian, Robert W. Kates, and Gilbert F. White. *The Environment as Hazard*. New York: Oxford University Press, 1978.

Calhoun, Craig ed. *Habermas and the Public Sphere*. Cambridge, MA: MIT Press, 1992.

Camus, Raymond M. "Fabrication industrielle de huit logements par jour dans la région parisienne." *Annales de l'Institut technique du bâtiment et des travaux publics* 101 (May 1956): 428–53.

Carlisle, Donald S. "Power and Politics in Soviet Uzbekistan: From Stalin to Gorbachev." In *Soviet Central Asia: The Failed Transition*, ed. William Fierman, 93–130. Boulder, CO: Westview Press, 1991.

Cattell, David T. "Soviet Cities and Consumer Welfare Planning." In *The City in Russian History*, ed. Michael Hamm, 257–75. Lexington: University Press of Kentucky, 1976.

Celik, Zeynep. *Urban Forms and Colonial Confrontations: Algiers under French Rule*. Berkeley: University of California Press, 1997.

Chebotareva, Z.N. "Opyt proektirovaniia eksperimental'nykh mikroraionov-makhallia v Tashkente." *Stroitel'stvo i arkhitektura Uzbekistana* 7 (1968): 11.

– *Tashkent v proshlom i nastoiashchem*. Tashkent: n.p., 1968.

"V zashchitu plotnoi maloetazhnoi zastroiki." *Stroitel'stvo i arkhitektura Uzbekistana* 11 (1974): 14–18.

– ed. *Rekomendatsii po proektirovaniiu drevesno-kustarnikovykh gruppirovok dlia ozeleneniia zhiloi zastroiki v gorodakh Uzbekistana*. Tashkent: n.p., 1976.

Chen, Beatrice. "'Resist the Earthquake and Rescue Ourselves': The Reconstruction of Tangshan after the 1976 Earthquake." In *Resilient City: How Modern Cities Recover from Disaster*, ed. Lawrence J. Vale and Thomas J. Campanella, 235–54. New York: Oxford University Press, 2005.

Chikov, T.M., and V. Zhuravlev. *Mesto podviga: Tashkent*. Tashkent: Izd-vo Uzbekistan, 1976.

Chornobil': Kniga pamiati pomerlykh ta zagiblykh vnaslidok chornobil's'koi katastrofy likvidatoriv evakuiovanikh i pereselentsiv, iaki meshkali v Kharkivs'ii oblasti. Kharkiv: Original, 1997.

Chornobil's'ka katastrofa v dokumentakh, faktakh ta doliakh liudei. Kyiv: Azimut-Ukraiina, 2006.

Clark, Katerina. *The Soviet Novel: History as Ritual*. Chicago: University of Chicago Press, 1981.

Clowes, Edith, Sam Kassow, and James L. West, eds. *Between Tsar and People: Educated Society and the Quest for Public Identity in Late Imperial Russia*. Princeton, NJ: Princeton University Press, 1991.

Cohen, Stephen F. *Bukharin and the Bolshevik Revolution: A Political Biography, 1888–1938*. New York: Vintage, 1975.

Collins, Kathleen. *Clan Politics and Regime Transition in Central Asia*. Cambridge: Cambridge University Press, 2006.

Comrie, Bernard. *Aspect: An Introduction to the Study of Verbal Aspect and Related Problems*. Cambridge Textbooks in Linguistics. Cambridge: Cambridge University Press, 1993.

– *Tense*. Cambridge Textbooks in Linguistics. Cambridge: Cambridge University Press, 1985.

Comrie, Bernard, Gerald Stone, and Maria Polinsky. *The Russian Language in the Twentieth Century*. 2nd ed. Oxford: Oxford University Press, 1996.

Conquest, Robert. *The Harvest of Sorrow: Soviet Collectivization and the Terror-Famine*. New York: Oxford University Press, 1986.

Corbin, Alain. *Village Bells: Sound and Meaning in the 19th-Century French Countryside*. European Perspectives. New York: Columbia University Press, 1998.

Cosentino, Donald J., ed. *In Extremis: Death and Life in 21st-Century Haitian Art*. Los Angeles: Fowler Museum at UCLA, 2012.

Cracraft, James. *The Petrine Revolution in Russian Architecture*. Chicago: University of Chicago Press, 1988.

Crews, Robert D. "Civilization in the City: Architecture, Urbanism, and the Colonization of Tashkent." In *Architectures of Russian Identity: 1500 to the Present*, ed. James Cracraft and Daniel B. Rowland, 117–32. Ithaca, NY: Cornell University Press, 2003.

Dal,' Vladimir I. *Tolkovyi slovar' zhivogo velikorusskogo iazyka*. Moscow: Gos izdatel'stvo inostrannykh i natsional'nykh slovarei, 1955.

Davidow, Mike. *The Soviet Union through the Eyes of an American*. Moscow: Novosti Press Agency Publishing House, 1976.

Dawson, Jane I. *Eco-Nationalism: Anti-Nuclear Activism and National Identity in Russia, Lithuania, and Ukraine*. Durham, NC: Duke University Press, 1996.

Dejevsky, Mary. "Armenia City Fetes Thatcher." *Times of London*, 11 June 1990.

Dekel-Chen, Jonathan L. *Farming the Red Land: Jewish Agricultural Colonization and Local Soviet Power, 1924–1941*. New Haven, CT: Yale University Press, 2005.

Dépelteau, François, and Aurélie Lacassagne. *Le Bélarus: L'État de l'exception*. Sainte-Foy: Presses de l'Université Laval, 2003.

de Tocqueville, Alexis. *Democracy in America*. New York: Perennial Classics, 2000.

Deutscher, Isaac. "Trotsky on Stalin." In *Heretics and Renegades*, 78–90. London: Jonathan Cape, 1969.

Dostoevsky, Fyodor. *Crime and Punishment*. Trans. Jessie Coulson. New York: Norton, 1989.

Dubrovina, E. I. *Zemletriaseniia v Srednei Azii. Ukazatel' literatury po seismologii i seismologicheskim metodam*. Tashkent: n.p., 1967.

Dunlop, John B. *The Faces of Contemporary Russian Nationalism*. Princeton, NJ: Princeton University Press, 1983.

Dupuy, Jean-Pierre. "Tchernobyl, le sarcophage de l'humain." *Écologie et politique* 32 (2006): 17–31.

Dvoichenko, P.A. "Chernomorskie zemletriaseniia 1927 goda v Krymu." In *Chernomorskie zemletriaseniia 1927 goda i sud'by Kryma*. Simferopol': Krymskoe gosudarstvennoe izdatel'stvo, 1928.

Egan, Timothy. *The Big Burn: Teddy Roosevelt and the Fire That Saved America*. Boston, MA: Houghton Mifflin Harcourt, 2009.

Elias, Norbert. *Time: An Essay*. Oxford: Blackwell, 1992.

Elie, Marc. "'Au centre d'un double malheur': Le séisme du 7 décembre 1988 en Arménie et l'expulsion des sinistrés azéris de Spitak." *Revue d'études comparatives Est-Ouest* 44, no. 1 (2013): 45–75.

Emmanuelli, Xavier. *Les prédateurs de l'action humanitaire*. Paris: Albin Michel, 1991.

Esaulov, Aleksandr. *Chernobyl': Letopis' mertvogo goroda*. Moscow: Evropa, 2006.

Feshbach, Murray, and Alfred Friendly. *Ecocide in the USSR: Health and Nature Under Siege*. New York: Basic Books, 1992.

Filtzer, Donald. *Soviet Workers and Stalinist Industrialization: The Formation of Modern Soviet Production Relations, 1928–1941*. Armonk, NY: M.E. Sharpe, 1986.

Fitzpatrick, Sheila. "Popular Sedition in the Post-Stalin Soviet Union." In *Sedition: Everyday Resistance in the Soviet Union Under Khrushchev and Brezhnev*, ed. Vladimir A. Kozlov, Sheila Fitzpatrick, and Sergei V. Mironenko, 1–24. New Haven, CT: Yale University Press, 2011.

Forsythe, David P. *The Humanitarians: The International Committee of the Red Cross*. Cambridge: Cambridge University Press, 2005.

Frachon, Benoît. *Au rythme des jours: Rétrospective sur 20 années de luttes de la C.G.T.* 1955–1967. Paris: Éditions sociales, 1968.

Frolic, B.M. "The New Moscow City Plan." In *The City in Russian History*, ed. Michael F. Hamm, 276–88. Lexington: University Press of Kentucky, 1976.

Furin, Stanislaw *Das Pionierlager Artek*. Moskau: APN-Verlag, 1975.

Fürst, Juliane. *Stalin's Last Generation: Soviet Post-War Youth and the Emergence of Mature Socialism*. Oxford: Oxford University Press, 2010.

Gaillard, Jean-Christophe, and Le Masson, Virginie. "Traditional Societies' Response to Volcanic Hazards in the Philippines: Implications for Community-Based Disaster Recovery." *Mountain Reserach and Development* 27, no. 4 (2007): 313–17.

Gale, Robert Peter, and Thomas Hauser. *Final Warning: The Legacy of Chernobyl*. New York: Warner Books, 1988.

Ganots'kii, Viktor. *Chornobyl' – nash bil': Zhertvam Chornobylia*. Kirovograd: Tsentral'noukraiins'ke vydavnitstvo, 2006.

Gestwa, Klaus. *Die Stalinschen Großbauten des Kommunismus: Sowjetische Technik- und Umweltgeschichte, 1948–1967*. München: R. Oldenbourg, 2010.

Gilbert, Claude. "Reply to Hewitt." In *What Is a Disaster? Perspectives on the Question*, ed. E.L. Quarantelli, 95–8. London: Routledge, 1998.

Gillespie, David. *Russian Cinema*. London: Pearson, 2003.

Gladkov, Fyodor. *Cement*. Trans. A.S. Arthur and C. Ashleigh. New York: International Publishers, 1929.

Goldman, Jasper. "Warsaw: Reconstruction as Propaganda." In *Resilient City: How Modern Cities Recover from Disaster*, ed. Lawrence J. Vale and Thomas J. Campanella, 135–58. New York: Oxford University Press, 2005.

Goldzamt, Edmund. *Städtebau sozialistischer Länder*. Berlin: Verlag für Bauwesen, 1973.

Gorbachev, Mikhail. *Perestroika: New Thinking for Our Country and the World*. New York: Harper and Row, 1987.

Gorits'kii, O. *Chornobyl': Pisliaavariina programa budivnytstva*. Kyiv: Ivan Fedorov, 1998.

Gorshkov, Boris B. *Russia's Factory Children: State, Society, and Law, 1800–1917*. Pittsburgh: University of Pittsburgh Press, 2008.

Goujon, Alexandra. *Révolutions politiques et identitaires en Ukraine et en Biélorussie 1988–2008)*. Paris: Belin, 2009.

Gould, Peter. *Fire in the Rain: The Democratic Consequences of Chernobyl*. Baltimore, MD: Johns Hopkins University Press, 1990.

Graham, Loren R. *What Have We Learned about Science and Technology from the Russian Experience?* Stanford, CA: Stanford University Press, 1998.

Graham, Stephen, ed. *Disrupted Cities: When Infrastructure Fails*. New York: Routledge, 2010.

Grandazzi, Guillaume and Frédérick Lemarchand, eds. *Les silences de Tchernobyl: L'avenir contaminé*. Paris: Autrement, 2004.

Grinberg, Ia. *Moskovskii teatr operetty*. Moscow: Moskovskii rabochii, 1967.

Guetta, Bernard. "L'aide étrangère aux sinistrés d'Arménie tente de pallier l'insuffisance des moyens locaux." *Le Monde*, 13 December 1988.

– "Opération-vérité." *Le Monde*, 14 December 1988.

Gur'ianova, L., and D. Vasil'ev. *Mertvaia zona: Goroda—prizraki*. Sankt-Peterburg: Vektor, 2006.

Gustafson, Thane. *Crisis amid Plenty: The Politics of Soviet Energy under Brezhnev and Gorbachev*. Princeton, NJ: Princeton University Press, 1989.

– *Reform in Soviet Politics: Lessons of Recent Policies on Land and Water*. Cambridge: Cambridge University Press, 1981.

Gutnov, A.E. *The Ideal Communist City*. New York: G. Braziller, 1970.

Gutnov, A.E., and I.G. Lezhava. *Budushchee goroda*. Moscow: Stroiizdat, 1977.

Habermas, Jürgen. *The Structural Transformation of the Public Sphere: An Inquiry into a Category of Bourgeois Society*. Trans. Thomas Burger with the assistance of Frederick Lawrence. Cambridge, MA: MIT Press, 1989.

Halfin, Igal, and Jochen Hellbeck. "Rethinking the Stalinist Subject: Stephen Kotkin's 'Magnetic Mountain' and the State of Soviet Historical Studies." *Jahrbücher für Geschichte Osteuropas* 44, no. 3 (1996): 456–63.

Hamm, Michael, ed. *The City in Late Imperial Russia*. Bloomington: Indiana University Press, 1986.

– *The City in Russian History*. Lexington: University Press of Kentucky, 1976.

Hanson, Stephen. *Time and Revolution: Marxism and the Design of Soviet Institutions*. Chapel Hill: University of North Carolina Press, 1997.

Hellbeck, Jochen. *Revolution on My Mind: Writing a Diary under Stalin*. Cambridge, MA: Harvard University Press, 2006.

Herbert, Christopher. *Victorian Relativity: Radical Thought and Scientific Discovery*. Chicago: University of Chicago Press, 2001.

Hériard-Dubreuil, Gilles, and Henry Ollagnon. "De la gestion de l'accident à la réhabilitation des conditions de vie." In *Les silences de Tchernobyl: L'avenir contaminé*, ed. Guillaume Grandazzi and Frédérick Lemarchand, 57–77. Paris: Autrement, 2004.

Hewitt, Kenneth. "Excluded Perspectives in the Social Construction of Disaster." *International Journal of Mass Emergencies and Disasters* 13, no. 3 (1995): 317–39.

– "The Idea of Calamity in a Technocratic Age." In *Interpretations of Calamity from the Viewpoint of Human Ecology*, ed. Kenneth Hewitt, 3–32. Boston, MA: Allen and Unwin, 1983.

– *Regions of Risk: A Geographic Introduction to Disasters*. Harlow, UK: Longman, 1997.

Hewitt, Kenneth, and I. Burton. *The Hazardousnesss of a Place*. Toronto: University of Toronto Press, 1971.

Hoffman, Susanna, and Anthony Oliver-Smith, eds. *Catastrophe and Culture: The Anthropology of Disaster*. Santa Fe, NM: Oxford: School of American Research Press, 2002.

Holloway, David. *Stalin and the Bomb: The Soviet Union and Atomic Energy, 1939–1956*. New Haven, CT: Yale University Press, 1994.

Honchar, Oles. *The Black Ravine*. http://www.utoronto.ca/elul/English/Bilenko/Honchar-Black-Ravine.pdf.

Hopkins, Arthur T. *Unchained Reactions: Chernobyl, Glasnost, and Nuclear Deterrence*. Washington, DC: National Defense University, 1993.

Hosking, Geoffrey A. *Beyond Socialist Realism: Soviet Fiction since Ivan Denisovich*. London: Granada, 1980.

– "Memory in a Totalitarian Society: The Case of the Soviet Union." In *Memory: History, Culture and the Mind*, ed. Thomas Butler, 115–30. Oxford: Basil Blackwell, 1989.

Hough, Jerry. *Democratization and Revolution in the USSR, 1985–1991*. Washington, DC: Brookings Institution Press, 1997.

Huber, Werner. *Hauptstadt Moskau: Ein Reiseführer durch das Baugeschehen der russischen Metropole von Stalin über Chruschtschow und Breschnew bis heute*. Zürich, 1998.

– *Moskau, Metropole im Wandel: Ein architektonisher Stadtführer*. Köln: Böhlau, 2007.

Hudson, Hugh D. *Blueprints and Blood: The Stalinization of Soviet Architecture, 1917–1937*. Princeton, NJ: Princeton University Press, 1994.

Iaroshinskaia, A.A. *Chernobyl': Dvadtsat' let spustia. Prestuplenie bez nakazaniia*. Moscow: Vremia, 2006.

Ignatkin, I.A. "Stroitel'stvo i arkhitektura sovremennogo Kieva." In *Istoriia Kieva*, ed. V.N. Boriakin and A.S. Kuznetsova, vol. 2, 641–62. Kiev: Izdatel'stvo Akademii nauk Ukrainskoi SSR, 1964.

Ikonnikov, A.V. *Rekonstruktsiia tsentrov krupnykh gorodov*. Moscow: Znanie, 1985.

– *Sovetskaia arkhitektura shestidesiatykh godov*. Moscow: Stroiizdat, 1972.

– *Soviet Architecture of Today, 1960s – Early 1970s*. Leningrad: Aurora Art Publishers, 1975.

Ikramov, K. "Giulistan – tsvetushchii krai." *Nauka i religiia* 11 (1967): 29–45.

"Interv'iu M.S. Gorbacheva korrespondentam tsentral'nogo televideniia i televideniia Armenii." *Pravda*, 12 December 1988.

Irbutaev, I. "V makhalle Iangi-Khaiat." *Nauka i religiia* 12 (1965): 7–10.

"Izuchenie prichin zemletriaseniia v Krymu." *Pravda*, 5 October 1927.

Kadyrov, Sh. *Ashkhabadskaia katastrofa*. Ashgabat: Izdatel'stvo Turkmenistan, 1990.

Kadyrova, T.F. *Arkhitektura tsentra Tashkenta*. Tashkent: Izdatel'stvo lit. i iskusstva, 1976.

Kadyrova, T.F., K.V. Babievskii, and F. Iu. Tursunov. *Arkhitektura sovetskogo Uzbekistana*. Moscow: Stroiizdat, 1972.

Karelin, Lazar'. "Zemletriasenie." In *Izbrannoe*. Moscow: Khudozhestvennaia literatura, 1982.

Kassof, Allen. *The Soviet Youth Program. Regimentation and Rebellion*. Cambridge, MA: Harvard University Press, 1965.

Kenez, Peter. *Cinema and Soviet Society, 1917–1953*. Cambridge: Cambridge University Press, 1992.

Khamidov, N. "O makhalle i ee vliianii." *Nauka i religiia* 6 (June 1966): 53–4.

Khasanov, Abdurakhim Khasanovich. *Zemletriaseniia: Problemy i suzhdeniia*. Dushanbe: Obshchestvo 'Znanie' TadzhSSR, 1987.

Kichin, Valerii Kichin. "Eksperiment, kotoryi ne sostoialsia." *Sovetskii ekran* 10 (October 1978): 4–5.

Kirby, Andrew. *Nothing to Fear: Risks and Hazards in American Society*. Tucson: University of Arizona Press, 1990.

Klinenberg, Eric. *Heat Wave: A Social Autopsy of Disaster in Chicago*. Chicago: University of Chicago Press, 2002.

Klychmuradov, K.K. *Ashkhabadskoe zemletriasenie i pomoshch narodov SSSR*. Ashkhabad: Ylym, 1977.

– *Edintsvo armii i naroda*. Ashkhabad: n.p., 1976.

Kniga pamiati k 25-i godovshchine avarii na Chernobylskoi atomnoi elektrostantsii. Cheliabinsk: ABRIS, 2011.

Kniga pamiati likvidatorov posledstvii avarii na Chernobyl'skoi AES. Donetsk: Iugo-vostok, 2008.

Koenker, Diane, and William G. Rosenberg, eds. *Party, State, and Society in the Russian Civil War: Explorations in Social History*. Bloomington: Indiana University Press, 1989.

Kollman, Nancy Shields. *By Honor Bound: State and Society in Early Modern Russia*. Ithaca, NY: Cornell University Press, 1999.

Kolokol pamiati: K 20-letiiu Spitaksogo zemletriaseniia. Moscow: Iuni Press SK, 2008.

"Komu stroit' Slavutich?" *Tribuna energetika*, 10 February 1987.

Kornilov, N. *Tashkentskii dnevnik*. Tashkent: Izd-vo Uzbekistan, 1970.

Korobovtsev, G.I. "Tashkent. "Staryi" gorod, kakim tebe byt'?" *Stroitel'stvo i arkhitektura Uzbekistana* 10 (1971): 19–26.

– "Tashkent. "Staryi" gorod, kakim tebe byt'?." *Stroitel'stvo i arkhitektura Uzbekistana* 12 (1971): 21–9.

– "Zhilishche v tsentre Tashkenta – izlishestvo ili neobkhodimost?" In *Sotsial'nye problemy arkhitektury Uzbekistana: Sbornik nauchnykh trudov*, 3–5. Tashkent, TashPI, 1989.

Korshunov, P.S. *Mogut li evrei rabotat na zemle?* Moscow: Der emes, 1930.

Koselleck, Reinhart. *Begriffsgeschichten*. Frankfurt am Main: Suhrkamp, 2006.

Kosinskii, A.S. "Bukhara. Novoe stroitel'stvo v drevnem tsentre." *Stroitel'stvo i arkhitektura Uzbekistana* 2 (1971): 18–27.

Kotkin, Stephen. *Magnetic Mountain: Stalinism as a Civilization*. Berkeley: University of California Press, 1995.

Kovalev, S.G. *Bol' nasha — Chernobyl': Zakonodatel'nye initsiativy, publikatsii v sredstvakh massovoi informatsii, deputatskie zaprosy, obrashcheniia, otvety*. Klintsy: Izd-vo Klints. gor. tip., 2004.

Kozirev, Iu. M. "Voni zakhishchali svoiu zemliu, svii narod." In *Chornobyl' 1986–1987 rr. Dokumenty i spogadi: Rol' NAN Ukraiiny u podolanni naslidkiv katastrofy*. Kyiv: Akademperiodika, 2004.

Kozlov, Vladimir A. "The Meaning of Sedition." In *Sedition: Everyday Resistance in the Soviet Union Under Khrushchev and Brezhnev*, ed. Vladimir A. Kozlov, Sheila Fitzpatrick, and Sergei V. Mironenko, 25–64. New Haven, CT: Yale University Press, 2011.

Kozlova, Elena. *Neizvestnye geroi sovetskoi epokhi*. Moscow: Sovetskii pisatel', 2006.

Kriukov, K.S., and Notkin, I.I. "Rekonstruktsiia drevnikh gorodov i problemy sokhraneniia pamiatnikov arkhitektury Uzbekistana." *Stroitel'stvo i arkhitektura Uzbekistana* 11 (1966): 28–30.

Krotov, Iakov. *Peredacha dlia radio "Svoboda": S khristianskoi tochki zreniia*. 2003. http://www.krotov.info/yakov/3_vera/3_radio/2003solovyev.html.

Kukhar, V.P. "Ia niz'ko im vkloniaiusia." In *Chornobyl' 1986–1987 rr.: Dokumenty i spogady: Rol' NAN Ukraiiny u podolanni naslidkiv katastrofy*, 405–7. Kyiv: Akademperiodika, 2004.

Kulaga, Lev Nikiforovich. *Rekonstruktsiia gorodov: Opyt zarubezhnykh stran*. Moscow: Izd-vo literatury po stroitel'stvu, 1967.

Kuzio, Taras. *Ukraine: Perestroika to Independence*. 2nd ed. New York: St Martin's Press, 2000.

Kydriavtseva, Galina Artem'evna. *Zemletriaseniia v SSSR. Zapisi oshchutimykh zemletriasenii 1965–1967 gg.* Moscow: Nauka, 1973.

Lahusen, Thomas, and Gene Kuperman, eds., *Late Soviet Culture: From Perestroika to Novostroika*. Durham, NC: Duke University Press, 1993.

Lavrov, Vitalii Alekseevich. *Rekonstruktsiia krupnykh gorodov. Metod. Posobie dlia proektirovshchikov*. Moscow: Stroiizdat, 1972.

Lazarenko, Anatolii. "Rostut' dobrotny budivli." *Molod' Ukraiiny*, 10 December 1989.

Legasov, V.A. *The Lessons of Chernobyl Are Important for All*. Moscow: Novosti Press Agency Publishing House, 1987.

Legault, Réjean. "The Idea of Brutalism in Canadian Architecture." In *Architecture and the Canadian Fabric*, ed. Rhodri Windsor Liscombe, 313–40. Vancouver: UBC Press, 2011.

Lemarchand, Frédérick. "Le futur pour mémoire." In *Les silences de Tchernobyl: L'avenir Contaminé*, ed. Guillaume Grandazzi and Frédérick Lemarchand, 139–55. Paris: Autrement, 2004.

– *La vie contaminée: Éléments pour une socio-anthropologie des sociétés épidémiques*. Paris: L'Harmattan, 2002.

Levin, Ia. *O pereselenii evreiskoi bednoty v Krym i Birobidzhan*. Moscow: Der emes, 1930.

Lewin, Moshe. *The Gorbachev Phenomenon: A Historical Interpretation*. Berkeley: University of California Press, 1988.

Libaridian, Gerard J. *Modern Armenia: People, Nation, State*. New Brunswick, NJ: Transaction, 2004.

Lindenmeyr, Adele. *Poverty Is Not a Vice: Charity, Society and the State in Imperial Russia*. Princeton, NJ: Princeton University Press, 1996.

Lovell, Stephen. *Russia in the Microphone Age: A History of Soviet Radio, 1919–1970*. Oxford: Oxford University Press, 2015.

L'vov, B, and I. Svirin. *Raduga nad epitsentrom. Reportazh iz Tashkenta*. Moscow: Sovetskaia Rossiia, 1968.

– "Raduga nad Tashkentom." *Stroitel'naia gazeta*, 28 October 1966.

Mackenzie, David. "Tashkent – Past and Present." *Russian Review* 28, no. 2 (1969): 207–16.

Maisurian, Aleksandr. *Drugoi Brezhnev*. Moscow: Vagrius, 2004.

Malia, Martin. *The Soviet Tragedy*. New York: The Free Press, 1994.

Mamaladze, T. "Probnyi kamen' temy." *Iskusstvo kino* 9 (September 1976): 70–8.

Manakova, V.N. "Arkhitektura kafe 'Golubye kupola' i chaikhany na bul'vare imeni V.I. Lenina." *Stroitel'stvo i arkhitektura Uzbekistana* 7 (1971): 33–4.

Man'kovskaia, L. "O rabote sektsii istorii arkhitektury, restavratsii i okhrany pamiatnikov, 1967–1971." *Stroitel'stvo i arkhitektura Uzbekistana* 8 (1971): 20–1.

Manley, Rebecca. *To the Tashkent Station:Evacuation and Survival in the Soviet Union at War*. Ithaca, NY: Cornell University Press, 2009.

Markevich, A.I. "Letopis' zemletriasenii v Krymu." In *Chernomorskie zemletriaseniia 1927 goda i sud'by Kryma*, 64–73. Simferopol: Krymskoe gosudarstvennoe izdatel'stvo, 1928.

Marples, David R. *Chernobyl and Nuclear Power in the USSR*. Edmonton: Canadian Institute of Ukrainian Studies, 1986.

– "The Greening of Ukraine: Ecology and the Emergence of Zelenyi Svit,

1986–1990." In *Perestroika from Below: Social Movements in the Soviet Union*, ed. Judith B. Sedaitis and Jim Butterfield, 133–44. Boulder, CO: Westview Press, 1991.

– *Heroes and Villains: Creating National History in Contemporary Ukraine*. Budapest: Central European University Press, 2007.

– *The Social Impact of the Chernobyl Disaster*. Basingstoke: Macmillan, 1988.

Martin, Terry. *The Affirmative Action Empire: Nations and Nationalism in the Soviet Union, 1923–1939*. Ithaca, NY: Cornell University Press, 2001.

Maslovskii, G. "Khronika podviga," *Sovetskii ekran* 15 (July 1980): 5.

Matchanov, N. "Tashkentskii khashar." *Novyi mir* 8 (August 1972): 205–16.

Mavlianov, Gani Arifkhanovich. *Tashkentskoe zemletriasenie: 26 aprelia 1966 goda*. Tashkent: Fan, 1971.

Medvedev, Zhores. *Nuclear Disaster in the Urals*. New York: Norton, 1979.

Meinhardt, Matthias. "Der Mythos vom 'Alten Dresden' als Bauplan. Entwicklung, Ursachen und Folgen einer retrospektiv-eklektizistischen Stadtvorstellung." In *Städte aus Trümmern: Katastrophenbewältigung zwischen Antike und Moderne*, ed. Andreas Ranft and Stephan Selzer, 172–200. Göttingen: Vandenhoeck and Ruprecht, 2004.

Melikov, G.G., ed. *Khronika istorii Ashkhabada (1881–1975 Gg)*. Ashgabat: Ylym, 1981.

Men'shikov, Stanislav M. *Sovetskaia ekonomika: Katastrofa ili katarsis?* Moskva: INTER-VERSO, 1990.

Merport, Il'ia Aronovich. *Novoe stroitel'stvo Tashkente*. Moscow: Stroiizdat, 1976.

Mersiianovaia, I.V., and L.I. Iakobson, eds. *Potentsial i puti razvitiia filantropii v Rossii*. Moscow: Izdatel'skii dom Gosudarstvennogo universiteta – Vysshei shkoly ekonomiki, 2010.

Meuser, Philipp, Jörn Börner, and Caroline Uhlig. *Zwischen Stalin und Glasnost: Sowjetische Architektur, 1960–1990*. Berlin: DOM Publishers, 2008.

Mickiewicz, Ellen Propper. *Media and the Russian Public*. New York: Praeger, 1981.

– *Split Signals: Television and Politics in the Soviet Union*. Oxford: Oxford University Press, 1988.

Miller, Donald E., and Lorna Touryan Miller. *Armenia: Portraits of Survival and Hope*. Berkeley: University of California Press, 2003.

Mitrokhin, Nikolai. *Russkaia partiia: Dvizhenie russkikh natsionalistov v SSSR, 1953–1985 Gody*. Moscow: Novoe literaturnoe obozrenie, 2003.

Moiseeva, S. "Narodnye traditsii i sovremennoe gradostroitel'stvo." *Ekonomika i zhizn'* 10 (1966) : 78–81.

Molotch, Harvey, and Marilyn Lester. "News as Purposive Behavior: On the

Strategic Use of Routine Events, Accidents and Scandals." *American Sociological Review* 39 (1974): 101–12.

Montaubrie, Aline. *La presse russe et la catastrophe de Tchernobyl, 1986–1995: Représentations et mémoire*. Toulouse: Groupe de recherche en histoire immédiate, 1996.

Morton, Henry W., and Robert C. Stuart, eds. *The Contemporary Soviet City*. Basingstoke: Macmillan, 1984.

Mote, Victor L. "BAM after the Fanfare: The Unbearable Ecumene." In *The Soviet Environment: Problems, Policies and Politics*, ed. John Massey Stewart, 40–56. Cambridge: Cambridge University Press, 1992.

Mukhamedshin, A. "Tashkent zavtra." *Stroitel'stvo i arkhitektura Srednei Azii* 1, no. 10 (1964): 9–10.

Mumford, Lewis. *The City in History: Its Origins, Its Transformations, and Its Prospects*. New York: Harcourt Brace Jovanovich, 1961.

Nalivkin, D.V. *Vospominaniia ob Ashkhabadskom zemletriasenii 1948 goda*. Ashgabat: Ylym, 1989.

Nature Protection in the Soviet Union. Moscow: Novosti Press Agency Publishing House, 1974.

Neverov, A.S. *Tashkent – gorod khlebnyi*. Moskva: Zemlia i fabrika, 1925.

Nietzsche, Friedrich. "Ecce Homo." In *Werke in drei Bänden*. Munich: Carl Hanser Verlag, 1977.

Nove, Alec. *An Economic History of the USSR*. London: Allen Lane, 1969.

– *Glasnost' in Action: Cultural Renaissance in Russia*. Boston, MA: Unwin Hyman, 1989.

Novikov, V.D. "'Chornobyl'tsi' Akademii z chestiu vikonali svoiu misiiu." In *Chornobyl' 1986–1987 rr. Dokumenti i spogadi: Rol' NAN Ukraiiny u podolanni naslidkiv katastrofy*, 423–32. Kyiv: Akademperiodika, 2004.

Novoe v etnograficheskikh i antropologicheskikh issledovaniiakh. Itogi polevykh rabot Instituta etnografii AN SSSR v 1972 godu. Moscow: n.p., 1974.

Nurmagambetov, Alkuat. *Zemletriasenie: zhizn' mozhno sokhranit': Fakty, prognozy, sovety*. Alma-Ata: Gylym, Vremia, 1990.

Oberg, James E. *Uncovering Soviet Disasters: Exploring the Limits of Glasnost*. New York: Random House, 1988.

O'dea, Michael. "Le mot 'catastrophe.'" In *L'invention de la catastrophe au XVIIIe siècle*, ed. Anne-Marie Mercier-Faivre and Chantal Thomas, 35–48. Genève: Librairie Droz S.A., 2008.

Officer, Charles B. *When the Planet Rages: Natural Disasters, Global Warming, and the Future of the Earth*. Oxford and New York: Oxford University Press, 2009.

Oliver-Smith, Anthony. *The Martyred City: Death and Rebirth in the Andes*. Albuquerque: University of New Mexico Press, 1986.

– "Theorizing Disasters." In *Catastrophe and Culture: The Anthropology of Disaster*, ed. Susanna Hoffman and Anthony Oliver-Smith. Santa Fe, NM: School of American Research Press, 2002.

– *Defying Displacement: Grassroots Resistance and the Critique of Development*. 1st ed. Austin: University of Texas Press, 2010.

Orekhov, I. *Velikii khashar*. Tula: Priokskoe knizhnoe izdatel'stvo, 1970.

Oreshkin, Dmitrii, B. *Aral'skaia katastrofa: Chernobyl'skaia katastrofa i tragediia Belorussii*. Moskva: Znanie, 1990.

Pamiat' o Chernobyle: Nizhegorodtsy - likvidatory posledstvii katastrofy. Nizhni-Novgorod: n.p., 2007.

Payaslian, Simon. *The History of Armenia*. New York: Palgrave Macmillan, 2007.

– *The Political Economy of Human Rights in Armenia: Authoritarianism and Democracy in a Former Soviet Republic*. London: I.B. Tauris, 2011.

Peris, Daniel. *Storming the Heavens: The Soviet League of the Militant Godless*. Ithaca: NY: Cornell University Press, 1998.

Perspektivy razvitiia sovetskogo gradostroitel'stva. Moscow: Stroiizdat, 1973.

Peskov, V. *Puteshestvie c molodym mesiatsem*. Moscow: Molodaia gvardiia, 1969.

– "Tashkent 700 dnei spustia," *Sovetskii fil'm* 10 (1968): 4–5.

– "Tashkent: Catastrophe and Courage." *Soviet Life* 10 (October 1966): 38–45.

– *This Is My Native Land: A Soviet Journalist's Travels.* Moscow: Progress, 1976.

Petrov, Evgenii, and Il'ia Il'f. *Dvenadtsat' stul'ev*. Moscow: Khudozhestvennaia literatura, 1967.

Petryna, Adriana. *Life Exposed: Biological Citizens after Chernobyl*. Princeton, NJ: Princeton University Press, 2002.

Pincent, Guillemette. *La réhabilitation des quartiers précoloniaux dans les villes d'Asie Centrale*. Paris: L'Harmattan, 2009.

Pipes, Richard. *The Formation of the Soviet Union: Communism and Nationalism, 1917–1923*. Cambridge, MA: Harvard University Press, 1954.

Pisateli Krymu: Literaturnyi al'manakh. Moscow: Izd-vo Narkomzdrava RSFSR, 1928.

Plakhov, A. "V razrezhennom prostranstve." *Iskusstvo kino* 9 (1978): 112–23.

– "Vse ruzh'ia streliaiut." *Iskusstvo kino* 12 (December 1980): 69–79.

Plesnevich, E.V. "Krizisy sovetskoi arkhitektury, ili kakaia nauka nam nuzhna." *Arkhitektura i stroitel'stvo Uzbekistana* 4 (1991): 6–7.

– "Prostranstvennoe myshlenie—novoe ili zabytoe staroe?" *Arkhitektura i stroitel'stvo Uzbekistana* 1 (1991): 14–17.

Pokhodnia, I.K. "Vse otsenili geroicheskuiu rabotu nashikh uchenykh." In *Chornobyl' 1986–1987 rr.: Dokumenty i spogady: Rol' NAN Ukraiiny u podolanni naslidkiv katastrofy*, 433–8. Kyiv: Akademperiodika, 2004.

Polian, P.M. *Against Their Will: The History and Geography of Forced Migrations in the USSR*. Budapest: Central European University Press, 2004.

Pryde, Philip R. *Conservation in the Soviet Union*. Cambridge: Cambridge University Press, 1972.

Putnam, Robert D. *Bowling Alone: The Collapse and Revival of American Community*. New York: Simon and Schuster, 2000.

Qualls, Karl D., *From Ruins to Reconstruction: Urban Identity in Soviet Sevastopol after World War II*. Ithaca, NY: Cornell University Press, 2009.

Quarantelli, E.L., ed. *What Is a Disaster? Perspectives on the Question*. London: Routledge, 1998.

Quenet, Grégory. *Les tremblements de terre aux XVIIe et XVIIIe siècles: La naissance d'un risque*. Seyssel: Champ Vallon, 2005.

Rabusseau, Raphaël. *Les neiges labiles: Une histoire culturelle de l'avalanche au XVIIIe siècle*. Geneva: Presses d'Histoire Suisse, 2007.

Raeff, Marc. *Understanding Imperial Russia: State and Society in the Old Regime*. New York: Columbia University Press, 1984.

Ranft, Andreas, and Stephan Selzer. "Städte aus Trümmern. Einleitende Überlegungen." In *Städte aus Trümmern: Katastrophenbewältigung zwischen Antike und Moderne*, ed. Andreas Ranft and Stephan Selzer. Göttingen: Vandenhoeck and Ruprecht, 2004.

Rasputin, Valentin. *Farewell to Matyora*. Evanston, IL: Northwestern University Press, 1995.

Rasskazovskii, V.T., et al. *Posledstviia tashkentskogo zemletriaseniia*. Tashkent: Fan, 1967.

Rassweiler, Anne D. *The Generation of Power: The History of Dneprostroi*. New York: Oxford University Press, 1988.

Razlogov, K. "Mezhdu zrelishchem i povestvovaniem." *Iskusstvo kino* 4 (1987): 63–7.

Remington, Thomas F. "Parliamentary Government in the USSR." In *Perestroika-Era Politics: The New Soviet Legislature and Gorbachev's Political Reforms*, ed. Robert T. Huber and Donald R. Kelley, 175–204. Armonk, NY: M.E. Sharpe, 1991.

Rimsha, Anatolii Nikolaevich. *Gorod i zharkii klimat*. Moscow: Stroiizdat, 1975.

Robbins Jr, Richard G. *Famine in Russia, 1891–1892: The Imperial Government Responds to a Crisis*. New York: Columbia University Press, 1975.

Ro'i, Yaacov. *Islam in the Soviet Union: From the Second World War to Gorbachev*. New York: Columbia University Press, 2000.

Romanov, Panteleimon. *Zemletriasenie*. Moscow: n.p., 1924.

Rosenstone, Robert A. "Introduction." In *Revisioning History: Film and the Construction of a New Past*, ed. Robert A. Rosenstone, 3–14. Princeton, NJ: Princeton University Press, 1995.

Rost, Iurii. *Armenian Tragedy*. London: Weidenfeld and Nicolson, 1990.

Roth-Ey, Kristin Joy. *Moscow Prime Time: How the Soviet Union Built the Media Empire That Lost the Cultural Cold War*. Ithaca, NY: Cornell University Press, 2011.

Rousselet, Kathy. "L'église orthodoxe russe entre patriotisme et individualisme." *Vingtième siècle. Revue d'histoire* 66 (Apr–Jun. 2000): 13–24.

Rousso, Henry. *La dernière catastrophe: L'histoire, le présent, le contemporain*. Paris: Gallimard, 2012.

Rubanenko, Boris Rafailovich. *Napravleniia razvitiia zhilishchnogo stroitel'stva v SSSR*. Moscow: n.p., 1969.

– *Perspektivy razvitiia zhilishcha v SSSR*. Moscow: Stroiizdat, 1975.

– *Zhilishchnoe stroitel'stvo v SSSR*. Moscow: Stroiizdat, 1976.

Ruble, Blair A., Anatole Kopp, and William Craft Brumfield. *Architecture and the New Urban Environment: Western Influences on Modernism in Russia and the USSR: A Special Report*. Washington, DC: Kennan Institute for Advanced Russian Studies, 1988.

"Russkomu narodu." *Turkmenskaia Iskra*, 15 February 1950.

Rüthers, Monica. *Moskau bauen von Lenin bis Chruscev: Öffentliche Räume zwischen Utopie, Terror und Alltag*. Wien: Böhlau, 2007.

Rutland, Peter. *The Politics of Economic Stagnation in the Soviet Union: The Role of Local Party Organs in Economic Management*. Cambridge: Cambridge University Press, 1993.

Ryzhkov, Nikolai. *Prem'er: Proekt 2017 – Mif ili real'nost'*? Moscow: EKSMO, 2011.

Saidbaev, Talib Sarymsakovich. *Islam i obshchestvo: Opyt istoriko-sotsiologicheskogo issledovaniia*. Moscow: Nauka, 1978.

Savel'ev, P.S. *Pozhary-katastrofy*. Moscow: Stroiizdat, 1983.

Savitsky, Yuli. "New Trends in Architecture." *Soviet Life* 3 (March 1966): 42–3.

Schmid, Sonja D. *Producing Power: The Pre-Chernobyl History of the Soviet Nuclear Industry*. Cambridge, MA: MIT Press, 2015.

Schmidt, Andreas. *"Wolken krachen, Berge zittern, und die ganze Erde weint." Zur kulturellen Vermittlung von Naturkatastrophen in Deutschland 1755 bis 1855*. Münster: Waxmann, 1999.

Schubert, Dirk. "The Great Fire of Hamburg, 1842: From Catastrophe to Reform." In *Flammable Cities: Urban Conflagration and the Making of the Modern World*. Madison: University of Wisconsin Press, 2012.

Searle, John R. *Rationality in Action*. Cambridge, MA: MIT Press, 2001.

Semeshko, N.A., ed. *Pomogite Krymu! Zhurnal komiteta sodeistviia bor'be s posledstviiami krymskogo zemletriaseniia pri narodnom komissariate zdravookhraneniia RSFSR*. Moscow: n.p., 1928.

Shakhov, A.T. *Likvidatsiia posledstvii tashkentskogo zemletriaseniia*. Tashkent: Uzbekistan, 1972.

"Shastri, 61, Dies after He Signs Pact with Ayub." *New York Times*, 11 January 1966.

Shearer, David R. *Industry, State, and Society in Stalin's Russia, 1926–1934*. Ithaca, NY: Cornell University Press, 1996.

Shestopalov, V.M. "Eto bylo kolossal'noe napriazhenie fizicheskikh i tvorcheskikh sil." In *Chornobyl' 1986–1987 rr. Dokumenty i spogady: Rol' NAN Ukraiiny u podolanni naslidkiv katastrofy*. Kyiv: Akademperiodika, 2004.

Shimanovskii, S.V. "Soobshchenie o Krymskom zemletriasenii 12 sentiabria 1927 goda." In *Chernomorskie zemletriaseniia 1927 goda i sud'by Kryma*. Simferopol: Krymskoe gosudarstvennoe izdatel'stvo, 1928.

Shirvanzade, Aleksandr. "Namus." In *Sobranie sochinenii*. Moscow: Izd-vo "Izvestiia," 1957.

Shkvarikov, V.A. *Gradostroitel'stvo SSSR*. Moscow: Stroiizdat, 1967.

– *Zhiloi raion i mikroraion: Posobie po planirovke i zastroike*. Moscow: Stroiizdat, 1971.

Shlapentokh, Vladimir. *Public and Private Life of the Soviet People: Changing Values in Post-Stalin Russia*. Oxford: Oxford University Press, 1989.

– *Soviet Intellectuals and Political Power: The Post-Stalin Era*. Princeton, NJ: Princeton University Press, 1990.

Shteinbakh, Valerii. *The Soviet Contribution to the Olympics*. Moscow: Novosti Press Agency Publishing House, 1980.

Shukov, Iurii. *Gor'kovskii metropoliten*. Gor'kii: Volgo-Viatskoe knizhnoe izdatel'stvo, 1986.

Shvidkovskii, O.A. "Puti rekonstruktsii drevnikh gorodov." *Stroitel'stvo i arkhitektura Uzbekistana* 10 (1968): 18–23.

Siegelbaum, Lewis H. *Stakhanovism and the Politics of Productivity in the USSR, 1935–1941*. Cambridge: Cambridge University Press, 1988.

Simon, Gerhard. *Nationalism and Policy toward the Nationalities in the Soviet Union: From Totalitarian Dictatorship to Post-Stalinist Society*. Trans. Karen Forster and Oswald Forster. Boulder, CO: Westview Press, 1991.

Skinner, Frederick W. "Trends in Planning Practices: The Building of Odessa, 1794–1917." In *The City in Russian History*, ed. Michael Hamm, 139–59. Lexington: University Press of Kentucky, 1976.

Smoliar, I.M. *Novye Goroda*. Moscow: Stroiizdat, 1972.

Sobolev, Romil. "Meniaiushchiisia i neizmennyi," *Sovetskii ekran* 14 (July 1975): 16–17.

Soiuz arkhitektorov Uzbekistan. *Svodnye otchetnye dannye o rabote pravleniia Soiuza arkhitektorov Uzbekistana v period mezhdu XI i XII s"ezdami arkhitektorov respubliki, 1980–1985 gg*. Tashkent: n.p., 1986.

Solnit, Rebecca. *A Paradise Built in Hell: The Extraordinary Communities That Arise in Disaster*. New York: Viking Press, 2009.

Solov'ev, Sergei Leonidovich. *Zemletriaseniia na Sakhaline*. Moscow: Nauka, 1967.

Solzhenitsyn, Aleksandr. *The Mortal Danger: How Misconceptions about Russia Imperil America*. New York: Harper and Row, 1980.

Sorokin, Pitirim Aleksandrovich. *Man and Society in Calamity*. New York: Dutton, 1942.

Spechler, Dina R. *Permitted Dissent in the USSR: Novy Mir and the Soviet Regime*. New York: Praeger, 1982.

Starovoitova, Galina. *Etnicheskaia gruppa v sovremennom sovetskom gorode: Sotsiologicheskie ocherki*. Leningrad: Nauka, 1987.

– *Galina Starovoitova*. Moscow: Novosti, 1990.

– *Sovereignty after Empire: Self-Determination Movements in the Former Soviet Union*. Washington, DC: United States Institute of Peace, 1997.

Starr, Kevin. *California: A History*. New York: Random House, 2007.

Steinberg, Ted. *Acts of God: The Unnatural History of Natural Disaster in America*. Oxford: Oxford University Press, 2000.

Stites, Richard. "Bolshevik Ritual Building in the 1920s." In *Russia in the Era of NEP*, ed. Sheila Fitzpatrick, Alexander Rabinowitch, and Richard Stites, 295–309. Bloomington: Indiana University Press, 1991.

– *Russian Popular Culture*. Cambridge: Cambridge University Press, 1992.

Stites, Richard, and James von Geldern, eds., *Mass Culture in Soviet Russia: Tales, Poems, Songs, Movies, Plays and Folklore, 1917–1953*. Bloomington: Indiana University Press, 1995.

Stone, Deborah. *Policy Paradox*. 3rd ed. New York: W.W. Norton, 2012.

Stronski, Paul. *Tashkent: Forging a Soviet City, 1930–1966*. Pittsburgh: University of Pittsburgh Press, 2010.

Strumilin, S., and M. Sonin. "Alkogol'nye poteri i bor'ba s nimi." *Ekonomika i organizatsiia promyshlennogo proizvodstva* 4 (1974): 30–44.

Sudarikova, A.A. *Luchshie proizvedeniia sovetskikh zodchikh, 1973–1974 gg.* Moscow: Stroiizdat, 1977.

Summers, Julie. *When the Children Came Home: Stories of Wartime Evacuees*. London: Simon and Schuster, 2011.

Sunstein, Cass R. *Laws of Fear: Beyond the Precautionary Principle*. Cambridge: Cambridge University Press, 2005.

Suny, Ronald Grigor. *The Revenge of the Past: Nationalism, Revolution, and the Collapse of the Soviet Union*. Stanford, CA: Stanford University Press, 1993.

Suny, R. Grigor, and Terry Martin. *A State of Nations: Empire and Nation-Making in the Age of Lenin and Stalin*. Oxford: Oxford University Press, 2001.

Takuma, Taketoshi. "Human Behavior in the Event of Earthquakes." In *Disasters: Theory and Research*, ed. E.L. Quarantelli, 159–72. London: Sage, 1978.

Tarakanov, Nikolai. *Dve tragedii XX veka: Dokumental'nye povesti*. Moscow: Sovetskii pisatel', 1992.

Tarasevich, Iu. I. "Mi stvorili novii metod dezaktivatsii vod, odiagu i tekhniki." In *Chornobyl' 1986–1987 rr. Dokumenti i spogady: Rol' NAN Ukraiiny u podolanni naslidkiv katastrofy*, 448–51. Kyiv: Akademperiodika, 2004.

Tashkent – 2000. Tashkent: Uzbekistan, 1983.

Tashkent – gorod mira i druzhby. Pamiatka chitateliu. Tashkent: n.p., 1971.

Tashkentskii gorodskoi komitet. *O plane rekonstruktsii goroda Tashkenta*. Tashkent: Gosudarstvennoe izdatel'stvo UzSSR, 1938.

Tashkentskii institut inzhenerov zh.-d. transporta: Tezisy dokladov. Tashkent: n.p., 1967.

Taubman, William. *Governing Soviet Cities: Bureaucratic Politics and Urban Development in the USSR*. New York: Praeger, 1973.

Taylor, Charles. "Liberal Politics and the Public Sphere." In *Philosophical Arguments*, 257–87. Cambridge, MA: Harvard University Press, 1995.

Toman, Irzhi. *Rossiia i Krasnyi Krest, 1917–1945*. Moscow: Mezhdunarodnyi komitet Krasnogo Kresta, 1998.

Toshkent 1966 iil silsilasi: gubokhlar khotirasi =Taschkenter Erdbeben 1966: Erinnerungen von Zeitzeugen = Tashkentskoe zemletriasenie 1966 goda: vospominaniia ochevidtsev. Tashkent: Nashriyotuyi Sug'diyona, 2008.

Travianko, L.N. "Kachestvenno proektirovat' i zastraivat' novye mikroraiony Tashkenta." *Stroitel'stvo i arkhitektura Uzbekistana* 4 (April 1968): 1–4.

Treml, Vladimir G. *Alcohol in the USSR: A Statistical Study*. Durham, NC: Duke Press Policy Studies, 1982.

Trifonov, I.V. *The Old Man*. Trans. Jacqueline Edwards and Mitchell Schneider. New York: Simon and Schuster, 1984.

"Turkmenistan: Urban Developments." *Central Asian Review* 2, no. 1 (1954): 76–84.

Turnerelli, Edward. *L'incendie de Kazan 1842*. St Petersburg: n.p., 1845.

"U druzhby sila radians'kikh narodiv." *Molod' Ukraiiny*, 7 September 1989.

Ulomov, Valentin Ivanovich. *Novye dannye po seismologii i seismogeologii Uzbekistana*. Tashkent: Fan, 1974.

– *Seismichnost' vostochnoi Fergany*. Tashkent: Fan, 1966.

– *Seismichnost' zapadnogo Uzbekistana*. Tashkent: Fan, 1972.

– *Vnimanie! Zemletriasenie*! Tashkent: Uzbekistan, 1971.

Utz, Peter. *Kultivierung der Katastrophe: Literarische Untergangsszenarien aus der Schweiz*. Munich: Wilhelm Fink, 2013.

Uzbek-English Dictionary. Ed. Natalie Waterson. Oxford: Oxford University Press.

Vail', Petr, and Genis, Aleksandr. *60-e—mir sovetskogo cheloveka*. Moscow: Novoe literaturnoe obozrenie, 2001.

Vale, Lawrence J., and Thomas J. Campanella. "Introduction: The Cities Rise Again." In *Resilient City: How Modern Cities Recover from Disaster*, ed. Lawrence J. Vale and Thomas J. Campanella, 3–23. New York: Oxford University Press, 2005.

Valkenier, Elizabeth Kridl. *Russian Realist Art: The State and Society – The Peredvizhniki and Their Tradition*. Ann Arbor, MI: Ardis, 1977.

Vanke, A.I., and V.M. Mikaelian. "Voprosy proektirovaniia tashkentskogo metropolitena." In *Metropoliten i planirovka krupneishego goroda*. Khar'kov: KhIIKS, 1980.

Vasil'eva, Vera. "Eto vysokoe trudnoe nebo." *Sovetskii fil'm* 6 (June 1980): 13–16.

Vender, D.V. *Chernobyl': Byl' i bol.'* Nizhnii Tagil: Media-print, 2006.

Verluise, P. *Armenia in Crisis: The 1988 Earthquake*. Trans. L. Chorbajian. Detroit, MI: Wayne State University Press, 1995.

Virabian, A., F. Arutiunian, S. Mirzoyan, M. Martirosyan, eds. *Spitakskoe zemletriasenie: Zona bedstviia vchera i segodnia*. Erevan: Natsional'nyi arkhiv Armenii, 2008.

Virilio, Paul, and Svetlana Alexievitch. "Être témoins de cet accident du temps." In *Les silences de Tchernobyl: L'avenir contaminé*, ed. Guillaume Grandazzi and Frédérick Lemarchand, 158–66. Paris: Autrement, 2004.

Voltaire. "The Lisbon Earthquake." In *The Portable Voltaire*, ed. Ben Ray Redman. New York: Penguin Books, 1977.

Vovk, A.A. "Nauchnaia mysl' operezhala tekhnicheskie vozmozhnosti." In *Chornobyl' 1986-1987 rr.: Dokumenty i spogady: Rol' NAN Ukraiiny u podolanni naslidkiv katastrofy*, 383–6. Kyiv: Akademperiodika, 2004.

"Vozrodit' goroda i sela." *Pravda*, 18 December 1988.

"Vsesoiuznyi khashar," *Sovetskii ekran* 13 (July 1968): 10–11.

Waldherr, Gerhard H. *Erdbeben. Das aussergewöhnliche Normale. Zur Rezeption seismischer Aktivitäten in literarischen Quellen vom 4. Jahrhundert v. Chr. bis zum 4. Jahrhundert n. Chr.* Stuttgart: Franz Steiner Verlag, 1997.

Walter, François. *Katastrophen: Eine Kulturgeschichte vom 16. bis ins 21. Jahrhundert*. Trans. Doris Butz-Striebel and Tresy Lejoly. Stuttgart: Philipp Reclam jun., 2010.

Ward, Christopher J. *Brezhnev's Folly: The Building of BAM and Late Soviet Socialism*. Pittsburgh: University of Pittsburgh Press, 2009.

Weiner, Douglas. *A Little Corner of Freedom: Russian Nature Protection from Stalin to Gorbachev*. Berkeley, CA: University of California Press, 1999.

Wenger, Dennis E. "Community Response to Disaster: Functional and Structural Alterations." In *Disasters: Theory and Research*, ed. E.L. Quarantelli, 17–48. London: Sage, 1978.

White, Stephen. *Russia Goes Dry: Alcohol, State, and Society*. Cambridge: Cambridge University Press, 1996.

Wilson, Andrew. *Ukrainian Nationalism in the 1990s: A Minority Faith*. Cambridge: Cambridge University Press, 1997.

Wittgenstein, Ludwig. *Philosophical Investigations*. Trans. G.E.M. Anscombe. 3d ed. Oxford: Blackwell, 2001 [1953].

Wortman, Richard S. *Scenarios of Power: Myth and Ceremony in Russian Monarchy*. Princeton, NJ: Princeton University Press, 1995.

Wyllie, Loring A., Jr, and John R. Filson, ed. *Armenia Earthquake Reconnaissance Report*. Special issue of *Earthquake Spectra* (1989).

Youngblood, Denise. *Movies for the Masses: Popular Cinema and Soviet Society in the 1920s*. Cambridge: Cambridge University Press, 1992.

– "Repentance: Stalinist Terror and the Realism of Surrealism." In *Revisioning History: Film and the Construction of a New Past*, ed. Robert A. Rosenstone, 139–54. Princeton, NJ: Princeton University Press, 1995.

– *Russian War Films: On the Cinema Front, 1914–2005*. Lawrence: University Press of Kansas Press, 2007.

Zairov, Sh. Sh. " Vklad komsomolu Ukraiiny u likvidatsiiu naslidkiv Tashkentskoho zemletrusu: 1966–68." *Ukraiins'kyi istorychnyi zhurnal* 9 (1982): 57–61.

Zarecor, Kimberly Elman. "The Rainbow Edges: The Legacy of Communist Mass Housing and the Colorful Future of Czech Cities." In *Without a Hitch: New Directions in Prefabricated Architecture* ed., Peggi Clouston, Ray Kinoshita Mann, and Stephen Schreiber, 238–45. Amherst: University of Massachusetts.

Zemletriasenie 3 ianvaria 1970 goda v Borzhomskom raione. Tbilisi: Metsniereba, 1973.

Zemletriaseniia u beregov Kamchatki v mae-iiune 1959 g. Moscow: Izdatel'stvo akademii nauk SSSR, 1960.

Zemletriaseniia v SSSR. Moscow: Nauka, 1967.

Zeynalov, Fazil. *Le conflit du Haut-Karabakh: Une paix juste ou une guerre inévitable*. Paris: L'Harmattan, 2011.

Zhores, Medvedev. *The Legacy of Chernobyl*. New York: W.W. Norton, 1990.

Ziiaev, A. *Tsentr Tashkenta — proshloe i nastoiashchee*. Tashkent: Izd-vo Uzbekistan, 1987.

Zopfi, Emil. *Kilchenstock*. Zürich: Limmat Verlag, 1996.

Zoshchenko, Mikhail. "Earthquake." In *The Fatal Eggs and Other Soviet Satire*, ed. Mirra Ginsburg, 215–19. New York: Macmillan Company, 1964.

Zubok, Vladislav. *A Failed Empire: The Soviet Union in the Cold War from Stalin to Gorbachev*. Chapel Hill: University of North Carolina Press, 2007.

– *Zhivago's Children: The Last Russian Intelligentsia*. Cambridge, MA: The Belknap Press of Harvard University Press, 2009.

Index